STEPCHILDREN OF THE SHTETL

Stanford Studies in Jewish History and Culture

STEPCHILDREN OF THE SHTETL

The Destitute, Disabled, and Mad of

Jewish Eastern Europe, 1800–1939

___

NATAN M. MEIR

Stanford University Press
Stanford, California

STANFORD UNIVERSITY PRESS
Stanford, California

Portions of chapters 2, 3, and 7 were originally published in "Home for the Homeless? The Hekdesh in Eastern Europe," in *Place in Modern Jewish Culture and Society*, ed. Richard I. Cohen, *Studies in Contemporary Jewry* 30 (New York: Oxford University Press, 2018), 3–16. Reprinted with Permission of Oxford University Press.

The epigraph to chapter 4 is an excerpt of page 6 from *Madonna in a Fur Coat* by Sabahattin Ali, translated from the Turkish by Maureen Freely and Alexander Dawe. Translation copyright © Maureen Freely and Alexander Dawe 2016. Reprinted by permission of Other Press LLC.

Portions of chapter 7 were originally published in "Charting the Outer Provinces of Jewry: The Study of East European Jewry's Margins," *POLIN: Studies in Polish Jewry* 29 (2017): 89–104. Reprinted with permission of Liverpool University Press.

Printed in the United States of America on acid-free, archival-quality paper

Library of Congress Cataloging-in-Publication Data

Names: Meir, Natan M., author.
Title: Stepchildren of the shtetl : the destitute, disabled, and mad of Jewish Eastern Europe, 1800–1939 / Natan M. Meir.
Other titles: Stanford studies in Jewish history and culture.
Description: Stanford : Stanford University Press, 2020. | Series: Stanford studies in Jewish history and culture | Includes bibliographical references and index.
Identifiers: LCCN 2020004504 (print) | LCCN 2020004505 (ebook) | ISBN 9781503611832 (cloth) | ISBN 9781503613058 (paperback) | ISBN 9781503613065 (ebook)
Subjects: LCSH: Jews—Europe, Eastern—Social conditions—19th century. | Jews—Europe, Eastern—Social conditions—20th century. | Marginality, Social—Europe, Eastern—History. | Poor—Europe, Eastern—History. | Mentally ill—Europe, Eastern—History. | People with disabilities—Europe, Eastern—History.
Classification: LCC DS135.E83 M345 2020 (print) | LCC DS135.E83 (ebook) | DDC 305.5/69089924047—dc23
LC record available at https://lccn.loc.gov/2020004504
LC ebook record available at https://lccn.loc.gov/2020004505

Cover photo: Jewish woman beggar on the stairs of a house in Cracow, Poland, 1920s. Ze'ev Wilhelm Aleksandrowicz (Beth Hatefutsoth Photo Archive, Israel)

Cover design: Rob Ehle

For Avinoam נ"י

CONTENTS

FIGURES

ACKNOWLEDGMENTS

This book would not have been possible without support and assistance from many quarters. Tony Kushner and Mark Cornwall, colleagues of mine at the University of Southampton, supported my successful application for a Yad Hanadiv / Beracha Foundation Fellowship at the Hebrew University of Jerusalem. That fellowship enabled me to spend a fruitful year of research at the National Library of Israel and the Central Archive for the History of the Jewish People, where the librarians and archivists graciously attended to my many requests and queries. I offer special thanks to Binyamin Lukin at CAHJP for his assistance. During that year I was fortunate to have Israel Bartal as mentor and guide. Once ensconced at Portland State University, I was the beneficiary of several internal grants that enabled me to devote precious time to research, as well as a PSU Vision 2025 Grant defraying publication expenses. The YIVO Institute for Jewish Research's Bernard Choseed Memorial Fellowship allowed me to travel to New York to work with historical documents at that institution's incomparable archive; I am grateful to the research staff there for their kind assistance. A travel grant from American Council of Learned Societies Committee on East European Studies (Title VIII funds) made possible an additional trip to Israel. Research in Ukrainian libraries and archives was facilitated by the assistance offered by the consummate professionals at those institutions, and especially Irina Sergeeva at the Vernadsky National Library's Judaica Division. The research and writing that I accomplished during my sabbatical year would not have been possible without the support provided by an International Fellowship in Jewish Studies from the Memorial Foundation for Jewish Culture and a Ruth and David Musher / JDC Archives Fellowship from the American Jewish Joint Distribution Committee. I thank Misha Mitsel for his assistance in the JDC Archives. Finally, my year-long fellowship at the New York Public Library's Cullman Center for Scholars and Writers provided me not only with time and space to write in one of the greatest research institutions in the country, but also with wonderful colleagues and friends who aided my research in various ways. I especially want to thank Jean Strouse, then director of the Cullman Center, Jonathan Stevenson, Nicole Fleetwood, Lauren Goldenberg, Paul Delaverdac, and Julia Pagnamenta, as well as the librarians at the Dorot Jewish Division, particularly Miryem-Khaye Seigel.

At Portland State University, my research was greatly facilitated by the outstanding librarians and staff at Millar Library, including Joan Petit and Min Cedillo. I am grateful to Stacey Johnston, Vicky Mazzone, and Suzane Van Amburgh for their help and support at various phases of preparing the manuscript, and thank my colleagues Moshe Rachmuth and Nila Friedberg for their counsel on some thorny translation issues. Lee Lipton helped me with research at an early stage of the project. Former dean of the College of Liberal Arts and Sciences Karen Marongelle and Associate Dean DeLys Ostlund offered support at crucial stages of this undertaking. My colleagues in the Harold Schnitzer Family Program in Judaic Studies have provided intellectual and moral encouragement at every step.

I am blessed with many wise colleagues who have been generous with their time and insight: Natalia Aleksiun, David Assaf, Eugene Avrutin, Lila Corwin Berman, Jeremy Dauber, Jonathan Dekel-Chen, Nathaniel Deutsch, Stanley Diamond, Havi Dreifuss, Valerii Dymshits, Glenn Dynner, John Efron, Paula Eisenstein Baker, Leonid Finberg, Jonathan Frankel z"l, ChaeRan Freeze, Sylvie Anne Goldberg, Eric Goldman, Todd Hasak-Lowy, Dan Kupfert Heller, Barbara Henry, Phil Hollander, Agnieszka Jagodzińska, Tomasz Jankowski, Hillel Kieval, Anatoliy Klots, Małgorzata Kośka, Rebecca Kobrin, Morgane Labbé, Shulamit Magnus, Michael Miller, Ken Moss, Benjamin Nathans, Avraham Nowersztern, Beth Omansky, Iris Parush, Yohanan Petrovsky-Shtern, Eddy Portnoy, Alyssa Quint,

Larry Rosenwald, Gabriella Safran, Gadi Sagiv, Aleksandra Sajdak, Ellie Schainker, Rivka Schiller, Sebastian Schulman, Ephraim Shoham-Steiner, Haim Sperber, Shaul Stampfer, Adam Teller, Scott Ury, Kalman Weiser, Marcin Wodziński, Deborah Yalen, Rakefet Zalashik, Motti Zalkin, and Arkadi Zeltser. I thank Alexandra Glebovskaia for her assistance in transcribing a very challenging Russian archival document, and the following people for their kind assistance in procuring images: Edyta Gawron; Erica Lehrer; Olga Levitan of the Israeli Center for the Documentation of the Performing Arts at Tel Aviv University; Yossi Raviv, son of Moshe Raviv-Vorobeichic (Moï Ver), whose work is analyzed in chapter 7; and Shaul and Sylviane Stampfer. Steve Zipperstein and the anonymous reviewer for Stanford University Press offered insightful comments and editing of the manuscript, and I thank Steve for his sage advice and heartfelt encouragement. My editor at the press, Margo Irvin, has made the publishing process straightforward; it has been a true pleasure to work with her and with associate editor Faith Wilson Stein, who has answered my many queries with aplomb.

A special thank-you is due to Don Zuckerman for his encouragement, coaching, and counsel, and for helping me get through some particularly difficult periods.

This book was a family affair. Chanan van Herpen accompanied me on this book's journey from its very beginning, and I thank him for the many ways he supported me along the way. To say that Ellen Singer gave generously of her time and wisdom is a tremendous understatement: she read several versions of the manuscript, discussed it with me, and spent many Sundays with my son so that I would have time to write. I am deeply grateful to her. My gratitude to my parents, Aryeh and Leah Nadich Meir, knows no bounds, but in addition to their moral and emotional support at every step of the journey, my father also served as my research assistant at the YIVO Archive, carefully reading and transcribing dozens of Hebrew petitions from the Guttmacher papers. His help was invaluable and I thank him from the bottom of my heart. My sister, Vered Meir, and my brother and sister-in-law, Adin Meir and Jordana Klein, lent their loving support along the way. As I write these words, I think of two beloved family members no longer among the living, Shoshana Ribalow and Reena Ribalow, who were passionate about both the written word and the millennia-long journey of the Jewish people. They were among my most enthusiastic cheerleaders, and they would have loved to see this book in print. I hope it would have met with their approval.

I dedicate this book to my son, Avinoam Yehudah Zane, who brings me much joy every day. Avinoam, this is Papi's chapter book.

NOTE ON TRANSLITERATION AND DATES

In rendering Russian, Ukrainian, and Hebrew into Latin characters, I have relied upon simplified versions of the Library of Congress transliteration systems. Yiddish transliteration is based on the system devised by the YIVO Institute for Jewish Research. With the exception of locales with commonly accepted English spellings, place names are rendered according to the historical period in question, with Yiddish variants provided in certain instances. Historical Hebrew terms are transliterated according to contemporary Israeli pronunciation; in some cases Ashkenazic pronunciation is provided as well. Dates for newspaper articles published in the Russian Empire are according to the Julian calendar, which was twelve days behind the Gregorian calendar in the nineteenth century and thirteen days behind in the twentieth century.

STEPCHILDREN OF THE SHTETL

INTRODUCTION

In a recent interview, by way of explaining his sense of alienness in the Israeli society he had entered as a thirteen-year-old refugee ("And it was demanded of me to be the new Jew. Why should I be a new Jew? I love the old Jews, you know"), the late Israeli novelist Aharon Appelfeld described a short story he wrote early in his career:

> It's about two characters, Max and Bertha. Max is somewhere around 27, Bertha is maybe 12, 13. He picked her up, somewhere during the war, and brought her to Israel. A retarded child. But he cannot leave her. She's retarded, but she has something magic in her blood. She is sitting, kneeling on the street. And he's always leaving her. Giving her food and some money and leaving her, and hoping not to find her. But always he comes back, and she's still sitting in the same place. I brought this story to a newspaper, it was a very short story. And the editor said, what are you trying here, why Bertha? We came to Israel to forget Bertha. You are taking a retarded girl as the hero of the story? What are you going to learn from such a story? How will this story help us build a new nation of new people? . . . Why are you are bringing these retarded, limited figures into our life?[1]

Bertha is a remnant of the old country, her "limited" nature a symbol of the deficient, defective nature of the Jews of eastern Europe. As Appelfeld's

editor says so cogently—and cuttingly—the goal of the Zionists who came
to the Land of Israel was to forget who they had been before, their alter ego:
the crippled, pitiful Jews of the diaspora. And yet, as Appelfeld's story shows,
Max could neither leave Bertha behind in Europe nor forget about her once
in Israel. Out of pathos and compassion, presumably, but also because of the
"magic in her blood."

In another meditation on the alienation he experienced during his early
years in Israel, Appelfeld wrote,

> I was strolling in the city [Tel Aviv] and finally sat on a bench in the
> boulevard. There were some beggars there who spoke Yiddish among
> themselves; Yiddish mixed with a few Russian words. I suddenly felt that
> the *nigun* [contour] of their language flowed within me. I knew that this
> was my tongue that was lost on the roads. Now, it was embodied in the
> beggars . . . [2]

The people speaking Russian-inflected Yiddish on the bench—a Yiddish
with which Appelfeld identified instantly—were beggars. They, like Bertha,
were the living embodiment of what Zionism thought it had left behind in
Europe: the sense of being the outcast, the rejected, the dregs of society.

The marginal individual is thus a figure of East European Jewish society,
since—like Bertha—he or she comes to stand in for that society as a whole.
At the same time, however, Appelfeld's beggars, unlike Bertha, are not fictional characters with a specific role to play in the drama unspooling in their
creator's mind but real people, with lives and emotions and agency of their
own. These, then, are the two paths of this book's exploration into the world
of marginal people, sometimes parallel, sometimes diverging, at other moments crossing back on each other: on the one hand, the outcast as person, as
historical figure, and on the other, as symbol.

This is a book about the other, the different, the uncanny in the Jewish
society of eastern Europe. At times marginal people were invisible, unseen,
nonpersons; at other times—crucial junctures in the modern era—they were
pulled to the center of the conversation within the Jewish collective about
what Jews should look like, or what they should not look like; how gentiles
viewed Jews, what they thought about them, why they hated them. Marginal people were consistently ridiculed, mocked, sometimes exoticized,

even fetishized; on rare occasions, they were held up as paragons, or even . . .
treated as fellow human beings.

At the core of the book's argument is the proposition that in the modern period, the Jewish marginal people of eastern Europe became a symbol for East European Jewry as a whole, a development that modernizers both advanced unwittingly and lamented and that modernists later embraced. Whether as recruits drafted into the tsar's army as substitutes for other Jewish boys, as denizens of the ubiquitous and contemptible Jewish *hekdesh* (poorhouse) that represented the ugliest and most despicable facets of Jewish existence, as central figures in a religious ritual that transformed them into vicarious victims of an epidemic in exchange for the salvation of the community, or as protagonists in classic works of modern Jewish literature—the undesirables of Jewish society frequently served as surrogates for the entire Jewish people, or at least for its subset in the Russian Empire. The internal Jewish discourse of modernization, progress, and integration required the creation of a despised Other to serve as a kind of doppelgänger to be cast out or transformed utterly—until the realization dawned that "they" were "us."

In his sweeping and thought-provoking study of the history of disability, Jacques Stiker writes:

> To begin with, let us admit the very *primordial* function that the disabled fill. Like the child for the adult, like woman for man (and vice versa), they are proof of the inadequacy of what we would like to see established as references and norm. They are the tear in our being that reveals its open-endedness, its incompleteness, its precariousness. Because of that, because of that difference, they can, like children and women, be considered expiatory victims, scapegoats. . . . They are the thorn in the side of the social group that prevents the folly of certainty and of identification with a single model.[3]

This book argues that not only the disabled but all of Jewish society's undesirable people served as scapegoats. Since in some sense they represented all of Jewish society, that society could, by sacrificing them, by placing the blame for Jewish suffering on them, redeem itself from its abject, suffering state.

I offer the following trajectory in Jewish eastern Europe for the complex balance of integration and exclusion that is the hallmark of any society's attitude to its marginals. We begin at the end of the early modern period with a traditional society that already held the consummate Other in its midst—the wandering beggar, lacking fixed abode, livelihood, and often family, and often perceived as undeserving of charity—in very low regard. Such vagrants were assisted, as religious law and communal norms dictated, but usually encouraged to move on as quickly as possible. As for disabled people, the mentally ill, and poor orphans, they were cared for by some combination of family, private alms, and charitable societies. But because such people contributed nothing to the communal purse, they could not but be seen as a liability for Jewish communities that were falling into ever greater debt and yet still had to find a way to pay the corporate taxes that they owed first to the Polish authorities and in later years to the Russian government. On the other hand, there was an element of the extraordinary and even the magical about people who did not conform to bodily, cognitive, or societal norms.

As is almost universally the case with social outcasts, marginals began, with the advent of modernity, to play a fraught role as the symbolic Other for Jewish society, which projected onto them its anxieties about its perception in the eyes of the Christian world, the rapid impoverishment of Russian/Polish Jewry, changing sexual mores, and more. Modernizing reformers and philanthropists were particularly concerned that large groups of marginal types, more visible to Christian society in the cities to which Jews were migrating in large numbers, might endanger the positive image of modern Jewry that progressives were attempting to cultivate. In the worst-case scenario, the surrounding society might even, it was feared, mistake the deformed part for the backward but fundamentally healthy whole.

When Jewish notables and progressives (*maskilim*) began to argue in the middle decades of the nineteenth century for the granting of full civic and political equality to Jews, they also had to explain why the Jews were deserving of such rights. In some cases, the argument about worthiness led inexorably to a statement about which parts of the Jewish people—in other words, which Jews—merited citizenship or expanded rights, and which did not.[4] Frequently, the debate revolved around productivity and model behavior: some occupations were considered to be useful to the state and society, and those pursuing them could serve as exemplars for their coreligionists. At the other end of the economic and social spectrum lay the marginals, and especially beggars, who were perceived as embodying traits that enemies of the Jews understood as characteristically Jewish—idlers, parasites, frequently deceitful, often physically repellent—and whom Jewish progressives saw as symptoms of Jewish backwardness. As Catherine J. Kudlick remarks, "Disability is a significant factor in the development of the modern state, by raising questions of who deserves the government's assistance and protection, what constitutes a capable citizen, and who merits the full rights of citizenship."[5] We could profitably expand her argument from one about disabled people, a significant category of marginal people, to one that includes all marginals.

But even as the process of defining the marginal person as outside the boundaries of the normal was under way, visionary artists were creating literature that challenged this model, emphasizing the essential humanity of Jewish society's undesirables and suggesting that their wounded condition was representative of the circumstances of Jewry as a whole. It is no coincidence that in addition to Glupsk (Foolsville), the Jewish towns that hold pride of place in the fictional Jewish universe of Sholem Yankev Abramovitsh (Mendele Moykher Sforim) are Kabtsansk (Pauperstown or Beggarstown) and Tuneyadevka (Leechville).[6] The work of writers like Abramovitsh adumbrated a profound shift in East European Jewish society heralded by World War I and the subsequent Russian Civil War and its accompanying massacres, which left tens of thousands of Jews homeless, destitute, orphaned, maimed, or insane. In newly independent Poland, while popular attitudes of disparagement and condescension persisted, the marginal type was to some extent no longer perceived as marginal at all, but rather as embodying a significant measure of Jewish society, which marshalled its resources to create institutional welfare networks to care for the most vulnerable. The undesirables merited attention from writers and filmmakers because their treatment illustrated both the cruelty and the kindness inherent in human nature and in Jewish communal life; from folklorists because they were both a subject of folk culture and a potential repository of folklore; and from nationalist leaders and social welfare activists because they exemplified the way that even the most abject could be lifted up and transformed into productive members of the Jewish nation. But nationalists, and especially Zionists, harbored profound ambivalence about the disabled Jewish body and psyche: they represented the persecuted, wounded, and deeply unhealthy Jewish nation, and therefore merited concern and sympathy. At the same time, however, they were also the clearest example of the Jews' degenerate state and therefore had to be done away with through the regeneration and transformation that Zionism promised.

Definitions

I embarked upon this project intending to explore the marginal people in Jewish society. I knew from my previous research project on the Jews of late imperial Kiev that those people existed, and I had a hunch that this was an important category in East European Jewish society. What I did not yet have was a clear understanding of which categories marginality embraced. Poverty? Then we were discussing beggars and paupers. Social status? Servants and *yishuvnikes* (rural Jews) had to be included. Familial condition? Orphans and widows, naturally. Physical and mental ability? People with physical and intellectual disabilities and the mentally ill. Other definitions might conceivably embrace the religiously lax, converts, prostitutes, and criminals.

Who the marginal people are depends, of course, on how we define marginality. One key factor is poverty. We might attempt to measure marginality in terms of economic position and self-sufficiency: was a given individual able to support himself or herself, or did he or she have to rely on charity or crime to survive? And even if some sort of livelihood was present, was it consistent or unreliable? Instability and unpredictability, as well as isolation—for marginals often fell into their difficult circumstances precisely because they had no family to rely upon—were often hallmarks of a socially marginal life.[7] Another indicator of marginal status is social deviance: identification, via behavior or membership, with a group that did not fit neatly into early modern society's "strict and rigid hierarchies . . . in which everyone knew, or was supposed to know, his or her place."[8] A deviant identity was associated with shame, stigma, and social ostracization, and sometimes even a perceived danger to the mainstream. "Outsiders or pariahs. . . . were considered to be a permanent threat to honorable people. At the same time. . . . their asocial behavior served as a reminder of the positive elements around which a societal consensus had formed."[9] (Had I written this study several decades ago, I might have drawn on sociological terminology to characterize its subject as "involuntary deviants" over and against other categories of deviants who must perforce be lumped together under the very unsatisfactory label of "voluntary"—as if criminals, prostitutes, and others perceived as "asocial" could truly be understood as having chosen their way of life free from societal and economic pressures, biases, and other circumstances. The term "deviant" has, of course, come to be seen as problematic.)[10]

If the threat posed by people on the margins to those in the center was a metaphysical one, imperiling the foundations of society, the danger represented by the underworld was usually much more concrete. Most obviously, criminals and bandits were clearly a menace to the well-being of all people, rich and poor alike.[11] However, the underworld is not identical with the margins of society; while the former evokes the vertical axis, the latter is mapped spatially along the horizontal. The criminal underworld includes those seen as outside the typical definition of proper society but not the disabled, the chronically ill, or the mad, or even ordinary paupers with no means of support.

Because poverty, crime, and marginality are interconnected, marginality can be a key marker for instability in times of social and economic transformation. At the dawn of the industrial age, rapid population growth greatly enlarged the ranks of paupers, and existing charitable institutions could not assist all those in need. Rates of crime and begging grew quickly, "heightening fears among propertied people about the basic social order."[12] That series of causal linkages could, with a few minor modifications, describe the situation of marginal people in Jewish society in eastern Europe in the late eighteenth century and well into the nineteenth. Not only were they a cause of social anxiety, but, as we shall see, "ordinary" Jews often projected onto them disquiet proceeding from other social disjunctions.

One of the primary litmus tests used in this work to determine social marginality is whether the people whose lives we are studying had to rely for survival on others outside of family members, whether through individual almsgiving, support from charitable confraternities, and/or (in the twentieth century) benefits from welfare networks or institutions. Hence the focus on indigence and pauperism in this study, as well as on the charitable and philanthropic institutions that attempted to alleviate those conditions. As we know from our own twenty-first-century societies, social isolation can be both a factor contributing to and a consequence of poverty. Although

in some cases marginal Jews were connected to some form of social network—one thinks of the bands of vagabonds who roamed the countryside en
masse—most were socially isolated because of their poverty, lack of familial
support, and/or alienating physical and mental characteristics.[13]

But abject poverty and isolation are not our only criteria for marginality.
Across European society, and in the Russian Empire in particular, there were
many, many poor people, but—though their lives were undoubtedly unimag-
inably difficult—not all were marginalized. Shame was a significant factor
as well—a factor highlighted by two significant historical phenomena, one
physical, the other socio-religious, around which marginal types clustered
together most visibly and which I use to define Jewish marginality.[14] These
were the hekdesh, or poorhouse, and the cholera wedding, a magical ritual
to stop epidemics that emerged in the early nineteenth century. During the
period that this book covers, the hekdesh was home to a motley crew of
itinerant and local beggars, vagrants, madwomen and madmen, chronically
ill people, and poor orphans. Similarly, the cholera wedding dragged under
the wedding canopy those considered the dregs of society, its misfits, freaks,
and monsters: paupers, beggars, "idiots," cripples, the deformed, the ugly, and
the unmarried indigent. Much more effectively than any conceptual philosophy, these two institutions highlight for us those whom Jewish society
considered to be marginal, devalued castoffs. Both are significant markers
of the transition in East European Jewish society from premodern to modern: the hekdesh underwent a gradual but perceptible transformation in the
early decades of the nineteenth century, a transformation linked to a broader
range of changes wrought by modernity. And even more starkly, the cholera
wedding was both a product of and a reaction to the coming of modernity,
a "traditional" (though in actual fact new and innovative) remedy intended
to surpass the remedies the modern world proffered for a very modern pandemic by reifying supposedly age-old dichotomies embedded within the
matrix of Jewish society.

The collective identity that the hekdesh and the cholera wedding highlight is the socially marginal, yes, but perhaps also the freak. In a perceptive
study of the process of "enfreakment," whereby people with extraordinary
bodies are categorized as Other by society and subsequently put on display

for a public that is by turns fascinated and horrified, Elizabeth Grosz argues that, paradoxically,

> at the same time that enfreakment elaborately foregrounds specific bodily eccentricities, it also collapses all those differences into a "freakery," a single amorphous category of corporeal otherness. By constituting the freak as an icon of generalized embodied deviance, the exhibitions also simultaneously reinscribed gender, race, sexual aberrance, ethnicity, and disability as inextricable yet particular exclusionary systems legitimated by bodily variation—all represented by the single multivalent figure of the freak. Thus, what we assume to be a freak of nature was a freak of culture.[15]

To be sure, the Jewish outcasts of eastern Europe were not limited to the disfigured or the deformed and were generally not called "freaks." But they *were* put on display in newspaper pictorial sections, ethnographies, and the cholera wedding. Grosz's insight helps us understand how Jewish society grouped marginal Jews together, collapsing their differences (to use her phrase) into one category of otherness.

In the traditional Jewish life-world of eastern Europe, marginal types were perceived as occupying a space that was neither fully within the boundaries that marked the norms of Jewish society, nor fully outside of them. They were betwixt-and-between people; in anthropological language, liminal. They lay outside two of the most central social structures of that society, livelihood and marriage, the first of which was usually critical for the attainment of the second. It was considered a great misfortune to be without independent livelihood, as evidenced—to give just one example—by the thousands of petitions sent to Rabbi Eliyahu Guttmacher in the 1870s by ordinary, mostly Polish, Jews asking for the blessing of *parnasah* (livelihood) and the large subset of those complaining about *dohak gadol* (great [economic] distress) or *parnasah be-tsimtsum* (reduced livelihood/income).[16] Jacob Katz's description of the early modern period applies just as accurately to modernity: Jewish "attitudinal patterns . . . encouraged and favored [a] desire for money and wealth far more than they restricted it," and poverty was perceived as a trial to be endured.[17] And without good prospects (for men) or a dowry (for women), a good match—or sometimes any match at all—was difficult to attain, a deplorable state in a community characterized by "tremendous pressure to marry."[18]

Beggars did not have a livelihood, at least not in the customary sense. Poor orphans could rarely hope to rise above their circumstances, even with support from relatives or charitable societies. For both groups, then, marriage was much less easily attainable than for ordinary people. For their part, physically disabled or deformed people did not conform to normative body types, and the cognitively impaired or mentally ill were perceived as lacking full functioning. In some cases, this meant that they were considered by rabbinic Judaism to be less than full members of the religious community; if they were men, that is, for women were never counted as full members. In terms of our larger categories, however, disability often meant that an independent life sustained by gainful employment was impossible, and that marriage and hence procreation would be difficult to attain.[19]

Such people were not, of course, the only unmarried members of Jewish society, who might also include servants whose circumstances made marriage impossible and widows and widowers who for some reason could not remarry.[20] However, servants did often manage to marry, and the expectation for widows and widowers was that they would remarry relatively soon after the death of a spouse. (A separate category altogether were *agunot*, "anchored" wives whose husbands had deserted them without a writ of divorce, who were technically married but functionally single.)[21]

Standing outside of society, marginal people were, therefore, marked as Other. They experienced liminality—an ambiguous identity that results from being on the boundary between two discrete, well-defined states of being— not for a limited period of time but for many years (in the case of orphans and beggars) or, among those born with a disability, even an entire lifetime.[22] The liminal figure is not only structurally invisible, since society's definitions do not allow for the existence of a category of "betwixt and between," but also structurally dead—or suspended between the living and the dead.[23] Liminality and ambiguity are also often linked with ritual pollution, because what is neither this nor that is viewed in many societies as ritually unclean.[24] As in many cultures, the symbols associated with marginal people in Jewish eastern Europe were drawn from the vocabulary of death; the realm of spirits and demons; disease and bodily un-wholeness (sores, wounds, missing body parts);

and filth and pollution. The institutions with which they were often linked—the hekdesh and the cemetery—also exhibited many of the characteristics associated with liminality: secluded, filthy or ritually unclean, inhabited by spirits and demons. And while marginals were sometimes among the most conspicuous people in a town—who could ignore the rantings of a town fool or the insistent pleading of the local beggar?—they were also, paradoxically, among the most invisible members of Jewish society in eastern Europe. The many different kinds of historical evidence upon which this study is based are testament to that invisibility: I had to scour the extant library of sources on East European Jewish culture in order to find documentation of the lives of these stepchildren of the shtetl.

This project started out as a study in social history that would draw on the usual sources of the social historian: archival documents, governmental memoranda, the press, memoirs, ethnographic studies, and statistical works. But over the course of the past decade, I discovered that a vital resource for understanding the place of marginal people in Jewish society, and perhaps even for getting some suggestion of the texture of their lives, was literature. Thus, in the space of a few pages we may begin with recollections from several memoirs, move on to a statistical survey and then a *pinkas* (communal register), stop briefly to ponder a Yiddish folktale, and conclude with an extended analysis of a late-nineteenth-century Yiddish novel and an early-twentieth-century Hebrew short story.

None of this historical analysis should obscure what lies at the heart of this study: the lives, and the suffering, of real people. These outcasts did not live to be the subject of a historian's inquiry. They were women and men, children and old people, who lived lives of extraordinary challenge, pain, and misery. Sometimes they were helped by their families or communities; frequently they were not, or that help was insufficient or crudely or insensitively proffered. Although their voices are almost completely absent from the historical record, it is my hope that this work will serve, in some small way, as testament to their collective experience.

Structure

The bulk of the book unfolds in the second half of the nineteenth century and the first decades of the twentieth century; in order to prepare the ground for that discussion, the first two chapters reach back to the origins of East European Jewry. Since the first Jews of the Russian Empire were, in fact, Polish Jews, I open with an exploration of the place of the socially marginal in Jewish society in the early modern Polish-Lithuanian Commonwealth and in Europe more broadly. Because we have vastly more evidence for beggars and vagrants in this period than for any other category of social outcast, much of the chapter is devoted to understanding the place of the beggar in preindustrial Jewish society and traditional Jewish approaches to charity and begging. Unlike mendicancy, physical disability and mental illness, and to some extent even orphanhood, had complicated socio-religious connotations that must be understood alongside the more prosaic and often tragic manifestations of these conditions in the physical world. The second chapter examines the decades immediately following the Partitions of Poland and the incorporation of hundreds of thousands of Polish Jews into the Russian Empire. The Romanov state's intervention in internal Jewish affairs, the beginnings of an extended process of impoverishment among Russian and Polish Jews, and the advent of the Haskalah, the Jewish Enlightenment, all had important influences on changing attitudes to marginal Jews—a shift we can assess best when examining the hekdesh and the military conscription introduced by Nicholas I in 1827. In this period, the hekdesh began its transformation from a hybrid sick house and hostel for vagrants into a neglected poorhouse for the riffraff of Jewish society. And the Nicholaevan draft witnessed the official Jewish community offering up poor orphans, homeless people, and other undesirables for the dreaded twenty-five-year military service, one of the first cases in this eastern European context of the use of marginal people as substitute (*kapore*), or a kind of scapegoat.

With the stage set, the following four chapters sketch various aspects of the lives of marginal people and attitudes to them from the mid-nineteenth century to the early decades of the twentieth century. Chapter 3 returns to the hekdesh, which by this period had so deteriorated as to become the physical embodiment of the contemptuous attitudes to marginal folk that were a hallmark of nineteenth-century Jewish modernity in eastern Europe. Memoirs, legends, and contemporary descriptions aid in a fragmentary reconstruction of this enigmatic institution, but it is literary works that provide the greatest insight into the nature of the hekdesh and its function in Jewish society—a physical locus for the grotesque, the uncanny, and the shameful in the Jewish collective unconscious. Chapter 4 follows with an in-depth exploration of the other institution that must lie at the heart of any investigation of attitudes to marginal people: the cholera wedding, an apotropaic ceremony in which the community's undesirables were wedded to each other in the town cemetery in a bid to end an epidemic. This chapter limns the nature and meaning of the ritual from its emergence during one of the Russian Empire's first cholera pandemics in the 1830s through later resurgences of the ritual in the 1860s, 1890s, and 1910s. The cholera wedding was a corrective ritual intended both to normalize marginal people through marriage in order to achieve a kind of cosmic reconciliation that would banish the epidemic, and to remove the calamity from the mainstream of the Jewish community to the community's chosen scapegoat: its marginals.

For Jewish modernizers and reformers in the late Russian Empire, marginal folk often shamefully exemplified all that was backward about Jewish society. The locus of that shame could be in marginal people's own behavior, as with beggars and vagrants, often perceived as social and economic parasites—an allegation often leveled by antisemites at all of East European Jewry—or in ostensibly backward Jewish charitable institutions such as the *Talmud-Torah*, the traditional school for orphans and poor boys. Chapter 5 examines the nature of the criticism aimed at traditional charity and some of the modern alternatives proposed as nostrums. Philanthropic activity was often motivated by persistent anxiety about the menace of the unproductive Jewish idler.

Chapter 6 examines the plight of mentally ill and cognitively disabled Jews by using the evidence of the Guttmacher *kvitlekh*, a collection of 1860s- and 1870s-era petitions from ordinary Jews to a wonderworking rabbi famous throughout eastern Europe for his medical knowledge. The petitions reveal the predicaments faced by family members of "crazy people" as they struggled to understand the nature of their illness, decide how to find treatment for them, and come to terms with the difficult future in store for their loved ones. At the turn of the century, by contrast, the discussion around madness and nervous illness was not so much about individual psychological infirmity as collective debility: insanity as a national Jewish concern.

The book's last chapter extends the analysis of the place of the marginal figure beyond the long nineteenth century into the interwar years, when Jewish philanthropic practice, political thought, and cultural production embraced the Jewish outcast as a potent symbol. Where traditional philanthropy had spoken of its wards as "unfortunates" to be assisted, mostly so that they could be made productive members of imperial society in pursuit of the eventual though far-off goal of social and economic integration of Jews, the nationalistically minded social welfare institutions and networks that emerged during this period saw the most vulnerable, and especially orphans and disabled children, as embodying the scars and hopes of the entire Jewish nation. Beginning with an assessment of the place of marginal people in the new discipline of folklore, I move on to examine literary works in which outcasts played central roles as true protagonists. The chapter also explores how Jewish nationalist discourse mobilized the trope of the social outcast, often to cast the entire Jewish people as the dispossessed of society, whom Jewish politics could transform into proud, self-respecting, and productive people. I conclude by examining interwar-era literary and cinematic representations of the cholera wedding in which the cholera bride and groom are now depicted as full human characters in their own right, warranting the sympathy of readers and viewers.

An epilogue extends the book's primary analytical concerns beyond the core chronological framework and into World War II and the postwar years. During the Holocaust, Nazi propaganda and persecution transformed all Jews into outcasts: literal beggars, madmen, and orphans. In the aftermath of destruction, several literary works—among them Isaac Bashevis Singer's story "Gimpel the Fool"—suggest that the marginal figure remains a persistent and compelling cultural representative of the vanished world of East European Jewry. In a brief conclusion, I consider the benefits of using gender studies, queer theory, and critical disability studies as tools in the study of East European Jewish history

A word about terminology. As is true for any history of disability, the contemporary terminology has long passed out of use and would almost certainly be considered both inaccurate and offensive today. "Madwoman," "madman," "idiot," and "cripple" are not meaningful or acceptable terms today; nor is there a straight line between any of these words and those we use today to describe and understand non-normative human experience in the realm of the psyche, the personality, the intellect, and the body: mental disorders; intellectual, developmental, or physical disabilities; or even depression or anxiety. In what follows, I do not distinguish consistently between different types of disabilities because the society in question did not do so, and I use both terminology that was current in the period in question but would be unacceptable today and twenty-first-century terms. The context makes clear which is appropriate.

CHAPTER 1

JEWISH MARGINAL PEOPLE
IN PREMODERN EUROPE

Short, fat, green as grass. . . .
She is pretty as a pretty apple
But her head is just a little bit dirty. . . .
Her father is a thief
And her mother lies in the cemetery together with all of you.
    —early modern *Purim-shpil*

In the nineteenth century, marginal people—beggars, physically and cognitively disabled people, the mentally ill, and poor orphans—became a virtual caste among the Jews of eastern Europe. But what of their counterparts in earlier centuries? Fragmentary source material shows that beggars were frequently associated with moral and physical decay, corruption, and filth. Physical disabilities and deformities were often perceived as originating in sinful acts. The notion of the undeserving poor that emerged in medieval European Jewish societies persisted for many centuries and would eventually play an important role in the thinking about poverty and begging that developed among the Russian Jewish intellectual and mercantile elite in the late nineteenth century. The attitudes we investigate in this chapter also gave rise to another modern phenomenon: the use of the most wretched and stigmatized Jews as a symbol for the Jewish people as a whole.

On the other hand, Jewish culture sometimes assigned a positive valence to the otherness of marginal people. Orphans had a unique connection to the heavenly realms; the possessed could prophesy; and even the disabled, if they were seen to have been struck because of sin, were evidence of the direct hand of the divine and of a Providential order.

This chapter explores categories of marginal identity in premodern Jewish society and culture in an attempt to understand the conditions that laid the foundations for the emergence of an underclass of outcasts in the modern period. We begin by examining poverty in history and in the writing of Jewish history.

Charity, poverty, and begging in Jewish history

There are two distinct trends in the historiography of Jewish charity; one optimistic, the other pessimistic. The first is a tendency to view charitable affairs and attitudes to the poor through rose-colored glasses; this approach often sets the Jewish community on a pedestal for its exemplary charitable ideals.[1] According to this interpretation, Jewish history "never knew a period of cruel treatment of the poor man," and Maimonides' ideal of anonymous charity reached its highest expression in the Jewish communities of Germany, Poland, and Russia, where many communities had a special box into which one could deposit contributions to charity or, if necessary, take out as much as one needed.[2] While it was not always possible to treat the poor exactly as one would anyone else in the community, rather than just providing the minimum, "the desire to reach this goal was almost always very apparent."[3]

Other historians have seen Jewish charity in a harsher, perhaps more realistic, light. While Judaism understood the "care for the poor as a sacred religious obligation," they contend that in reality impoverished premodern Jewish communities could often provide only "the most elementary type of sick-care and alms."[4] Shame also played a pivotal role: examining the interrelationship among charity, the poor, and social control in premodern Jewish communities, Elliot Horowitz noted that specific communal regulations or rabbinic responsa sometimes betrayed the ambivalence or even disgust of middle-class Jews at their destitute coreligionists. In the Polish-Lithuanian Commonwealth, in particular, communal documents revealed a certain aversion to "direct and ongoing contact with the poor, and especially to the foreign poor."[5] A seventeenth-century regulation from Poznań, for example, banned the poor from begging house to house on Purim so that householders would not suffer shame (*kedei she-lo yevuyash ha-ba'al bayit me-aniyim*).[6]

Charity also functioned to elevate the social status of the donor; Isaac Levitats argued that Jewish charity in tsarist Russia was arranged more for the benefit of the donor than the recipient, since charitable societies—as seen through the prism of their minute books (*pinkasim*)—were more concerned with "defining the rights and privileges of the members than with the ways and means of distributing the charities."[7]

Many scholars of charity in the premodern world have noted the tendency to distinguish between the pious poor who have descended temporarily into poverty—sometimes called conjunctural poverty—and the undeserving poor who were born into poverty and, according to some religious authorities, were not to be given charity at all. The latter phenomenon is known as structural poverty.[8] In the former category were included the so-called "shamefaced" poor—former people of substance whom circumstances (fire, illness, etc.) had brought low but were often recognized as more "worthy" than ordinary paupers. By contrast, alien or unknown beggars and vagrants were frequently viewed with great suspicion in medieval and early modern Europe, since one could never be sure if the condition preventing them from working—a physical disability, for example—was genuine or faked. Timothy Smith contends that "the image of the 'professional beggar' was in fact grounded in reality. . . . Every European town had its share of occasional and professional beggars."[9]

Paradoxically, it was frequently those born into structural poverty who were most in need of help, for they—and especially the disabled and those without family to support them—had little chance of ever rising out of a life of misery and want. According to pioneering scholar of poverty Michel Mollat, poverty was "a situation of weakness, dependence, or humiliation, characterized by privation of the means to power and social esteem. . . . Living from hand to mouth, [the pauper] had no chance of rising without assistance."[10] Mollat's subject was medieval Christian society, but his *Annales*-based approach to the texture of everyday life can profitably be applied to Jewish society in the Polish-Lithuanian Commonwealth and even, to an extent, in the Russian Empire, which until at least the mid-nineteenth century operated on essentially traditional—that is, premodern—foundations. Jews born into structural poverty, and especially the disabled and those without family to support them, had little chance of ever rising out of a life of misery and want. Many had little other choice but a life of begging.

As Derek Penslar and Tirtsah Levie Bernfeld have demonstrated, the first European Jews to differentiate formally between worthy and unworthy recipients of charity were the Sephardim of early modern Amsterdam. The leaders of that community—like their Christian counterparts in much of western and central Europe—understood poverty as both an economic and a moral problem.[11] Faced in the seventeenth century with an onslaught of poor Ashkenazic Jews, many of them refugees or economic migrants from Poland-Lithuania who ended up begging on the streets of Amsterdam, Sephardic communal leaders decided that relief would only be granted to those who could not work due to poor health, old age, or genuine unemployment.[12] Also deemed worthy of assistance were widows and disabled people, including blind people and "deaf-mutes."[13] This was perhaps the only Jewish community in Europe to establish a workhouse to keep Jewish paupers from begging or, worse, ending up in the city's jails. As Levie Bernfeld shows, another significant motivation for curbing mendicancy was protecting the good reputation of the Sephardic community. "Therefore, they tried to curtail begging by Ashkenazi Jews, so as 'to prevent scandal and annoyance to the inhabitants of our country and the magistracy.'"[14] Indeed, the communal worthies also tried to keep undesirables out of the city altogether, a practice followed in many Jewish communities across Europe.[15]

The *Betteljuden* of early modern Europe

The gradual impoverishment of German Jewry in the late medieval period owing to ongoing expulsions, as well as a weakening legal status, led to the emergence of "a class of impoverished vagrants known as *Schalantjuden*, or, in Hebrew, *archei u-farchei* (flotsam and jetsam)."[16] This was part of a much wider pan-European process of pauperization caused by the rapid socioeconomic changes of the sixteenth century.[17] The Hebrew term persisted into the early modern period, but a new German designation for these vagrants appeared in the seventeenth century: *Betteljuden*.[18] These "beggar Jews" tended to follow fairly fixed routes from community to community, since the accepted custom was for charity overseers to provide them with food and lodging for one night (or two if they arrived on Friday) and then to send them to the next locale with a Jewish population.[19] On a larger scale, the general path of Jewish beggars in the early modern period was from east to west, that is, from Poland to Germany (a reversal of the direction of Jewish migration in the late Middle Ages).[20] By the late seventeenth century, surges of Jewish refugees from Poland, along with government policies, had exacerbated the problem to the extent that "Jewish vagrancy had become a serious social problem" in the lands of central Europe.[21] "It was the flood of Jewish refugees created by the Thirty Years' War and the Russo-Polish-Cossack wars of the mid-1600s that prompted wide-ranging efforts by Jewish communities to stanch the flow of beggars and limit communal resources on care for the foreign poor," Derek Penslar writes.[22] Medieval Jewish communities had been relatively open to strangers, but a clear preference for locals over aliens emerged in the early modern period, one symptom of "the growing geographic diffusion and communal separatism of early modern Jewry," Salo Baron maintains.[23] In the large Jewish community of Frankfurt am Main, there were signs early on that long-established charitable customs that brought rich and poor together, most notably the *Pletten* system (from *Billeten*, "tickets," referring to the vouchers that the poor were given), which assigned the alien poor to eat and lodge in the homes of householders, often for a maximum of three days, were giving way to a widespread aversion to direct contact with the underclasses: instead of having *Betteljuden* eat at the family table, Jews with residence privileges (*Schutzjuden*) began to seat them at separate tables.[24] Yacov Guggenheim argues that although by the end of the eighteenth century the "depersonalization" of charity for the poor had made significant progress, the Pletten system prevented the full-scale isolation of the Schutzjuden from their "unfortunate" coreligionists.[25] Nonetheless, more than one contemporary Jewish publication made clear that Betteljuden were of a different class from "ordinary" Jews: one pamphlet described "their physical and moral decay, their apathy and filth."[26] German states introduced various policies to compel Jewish communities to withhold assistance from wandering Jewish beggars; in some cases communal authorities agreed to cooperate with the government in such initiatives.[27]

This trend was far more marked in the Polish-Lithuanian Commonwealth. The principle of *hezkat ha-yishuv*, the restriction of the right of residence to a limited number of people, made it very difficult for the poor simply to settle in a new community, and over the course of the seventeenth century, the Jewish supracommunal bodies of the Polish-Lithuanian

Commonwealth (the Council of the Four Lands and the Council of Lithuania) both passed regulations making it more difficult for itinerant beggars and paupers to settle in a new community, or—in the case of Lithuania—even to stay for longer than twenty-four hours.[28] From an economic point of view this made good sense, since anyone who could not pay taxes was essentially dead weight for a communal structure that depended on the taxes it collected from its members in order to fund the day-to-day functioning of the *kahal*, the governing board of the organized Jewish community, and to pay the collective taxes that it owed to various Jewish autonomous bodies.[29] The Council of Lithuania, in particular, issued ordinances that came down very harshly on itinerant beggars. Among the very earliest ordinances recorded (the council had been in existence for at least a half-century prior to the start of regular documentation) is one from the year 1623 that referred to the "crooked ways" and "dark deeds" of the beggars who roamed the land.[30] The *takanah* levied the accusation that many of these mendicants were charlatans masquerading as rabbis and scholars when in fact, in the excellently worded paraphrase of Salo Baron, "they were often found drinking in inns, dissipating in houses of ill-repute and committing other unmentionable wrongs."[31] The allegation of sexual licentiousness is significant, since the latter was often associated with marginal people, a linkage that would continue to be made in the modern period. It is also noteworthy that the alien poor were accused of being imposters. There was a long tradition in Jewish legal literature of associating the poor with the taking on of a false identity.[32] Finally, "communal officials feared that Jewish vagrants would commit crimes against Gentiles and thereby bring the wrath of the authorities down on the Jewish community as a whole."[33]

The Council continued as follows:

> No beggar whatsoever shall be given anything except transportation to send him away on pain of *herem*, *shamta* [both variations on excommunication], and large fines; neither shall he be kept in one's house for more than twenty-four hours. . . . If one is unable to get rid of him and expel him by the power of the Jewish authorities, one may invoke the aid of the Gentiles, and there is no sin or wrong in so doing.[34]

The tone of the ordinance is unmistakably severe, though it is notable that punitive measures are threatened not against the mendicants themselves but communities or individuals that aided them. It is also remarkable that the Council permitted communities to resort to the Christian authorities, since as a general rule Jewish communal institutions preferred not to ask Christians for assistance. About a decade and a half later, the Council decreed that Jewish communities near the Polish border were required to deport itinerant beggars posthaste, an admonition that later sessions of the Council in the seventeenth century repeated. The harsh line was again taken in a 1761 regulation that forbade communities to admit itinerant beggars from Poland.[35]

As is often the case with these kinds of ordinances, the severity that we see here may in fact have been intended as a response to what communal officials on the highest level perceived as undue laxity vis-à-vis Jewish vagrants; the legislation may thus actually be testimony to rather more lenient attitudes on the part of ordinary Jews and even kahal elders at the local level.

We find fewer harsh regulations on the alien poor among the Jewish communities of Poland, but a 1595 communal ordinance in Kraków forbade begging anywhere in the city (the poor were instead given a fixed sum for the week), while Poznań similarly banned itinerants from begging house to house and, in addition, ended the previous custom of offering them transport to the next locale.[36] In the late 1700s, one of the beadles of the Swarzędz kahal was obligated to monitor poor visitors so that they would not remain in the town longer than permitted, usually twenty-four hours, even when this meant ensuring their departure on Friday if they had arrived the afternoon before. At gatherings of supracommunal bodies, representatives of Jewish communities would often warn their peers not to send them beggars, or "announced that poor people from other locations could not count on them due to general impoverishment."[37]

In the course of the eighteenth century, more and more Polish Jews fell into penury owing to a range of factors, and a new lumpenproletariat underclass was clearly emerging.[38] There was also a marked growth in the number of Jewish beggars and vagrants, who, according to one estimate in the early 1790s, numbered some 81,000—the equivalent of about 9 percent of the entire Jewish population of the Polish-Lithuanian Commonwealth. A social and demographic study by Y. Y. Trunk of the community of Kutno in the late eighteenth century provides a remarkably similar statistic for what it classifies as "the poor"—9.2 percent—but this category includes not only those living off of communal and private support but also poor artisans, day laborers, peddlers, and others members of the working poor.[39] Of course it stands to reason that the itinerant poor would not have entered into Trunk's calculations, since they were not considered permanent members of any community.[40]

Efforts at reforming and "productivizing" Jews in both western and eastern Europe from the late eighteenth century on usually included references to the Betteljuden as symbols of Jewish parasitism, and large groups of them were expelled from Prussian- and Austrian-annexed Poland into the rump Rzeczpospolita after the first partition in 1772.[41] A reform plan put forward in 1792 proposed that the government divide Polish Jewry into five categories, the lowest of which would include both poor people who were able to work and those so destitute and frail as to require community support.[42]

Jacob Goldberg argues that Jewish vagrants "took on the way of life and characteristics of the so-called 'unbound people' (ludzie luźni)," a motley crew of peasants unattached to the land and others—destitute townspeople, former soldiers or deserters, pilgrims—who wandered from town to town, finding occasional work as day laborers and sometimes resorting to begging.[43] This was a marginal element in Polish society both in its lack of geographic permanence and position outside the feudal hierarchy. The fact that a number of Jews felt comfortable enough to enter into the company of the unbound suggests the extent of their marginalization from Jewish society. Indeed, Goldberg suggests that a good number of them ended up converting to Christianity.[44]

Were Jewish itinerant beggars linked to criminality, either in reality or in popular perception, as was often the case with their Christian counterparts? The links between vagrancy and criminality in Jewish society are unclear. The leading scholar of the late-medieval Schalantjuden of central Europe, the predecessors of the Betteljuden, claims that, unlike their Christian counterparts whose extreme marginalization pushed them to criminal behavior, there is little evidence of that phenomenon among the arhei u-farhei, in large measure because they were in some sense still members of the established Jewish community. The Jewish vagabond "was not entirely disenfranchised," Yacov Guggenheim writes. "As long as they did not convert, destitute Jews retained an organized reference group, namely, their fellow Jews, to which they still belonged and which took responsibility for them."[45] Scholars examining the case of the early-modern Betteljuden, by contrast, argue that it was just a few steps from destitution to "acute social distress," and thence to crime.[46] Emanuel Ringelblum, one of the only historians of Polish Jewry to examine the question, concluded that in eighteenth-century Polish Jewish communities, it was the competition between local and alien beggars that resulted in some beggars turning to crime. In turn, the existing thieves were pushed "to the very edge of the underworld" and became murderers and bandits.[47]

The Beggar's Comedy: a farcical wedding of marginal folk

Given the beggar's dubious reputation among Polish Jews, our next piece of evidence—among the few we possess that offer a clear window into attitudes to marginal people among early modern Jews in eastern Europe—comes as no surprise. The *betler-shpil* (beggar's farce or beggar's comedy), one of most popular *Purim-shpiln* (popular plays put on during the one-day carnival holiday of Purim) in early modern Jewish communities, presented scenes from a beggar's life as a kind of interlude between acts of the *Akhashveyresh-shpil*, a burlesque of the Purim story as recounted in the Scroll of Esther.[48] In his history of Jewish theater, Ignacy (Yitskhok) Schiper compared several tsarist-era fragments of a surviving text, the earliest version of which he dated to the fifteenth or sixteenth century, which has remarkable connections to other topoi associated with marginal people—ugliness, filth, illness, demons and the world of the dead (including the cemetery). These fragments of the Beggar's Comedy—examined at greater length in the analysis of the cholera wedding in chapter 4—parody of a marriage between two beggars. In the first section, a matchmaker introduces the beggar woman, who is both an orphan and an old maid:

Short, fat, green as grass.
[. . .]
She is pretty as a pretty apple
But her head is just a little bit dirty.
[. . .]
She's a real housewife at home:

She polishes the cup with her sleeve
And sweeps the room with her apron
And when she has to heat the oven and make the bed
She makes the oven and heats the bed.
[. . .]
Her father is a thief
And her mother lies in the cemetery together with all of you.[49]

The orphaned beggar maiden is associated here with ugliness, filth, and stu-
pidity.[50] There is also an explicit reference to illness and the cemetery.

In the *tnoyim* (engagement contract) scene, the couple are told:

So, shall we read the contract?
This is the contract:
You are both totally ignorant Jews [*groyse goyim*]!
These are the garments:
Absolutely zilch! [*kadokhes mit koshern fodem*]
For a dowry, I give nine thousand demons,
Lodging—in the poorhouse,
Support—begging door to door
A position—at the cemetery.
And all is valid and binding.
Listen, children, tell me word for word
May boils cover you in abundance![51]

We can imagine a Purim-shpil audience, its customary social strictures loos-
ened by alcohol, laughing uproariously at this fun-house-mirror version of
Jewish wedding traditions. The primary themes are deficiency and illness.
The beggars have *no* education or knowledge, *no* garments, *no* dowry, *no* real
accommodation, *no* true occupation other than the community's permission
to beg (the cemetery was a good place to beg because Jews visiting graves
often wished to give charity; Proverbs 11:4 declares that "righteousness will
save one from death"). As if that were not bad enough, they are then cursed
with boils and illness (*kadokhes mit koshern fodem* idiomatically means "nothing at all," but *kadokhes* also signifies some kind of fever or illness).

Traditional engagement contracts often had the newlyweds living with

FIGURE I.I. Two beggars at cemetery wall (Lwów, 1930s). The long association of beggars and other marginal people with the cemetery extended into the interwar period. The meaning of the markings on the photograph is unknown. Archives of the YIVO Institute for Jewish Research, New York, RG 120 (Territorial Photographic Collection) PO 2149.01.

either the wife or husband's parents for a set period, but the betler-shpil has, of course, a mockery of *kest*: living in the poorhouse and procuring food by begging. (A Yiddish expression recorded in the late nineteenth or early twentieth century is testament to the longevity of this kind of parodic humor: "An orem-man hot kest in di hayzer un dire in hekdesh"—[after his wedding,] a poor man gets his board by begging and has his lodging in the poorhouse.)[52] And once again, the cemetery makes an appearance, in addition to demons.

Under the wedding canopy, the solemnizer intones:

I hereby wed you,
You two stains . . .
On you [the bride], my child, a plague
And on the lout, two.[53]

If the Purim-shpil is a reasonable gauge of popular Jewish attitudes to beggars, those attitudes were negative in the extreme. They were, it seems, associated with ugliness, ignorance, filth, disease, and death. (The connection with disease is particularly interesting in light of the fact that Christian perceptions of Polish Jews were often colored by the notion that Jews were predisposed to specific illnesses.)[54] The apparent hostility to the destitute and the beggar in Jewish society had significant consequences for the development of the hekdesh, the Jewish sick house–poorhouse. Since the following chapters will trace the development of the hekdesh into the twentieth century, a brief study of its origins is in order.

The origins of the hekdesh

How the rabbinic term *hekdesh*, from a Hebrew root denoting holy or sacred, evolved from denoting something consecrated as sacred or Temple property to a shelter for the sick and poor is unclear.[55] One explanation argues that "the term *hekdesh* originally meant the Temple treasury" but in later centuries came to be applied to the charity and endowment funds of the medieval synagogue-community, and was finally used, by extension, for the communal hospice.[56] Another account explains that in the Middle Ages, both Christians and Jews viewed their sick houses and hospices, maintained by charity for the poor, as adjunct, in a metaphorical sense, to their holy places—consecrated to God for the benefit of the poor.[57] Just as Christians called their home for the sick poor a "house of God" (e.g., French *hôtel-dieu*), Jews called their hostel—a shelter for poor travelers and for the sick—"a consecrated place": hekdesh.[58] But Christian society developed a wide array of hospitals, almshouses, and other eleemosynary institutions, all of them connected intimately with the church, while Jewish communities, relatively small in size, usually maintained only one institution, which, unlike Jewish charitable confraternities, did not usually attain any particular religious significance (for example, fourteenth-century sources suggest that "Jewish communal charitable institutions for the indigent or ill" [*batei hekdesh*] may also have served as leper hospitals, Ephraim Shoham-Steiner notes).[59] It is unclear whether the premodern hekdesh in central Europe primarily served local Jews or outsiders, likely because community policies differed from place to place and region to region (analogous Christian institutions served both locals and aliens).[60] Itinerant Jews arriving in towns where the institution was primarily for locals had to submit to an assessment by the kahal and might be compelled to depart posthaste.[61]

In early modern Poland, the primary function of the hekdesh had been that of sick house, but at some point in the eighteenth or nineteenth century, the institution began to serve chiefly as a beggars' hostel.[62] The sources make it very difficult to pin down a more precise date for this transition (explored in more depth in chapter 2), in part because in premodern societies poverty, vagrancy, and illness were often intimately intertwined. Mollat and other medieval historians have noted the dynamic relationship between poverty and illness or infirmity of some kind; the chronically ill and mentally disabled were more likely to live lives of destitution and dependence, since they lacked the means to support themselves, as is still often the case in the twenty-first century.[63] Disabled and infirm people who lacked security in the form of property or family were usually at the mercy of society, reliant on whatever aid their community, corporation, or religious institutions chose to provide.[64] Amplifying Mollat's thesis in his study of Jewish marginals in medieval Europe, Shoham-Steiner observes that "poverty was also often correlated with madness, deformities, and disease, on the one hand magnifying the negative image of both these groups, but on the other hand making a response to their needs more urgent."[65] In early modern Poland, to separate the poor from the rest of society, alms and poor relief were often provided in the local hospital.[66] In some cases, hospital wardens even sought out beggars and hauled them to the hospital, sometimes against their will.[67]

Disability in classical and medieval Judaism

Before exploring medieval Jewish attitudes to disability, it is vital that we go back even further in time to the foundations of those attitudes found in seminal rabbinic works. In her path-breaking work on disability in Judaism, Judith Abrams argues that "in the [Talmudic] sages' system, persons with hearing, speaking, and mental disabilities . . . were deemed unable to receive, retain, and retrieve [Judaism's] *sacra*."[68] This was so because they lacked *da'at*, a quality essential to participation in the Jewish society envisioned by the rabbis of the Mishnah, which is "a complex combination of cognitive and cultural skills involving the ability to discern the difference between right and wrong and an insight . . . that allows for a comprehension and judgment that is greater than the senses."[69] Thus, the mentally ill and cognitively disabled person (*shoteh*) was grouped together with the minor (*katan*) in exclusion from full legal personhood in rabbinic Judaism. So too was the so-called deaf-mute (*heresh*), since in the premodern world, deaf people were perceived as mute, and thus could not show that they were capable of the mindfulness that was necessary for full participation in Jewish life.[70] Deaf people may actually have suffered developmental disabilities due to their frequent exclusion from educational frameworks of any kind.[71] (It bears mentioning here that all the categories in question were understood to be gendered male, since the rabbinic system excluded all women, regardless of physical ability, from legal personhood.)

As for physical disability, there is evidence that the ancient sages believed that it was caused by sin; in the case of leprosy, for example, "consequences of sin committed through the body are experienced through the body.[72] In a particularly compelling and, in the context of the present work, germane line of reasoning, Abrams also argues that the suffering that was understood to accompany disability could serve as atonement for sin, following the rabbinic principle of *midah ke-neged midah*, or measure for measure. In the stories of the legendary Nahum Ish Gamzo found in the Palestinian and Babylonian Talmuds, the righteous Nahum curses himself with physical disabilities as punishment for having postponed a charitable deed, as a consequence of which the erstwhile recipient died.[73] Further, Abrams postulates that the Jewish people, or a part thereof, is sometimes portrayed in rabbinic literature as a physically disabled person. In the former case, the disability is a symbol of immoral or sinful deeds committed by the entire nation; in the latter, such as that of Deutero-Isaiah's suffering servant, it is an atonement for sins committed by other Jewish groups:

> In the powerful prophetic image of Isaiah's suffering servant we find an explicit linking of sin, disabilities, suffering, and atonement. The suffering servant is clearly disabled and wounded. His wounds, like the sacrifice in the Temple, make an expiation for sin. . . . The servant suffers as the faithful of Israel suffer. He is downcast as the exiles are downcast. To be stripped of one's country and cult is to be disabled.[74]

The belief that bodily disfigurement was a punishment for sin persisted into the Middle Ages, since the whole, intact body was seen as the ideal vehicle for worship and following God's commandments.[75] That perception, however, coexisted with an understanding of disability as a natural phenomenon that was simply an aspect of God's creation.[76] As Shoham-Steiner explains, *Sefer Hasidim*, a twelfth- or thirteenth-century foundational work of the pietists of medieval Ashkenaz, taught that no matter what the cause of a physical disability, Jews were religiously and ethically obligated to care for a disabled or deformed person as one would care for a parent.[77]

But Shoham-Steiner also demonstrates that this attitude was not always the norm among ordinary Jews. When in the thirteenth century a group of petitioners asked Meir of Rothenburg, a great rabbinic figure of medieval Franco-German Jewry, whether a disabled man could serve as prayer leader, they referred to the man as having been "struck by [God's] attribute of justice."[78] God had rendered a severe judgment against such an individual and therefore there was grave doubt as to whether he could rightfully lead the congregation in prayer. R. Meir's response was notable in its compassion: "It is better if the reader is deformed. God is not like a king of flesh and blood who uses whole vessels and throws away those that are broken. God prefers broken vessels, as the Psalmist declares, 'A broken and contrite heart, O God, Thou wilt not despise' (Ps. 51:19)."[79]

It is also important to note that in the context of the medieval

Christian-Jewish polemic, Christian theologians frequently portrayed Jews as ugly and deformed, even suffering from physical afflictions, because of their rejection of the truth of Christianity.[80] The actual deformities of disabled Jews thus echoed long-standing Christian superstitions about Jewish bodily anomalies (e.g., the Jewish hunchback) embodying Jewish immorality. This notion adumbrates an idea encountered in modern eastern Europe: Jewish marginal people as a symbol for the entire Jewish nation, perceived by gentiles or sometimes even by Jews themselves as inadequate, pitiable, malformed, and corrupted by their unnatural economic and social circumstances. The idea of the part representing the whole is intrinsically related to the way social theory understands the perception of the disabled or deformed person as focusing on the non-normative aspect of that person's appearance. That "trait can come to designate the person as a whole. . . . This phenomenon, which we may call 'identity spread,' is a key factor in the production of attitudes toward marginal individuals."[81] It is integrally linked to fear and the uncanny.

Mental illness in the premodern world: possessed, holy fool, lunatic, idiot

"The labeling or identifying of insanity has been primarily a social act," the historian of disability Herbert C. Covey writes.[82] In medieval Europe, among Jews as among Christians, madness was viewed variously as an illness, a product of witchcraft and/or demonic possession for which the sole remedy was exorcism, and a severe, albeit mysterious, punishment from God.[83] Sometimes the latter two were conflated, since heavenly punishment could be understood as coming through Satan and the demonic forces. There was no conception of a specific refuge for madmen and madwomen; if they were "serene," that is, nonviolent, they could be cared for—or mistreated, as the case might be—at home or (for men) permitted to wander freely within the local community or more widely. Violent madwomen and madmen of course had to be confined in some way.[84] Roy Porter comments that the integration of lunatics into the mainstream of society may have fostered "some residual sense of common humanity," and at the very least inhibited a widespread perception of mad people as alien others.[85]

Christianity offered additional, positive interpretations of madness. Some theologians postulated that God might permit demonic possession in order to manifest His own glory and the power of the sacraments.[86] A more potent belief was the concept of the holy fool, a notion deeply rooted in Christian thought; as Roy Porter argues, "a faith . . . which valued the spiritual myster-ies of contemplation, asceticism, and the mortification of the flesh . . . could not but see gleams of godliness in the simplicity of the fool or in ecstasies and transports."[87] The tradition of the fool in Christ (based, some argue, on 1 Corinthians 4:10: "We are fools for Christ's sake . . .") goes back to early Christian traditions in the Near East and medieval Byzantium and seems to have taken root in Russian principalities such as Novgorod by the fifteenth century.[88] In Muscovy, the holy fool, or *iurodivyi*, was a highly regarded fig-ure whom people would come to for advice—it was understood that he had the power of prophecy—and for a time the holy fool played a role at the royal court, having the unheard-of freedom to speak openly to the tsar and even criticize him.[89] As the phenomenon became more widespread in the seven-teenth century, the iurodivyi lost its luster; by now, it seems clear, some holy fools were perceived as mentally ill.[90]

As Shoham-Steiner argues persuasively, Jewish culture had no analogy to the Christian holy fool, in large measure because normative Judaism prized the rational intellect as the seat of judgment so necessary for comprehension and punctilious observance of the commandments. If madness was linked to the divine or the supernal realm, it was either as an inexplicable punishment or as a consequence of demonic possession. As was true of many traditional societies, premodern Jewish society commonly attributed madness to spirits and demons, and there seems to have been an uptick in such manifestations in eastern Europe in the seventeenth and eighteenth centuries.[91] Then, in the late 1700s, the popular linkage of madness to the realm of the supernatural began to wane—perhaps a testament to the gradual encroachment of mo-dernity—and the tsaddik took the place of the insane person in his ability to perceive hidden things and thus strengthen ordinary people's faith.[92] At approximately the same time, responsibility for the insane in the Russian Empire was beginning to shift from the church to the state and science.[93] Starting in the sixteenth and seventeenth centuries, states across the Euro-pean continent had moved to segregate the insane from society by confining them in specialized institutions.[94] This trend reached Russia in 1762, when

Tsar Peter III decreed that madmen and madwomen were not to be sent to monasteries, as had long been customary, but to a "special house," that is, a lunatic asylum.[95] (It was usually individuals from privileged families whose relatives could or would not care for them at home who were housed in monasteries; in peasant society, lunatics were more likely simply to be shackled.[96] Such people were consigned to a life of misery, isolated from society and subject to abuse and maltreatment.) Under Catherine the Great (r. 1762–96), newly established local departments of public welfare created insane asylums on the Western model: madhouses to segregate the insane from society and ensure that they did not cause harm.[97] Those institutions were "regarded as places of horror to be avoided at all cost," Julie Brown writes.[98]

That the early decades of Jewish life under Russian rule (late eighteenth and early nineteenth centuries) coincide with the advent of the medicalization of mental illness is clear from the case of Moshe Schneerson, scion of the first tsaddik of the Lubavich dynasty, Shneur Zalman of Liady. Moshe suffered from mental illness from a young age and throughout his life his family spent considerable time, money, and effort seeking medical advice and care for him in the Russian Empire and Prussia.[99] This path was, of course, open only to families of means; most ordinary folk, Jewish and Christian alike, could only dream of soliciting the advice of medical experts, and in any case would only turn to modern medicine with the greatest reluctance (more on this in chapter 6). Most mentally ill people were cared for at home, treated with prayer and folk remedies.[100] Although it was generally understood that intellectually disabled people (often called idiots or imbeciles) were qualitatively distinct from lunatics, they were frequently lumped together with all others perceived as being mentally infirm.[101]

Orphans

Unlike the other categories we have surveyed thus far, poor orphans only became marginal figures in the modern period. In medieval and early modern Jewish communities, orphans were generally well looked after by the kahal or the myriad *hevrot* (charitable societies) that were a fixture of the medieval Jewish community. Every community had a confraternity to support poor orphans, and especially to find matches for them (particularly for dowryless orphan girls) and provide for their weddings.[102] Jewish communal organs took the care of widows and orphans very seriously, especially with regard to any funds or property that they might have been deeded by their deceased family members, and often released them from communal taxes.[103] A special overseer called *avi yetomim* ("father of orphans," a term is found in Mishnah Gittin 5:4) was sometimes assigned by the kahal to ensure that an appropriate guardian (*apotropos*) was appointed to look after an orphan's property until he or she reached the age of majority.[104] Of early modern Ashkenazic communities, Jacob Katz writes, "The raising of a poor orphaned relative and the arranging of his or her marriage was considered an especially meritorious deed, which charitable persons took pride in fulfilling."[105] Given what we have already learned about the Sephardic community in early modern Amsterdam, it will come as no surprise that the first Jewish orphanage was established in that city in 1648, and the nineteenth century saw the founding of numerous such institutions across the European continent.[106]

For the purposes of education, Jewish orphans in eastern Europe—who could be full orphans, half-orphans, or children whose parents were alive but could not care for them—were often grouped together with the children of the poor, and associations or brotherhoods independent of the official community were often established to endow and run schools to provide these children, usually boys but sometimes girls as well, with a basic Jewish education.[107] Where such associations did not exist, the kahal itself provided for the education of orphans and poor children. Most of the charges stayed in these schools until their early or mid-teenage years, when they would go into domestic service or apprenticeship to an artisan.[108]

In the late 1700s and early 1800s, Polish Jews newly living under the tsarist regime faced a financial crisis, making it much more difficult for communities to care for needy orphans and causing them in some cases to offer orphan boys as substitute recruits for children of more prosperous families. During the decades that followed, down to the end of Romanov rule, Russian and Polish Jews experienced a population explosion, large-scale impoverishment, and far-reaching urbanization, and the number of poor orphans correspondingly soared, most visibly in the large cities of the empire. This, it seemed to some, imperiled the political and social advances that East European Jewry was making in the 1860s and 1870s, and thus posed a serious problem.

The Other in premodern Jewish religious culture: heroes and freaks

Irrespective of their particular difference, marginal people are bound together by their status as outsiders. Disabled people are visibly other in terms of the physical body; mentally ill people fall outside the cognitive mainstream that we are familiar with in everyday life; itinerant beggars and vagrants lack the fixed abode associated with ordinary settled life. These differences represent a tear in the fabric of everyday life and serve as a reminder of all that is base, ugly, unfair, repulsive in this world. Such a reminder can arouse pathos—but also fear and revulsion, and such people were the targets of disgust, ridicule, and persecution in the early modern world.[109] Ugliness, deformity, or disability such as missing limbs hinted of witchcraft, and they were often associated with the devil.[110] Indeed, their very humanity could be called into question.[111]

But their difference could also have a positive valence, perhaps a consequence of the awe with which ordinary folk regarded the extraordinary, the exceptional, even the bizarre. In the preindustrial world, Rachel Adams writes, "freaks were not always understood as the flip side of normality; at one time, their bodies were read as figures of absolute difference who came from elsewhere and bore the portentous imprint of divine or cosmic forces."[112] For both Jews and Christians, the clairvoyance attributed to "mad" men and women thanks to the spirits that had entered them confirmed people's beliefs in the supernatural and strengthened their faith.[113] (The Yiddish saying "A whole fool is a half a prophet" [A gantser nar iz a halber novi], perhaps derived from the Talmudic assertion in Baba Batra 12a that after the Temple was destroyed, prophecy was given to fools, is clearly linked to this notion.)[114] Referring to wonder tales about the founder of Hasidism, Israel Ba'al Shem Tov, Zvi Mark argues that "in the stories recounted in Shivhe ha-Besht we find the Besht described and characterized with the precise properties of the insane and the *hiner bet* [a kind of trancelike experience of the supernal worlds], by whose merit faith had previously been increased and many had repented."[115] Similarly, Rachel Elior notes that during early modern exorcism rituals, the dybbuk relates hidden sins of the living and the dead and divulges communal secrets, and sometimes even sees into the future based on communications with demons and angels.[116] Thus, the insane were actually proof of the existence of God or at least of an entire supernatural world that could not be explained in normal terms. This holds true despite the fact that, as Yoram Bilu argues, Judaism generally perceived possession in negative terms, unlike the possession cults of other traditions in which adepts sought "to establish a symbiotic relationship with the possessing agent."[117]

One tantalizing source that corroborates the perception of the mad as linked to the supernatural is an entry in the *pinkas* (minute book) of the Hevra kadisha (burial society) of Kiev dating to 1793. The pinkas records that one Barukh ben R"R Mordekhai Shamash of Tarashcha (a town about sixty miles from Kiev) had been institutionalized in the Kiev insane asylum on account of his madness—making this perhaps one of the first recorded cases in eastern Europe of a Jewish madman being confined to an asylum. Barukh subsequently died in the hospital and was given a non-Jewish burial. When this became known to the members of the society eight months later, they requested and received permission to bury him with Jewish rites. Upon exhuming the body, they were astonished to find that it was entirely whole: "not a worm had touched it."[118]

Orphans, too, were perceived as having a special connection to the supernatural. *Mahzor Vitry*, an eleventh-century compendium of liturgy and law, records the widespread custom in Jewish communities of medieval northern Europe of having an orphan lead the evening prayer marking the close of the Sabbath. With the souls of the unrighteous dead about to return to hell after their Sabbath reprieve, the orphan's prayer was considered particularly effective in delaying the fateful moment for as long as possible, presumably because his link to the world of the dead was more tangible than that of anyone else in the community.[119] Slavic mythology held similar beliefs with regard to orphans. "The orphan, like the beggar, had the status of intermediary between the world of people and the 'other' world. The utterance of the orphan, like that of the beggar, comes more quickly before God."[120]

Conclusion

In premodern Jewish society, marginal people were viewed with profound ambivalence. The itinerant beggar could be expelled from the town after a fixed period—twenty-four hours, or three days—but the local beggar, the disabled person, the madwoman, the poor orphan—these people had nowhere else to go, especially since modern philanthropic and medical institutions were not to emerge in eastern Europe until the nineteenth century. In the small or middling settlements which most Jews called home, such marginals were simply part of the landscape. Their lives, frequently disfigured by grinding poverty, were often difficult, if not dismal, though they were sustained by personal alms and communal charity.

Beyond the religious limitations imposed by Jewish law on deaf people and those perceived as mentally deficient, on the level of the symbolic, marginals were often perceived as variously linked not only to sin, filth, and physical ugliness but also to the realm of death, clearly a weighty stigma.[121] And while there were some manifestations of marginality that could bear positive connotations, those likely had little impact on the everyday lives of marginal individuals. By the eighteenth century, those perceptions were beginning to wane with the advent of modern science. As Rosemarie Garland Thomas writes with regard to people with bodily deformities, what had previously been marvelous would soon become deviant; "what aroused awe [would] now inspire horror."[122]

CHAPTER 2

BLIND BEGGARS AND ORPHAN RECRUITS

The Russian State, the Kahal, *and Marginal
Jews in the Early Nineteenth Century*

> Zushe Rakover has seven sons
> Not one was drafted
> But Leah the widow's only son
> Is made to pay the price for the *kahal*'s sins.
> —nineteenth-century Yiddish folk song

After the 1772–95 Partitions of Poland and the incorporation of hundreds of thousands of Polish Jews into the Russian Empire, an array of socioeconomic and cultural factors led to the creation of a Jewish underclass of beggars, vagrants, and paupers. These included the predisposition of the physiocratic tsarist state to intervene in internal Jewish affairs, a sharp rise in the numbers of destitute Jews, and the first influences of modernizing thought. In this period, individual contact between ordinary householders and itinerant beggars was apparently on the wane, while the hekdesh began taking on an aura of ignominy that would intensify over the coming decades. The nadir of this early period was undoubtedly the brutal conscription regime introduced under Nicholas I in 1827, during which some Jewish communal leaders, compelled by the state to compile lists of draftees, attempted to draw recruits solely from among socially marginal people. Other Jewish communities drafted poor orphans as so-called voluntary substitutes for the sons of prosperous families. Once they disappeared into the interior of the empire to start their decades-long military service, these boys were perceived in the folk consciousness as victims sacrificed for the greater good of the Jewish people—or for the self-interest of the powerful and wealthy.

The image of the beggar in Jewish and Slavic societies

Chapter 1 has shown the generally negative attitude to beggars in early modern Jewish society. In the surrounding Slavic cultures, attitudes to beggars were ambivalent. "Russian Orthodox doctrine adopted a strikingly lenient attitude toward the poor," identifying them with Christ and emphasizing their "special suffering and sanctity," Adele Lindenmeyr observes.[1] Throughout the nineteenth century, religious thinkers and writers continued to view the poor as "victims, not threats to the social order."[2] The Orthodox concept of charity had a reciprocal, even transactional, nature: the poor enabled the prosperous to fulfill their obligation to give and gave them an opportunity to earn divine blessings and attain spiritual perfection, and it was the duty of the poor in turn to pray for their benefactors; there was even a notion of the beggar as intercessor (*khodatai Boga*).[3] Almost every church or cathedral had a hut where beggars lived.[4] It follows, therefore, that "Orthodox doctrine idealized direct, person-to-person charity."[5] Lindenmeyr argues that church teachings were both reflected in and influenced by popular attitudes, which similarly tended to see paupers, beggars, and even criminals in a positive light.[6] Beggars in Moscow, while repellent to some for their filth and widespread physical defects, were seen by others as "picturesque extremes of the ordinary life of the streets" and even "possessors of some inner virtue, as quintessential representatives of the Russian people."[7]

The nexus between beggars and the sacred—which anthropologists would explain with reference to beggars' permanent liminal state—was perhaps most apparent in the cultural type of the holy vagrant found in many Slavic cultures.[8] In Russia, itinerant religious singers, *kaleki* (or *kaliki*) *perekhozhie*, were beggars, often blind, who sang spiritual songs for alms "to rapt audiences in markets and outside of churches and monasteries. Their songs glorified poverty and begging, while lamenting the sufferings of the poor."[9] In the Polish lands, *dziady*, itinerant beggars who frequently sang religious songs, were perceived as having a special connection to "the other world" and the realms of the sacred and the magical. In traditional culture, offering shelter, food, and alms to such men was understood as propitiating the spirits of the ancestors (the literal meaning of *dziady* is "forefathers"). In some cases, dziady not only sang but also healed, did magic, and conducted religious rituals.[10] There was, not surprisingly, also a negative facet to the image of the dziady, one associated primarily with the modern era: that of idler, swindler, and general annoyance. This image emerged as a result of the fading of premodern beliefs about the magical powers of the dziad, who gradually ceased being treated as a healer or a "holy wanderer."[11]

Russian government policy from the reign of Peter the Great on began to incorporate elements of the punitive approach to begging and vagrancy that had been common in western and central Europe since the advent of the early modern period.[12] Peter himself (r. 1682–1725) attempted to do away with almsgiving in favor of the institution of the almshouse, introduced a distinction between the deserving and undeserving poor, and decreed that local police would be "responsible for poor relief and the eradication of begging" and that municipal governments must establish workhouses for "beggars, idlers, incorrigible children, debtors, disobedient servants, and other undesirables."[13] In 1775, reorganizing provincial administration, Catherine the Great (r. 1762–96) instituted provincial social welfare boards, which were to establish charitable institutions such as almshouses, orphanages, insane asylums, and workhouses, and these "became the major providers of medical and charitable aid in preemancipation Russia."[14] Catherine continued Peter's policy of criminalizing and penalizing begging and vagrancy since, as Lindenmeyr notes, "begging and especially vagrancy threatened to undermine Russia's rigid social structure."[15] Various governmental reports and committees in the 1820s and 1830s encouraged the categorization of beggars into deserving (the truly poor and needy) and undeserving (professional beggars, able-bodied people who were presumably shirking work), but these efforts seemed to have had little impact on the masses, and popular tolerance for begging persisted.[16]

Such tolerance existed in Jewish society as well, thanks to Judaism's command to care for the needy and to charitable traditions dating back to the Middle Ages, but there was no Jewish analogue to the Slavic idea of the holy beggar. Beggars appeared, of course, in legends and folktales, but they had no consistently positive valence.[17] As a brief excursus into one of Jewish literature's most famous creations centering on beggars will reveal, the lionization of the beggar that seems to lie at the core of R. Nahman of Bratslav's "Tale of the Seven Beggars" may actually point to the very opposite.

R. Nahman of Bratslav's "Tale of the Seven Beggars"

Nahman of Bratslav (1772–1811), a great-grandson of the so-called founder of Hasidism, Israel Ba'al Shem Tov, emerged as a charismatic Hasidic leader in his own right in the last years of the eighteenth century and went on to develop a body of often controversial mystical teachings. Those teachings were communicated in the form of homilies until 1806, when he began to share with his followers a series of thirteen tales that were eventually published after his death in a bilingual Hebrew-Yiddish edition titled *Sipurei ma'asiyot* (1815).[18] Simultaneously captivating and impenetrable, R. Nahman's tales were highly innovative in the world of Jewish religious discourse, since they made no reference to traditional Jewish concepts and seemed to draw on the personae and tropes of folklore: kings and emperors, princes and princesses, pirates and demons, magical charms, and lifelong quests. They soon became famous well beyond the circle of Bratslav Hasidism, entered into the Jewish canon in eastern Europe, and had a major impact on the eventual development of modern Jewish literature.[19]

R. Nahman's last tale, told in the spring of 1810, was the "Tale of the Seven Beggars," which centers on two orphans who, after having been abandoned as children, are rescued by seven different beggars, each with a different physical disability or defect. The orphans eventually become beggars themselves, marry each other, and after their wedding receive mystical gifts of great value (e.g., a long life, a good life) from the seven beggars, each of whom tells a fantastical tale. In the course of the visits by the beggars, the orphans discover that the beggars' disabilities and deformities are illusory and are in fact hints of amazing powers that are just the opposite of their supposed defects. "Do you think that I am blind? Not at all. It is just that the entire world does not amount to the wink of an eye for me," the blind beggar declares, for example, and the storyteller notes, "He looked like a blind man because he did not look at the world at all."

Similarly, the stuttering beggar informs the couple that he only pronounces imperfectly those words that are not components of prayers. Not only is he not a stutterer, he is in fact "an extraordinary orator."[20] The seven beggars represent the nexus between alienness and deformity, on the one hand, and the supernatural and fabulous, on the other. Each beggar is simultaneously of his own place and time—the beggars' wedding, occurring in a pit of filth—and of a legendary past or a salvific future.[21]

One seminal interpretation is common to most, if not all, of the many readings of "The Tale of the Seven Beggars": that the beggars represent the true world that lies underneath or beyond the "illusory world of our daily experience."[22] The sheer incongruity of the simultaneous existence of those two worlds is made clear in R. Nahman's choice of physically deformed beggars, since in his sociocultural context, this category of human existence was generally reviled—and yet it is precisely those degraded, repellent humans who are the bridge between this world (exemplified by the pit in which the wedding takes place) and the transcendent world, or between this world as it is today and its redeemed form as it will be at the end of days.

The implications of this idea are twofold and contrasting. On the one hand, R. Nahman's decision to place beggars at the center of the last and arguably the holiest of his tales could be understood as radical, since Jewish tales did not ordinarily feature such characters as protagonists in their own right. Ordinary people may have been, in some sense, in awe of beggars because they had few of the usual ties to ordinary life—occupation, communal obligations, social and even religious norms—and were thus free of the burdens associated with those (though they were of course also bereft of their benefits). R. Nahman may even have seen himself in the role of spiritual beggar. According to Joseph Weiss, he identified with the protagonists of his tales and was quoted in his biography as saying, "I am poor and destitute."[23]

One the other hand, the tale itself reveals that the beggars are not who they seem to be—their deformities and disabilities are illusions, and rather than soliciting alms, their primary role in the tale, in addition to telling stories, is to do just the opposite: give gifts of infinite value. From this perspective, Nahman's beggars are familiar personae, since the trope of the beggar-who-is-not-really-a-beggar had a respectable pedigree before Nahman told his tales. As is true of folktales in many cultures, beggars who featured in Jewish tales were often wealthy or pious men (or, more rarely, women) who had fallen on hard times and were compelled to beg to survive, or for some reason had to disguise themselves as beggars.[24]

The same was often true of Hasidic tales. One such tale, included in an 1866 collection entitled *Sipurei kedoshim* (Stories of Holy Men), recounted the turns of fate of a wealthy man, a member of the Jewish elite and a supporter of the tsaddik Rabbi Leib Sores/Sarah's (1730–91). After a fire kills the man's family and renders him destitute, he has no choice but to become a beggar. The tsaddik tells him to go to a wealthy woman in a certain city. When he arrives there, he is mocked by the woman's associates because of his appearance and called a madman, but eventually he manages to secure an audience with her. When the woman receives a magical sign that this man has been sent to her by the tsaddik, she immediately agrees to marry him to fulfill a pledge she has previously made to the holy man.[25] Once the beggar's clothes are taken off of him, he "became another person."[26] Thus, the state of beggardom is a transient one—and the reader knows that this is not a beggar at all but a Jewish notable in disguise.

Beggars in the post-Partitions world

After the Partitions of Poland, the problem of the itinerant poor persisted, or even worsened, due to the indebtedness of Jewish communities and onerous tax burdens imposed by the government. As Iiulii Gessen notes, the Russian Minister of Finance wrote in 1820 that the Jews were "in large measure falling into poverty and, turning to begging and vagrancy, are finding it impossible to support their families or to pay taxes, which in large measure remain in arrears."[27] The government's short-lived attempt to eliminate Jewish tavernkeeping and distilling in the Pale of Settlement resulted in the expulsion of thousands of Jewish families from rural locales starting in 1808.[28] Expulsions from the countryside continued sporadically until 1830, with horrific consequences, followed by another mass expulsion from the border region starting in 1843; these undoubtedly increased the numbers of destitute and homeless Jews wandering from town to town.[29] In his *Sefer mi-dor le-dor* (1901), a popular, traditionalist history of a period in Russian Jewish life corresponding approximately to the second quarter of the nineteenth century, Hirsh Kolp described the "great band of vagrant poor" made up of the wretchedly poor, the burned out, and expellees from villages in Vitebsk and Mogilev and, after 1844, throughout the Pale.[30]

Glenn Dynner estimates that approximately one-fifth of the Jews of the Kingdom of Poland, a nominally independent rump state ruled by the tsar, lost their livelihoods as a result of the steady rise in the price of liquor concessions that were intended to "gradually squeeze Jews out of the liquor trade"while also generating revenue for the state.[31] There, too, the authorities expelled Jews from the border region.[32] A rapidly growing population only worsened the situation.

The increasing stratification of the Jewish economy that took place under the reign of Nicholas I—and in large measure thanks to his policies, as Michael Stanislawski explains—meant that from the late 1820s and into the 1850s, more and more petty traders were driven out of their field of economic activity with no clear fallback option.[33] This trend, coupled with the rapid growth in the Jewish population of the Russian Empire and the expulsions from rural areas, led to the impoverishment of large numbers of Russian and Polish Jews, some of whom slid into outright penury.

An 1808 petition to the Vilna kahal from a group of householders in reduced circumstances makes clear the growth in the number of destitute Jews, both local and itinerant. The petitioners claimed that the kahal's ordinance banning mendicants from begging from house to house (clearly a legacy of the statutes of early modern Lithuanian communities) had been enforced the previous year, but since then had been disregarded. The subsequent return to "knocking on the doors," as the memorial put it, brought shame upon the householders of the city, "for they go around naked and barefoot."[34] The petitioners contended that many previously comfortable families such as themselves were now in difficult economic straits and could no longer be expected to support the large numbers of paupers—both local and itinerant poor (*arhei parhei*)—who were seeking alms. It is very likely that among the wandering destitute described here were victims of the expulsion of Jews from villages that was decreed in 1804 but that actually began in early 1808.[35] To make matters worse, the petition continued, some of the most generous members of the community had ceased respecting the customary regulations on charity to the poorest, which required them to donate to a general fund from which the wardens of the *Tsedakah Gedolah*, the main charitable organ of the community, maintained destitute vagrants for several days and then provided them with transportation to the next locale. Apparently the wardens were not enforcing those regulations, which was the motivation behind the petition: the less prosperous community members were appealing to the highest communal authorities to call the Tsedakah Gedolah to order, since the entire system was now in jeopardy. Vilna Jews were now saddled with a large number of itinerant poor who were neither being cared for by the relevant communal authorities nor moved out of the city in a timely fashion.[36] That the petition was submitted in August suggests that its authors were particularly worried about the upcoming fall holiday season, with its accompanying greater demands for charitable giving.

Perhaps the refusal of the well-off Jews to provide (or pay for) lodging or food to vagrants and thus flaunt heretofore accepted norms of charity was prompted by the increasing numbers of beggars in the community. It may also be evidence of a more fundamental shift in social standards that would see beggars—especially in large groups—given shelter not in private homes but in the hekdesh. We must also understand this document in its Russian imperial context, specifically the introduction of provincial social welfare boards in 1775, which established a range of institutions for the sick and indigent, including almshouses. At the same time, begging and vagrancy continued to be punishable offenses.[37] Thus, the shift described in the Jewish sphere may have been part of a larger change of emphasis in imperial society from individual alms-giving (though that of course continued) to institutional care for the poor. Some of the disquiet communicated in the language of the petition may also stem from its authors' anxiety about having large numbers of Jewish beggars roaming the city streets, clearly a liability for the community itself.

The picture that emerges from the 1808 document is similar to one described in another petition, this one from the Tsedakah Gedolah wardens themselves to the kahal leadership in 1821. Here, too, an untenable state of affairs had arisen from the refusal of a particular group (in this case the local butchers) to adhere to long-standing communal customs with regard to charitable giving. (Significantly, of the long list of charitable obligations of the Tsedakah Gedolah provided in the petition, the first two are weekly allotments to the city's poor and the hiring of wet nurses for orphans.) As a result, the Tsedakah Gedolah was in danger of not being able to meet its regular commitments to provide charitable aid, let alone the additional demand that came before and during the approaching Passover holiday.[38] Mordechai

Zalkin correctly sets that set of circumstances in the context of an economic downturn related to Russia's grain trade, but he also interprets the butchers' resistance as a challenge by a group with financial clout to the authority of the established communal leadership. In both cases, what emerged was a larger pattern of prosperous members of the community—who were not part of the leadership of either the kahal or the Tsedakah Gedolah—flaunting communal norms in relation to charity and welfare. This trend was likely linked to the emerging desire for separatism on the part of Vilna's Jewish merchants, relatively recently ensconced in a different estate category from their coreligionists, demonstrated by their request in the same year to be excluded from the list of taxpayers that included almost all of the city's Jews.[39] Also noteworthy is that, although the 1821 petition to the Vilna kahal did not mention an increase in the number of destitute Jews as a motivating factor, in both cases the prosperous Jews' separatist aim (if that is what was involved) was linked in some way to aid to the poorest of the community. This was the first stirring of tensions that would soon, with the advent of Nicholas I's conscription, become much more visible. But before we come to that difficult historical episode, we should examine another symptom of emerging new attitudes to the most vulnerable: the gradual transformation of the communal poorhouse into a beggars' hostel.

The hekdesh in the early imperial period

Our few sources suggest that, up to some point in the first few decades of tsarist rule over formerly Polish Jewry, the hekdesh in the Russian Empire was primarily for the indigent sick of the community; after this time, it seems increasingly to have served as a shelter for itinerant beggars. The hekdesh usually housed the infirm and the poor indiscriminately, and the sources are often opaque in distinguishing between the two. For example, in eighteenth-century Vilna, the Bikur Holim confraternity for visiting the sick had two sets of wardens (*gabaim*), one for "the hekdesh for the sick" and another for "the hekdesh for the poor," though most documents confirm that there was only one institution for both cohorts.[40] (Statistics from 1765 indicating that there were eighteen sick people and three poor people in the Vilna hekdesh suggest that it was likely primarily a sick house.)[41] Hirsh Kolp writes of two categories of hekdesh: one for the sick and another, "the hekdesh of the healthy," that housed only beggars.[42] But elsewhere Kolp uses the term *hekdesh* to refer only to beggars' hostels.[43] Another example of the blurring of boundaries between sick and poor can be found in the hekdesh of Birzh (Birzhi), where according to the 1804 regulations of the Hevra Kadisha, the Jewish burial society, servants who had been ill for longer than three days, and had no parents to pay for their medicine and care for them at home, were to be transferred to "the hekdesh for the poor in our community."[44]

Similarly, the 1802 regulations for the hekdesh of the Minsk Bikur Holim society speak of both sick people and beggars. It may be significant that the first ten sections of the regulations speak only of sick people, other than a reference late in the fourth section to "needy healthy persons," presumably itinerant beggars lodging in the hekdesh.[45] Is it possible that the existence of such a large passage of text that seems to speak almost exclusively of the hekdesh as a shelter for the poor sick, complete with funds provided to residents for "medicine and healing," is evidence of an earlier iteration of this institution as hospice? Such a supposition would mean that regulations governing the lodging and conduct of itinerant beggars—such as sections 12–14—were interpolated later, though there is no clear evidence for that. Section 12 begins with a directive that the hekdesh overseer accept into the institution any stranger (*prikhodiashchii*), without exception. The overseer was also required to report about the arrival of such a person to the Bikur Holim brotherhood so that the time of arrival could be recorded on a special chit to ensure that the visitor did not stay longer than three days. Only then may "that person collect alms around the town for three days."[46] The subsequent two sections enjoin town residents, on pain of communal ban (*herem*), not to give alms to any beggar lacking the appropriate chit or who stays in town longer than three days, and not to lodge itinerant beggars in their homes. "Itinerant beggars must without exception lodge in the hekdesh." It is noteworthy that throughout the document, the poor sick and itinerant beggars are treated as two totally separate categories of people eligible for lodging in the hekdesh.

The very fact that the Minsk regulations strictly forbade local Jews from providing lodging to non-local beggars in their homes is significant, and suggests that until recently it had been the custom for locals to put up vagrants.[47] (The regulations for the Grodno hekdesh list the same prohibition.)[48] It is also of some note that the communal authorities wanted to keep strict control over who was permitted to beg in the town. Evidently, at least some Minsk Jews decided to ignore these prohibitions, for three years later, the kahal found it necessary to require that they be read out loud in all the synagogues; in this case, householders were prohibited from giving "even a quarter-kopeck" to a beggar without the appropriate document from the kahal.[49]

Clearly, the age-old custom of housing the itinerant poor in one's home died hard. So why were communal leaders so intent on this change? Was it because of the growth in the numbers of the itinerant poor? Were the leaders trying to consolidate control of charity? Kolp's description of communal trustees using the hoary *Pletten* system on Fridays to provide Sabbath hospitality for the residents of the hekdesh provides a clue. The tickets assigned each householder one or more poor people as guests for the Sabbath meals, but—unlike the practice in the early modern period—*not* for lodging. The paupers were to make their way back to the hekdesh for the night. Kolp's explanation of this practice is the Hebrew maxim *kabdehu ve-hashdehu*—the equivalent of "trust, but verify." These were, after all, unknown people, and one can imagine that distrust increased in an era that saw ever more destitute Jews on the road.[50]

The traditional Jewish practice of providing shelter to marginal people was not dissimilar from the Russian peasant system of *po ocheredi* (lit., "in turn"), "whereby each family would in turn offer shelter to the village's 'idiots,' its homeless widows, and whichever other unfortunates happened to belong there."[51] However, in actuality, most such people had to turn to begging to survive; according to an 1856 government study, for example, over half of the "73,000 disabled, handicapped, homeless, or otherwise needy state peasants received some aid from relatives, communes or charity. The rest fended for themselves, principally by begging."[52] Most ordinary Russians, then—especially those who lived in the countryside—had no recourse to even as mean an institution as the hekdesh. The few formal charitable institutions that existed in the early nineteenth century were located only in cities and large towns.

Reading the Minsk regulations, one gets the clear impression that its function as a hospice for the sick was deeply ingrained in the religious and charitable culture of the Jewish community. Anyone requesting that the *Mi she-beirach* prayer be recited for the healing of a sick person, or that the *Birkat ha-gomel* prayer of thanks for deliverance (in this case, from illness) be recited at a local synagogue was required to donate a fixed sum to the hekdesh.[53] Another regulation required new mothers desiring that the *Mi she-beirach* prayer be recited for an infant to make an offering for the hekdesh. Three other sections deal with additional circumstances in which community members were required to make donations to the hekdesh.[54]

The Minsk regulations provide little hint as to the actual condition of the hekdesh other than that the overseer was required to maintain order, provide water in every room, and remove night soil on a daily basis. The overall impression, however, is of an institution with multiple streams of income from various kinds of charitable donations and with adequate, even strict, oversight by not one but two charitable brotherhoods. It is striking, then, to read the description of the Minsk hekdesh in the 1833 travel account of an English missionary, Robert Pinkerton:

> In the Jewish Hospital we saw forty-five young or old of both sexes, seemingly without classification of disease, placed in several small rooms; they certainly presented one of the most appalling scenes of wretchedness I ever witnessed; filth, rags and pestilential effluvia pervaded the whole place. A small apothecary's shop, with a kind of chapel, occupied one end of the building. The government contributed 16 *l.* [pounds] per annum towards its support; and the rest of the miserable pittance allowed to this lazar-house is derived from the Jewish Kahal and from private charity.[55]

Even accounting for Pinkerton's prejudices—elsewhere in this volume he described Russian Jews as being infamous for their "low cunning, imposture, and every species of circumvention"—this is a dark picture indeed.[56] Had there been such a radical change over the course of the preceding three decades? In 1807, the communal record book referred to the hekdesh as serving itinerant beggars exclusively, with no mention at all of the indigent sick. Similarly, the regulations of the society for visiting the sick in Grodno, while opening with a reference to "the sick of the Hekdesh," moved on immediately to discuss the poor people residing in the hekdesh. Even when there were no sick inmates in the hekdesh, the warden was nonetheless obliged to go there twice a week "to take care of the poor and to decide who shall be sent away from the city on foot and who by vehicle."[57] This evidence, while fragmentary, suggests that the bulk of the inmates were in fact paupers.

Our fragmentary sources, then, point to a slow transition during the early decades of tsarist rule from the hekdesh as an infirmary of sorts for the local sick poor to a shelter for the growing numbers of homeless, wandering poor Jews. This evolution was one of the first signs of a larger shift in attitudes to the most vulnerable of the Jewish community that would unfold over the following decades. Another such sign was the decision on the part of communal Jewish leadership to offer marginal people for conscription into the tsar's army.

Drafting the undesirables

Generations of scholars have from a variety of angles examined the painful episode of the draft introduced in 1827 by Nicholas I in the provinces of the Pale of Settlement, which required Jewish communities to select recruits for twenty-five-year terms of service in the tsarist army.[58] But this sad chapter in the annals of Russian Jewry history, often referred to as the *rekrutchina*, is also an important aspect of the history of marginal people. The decree of 1827 demanded that military obligation be determined according to the official conscription lists compiled by each community, but section 34 permitted the latter "to offer for conscription any Jew at any time for failure to pay taxes, for vagrancy and other disturbances [*besporiadki*] which are not tolerated by them [the communities]."[59] Michael Stanislawski notes that this provision "was entirely in keeping with the procedures established for all other categories of Russian draftees" and was, as the law suggests, intended as a means of social control.[60] Not long after the promulgation of the decree—in spring 1828, to be exact—the kahals of Mogilev, Shklov, and Grodno petitioned the authorities for permission to select conscripts *solely* from among the socially marginal people covered by section 34 without relying on regular conscription lists at all, or at least, in the words of the first Mogilev petition, submitted in April, "until such people disappear."[61] The petitions listed in inconsistent fashion those who did not pay taxes, those in arrears, and perpetrators of anti-social acts (*neterpimykh za proizvodimye besporiadki*), as well as two categories not specified in the law: idlers (*prazdnoshataiushchikhsia*) and those without the means to support themselves.[62]

The first petition from the Mogilev kahal, for example, proposed as eligible for the draft Jews in tax arrears, those who could not support themselves, and those accused of anti-social behavior, and referred to the example of the local Christian community, which "always presents similar [categories of people as recruits]."[63] In one case, these were not just theoretical proposals. The petition from Grodno, dated May 25, noted that, in the most recent draft, the kahal had submitted as recruits "with the greatest success" idlers, those who did not pay taxes, and similar undesirables (*tomu podobnykh neterpimykh v obshchestve*—literally, people the community could not tolerate).[64]

These petitions, which were clearly coordinated among the three kahals (Mogilev and Shklov are separated by a little over twenty miles; Grodno is much further away), requested more than just official permission to select social undesirables as recruits. They also asked the government to prohibit the military authorities from compelling Jewish recruits to do anything forbidden by the Jewish religion, since such a prohibition would "awaken in many the voluntary [!] inclination to present themselves for conscription."[65] The former may have been the kahal leaders' way of assuaging their consciences about the socially marginal people they were selecting to fill the draft quota: these men and boys might be leaving all that was familiar to them for a totally foreign and likely hostile environment—and for a length of time equal to a good chunk of the average life expectancy—but at least they would be able to remain observant Jews. It is very unlikely that the explanation offered in the petition was meant sincerely, since even the most robust assurances on the part of the regime that freedom of religion was guaranteed in the army would not have prompted Jews to "present themselves" voluntarily for the draft.

The petitions also asked that the government permit Jews to engage in a range of economic activities that had recently been circumscribed by the authorities, since those restrictions had led to the impoverishment of many Jews and to expulsions, causing overcrowded conditions in towns and cities. What was the connection to the conscription crisis? As we have seen, many expellees were compelled to join the itinerant poor or, if they managed to settle down in a town, were almost certain to be seen as outsiders and perhaps even as a burden to the community.[66] In their reduced state, there was little chance of them contributing to the corporate tax obligation.

In any case, the "legalized social discrimination" that these petitions requested was already being put in place in other ways.[67] In 1828, the government without explanation added an amendment to the conscription statute that "permitted the Jewish community to divide large families into smaller ones and to combine several small families into a large one in the queue books, even when these permutations had no basis in real life. At the same time, the kahal leaders were allowed to draft village Jews before city Jews."[68] Many kahals would use this authority to select sons of poor families—sometimes even only sons— for the draft, while protecting the sons of the prosperous and well-connected (the truly wealthy were not at risk because members of the merchant guilds were not liable to conscription).[69] In addition, some clearly cooked the books so that the sons of poor families always appeared at the top of the conscription lists.[70] A standard trick was one described by a Berdichev Jew by the name of Usher Vol'f (Asher Wolf) Zhol'kber when he wrote to the authorities to denounce the Berdichev kahal for "merging" poor families with one son with prosperous families with numerous children in the conscription lists, so that if needs be the son of a prosperous family could be listed an only child of the poor family and therefore ineligible for conscription. According to Zhol'kber, this was done upon payment of 700 rubles—a princely sum—to the Jew who compiled the lists, under the direction of the kahal deputies.[71] Unmarried men and illiterates were also at the top of the lists. The pool of undesirables from which the kahals wished to draw their recruits was necessarily limited, and the government was not supposed to allow the kahals to circumvent the legally required conscription lists, which were supposed to include every eligible family in descending order of the number of sons they had. In addition to the venal side of human nature that led some leaders to protect the powerful and the well-connected, it was also logical for them to protect taxpayers from being drafted. Most of the kahals were already deeply in debt, and the vicious cycle created by the *rekrutchina* only made things worse: debts on taxes were punished by demanding additional recruits, and any failure to present recruits as per the quota was punished by exacting even more recruits.[72]

Still, the lion's share of the burden frequently continued to fall on the socially marginal. The Jews who were of least use to the kahal were those who did not pay taxes, the "idle and useless," and individuals who contravened the social order. An excellent case in point is the Minsk kahal in 1829, which Stanislawski describes in some detail. The kahal's first list of recruits includes seventy men and boys, of whom almost half were without occupation, while fourteen were artisans, thirteen were servants, three were unskilled laborers, and three were beggars. Thus, fully 90 percent of those on the list were poor or destitute. Moreover, twenty of the seventy were either vagrants or villagers, often regarded by town Jews as ignorant and contemptible. However, when it came time for the conscripts to present themselves, most of those listed could not be found or were able to present a valid exemption. When a second list was drawn up, over half (twenty-eight of fifty-four) were vagrants or villagers.[73]

The kahals committed great injustices, but communities faced horrific decisions and, as Shoyl Ginzburg argues, blaming the excesses of the *rekrutchina* exclusively on them is unjust. So many families tried to shield their sons from the draft in one way or another that the kahals simply could not make their quotas.[74] The ultimate responsibility lay with the brutal Nicholaevan regime, which had already made the task difficult enough by freeing prosperous merchants from the draft. The kahal was forced to be act callously in order to cope with the demands made of it.[75] Isaac Levitats argues convincingly that kahal elders felt justified in presenting the poor as conscripts not only because reducing the number of communal poor automatically reduced the tax burden but also because middle-class householders had been paying taxes on their behalf for decades. Now it was the turn of the poor to repay that debt.[76]

Orphan recruits

One particularly bleak aspect of the *rekrutchina* was the drafting of children, sometimes as young as ten or eleven years old.[77] A series of cases in 1840 from the archives of the Minsk kahal, preserved in the YIVO Archive, reveals that among the most vulnerable to such conscription were poor orphans, and especially those who were homeless. The kahal made it possible for the families of such children to strike agreements in which the poor sons hired themselves out as "voluntary" substitutes for the sons of other families of means. The Klots brothers—Berko (Ber), aged twenty-three, Itsko (Itsik), thirteen, and Iankel' (Yankel), eleven—were orphaned of both parents, their father having died eight years earlier (the documents make no mention of their mother). The petition that they submitted to the kahal, which was without question written for them, deserves to be reproduced in full:

> After the death of our parents, we and our third brother Iankel' were left very young without any means or shelter [*bez vsiakogo sposoba i pristanishcha*]. I, Berko, am barely able to feed myself and my younger brother, and I, Itsko, not having any occupation or shelter [*priiut*], am roaming the city—we cannot and do not have any circumstance or possibility of paying the state taxes to the community, therefore in order not to burden the community with paying our taxes for us and with my, Berko's, agreement as eldest brother and head of the family, I, Itsko, desire willingly to enter into military service as a voluntary replacement [*po dobrovol'nomy naimu*], hired by local townsperson [*meshchanin*] Gerts Slepiak, and therefore request the Kahal and community to allow me, Itsko, to enter into this agreement.[78]

Ber was clearly trying to care for the youngest brother, Yankel, as best he could, while middle brother Itsik was for some reason not even living with his brothers. That he was illiterate—someone else had to sign this poignant document for him—is hardly surprising; it is unlikely that he had ever had any schooling. (Ber was able to sign his name in Hebrew.) Other documents in the Klots file show that the family owed three rubles in taxes. There are also inconsistencies in the file about the actual ages of the younger two boys: was Itsik actually thirteen, or was he eleven? Malfeasance when it came to the ages of hired child recruits was widespread. A larger question is that of consent: to what extent were Ber and especially Itsik entering into this agreement voluntarily? One can imagine without much difficulty that the Slepiak family, faced with the possibility of losing a son to the military, were more than willing to pay a few rubles (and perhaps a fee of some kind to the kahal as well) for a chance of having their family's name taken off the conscription list. Nor is it hard to conceive that a great deal of pressure would be brought to bear on the destitute orphans to enter into this agreement. Or perhaps Ber simply could not resist the lure of whatever money might have been offered him in exchange for his brother.

A similar case from the same year was that of the Chertov family, four sons and two daughters whose father had died nine years earlier and mother four years earlier. The eldest brother, Peisakh, aged twenty-three, the legal head of the family, approved the stated desire (according to the documents) of his seventeen-year-old brother Girsh (Hersh), to hire himself out as a recruit in place of a son of the Margolin family. Like the Klots brothers, the Chertov orphans owed three rubles in back taxes. The documents also made clear that despite losing Girsh to the army, the family—that is, brothers Tevel' (Tevye) and Abram (Avrom), whose ages are not provided in the file—would still be eligible for conscription two draft cycles later.[79]

Also hired out as a "volunteer" in 1840 was Aba, the sixteen-year-old son of the widow Rasia Mozhilkov, whose elder brother Khaim had been drafted ten years earlier; Aba's departure would leave Rasia with only one son, nineteen-year-old Iosel' (Yosel). Their father Ovsei (Yosef) had died in 1835, leaving behind a tax debt of two rubles and eighty kopecks. The family whose son Aba would replace agreed to pay that debt and all the family's taxes until the next revision (household census), something that took place approximately every ten to fifteen years.[80] Of particular interest in the attestation that Rasia and Aba, both illiterate, had to have others sign for them, is the formulation that was put in Aba's mouth, since he of course did not write the document himself: "With the knowledge and consent of my mother, I, Aba, being orphaned of father and without shelter [ne imeia pristanishcha], desire to hire myself out and enter into military service."[81] The fact that Aba—and presumably the entire family—was homeless reveals the depth of their destitution and despair. Again, there is no way to gauge to what extent coercion by kahal officials was a factor, but it is difficult to imagine that it was completely absent.

A document from the archives about the conscription of a poor orphan in Minsk was reproduced in the journal of the Jewish Section of the Institute for Belorussian Culture, a Soviet state institution, together with other tsarist-era documents on the theme of conscription. Sora Abramova and Raina Sarnovaia, aunts of the orphan Leib Sarnov, aged thirteen, submitted a petition to the kahal on May 16, 1840, protesting that after they had placed their nephew with one Iosel' Leibovich, a cobbler, for an apprenticeship, the latter falsely claimed to be related to the boy and presented him for conscription in exchange for payment from another family. The two aunts vociferously objected to this action, noting that Leib was a minor and that they were his

closest relatives and therefore bore responsibility for his welfare. Since both
women were illiterate, they were unable to sign the petition themselves and
another person therefore signed for them. On June 6, however, they submitted another petition asking that their original entreaty be disregarded and
"consigned to eternal oblivion," since their nephew Leib had disregarded all
their exhortations and, "his soul firm, remained fast in his earnest desire to
zealously enter into military service as a hired conscript." They would therefore no longer express any objections to his being drafted.[82]

One senses instinctively that the paper on which this second document
was written is hiding a dark and sinister set of circumstances. Why would a
thirteen-year-old have insisted on being drafted under the circumstances of
the Nicholaevan conscription? And even if he had, why would his aunts have
decided to retract their appeal to the kahal, given the sentiment they had
previously expressed that they had taken the place of his parents after their
deaths? Perhaps the family that had hired Leib as a recruit from the cobbler
was particularly influential within the Minsk Jewish community and applied
pressure after the aunts submitted their first petition on May 16. Perhaps the
kahal itself, which had a stake in having such transactions go off without a
hitch, coerced the aunts into dropping their objection. Or perhaps, as Isaac
Levitats surmises, "their change of heart was brought about by a satisfactory
share in the spoils."[83] A similar set of circumstances is suggested by a case in
which a couple allowed their eleven-year-old orphaned grandson to "volunteer" as a hired recruit.[84]

The government did not always turn a blind eye to this kind of corruption,
especially given its pervasiveness. Moreover, not a few Jews were prepared to
take their grievance against the kahal to the authorities, as evidenced by hundreds, likely thousands of archival files, each corresponding to an individual
case brought by Jews who complained bitterly about having had their only
son drafted or who, without any clear personal link to the conscription issue,
were simply ratting on the kahal elders.[85] The YIVO Archive also contains a
copy of a very long archival file from 1841 entitled "Corruption: Jewish Conscription" with dozens of official documents revealing a government inquest
into the practice of hiring "voluntary" recruits from among the indigent. The
authorities were particularly interested in the common practice of having the
family that wished to free their son from conscription duty pay not only for

the back taxes of the hired recruit's family but for those of other poor families as well.[86]

Kapore: the conscript as scapegoat, substitute, and symbol

The collective experience of having as a community offered its sons, usually
those of its poorest and most vulnerable families, to the tsarist beast weighed
heavily on Russian Jewry. Scholars have assessed the long-term impact of the
debacle on the leadership of Russian Jews, which amounted to its near-total
delegitimization in the eyes of the masses, or, at the very least, the breakdown
of communal solidarity.[87] A handful of sources hint that the conscripts may
have become a potent symbol in the consciousness of ordinary folk, who, not
surprisingly, viewed them as sacrificial lambs given up for the greater good
of the collective.

An 1833 entry in the communal register of Pruzhany (Yid., Pruzhene), a
town in Grodno province, vividly shows how the Jewish draftees were viewed
by the community, members of which had recently received letters from
them. (The immediate issue at hand was the need to collect funds to send to
the boys so they could bribe their superiors to permit them to practice Judaism.)[88] The entry laments: "We have seen in the writings of the depressed of
spirit whose souls are suffering [*metsukei nefesh*, i.e., the soldiers], redeemers
of many souls among the inhabitants of our town, who went into the darkness and have no light, who risked their lives to take upon themselves the
king's labor with dominion and fear [*be-hamshel va-fahad*] for the sake of the
community."[89]

It is striking that the language of the communal register, usually rather
dry and formulaic, here uses language that is not only dramatic, but indeed
religious in nature and tone. The anonymous writer portrays the draftees as
protagonists in a spiritual drama; in what could be read as a kabbalistic text,
he portrays them as having entered the realm of darkness in order to "redeem
many souls"—since each of them went as a substitute for many other potential recruits. Thus, the fearsome labor they have taken on is for the sake of the
entire community.

In Saul M. Ginsburg and P. S. Marek's 1901 collection of Jewish folksongs from imperial Russia, we find an oft-quoted song that the compilers
called "Rekrutchina Lament."

Tears flow in the streets
One could wash oneself in children's blood
Woe, what a misfortune is this
Will dawn never come again?
They drag little chicks from school
Dress them in military uniforms
Our elders, our rabbis
Help to force them into service [in the Christian army].
Zushe Rakover has seven sons
But not one was drafted
But Leah the widow's only son
Is made to pay the price for the kahal's sins [*Iz a kapore far koholshe zind*]
It's a *mitsve* [good deed] to draft the common folk [*prostakes*]
Cobblers and tailors are scoundrels [*leydakes*], don't you know
Brutish kids from a prosperous family
Can never leave their families, not a one.[90]

Ginsburg and Marek noted that the song had been submitted by one Iu. M. Neifakh in Minsk province, one of many amateur collectors who sent the compilers songs in response to their appeal in the press in 1898.[91] It is impossible to ascertain the song's "authenticity" (if such a thing exists), but at the very least it undoubtedly reflects an authentic memory of the unjustness of the Nicholaevan conscription and its tragic impact on poor Jews. The kahal, not the tsarist authorities, is the villain, while the common folk are the victims. Two lines are of particular significance for our purposes: "But Leah the widow's only son / Is made to pay the price for the kahal's sins." The Yiddish word *kapore*, "scapegoat," is intimately linked in Judaism to the ritual of symbolically transferring one's sins to an animal—in the Bible, the literal "scapegoat" (*se'ir la-azazel*) and, in a Day of Atonement eve ritual that emerged in the early Middle Ages called *kaparot* (*kapores* in Ashkenazic Hebrew), a rooster. A significant difference between the two practices, of course, is that the ritual described in the Bible and rabbinic writings is a national one, since the scapegoat accepts the corporate sins of the entire Israelite people, whereas the medieval custom is carried out by individuals. In the "Rekrutchina Lament," the marginal individual—the poor orphan—is called a scapegoat for the collective sins, not of the entire community, but of its leadership. But in order to fully understand the lyric, we must look to another definition of *kapore* in Yiddish, in the context of the phrase *geyn a kapore fir emetsens zind*: to suffer for someone else's sins.[92] The key lines thus become: "But Leah the widow's only son / is a scapegoat for the kahal's treachery." The genius of the folk creation puts a fine nuance on the original meaning of the word: the orphan is not a scapegoat in the sense that he enables the wiping away of sins; rather, the suffering that he experiences as a result of those sins makes him a visible symbol of their dastardly nature.

Another, later folk song about the draft—this one dated by Ruth Rubin, a scholar of Yiddish folk song, to the advent of universal conscription in 1874—also uses the term *kapore* to great effect. Phrased as a bitter warning to the householders of the community who never experienced the suffering of having a child conscripted, it promises that they too will soon know such sorrow.

> Until now you have never known worry
> Never known grief, never known sorrow.
> When the beggar, poor thing, was the substitute/scapegoat (*kapore*),
> There was rejoicing in your house.[93]

In another verse, the singer puts the worthies and pillars of the community on notice with a reference to the "volunteer" conscripts of yore:

> Volunteers will no longer go in your place
> You will no longer use them as scapegoats/substitutes [for your sins] [*Ir vet*
>   *shoyn keyn kapores nit shlogn*]
> The substitutes will be you yourselves
> You'd better cry and weep.

In a marvelous wordplay, the second line reads literally, "You will no longer *shlogn kapores*" in a reference to the use of a rooster as a ritual scapegoat on Yom Kippur eve—but the implied meaning is *kapore* as substitute for the draft. Elsewhere, the song assures those who have until now been protected that when their children finally go off to the military together with the beggars' children, their own sins will have brought this about.[94] Thus, the relationship of sin to *kapore* (substitute and scapegoat) in the song is quite complex: the original sin of the Jewish establishment was to force the poor folk and marginals into conscription as substitutes (*kapores*) for its own children. In doing so, on a metaphysical level it also hoped that the cantonists would serve as scapegoats (*kapores*) and "take away" their sins, as it were, when they disappeared into the ranks of the tsar's army. Not only was that conclusion never to be, the song warns, but those sins will come back, decades later, to be visited upon their children.

The nexus between marginal folk and the scapegoat is a trope that appears over and again in the history of Ashkenazi Jews. For example, in an early sixteenth-century work by Victor von Carben, a convert to Christianity, itinerant Jewish beggars are described as willingly eating the chicken or rooster used in the *kapores* ritual, which rich Jews refused to eat since it was "loaded with sins."[95] As we saw in chapter 1, a Purim-shpil from the early modern period has a jester-like figure telling a beggar couple under the wedding canopy: "May you both be punished [*a kapore zolt ir vern*, lit., may you both serve as scapegoats] instead of me and the whole Jewish people."[96] And the ritual of the cholera wedding, explored in depth in chapter 4, sets the marginal people of the town apart from everyone else in a ritual of degradation that may be interpreted as creating scapegoats of the bride and groom so that the epidemic will lift from the town.

Similarly, in the folk culture of Wales and the Welsh Marches, a socially marginal person called the sin-eater was hired to play the central role in a ritual that had him eating a piece of bread that had been placed upon the breast of a recently deceased person. It was believed that in this way he took upon himself the sins of the departed, and he was therefore regarded by locals "as one irredeemably lost." The folklorist who described the sin-eater practice in the late nineteenth century noted that it might have some relationship to the biblical idea of the scapegoat.[97]

Conclusion

The Russian state played no little role in the increasing stratification of Russian and Polish Jewry starting in the early nineteenth century, which contributed to the growing marginalization of beggars, paupers, and the homeless. But the Jewish establishment—primarily the kahal leadership, a new economic elite, and to some extent the rabbinate as well—played a part too, whether by funneling the destitute into charitable institutions such as the hekdesh, rather than advancing the personal charity that had been the norm in the early modern period, or by facilitating the conscription of poor orphans and other vulnerable individuals.

The catastrophe of the *rekrutchina* and the use of the marginal individual as substitute or *kapore*—which, as we have seen, was not an entirely new trope in Jewish culture—set the stage for an intensified perception in the coming decades of marginal people as both scapegoat and stand-in, as it were, for all of Russian Jewry. This would emerge most clearly and distinctively in the ritual of the cholera wedding, discussed in chapter 4. First, however, we must turn back to the hekdesh and its further development as a historical institution and a cultural symbol.

CHAPTER 3

"A PILE OF DUST AND RUBBLE"

Poorhouses, Real and Imaginary

The symbolic function of the hekdesh as a liminal space at the figurative edge of a small-town Jewish community in the Russian Empire was just as important to its charitable economy as the poorhouse building itself. The undesirables who resided there were perceived by many as otherworldly and yet somehow firmly—too firmly, perhaps—lodged in this world. This chapter explores the nature and function of the Jewish poorhouse of eastern Europe. Its role is illustrated inter alia by the stories of two extraordinary fictional *hekdeshim*. Sholem Yankev Abramovitsh and Shmuel Yosef Agnon both employed the hekdesh as a terrifying—but fundamentally undistorted—reflection of the darkest and most sinister aspects of Jewish society, into the murky corners of which they felt compelled to shine the bright light of literature. The Jewish community might prefer to ignore its undesirables or lodge them out of sight, since they represented a facet of it that was psychologically damaged and emotionally deformed. But, as one of Abramovitsh's characters discovers, there is in fact very little that separates "them" from "us": "All of Jewry—nothing but beggary!"

Orphan institution: the hekdesh at mid-century

Chapter 2 argues that in the first half of the nineteenth century, the hekdesh transitioned from sick house to beggars' hostel, at least in some locales. That hypothesis is strengthened by the many sources from mid-century that clearly indicate that the hekdesh was primarily or even exclusively for wandering beggars. For instance, Yekhezkel Kotik, whose descriptions of his childhood home date from around 1860, maintained that the hekdesh in Kamenets Litovsk was not "intended, heaven forfend, for the sick, but for impoverished itinerants or beggars [*far di orkhim, far di orime layt*] passing through our shtetl."[1] And while Ephraim Deinard called the hekdesh "a wayfarers' hostel and hospital," his description—probably pertinent to the 1850s or early 1860s—makes it clear that it was really intended for the wandering poor, though they could also take advantage of it as a place to recover from illness. Indeed, according to Deinard, "a poor wanderer who came to a town knew that he should direct himself to the hekdesh."[2] As a correspondent from Płock to the Polish Jewish organ *Izraelita* noted in 1888, the institution was "a refuge for the crowd of itinerant beggars and cripples who end their lives there in misery."[3] But this was not the case everywhere: for example, Andrei Subbotin reported in 1887 that both the chronically ill and beggars lodged in the hekdesh in Kovno.[4]

The apparent shift from sick house to beggars' hostel may have been closely related to another phenomenon: the abolition of the kahal in the first half of the nineteenth century and the subsequent apparent abandonment or neglect of the hekdesh by the communal associations that had previously overseen it. Before the abolition of the kahal, the hekdesh had been maintained by the community itself or by hevrot (charitable societies; Yid., *khevres*). As we have seen, hekdesh regulations from this period often required that a warden of the association or even a doctor visit its residents on a regular basis, usually twice weekly, while the *shamash* (beadle or overseer, also known as *hekdesh-man*) was to visit twice or even three times daily. Such rigorous management, even if not always carried out according to the letter of the ordinances, suggests an institution that was basically orderly and well-maintained.

After the 1822 abolition of the kahal in Russian-ruled Congress Poland and its replacement by the so-called congregational board, many hevrot had to go underground to some degree.[5] This change was due in some measure to the narrowing of the new institution's jurisdiction to strictly religious matters, though it was later expanded; much more important was the fact that the individuals who sat on the boards tended to have very little understanding of the fields that they were meant to oversee, which included charity and welfare.[6] In the Pale of Settlement, the government's abolition of the kahal in 1844 meant that hekdeshim were now illicit institutions, since most had no official constitution or regulations (*ustav*) and no formal governance structure.[7] Oversight of the hekdesh was continued by whichever institution had taken over the kahal's functions, such as the Tsedakah Gedolah, the charitable association attached to the synagogue.[8] In other localities, the burial society or the society for visiting the sick was responsible for its upkeep.[9] Because the hekdesh was not an officially recognized institution, it was ineligible to receive support from proceeds of the *korobka*, the kosher meat tax that was allocated within each community for communal and charitable needs; it thus had to rely on a meager stream of collections, donations, and bequests.[10] And while in some locales the hekdesh fell under the supervision of the Bikur Holim, in many towns the hekdesh was apparently an orphan institution, not sponsored by any *hevrah*, lacking any fixed fiscal or institutional support. This helps explain why living conditions for those sheltering under its roof are so often described in abysmal terms. In this respect the hekdesh was unlike almost all other charitable institutions or activities in the typical shtetl, which were supported by the many charitable societies that had characterized autonomous Jewish existence for centuries: *Hakhnasat kalah* for dowering needy brides; *Mahzikei yetomim* to educate poor boys and orphans; *Lehem evyonim* to distribute food to the poor.

So it is no surprise that from at least as early as the 1860s, it was often *gabetes*—self-appointed women who collected and distributed charity outside of any institutional framework—who saw to it that the hekdesh would have the funds necessary to operate and that its residents would not go hungry.[11] While the proper functioning of communal charity seemed to assume and indeed rely on the existence of the *gabetes*, these women usually had no official status and held no position in any organization.[12]

The exclusion of the hekdesh from the regular funding stream for Jewish communal institutions had dire consequences. By the mid-nineteenth century, the institution is almost universally described as filthy and unsanitary, either totally unfurnished or else outfitted with crude improvised furniture. Even those who describe it as relatively clean remembered that it had "a specific smell."[13] The hekdesh was for the poorest of the poor and the lowest of the low; in general, it was meant for those who had nowhere else to go and no one to support them. ("Respectable" travelers lodged in another community institution, known as the *hakhnasat orhim,* or in private homes.)[14] Kotik writes:

> One could always find three or four poverty-stricken families living there. The building's façade was awful. It looked like some kind of dilapidated ruin whose roof was about to cave in, whose shattered windowpanes were stuffed with black, grimy rags, and whose door was open. Very often families lived there with their little children. It is indescribable, and even now I cannot recall without a shudder the squalid conditions, the gloominess, and the horrible poverty suffered by both the older folk and the very young living there.[15]

In those places where the hekdesh retained a quasi-medical character, its residents were likely to be drawn from across the spectrum of the Jewish down-and-out, including orphans and people who in the language of the time would have been characterized as crippled and insane. Many observers and memoirists, such as Gershon Levin, who wrote about the 1860s-era hekdesh in Lublin, noted that any pretense that this was a medical institution was wholly accidental, and that the wardens and caretakers had no training whatsoever.[16] Moreover, there were often charges that the overseers of the hekdesh were corrupt and were lining their own pockets at the expense of the inmates.

Indeed, starting in the 1860s the hekdesh began to come in for criticism from a number of fronts, and especially by maskilim, proponents of the Jewish Enlightenment and advocates of social reform in the Jewish community. According to Lisa Epstein:

> The terrible state of the hekdesh was noted by visiting foreigners and Russians over the course of the nineteenth century. This public notice made the issue one of concern for reformers of Jewish life, [who wanted to] transform health care institutions to bring them into accordance with their standards and goals for the Jewish community, both for the betterment of Jewish life and as a sign to the outside world of the civilized, sanitized nature of Jewish life.[17]

The maskilic writer Moyshe-Arn Shatskes, for example, painted a bleak picture of the hekdesh in his *Der yidisher far-peysekh* ("Passover Eve"; 1881), noting with bitter irony how the original meaning of the hekdesh, derived from the Hebrew root for "holy," had become twisted over time:

> The word *hekdesh* means . . . a house full of stench and dirt, clutter, cold, smoke, damp, with all the windows broken, the walls peeling, darkness and gloom, black as chimney soot. . . . Why is this called hekdesh? What is sacred about it? . . . To this very day, in many towns the sick houses which Jews call *hekdeyshim* . . . are the worst buildings of the entire town; the town's house-holders pay no attention either to the air of the hekdesh, which is poison for the sick, or to the vilenesses the hekdesh-*man* commits, along with the hekdesh doctor.[18]

The corruption of the hekdesh-*man* is a frequent trope in descriptions of the hekdesh. An exposé in a Vilna newspaper of the hekdesh in Grodno, where filth and corruption were also the order of the day, dates from a slightly later period but is consistent with descriptions encountered through the late imperial era:

> It's difficult to describe the terrible images that emerge from the hekdesh here. The sick people suffer from cold and hunger; the first meal they receive is at noon. The crazy people often break the windowpanes out of hunger. The linen is terribly dirty; it probably hasn't been changed in about ten weeks. The inmates don't even sleep on straw mattresses; the lamps smoke a great deal and no one fixes them. Only those who have the money to bribe the staff get to have a bath. The kitchen is full of dirt and mud, and the food is inedible because they are always looking to buy cheap stuff. There is only one supervisor [*mashgiekh*] for the entire hekdesh; he goes around to all the sick people and cuts their portions, and thus the illnesses are spread around from one bed to the other. The instruments for operations are dull and the sick people suffer terrible pain. The sick people are treated just like animals.[19]

The writer incriminates one person in particular—a supervisor named Shteynberg, who, it was alleged, practiced nepotism in the staffing of the hekdesh, and whose personal disputes with others (such as a local pharmacist) caused suffering to its denizens. One must of course treat this with a modicum of suspicion—since the author wrote under a pseudonym, there is no way of knowing whether he had a stake in making these allegations—but it is generally consonant with what we hear elsewhere about corrupt shtetl institutions.

In the Yiddish language itself, the very word *hekdesh* became synonymous with filth, chaos, and decay. Nahum Stutchkoff's 1950 Yiddish thesaurus lists *hekdesh* as a synonym for "dirty," along with *drek* (filth, shit), *tinoyfes* (excrement), and *neveyle* (carcass), citing idioms like "*shmutsik vi in altn* hekdesh" ("dirty as in the old hekdesh").[20] It is hardly surprising, then, that it was considered shameful for the sick to end up in the hekdesh, presumably because their family could not care for them at home (for financial or other reasons).[21] "Better to die younger at home than older in the hekdesh," a Yiddish saying declared.[22]

Despite the eclipse of the custom of community members' accommodating transient paupers, in many communities the hoary practice of providing meals for paupers and beggars on the Sabbath persisted. Kotik recalled that in his youth (late 1850s–early 1860s), his prosperous grandfather "often invited as many as twelve paupers to his table. Then, the rest of the family, who were themselves famished, would have to give up their places in order to make room for the guests. . . . The welfare of 'his' poor was closer to his heart than that of his wife and children, who, more often than not, went hungry on that account."[23] Note here that—whether for Kotik himself or for his grandfather—the latter's support of paupers translates to a kind of ownership ("'his' poor").

The hekdesh and its denizens in the socio-religious geography of the shtetl

In his *Sefer mi-dor le-dor* (1901), Hirsch Kolp writes that the beggars' hekdesh in the pre-Reform era was where

> the dregs of humanity lived, all the lepers and diseased, anyone with a physical or mental disability, all the riffraff in their multitudes, teeming like a swarm of locusts, one group leaving and another coming in, each one leaving after it the filth and contamination from the disgusting remains of the bread and soup that they ate and trampled underfoot, and the mud and refuse that they picked up on their feet . . . until the hekdesh was like a heap of trash and dung.[24]

Kolp makes clear that wandering beggars were not just poor people, but the rejects of Jewish society: the chronically ill; the crippled, maimed, and deformed; the mentally ill and insane. It would be hard to achieve a more negative and, indeed, dehumanizing depiction of such people: "the dregs of humanity"; "riffraff"; "filth . . . contamination . . . trash . . . dung." The description is strikingly similar to one that we find several years earlier in an article entitled "Tramps, Mediæval and Modern," a review of a new book on the history of begging and vagrancy that appeared in the liberal British *Westminster Review*: "The modern professional tramp is a repulsive creature—few more so—equally filthy and degraded in mind and body, a noxious parasite of the most disgusting kind."[25] In colloquial Yiddish one speaks of "scratching like a beggar," "scratching like a lousy person," "scratching like a pig against a fence," or "scratching as in a hekdesh."[26]

Kolp's depiction of the flotsam and jetsam of Jewish society who ended up in the mid-nineteenth century hekdesh is also reminiscent of Michel Foucault's description of the Great Confinement in Europe's Classical Age (i.e., the seventeenth and eighteenth centuries), which incarcerated beggars, vagabonds, petty criminals, prostitutes, idlers and the unemployed, and the insane in new institutions such as Paris's Hôpital général. (Foucault argues that the common element among all these categories was society's perception of them as idle, a concept that we shall return to in chapter 5.)[27] A similar miscellany of people deemed unworthy by society inhabited hospitals for the rural poor in sixteenth-century Germany, suggesting that the Russian-Polish-Jewish poorhouse was in some sense a modern institution with early modern characteristics.[28]

The hekdesh was a liminal space that lay on the boundary between ordinary life and . . . something else. In a very practical sense, the itinerant poor were, in fact, outsiders, since they did not belong to the local community and, of course, paid no communal taxes.[29] In the relatively tight-knit world of the shtetl, they were unknowns to the local residents, and the community's main concern was usually how to encourage them to move on to the next town as quickly as possible. The hekdesh, moreover, was often located next to the cemetery, since in the medieval and early modern periods (and, to some extent, later as well) it was logical to place buildings housing the sick far from the bulk of the population in order to keep contagious diseases at bay. It also made sense to situate a shelter for itinerants on the outskirts of town, close to a road leading somewhere else.[30] Those residing in the hekdesh—at least those residing there temporarily—were thus clearly identified as foreign to the community. As we saw in chapter 1, some communities even provided transportation to the next town to ensure that the itinerants did not overstay their welcome.[31]

But the liminality of the hekdesh and its residents went beyond such pragmatic matters. The cemetery itself was a liminal site, marking the border between the worlds of the living and the dead.[32] As Avriel Bar-Levav notes, the cemetery was a "fringe neighborhood . . . inhabited by fringe entities: not only the dead but also the insane and demons."[33] (It was the cemetery's impurity that made it a suitable home for demons, while the link to insanity may have been provided by the Talmud's definition of madness, preserved in medieval and early modern legal codes: "The rabbis taught: Who is a madman [*shoteh*]? One who goes out alone at night, and [one] who sleeps in a cemetery at night, and [one] who rips his garments").[34] Marginal types who lived in the hekdesh were perceived as half-dead, and some of them, as we shall see, were insane as well. There is also some evidence that they were linked to the demonic. In Yiddish, if one wanted to describe someone dressed in tatters, one could compare them to a beggar (*opgerisn vi a betler*)—or to a demon or spirit (*opgerisn vi a shed, vi a ruekh*).[35]

The hekdesh "is a grave, giving shelter to living cadavers. Even outwardly it resembles a grave," the American Jewish author S. M. Melamed reflects in a short story. The hekdesh itself was viewed as a place of death, and those in it were regarded as being closer to the realm of the dead than to that of the living.[36] The link between death and the marginal individual, or at least the figure of the beggar, has deep roots in Jewish lore. Several medieval Jewish narratives feature the trope of "the pauper who is a guest at the wedding feast," a personage of deep ambivalence: he is a positive figure in the sense that his presence enables the fulfillment of the *mitsvah* (commandment) of charity, but at the same time, he is the Angel of Death disguised.[37] The maskilic writer Ayzik-Meyer Dik picks up on this theme in his biting 1867 satire *Di nakht fun tes-vav kislev* (The Night of the 15th of Kislev), in which the Angel of Death initiates the creation of the hekdesh as a way to make his work easier, since "the goal of this institution was more to be a place to die than to be healed. . . . [It was] an expensive death-house [*shterbe-hoyz*]."[38] According to Kolp, dead bodies were brought to the hekdesh building in order to be prepared for burial. Why? Because—and here Kolp slyly tweaked a rabbinic maxim, *ani hashuv kamet*—"the poor [were] considered as dead."[39] Given the isolation of the hekdesh from the mainstream of shtetl society and space, this made some sense: no one who was "normal" would want to have contact with the dead souls, as it were, of the hekdesh. (Kolp's claim is confirmed by the regulations governing the Bikur Holim in Minsk, which required the *shamash* of the hekdesh to get permission from the burial society before bringing corpses from outside the city into the building.)[40]

The cemetery was the shtetl institution with the most obvious ties to the hekdesh, but there were others as well.[41] Strangely enough for an institution synonymous with filth and unsanitary conditions, the hekdesh apparently often shared a building with the communal bathhouse or stood next door to it. Perhaps this juxtaposition had its origins in the fact that both institutions were connected with the health of the community. The bathhouse was where one could usually find the local barber-surgeon engaged in cupping, while folk wisdom common to Jews and Christians across eastern and northern Europe dictated that bathers stimulate the circulation by beating each other with birch branches. Moreover, the bathhouse attendant, a low-level communal employee and often an indigent person himself, sometimes lived in the hekdesh building. Like the hekdesh, the bathhouse was a liminal space: with its nudity, intimations of sexuality, and reminder of the porousness of the body, it stood on the border between the realms of the ordinary and the repressed.[42]

A third possible location for the hekdesh was quite central, near the *shul-hoyf* (synagogue courtyard) or in the *shul-gas* (synagogue street), close to the prayer houses and houses of study.[43] Perhaps this alternate siting of the hekdesh, in the very center of the shtetl, indicates that in some cases, it was more integrated into shtetl life than one might have expected. Similarly, there is evidence that the local madman or "town fool" sometimes slept in the house of study, also a central institution in the shtetl. How ironic that the individual who spent the most time in the house of study was the community's most peripheral figure; as with a picture or piece of furniture in the most-used room in the house, one does not notice it because it's always there. An intriguing comparison can be found in premodern western Europe, where in some French and German towns "the *pauvres honteux,* or shame-faced, locally known poor, were . . . granted a regular spot in annual processions. Thus marginals were often fully integrated, symbolically as well as materially, into society."[44]

One tantalizing piece of evidence that might serve as confirmation of that integration can be found in Gershon Levin's turn-of-the-century memoir of a mid-nineteenth-century Lublin childhood:

> One of the Sabbath pleasures was to go to the Jewish hospital [elsewhere he explains that this was actually the precursor to the hospital, that is, the hekdesh], even if one did not have any relatives to visit there. Some would distribute food . . . to the patients; others would go just to pass the time looking at the patients and, most importantly, to tease the crazy people a little. . . . These visits to the hospital disturbed the Sabbath rest, because it became a real trade fair [that is, a hubbub] there. We ran there from all over the whole city, dirtied everything, and it looked like the marketplace after the market. And of course we also disturbed the sick people with our talk. We joked with the wardens, cursed, and teased the crazy people.[45]

The first reason that Levin gives for visiting the hekdesh is fairly straightforward: to do a charitable deed by bringing food to the residents. But the second—to while away the time on Sabbath afternoon by looking at the patients and teasing the insane inmates—suggests a common human fascination with the abnormal, the ugly, and the repulsive. Levin's description is eerily reminiscent of the eighteenth-century custom of publicly exhibiting lunatics that Foucault analyzes in his *Madness and Civilization*: "As late as 1815 . . . the hospital of Bethlehem exhibited lunatics for a penny, every Sunday. . . . In France, the excursion to Bicêtre and the display of the insane remained until the Revolution one of the Sunday distractions for the Left Bank bourgeoisie."[46] Foucault's linguistic sleight-of-hand here is that madmen were perceived as monsters, which in etymological terms, he contends, would seem to derive from the Latin verb *monstrare,* "to show, display."[47] (He is mistaken, however; "monster" derives from *monēre,* "to remind, warn.") The idea of visiting the *hekdesh-layt,* the people of the hekdesh, in order to view a spectacle or even a kind of freak show is reinforced by the ritual of the cholera wedding, which, as we shall see in chapter 4, was also a putatively charitable act but in some sense a spectacle for entertainment as well. And like the cholera wedding, the hekdesh visit provided the opportunity to infringe traditional norms within the wider structure of accepted custom and convention (although described as a Sabbath pleasure, the children's visit to the hekdesh actually contravened the spirit of the day of rest, since their presence disturbed the peace of the inmates).

One folktale, while supernatural in its content, provides a vivid illustration of the stigmatization of the people of the hekdesh. In this tale, an orphan raised in a hekdesh with no one to care for him is fed on scraps thrown to him by the other residents. The townspeople will have nothing to do with him; to avenge himself, he becomes the town informer, who sows discord wherever he can: "Thus I lived my miserable life, unwanted by God and my fellow human beings, until one fine day I stopped existing. No one cried for me, no one mourned for me. They buried me beyond the cemetery wall, without a stone and without a monument, not far from the hekdesh. No one said kaddish for me."[48] How is it, then, that we are hearing this tale of woe? Because after his death, the orphan has become a dybbuk possessing the body of a fifteen-year-old boy. "I was abandoned and cursed by everyone in my life," the dybbuk has the boy say. "I was not a man but a shadow."

For someone who lives his life outside the realm of normal human existence—without family, without home, without normal intercourse with his fellow Jews; who indeed, in his own words, was "not a man"—what could be a more appropriate domain to start off life than the hekdesh? And what could be a more fitting locale to end it than in the area of the cemetery set aside for suicides, apostates, and infamous sinners, not far from the hekdesh? And yet, if we approach the tale knowing that the archetypal Jewish town (as it was often portrayed in belletristic and memoir literature, as well as folklore) had an array of set characters—the fool, the cripple, the informer, perhaps even the town ghost—then the place of the dybbuk becomes clear.[49] He was as much a part of the community as he was cut off from it.

This story is fascinating for another reason: it overturns the conventional roles of accuser and accused in the traditional *dybbuk* narrative. Usually, the dybbuk was the soul of a deceased individual who had committed a sin and had thus gotten ensnared in the dominion of Gehenna. The public ritual of the exorcism thus served to reinforce the communally held values against which the dybbuk had transgressed.[50] In our story, however, the orphan was as much sinned against as sinning, and he accuses the community that abandoned him to his miserable existence through the voice of the boy whom he has possessed.

Literary interventions

Because of the fragmentary nature of historical sources on the hekdesh, we turn now to fiction to enhance our understanding of the place of the poorhouse—and marginal people more broadly—in East European Jewish society and culture. Two writers who devoted significant room in their oeuvres to Jews on the margins of society were towering figures in the formative era of modern Jewish literature: S. Y. Abramovitsh, whose works we examine in this chapter, and Itskhok Leyb Peretz, whose writings we shall consider in later chapters.

Sholem Yankev Abramovitsh (known later also by the name of his most famous protagonist, Mendele Moykher Sforim, or Mendele the Book Peddler) made his debut in Hebrew and Yiddish letters in the central Ukrainian city of Berdichev in the early 1860s. His early literary output was that of a typical *maskil* (proponent of the Jewish Enlightenment): positivist works intended to encourage his fellow Jews in the Russian Empire to embrace Western-style education and the social integration and economic productivity that would surely come in its wake. But towards the end of the decade, his art became more radical, "in touch with the new European wave of interest in poverty [and] the lower depths of society."[51] This shift in artistic sensibility resulted in two very different works: *Fishke der krumer* (Fishke the Lame), subtitled "a story of poor folk," in which Abramovitsh limned the world of Jewish beggardom, and *Di takse* (The Tax; 1869), an exposé of the corruption and venality of the Jewish bourgeoisie.

Abramovitsh was to meditate on these themes for decades to come: *Fishke der krumer* was first published in 1869 as a novella and later expanded into novel form and published in 1888. In the intervening years, he moved to Odessa to take up the position of principal of a new Jewish school there, a reformed Talmud Torah (school serving orphans and poor children).[52] Starting in the 1880s and continuing to the end of his life, he recast his Yiddish works of long fiction in Hebrew in addition to writing new work in Hebrew. The reworked Hebrew-language version of *Fishke*, entitled *Sefer ha-kabtsanim* (The Book of Beggars) was published in the 1909–12 anthology of Abramovitsh's collected works.

After his license to practice law was revoked in 1887 "for allegedly promoting Polish nationalism and socialism," I. L. Peretz, Yiddish literature's giant of modernism, had a second career as a bureaucrat in the Warsaw Jewish community council (ironically, given the heavy use of the cemetery and death imagery in some of his works, he worked in the burials department).[53] His entrée into the world of statistics in the service of the community was the invitation he received from a wealthy financier and convert named Jan Bloch to accompany Nahum Sokolow on an 1890 journey through the Tomaszow region to collect statistics that would counter the prevailing image of Polish Jews as economic parasites. The expedition came just a few years after Peretz's formal entrance into the world of Yiddish letters with the publication of his modernist ballad "Monish."

Given that both Abramovitsh and Peretz had significant experience as bureaucrats and administrators in Jewish philanthropic institutions and communal governance, it is no accident that significant portions of their oeuvres are dedicated to exploring the plight of the vulnerable and marginalized. In each case, the writer came into close contact with those populations: Abramovitsh worked with orphans, a marginalized group that he strove to transform through education, an undertaking that Olga Litvak comments was bound up with his own literary endeavors: "In taking a job at the Talmud-Torah, Abramovitsh did not simply secure a position; he performed the act of rescuing poor Jewish children, a task he had assigned to [his ubiquitous protagonist] Mendele in *The Little Man*."[54] For his part, Peretz interacted with people on the margins in order to collect data that would help to defend the Jewish community from the injurious image of the Jewish parasite and exploiter, and later, in his role as communal functionary, doubtless in his dealings with the many requests for free burial that were brought to the Warsaw Jewish community board.

We find in the mature work of Abramovitsh and Peretz a radical response to the plight of the marginalized in Jewish society and their treatment at the hands of the modernizing Jewish elite, a response that it seems unlikely could ever have been fully articulated in their day-to-day work in the Jewish community, where the watchword was gradualism. In *Fishke der krumer* (1888), Abramovitsh went beyond providing a detailed and gruesome, albeit fictionalized, account of the lives of itinerant Jewish beggars; his non-beggar characters ultimately came to the paradoxical realization that this underworld of begging and parasitism actually embraced all of Jewish society: "All of Jewry—nothing but beggary!" (*Kol yisroel—eyn kabtsen, un gornisht.*)[55] Here Abramovitsh was standing on the shoulders of literary predecessors in two worlds. In Yiddish, Ayzik Meyer Dik created a satirical Jewish world in the 1860s and early 1870s consisting almost entirely of many layers and categories of beggars and shnorrers, and in Russian A. Golitsynskii, whose *Ulichnye tipy* (Street Types, 1860) catalogued the various kinds of beggars to be found in Moscow's streets, is perhaps the best parallel to Abramovitsh within the literary tradition of the "physiological sketch"—portraits of lower-class types.[56] This discursive strategy exploded the standard Jewish philanthropic approach to the Jewish lumpenproletariat, which insisted on the fundamental marginality of such people—that they were outside the norm of the Jewish community and did not represent a "true" picture of Jewish life. That approach necessitated, of course, the elimination, transformation, or at least concealment of such undesirable elements.

In two works exploring madness—"The Mad Talmudist" (1890), discussed in chapter 6, and "From the Madhouse" / "In the Insane Wing," a short story cycle published in Hebrew and Yiddish versions between 1895 and 1901 and evaluated in chapter 7—Peretz questioned the boundary between sane and insane, and thus, like Abramovitsh, cast into doubt the putative boundary between normal and abnormal, center and margins, mainstream and aberrant. For example, Leyb the Philosopher, one of the madmen in the fictional insane asylum that lies at the heart of the story cycle, maintains that "there is no truth and falsehood in the world, and a fortiori there is no madness or madmen."[57] And the narrator states plainly: "We are all mad or we are all sane!"

But in order to make these radical narrative moves, Abramovitsh and Peretz had to do something more fundamental first: they had to risk placing marginals—beggars, cripples, madmen, orphans—at the center of their works and thus, perhaps, casting them as seminal figures in Jewish culture.

Indeed, I would suggest that that both of these literary giants prefigured a development that was about to emerge with the rise of modern Jewish politics: the reclaiming of the marginal figure as a symbol of the wretched state of the entire Jewish nation (or at least its eastern European cohort) and a rejection of Jewish self-hatred as a reflection of antisemitic stereotypes. We shall explore this thesis at greater length in chapter 7.

Fishke's hekdesh: Abramovitsh's poetics of the Jewish grotesque

One of the richest and most suggestive portrayals of the hekdesh is the fictional one found in Abramovitsh's *Fishke der krumer* (1888). To summarize briefly the plot of the novel: after Mendele the Book Peddler encounters his fellow bookseller Alter Yaknehoz on the road, we are introduced to a hapless cripple by the name of Fishke and learn his sad story. In his hometown of Glupsk (the equivalent of Stupidville) he was forced to marry Basya, a blind orphan (who was a widow to boot; this was her second wedding) as a substitute for the original groom, who never showed up at the wedding canopy. After the couple joined a band of itinerant beggars, Fishke's wife took up with Faybush, a boorish rogue, while Fishke himself fell in love with the hunchbacked Beyle, abandoned by her parents in childhood and subsequently the victim of terrible abuse and neglect at the hands of her guardians that led to her disfigurement. Experiencing many adventures and calamities, including a trip to Odessa, Fishke and Beyle were separated, reunited, and then parted again. As Fishke is relating the last of his mishaps to Mendele and Alter, Mendele asks him for the name of the loutish father who abandoned Beyle—and it turns out that he is none other than Alter Yaknehoz himself.

During their wanderings, the band of beggars, including Fishke and Beyle, take shelter in a hekdesh. Abramovitsh's poorhouse is a consummate example of hyperbole and is thus a perfect way for him to embody in a place, an institution, the characteristics of society's castoffs who come to take shelter there. Fishke relates that he had seen plenty of poorhouses, but "this one was different." It is different because it stands at the nadir of existence, *anus mundi*—seemingly an entrance to hell, given its hellish conditions, a state ironically emphasized by Fishke's statement in the Hebrew version: "This was the heavenly gate for the ascension of their souls." (Whether all the beggars will "ascend" is indeed a matter for dispute, given what we learn about the depraved beggar Faybush; as Fishke says, "May he never rise on Judgment Day.)[58] The lengthy description is worth quoting in full:

> This poorhouse was a very old inn, a ruin with crooked walls and a roof like a crumpled cap, turned up in front and very low in the back, almost down to the ground. This tired old poorhouse looked ready to faint. The poor building wanted to collapse and lie down to rest on the ground in a pile of dust and rubble. But the townspeople had talked it out of such nonsense. They propped it up with sticks, tied it up with string, and begged it to last for another hundred and twenty years.
>
> What used to be a gate led into a large house. You could see daylight through the cracks in the crumbling walls. The ground was full of holes and puddles. Some of them were filled with moldy, stagnant water from slops and similar things and dirty rain water that had come in through the rotten roof. Pieces of rotten straw lay all over mixed with all sorts of rags and junk: pieces of baskets, chopped-up matting, dried-out uppers of shoes, old heels and soles with rusted nails, pieces of pottery, broken barrel hoops, spokes from wheels, hair, bones, broom reeds and other trash. All this rotted on the ground and made the air so thick and stinking you could faint.
>
> On the left side of the house was a greasy old door. It opened with a creak into a room with small, narrow windows that didn't set right. Most of the panes were missing; the holes were covered with fish paper, or stuffed with rags. The whole panes were very dirty and had thick layers of mold in the corners. Some were so old that they were covered with glaring yellowish-green film whose sharp reflections hurt your eyes just as scraping on glass hurts your ears. Long benches—boards lying on wooden blocks and stumps—stood along the crumbling walls and around the big stove. Wooden hooks were knocked into the walls over the benches. From the black ceiling hung several nooses with wooden rods through them. On these hooks and rods hung the greasy old cots, dresses, and baskets of all the beggars who came there, some on foot, some by van. Young and old, male and female—all stayed together.
>
> The poorhouse was also the charity hospital [*a biker-khoylim*]. This was the place where the town's sickest, ugliest beggars died. The doctor did every-

thing he could: he cupped them, he bled them, he physicked them [lit., he cupped them, he applied leeches, he bled them] at the expense of *Kahal*, until their kosher souls fled from his treatment. Then the poorhouse keeper, who was also the town grave digger, buried them for free.

The poorhouse keeper and his family lived there too in a little alcove that was an excuse for a room. Aside from being poorhouse keeper, grave digger, official in the Burial Society, inspector of the charity hospital, Queen Vashti in the Purim play, a bear during Simkhes-Toyre, a waiter, and a punster at all weddings and circumcisions, he had another business: he made wax candles. All the rich families and all the synagogues in the town bought their candles from him. And when he made a batch, there was a stink for miles around. . . .

That night the ground, the benches, the stove were swarming with droves of people. They pushed, shoved, cursed and fought for a place to sit. It was a war between cavalry and infantry. Each tried to show the other who was stronger. During the whole uproar, a sick old man, who had been brought in the day before, was groaning in a corner. A little baby, whose foot someone had stepped on during the shoving, screamed deafeningly.[59]

In this tale the hekdesh is fitting metaphor for how the marginals are perceived by Jewish society. The building's many physical deficiencies—crooked and crumbling walls, sagging roof, missing windowpanes—are reminiscent of human disability. The benches have blocks and stumps instead of proper legs, in this resembling Yontl, a character introduced earlier in the novel, "who had no legs and moved around on his buttocks by pushing himself with two little wooden blocks." The front room is littered with the detritus and leftovers of ordinary life—fragments of pottery, barrels, shoes, baskets, wheels—in addition to various varieties of wastewater. What more appropriate place to toss the waste material of shtetl life than the house that shelters those who are perceived as human rubbish, human wreckage? Abramovitsh's description also makes clear that the hekdesh is an assault on the senses: the stench of the rotting trash and candle-making from tallow,[60] the glare of the reflection from the filmed-over windows; the hubbub of the beggars fighting each other for a place to sleep, the howling of the wind, the scraping and squeaking of the door; the indignity to the body of vermin, cold, and rain.

That the building "wanted to collapse" suggests that this archaic, medieval institution has survived far beyond its natural lifespan and has no business existing in the nineteenth century, but the shtetl residents have no intention of allowing it to disappear. They need the hekdesh—perhaps as a convenient place to dispose of their undesirables?—and implore it "to last for another hundred and twenty years," the full lifespan of a person in traditional Jewish terms. For if it caves in, they will be forced to confront and contend with their marginals some other way.

There are clear elements of the literary theorist Mikhail Bakhtin's notion of the grotesque here as well. In his analysis of Rabelais's oeuvre, Bakhtin's "grotesque body" is centered around physical functions that blur the boundaries between the body and the outside world, especially hints about sexual and excretory functions. "The artistic logic of the grotesque image ignores the closed, smooth, and impenetrable surface of the body and retains only its excrescences . . . and orifices."[61] The puddles in the front room of the hekdesh contain "moldy, stagnant water from slops and similar things [*un nokh azelkhe zakhn*]"—perhaps a reference to human waste—and in the back room "male and female . . . stayed together" (also a suggestion of sexual license).[62] Since the hekdesh also serves as a primitive hospital, the boundaries of the body are further violated in the acts of leeching and bleeding. In the grotesque, moreover, "the beginning and end of life are closely linked and interwoven," a condition represented in Abramovitsh's hekdesh by the baby, on the one hand, and the sick old man who expires during Fishke's stay and all the "sick beggars" who go to the hekdesh to die, on the other.

Bakhtin added that this "grotesque logic" could also be applied to "objects in which depths (holes) and convexities are emphasized"—a superb description of Abramovitsh's hyperbolic hekdesh, a central element of which are its innumerable cracks, holes, and other apertures.[63] There is, indeed, very little separating outside from inside. It bears noting, however, that on the whole Bakhtin's grotesque has a positive valence, whereas Abramovitsh's grotesque is monstrous.

The acme of Abramovitsh's irony is reached in the passage about the poorhouse as charity hospital (*biker kholim/bet holim*). In the looking-glass world of Abramovitsh's shtetl, a hospital is a death house, and a doctor is a butcher. In his next breath after uttering the word "hospital," Fishke explains—deadpans?—that the term "hospital" is actually the shtetl's word for a charnel-house: the hekdesh is where beggars go to die (and in some cases possibly even to be killed by the so-called doctor, who "did everything he could"—but whether for good or evil is left up to the reader to decide). The Hebrew version heightens the irony by making the poorhouse literally death's door: "This is where sick beggars find their death and this is the heavenly gate for the ascent of their souls."[64] It comes as no surprise, then, that the hekdesh-*man*—who, by the way, helpfully also wears the hat of the charity hospital inspector—is also the gravedigger, since the two institutions—poorhouse and cemetery—are so close to each other in function. Nor is it entirely astonishing that on the carnival holiday of Purim, he plays Queen Vashti, associated in rabbinic legend both with nudity (according to the Talmud, Vashti refused King Ahasuerus's order to appear naked before his court) and with disease and deformity, since she is variously described as having contracted leprosy or grown a tail.[65] Her ultimate banishment from the royal court is a fate with some affinity to the status of Jewish marginals.

In a study of Byzantine miracle narratives, Stavroula Constantinou perceptively links the grotesque with Freud's uncanny—that which is strangely familiar, evoking fear and dread, because it has previously been repressed and therefore estranged from the psyche.[66] In Constantinou's words, "Bakhtin's grotesque body also refers to aspects of human life and experience that have been rejected and repressed. The lower bodily stratum and its functions and products, which the official culture treats as taboo and eliminates, are celebrated and stressed by the grotesque body, which situates them as the center of human activity."[67] The Hebrew literary critic Gershon Shaked draws on the uncanny in his evaluation of *Sefer ha-kabtsanim*, writing that the novel's marginal characters are "repressed and depressed by society, but [or, rather, and therefore] they are also a kind of synecdoche of the society they live in."[68] It is precisely *because* these "non-persons," as Shaked puts it, in some way represent the whole of that society that they are treated with such disgust and contempt. They are the aspect of human life that has been, in Constantinou's words, rejected and repressed.

It is worth noting that the hateful accusations made against poor Jews by Russian antisemites not infrequently bore a sharp resemblance to Jewish perceptions of the marginals. The Anglo-Irish journalist and author E. J. Dillon, who spent many years in the Russian Empire, collected some choice excerpts from antisemitic descriptions of Berdichev and Vilna, like this one from the Judeophobic monarchist newspaper *Novoe vremia*:

> All the narratives of travellers about Asiatic and African cities dwindle down to the level of the commonplace in comparison with the sights that meet your eye here; even the glorious city of Berditscheff, the very name of which is become proverbial as a synonym for dirt and rottenness, is as nothing when confronted with this pearl [i.e., Vilna]. . . . Glance at the Jewish Synagogue. The dirt in the courtyard is indescribable, the noise and tumult like unto that which accompanied the confusion of tongues. But the atmosphere! You should breathe it, to be able to conceive what it is like. Beside the women's wing of the synagogue are the baths in which the sons and daughters of Israel cleanse their sinful flesh. You can judge the internal tidiness and cleanliness of these baths by the high dunghill carefully heaped up beside the steps of the entrance.[69]

The newspaper's description of the barbarous conditions of the synagogue and its courtyard—the dirt, the hubbub, the stench—bear a striking resemblance to Fishke's description of the filthy, noisy, foul-smelling hekdesh. There is also a suggestion of sexual licentiousness, since the baths where "the sons *and* daughters of Israel" bathe is adjacent to the women's wing of the synagogue. The reference to "Asiatic and African cities" hints broadly that the tsar's Jewish subjects are even less civilized than the primitive denizens of those far-off locales.

"All of Jewry—nothing but beggary!"

At the dramatic turning point of *Fishke der krumer*, Reb Alter realizes that he is Beyle's father, that the story of poor folk of which he had been an onlooker, a member of the audience—is actually *his* story. He was complicit in Beyle's downward spiral from a life of ordinary poverty to her miserable existence among the castoffs of society. At the same time, the reader realizes—and this is, of course, Abramovitsh's strategy—that he or she, too, may not be "just" a reader, listening to Fishke's tale as a form of melodramatic entertainment. Just as Beyle was sacrificed by her father, Reb Alter, when he abandoned his family, so are all the castoffs victims of the immoral choices of society. In Gershon Shaked's words, these "non-persons on the margins of society . . .

have a name but no identity [and are] repressed and depressed by society."[70] More specifically, Beyle is the victim of her parents' sexual sins (her father left her mother for a younger woman, and then her mother abandoned Beyle, for a lover), while Fishke's symbolic parent, the kahal, has abused and exploited him.[71]

But Reb Alter and Abramovitsh's readers must not only understand how they have helped create Jewish society's marginals; they must also realize that the repulsive mass of wandering beggars that has so cruelly oppressed Beyle (and Fishke too) is an aspect of the Jewish collectivity that has been repressed, or that society would like to repress: the homeless, the ugly, the deformed, the monstrous, the sexually licentious Other, the inhuman. All these are also used by the Christian world to describe Jews, which Jews then displace onto their destitute and disabled.[72] Just as the Jewish body was perceived as different and other, so is the marginal body seen as grotesque, as uncanny. As Shaked points out, defects, deformities, and disabilities permeate the novel's fictional world, which is both the realm of poor folk and beggars but, via synecdoche, also represents Jewish society, or at least its lower middle-class segment.[73]

> The handicapped characters with distorted lives are a social underworld, but they are also symbols of something pathological, repressed, and distorted in the lower-middle-class strata of Jewish society and in the lower strata of that society's collective unconscious. . . . The very appearance of the beggars is a metaphor for the distortions and flaws of the society into which they have been thrust.[74]

Nor does Abramovitsh proffer a cure. The novel—unlike the 1939 film adaption, discussed in chapter 7—offers no resolution, no happy ending, since the deeply rooted problems that the author describes have no easy solution. As Shaked remarks with compassionate insight: "The victims of this tale are ugly victims who will never be redeemed from their ugliness; wretched victims who will not be saved even by miracles; their suffering verges on the grotesque because their hope for salvation is so ridiculous."[75]

But as Dror Mishani points out, in Shaked's insistence that the body of Jewish beggars and poor folk portrayed in the novel is actually a synecdoche for all of Jewish society, he is continuing a long tradition of nationalizing

Sefer ha-kabtsanim, a tradition that Mishani traces back to a 1913 article by Yosef Hayyim Brenner.[76] Mishani urges us to see the novel in its original historical context and to read the class-based society of East European Jewry back into the text, contra the "erasure" performed by Brenner and many others (and, Mishani adds, by Zionism itself). By using poststructuralist critical theory, he argues, we can listen to the many voices in the text "that speak outside of the bounds of the nationalist allegory."[77] The nationalist reading of Abramovitsh that Mishani rejects is yet another example of mainstream bourgeois society quite literally reading marginals out of history.

Another possibility for understanding the nexus between Abramovitsh's marginals and Jewish society as a whole is hinted at in a passage that we may describe as the taxonomy of beggardom, in which Fishke describes the many different kinds of beggars that he encountered on his journey, such as tramps, idlers, loafers, *batlonim* (Talmud recluses), *mekubolim* (kabbalists), and many, many others.[78] Mendele then continues the taxonomy by offering even more categories, including paupers in religious service such as shofar-blowers and mezuzah inspectors, charity collectors who wander from town to town, hidden paupers who accept charity in secret because of their previous patrician status, and "semi-beggars," including some teachers and rabbis.[79] An additional list encompasses sick Jews, deserted wives, writers, and—last but certainly not least—peddlers. It is obvious that we have long ago left behind beggars as they would ordinarily be defined; it seems that there are, indeed, very few Jews in the Russian Empire who would not be classified as beggars! And that is exactly the point that Alter Yaknehoz makes at the conclusion of the passage: "Enough of your beggars! . . . As far as I'm concerned, you can cut the whole story short: all Jewry's Beggardom! And an end to this nonsense."[80] But rather than understanding this passage as telling us that the novel is actually a metaphor for the circumstances of the entire Jewish people (or, to be more precise, Jews in eastern Europe), as Zionist critics usually read it, or, as Shaked argues, that the poor folk in the novel serve as a synecdoche for the larger Jewish society, we can see this as Abramovitsh slyly expanding the circles of beggardom wider and wider until they encompass the narrator of the tale himself and ultimately *all* Jews. In so doing, he causes the reader to realize that the beggars of the story are not the Other, outcasts to be pitied and viewed with disgust, but that, when one thinks about it, there is not all that much separating "ordinary" people from pauperdom. In essence, Abramovitsh is saying: the vast majority of Russian-Polish Jewry is poor, living off of the community, other people's hard work, or even, from time to time, charity. Thus it often seems as though we are all beggars, which is exactly why most Jews want nothing to do with the marginal folk and look down upon them with such disgust—because they fear *becoming* them! There but for the grace of God go I.

Agnon's hekdesh: bodily putrefaction and sexual shame

Some three decades later, the eminent Hebrew writer S. Y. Agnon (1888–1970) offered a fictional portrait of a traditional hekdesh that bears a striking resemblance to Abramovitsh's in its resonances of fleshly decay and sexuality. Agnon, who devoted much of his oeuvre to fictional reworkings of his hometown shtetl of Buczacz, Galicia, and of traditional Jewish society more broadly, touches on themes relating to marginal people in his story "Ovadiah the Cripple" (*Ovadiah ba'al mum*). Its narrator describes the old hekdesh of Ovadiah's town as "the place for all the contemptible and worthless people as well as for brigands who wander from land to land and for the chronically ill [*holeh muhlat she-ein lo takanah*]."[81] As is always the case with Agnon, the Hebrew phrasing here is rich with nuance and intertextuality. *Kol tsaru'a ve-khol zav*, Agnon's "contemptible and worthless people," is a phrase from Numbers 5:2 in which God instructs Moses to have the Israelites "remove from camp anyone with an eruption [or "anyone who is leprous"] or a discharge and anyone defiled by a corpse" (NJPS). Since the *tsaru'a* is a leper (in the traditional understanding of the skin affliction called *tsara'at*) or someone with an eruption of the skin, while the *zav* is a person suffering from sexual discharge, Agnon's "worthless people" are not only chronically ill, possibly disfigured, and physically repulsive, but also perceived as impure and thus liable to defile others. For that reason, they must be put out of the camp, isolated from the body of the people—a fate true of both the context of biblical Israel and of modern eastern Europe. In the former, however, the tsaru'a and zav could hope to regain purity and be welcomed back into the camp once the skin eruption or discharge had passed; it is very doubtful whether anyone in the hekdesh could be so optimistic about a change in his or her status.

As for the chronically ill, when the story was first published Agnon used the phrase "every sick person who had lost hope" (*kol holeh asher avdah tikvato*), but in the final version he substituted *holeh muhlat she-ein lo takanah*—chronically and incurably ill person. Perhaps Agnon was suggesting an intertextual reference to a Talmudic story (BT Sanhedrin 75a) about the intersection between illicit sexual activity, death, and sin. A certain man fell in lust with a particular woman to the point that he became deathly ill, and a debate ensues between doctors and sages, with the former urging that the man be allowed to have sex with the woman: "And the doctors said: He will have no cure [*ein lo takanah*] until she engages in sexual intercourse with him" (they later temper their prescription to the condition that the man at least be allowed to see the woman naked, and then that he be permitted to converse with her through a fence).[82] The sages insist in all these cases that the man must rather die than be permitted to assuage his lust, which the Gemara ultimately questions: why is this necessary? Rav Pappa answers that it is because of the danger of bringing shame on the woman's entire family. It is not the details of the story and the debate around it that are relevant to the hekdesh but the conceptual associations and connotations. The chronically ill people in the hekdesh—and by extension, all marginal people—are associated not only with death but also with illicit sexual activity, nudity, shame, and the crossing of borders (the conversation through the fence).

Agnon's subsequent portrayal of the inglorious end of the hekdesh—after the authorities declare its compulsory closure, the community pulls it apart bit by bit and its constituent components are cannibalized for use in other building projects—also hints at the character of the institution:

> The roof started to sag and the walls started becoming unsteady [*ad she-makh ha-mekareh va-yerofefu ha-ketalim*], and the authorities declared that it must be closed. And from then the building was deserted. Whoever built a house in that neighborhood took some stones and columns, chopped up the hekdesh doors and took away the cornices [*atarot*] and the engravings [*pituhim*] and the threshold [*asqopah*] and the crevices [*sheqifim*] until the great fire came and burned up the remainder and nothing remained of the building but a pile of stones.[83]

Three of the Hebrew terms for architectural elements—*atarot, pituhim, shekifim*—are used in the Mishnah's discussion of what conveys impurity within a building (m. Ohalot 14:1). The fourth, *askopah* (threshold), is a clear reference to liminality.

The first sentence in the passage above also lends itself to intertextual exegesis. The first phrase is a reference to Ecclesiastes 10, a comparison of wisdom and folly with frequent mention of the fool (*sakhal* or *kesil*). The specific verse from which the phrase "the roof started to sag" is borrowed reads, "Through slothfulness the ceiling sags; through lazy hands the house caves in" (10:18). Is this Agnon's way of gesturing at the frequent characterizations of marginal people as idlers, while simultaneously hinting that the truly lazy are the community members who did nothing, or next to nothing, while their coreligionists rotted away in the hekdesh? "The walls started becoming unsteady" alludes to Job 26, which begins with a reference to Job's (and by extension, God's) support of those without strength or wisdom.[84]

In Agnon's telling, the hekdesh was eventually replaced by "something like a hospital for the poor"—not a true hospital, but a place where the chronically ill with connections among the institution's trustees could find a bed and some kind of treatment until death. The efficacy of that treatment is revealed by the mortality rate in the hospital: "Once daily the town doctor came to visit his patients and twice or thrice weekly the beadles of the *hevra kadisha* came to prepare the dead for burial"[85]—an echo of Fishke's reference to the hekdesh doctor who did "everything he could."

Conclusion

These rich literary sources provide profound insight into the nature of the hekdesh and its function in Jewish society. The hekdesh was both a physical and imaginary locus for the grotesque, the uncanny, and the shameful in the Jewish collective unconscious. And just as Alter Yaknehoz recognizes that the story of the marginal people to which he has been listening is actually his own, the contemporary reader will grasp one of the central ideas in Abramovitsh's text: that the marginal individual is not out there "somewhere" but instead is an integral part of the Jewish narrative. In fact, the line between ordinary poor Jew and pauper or beggar is so fine that it is only because the former is in such great need of reifying it that it exists at all. This circumstance also helps to explain why at times the Jewish mainstream is seemingly so eager to displace onto its marginals the opprobrium heaped upon Jews by antisemites.

That is also the ultimate lesson of the dybbuk tale of Piesk and Most. The protagonist of the story represents the undesirables of Jewish society in all their guises: as the orphan in the hekdesh, a member of the Jewish community by birthright but neglected and spurned because of his condition; as informer, an internal enemy who threatens the very existence of the community; and finally and most powerfully, as dybbuk—an entity that possesses from within, threatening to take over the Jewish collective's very essence, its very soul. There could hardly be a more eloquent articulation of the deep-seated fears of the Jewish societal mainstream vis-à-vis its marginal people.

CHAPTER 4

THE CHOLERA WEDDING

> When misfortune visits those who once walked alongside us, we do tend
> to feel relief, almost as if we believe we have ourselves been spared, and
> as we come to convince ourselves that they are suffering in our stead, we
> feel for these wretched creatures. We feel merciful.
> —Sabahattin Ali, *Madonna in a Fur Coat*

The cholera wedding was one of the most peculiar folk rituals to emerge
from the rich spiritual matrix of East European Jewry. In this magical ceremony, marginal people were wedded to each other in the town cemetery in
a bid to end a cholera epidemic. This chapter limns the nature and meaning
of the cholera wedding from its emergence during one of the Russian Empire's first cholera pandemics in the 1830s through later resurgences of the
ritual in the 1860s and the 1890s and down to its (nearly) last appearance in
the 1910s. Accounts of the cholera wedding in the press, memoir literature,
rabbinic works, and Hasidic tales show not only how the ritual developed
over time but also, more important, what it can tell us about the changing
place and role of the marginal individual in Russian and Polish Jewish communities. The cholera wedding, despite being firmly rooted in mystical and
folk beliefs, was in fact a modern innovation masquerading as a hoary rite.
It functioned as a corrective ritual intended to normalize marginal people
through marriage and restore them to a respectable place in the community
in order to achieve a kind of cosmic reconciliation that would banish the
epidemic. The cholera wedding may also have been intended symbolically to
displace the epidemic from ordinary Jews to marginal people.

Cholera and social marginality

Cholera was at once a symbol of barbarism and an icon of modernity. Spilling forth from the Indian subcontinent where it had been endemic for centuries, in six pandemics in rapid succession through the nineteenth century and into the twentieth, it spread to Central and East Asia, the Middle East, North Africa, Russia, Europe, and the Americas. In the Western imagination, both expert and popular, cholera was often associated with the ostensibly primitive societies of the East, particularly as people learned that Hindu and Muslim pilgrims were an important vector for the epidemics.[1] It also came to be associated with poverty, filth, immoral behavior, and debauchery. But paradoxically, it was the modern age and its scientific innovations—particularly in the realm of transport—as well as the spread of colonialism, binding far-flung corners of the world together in unprecedented political and economic relationships, that made global cholera pandemics possible.[2]

In a world that did not understand the bacterial basis of infectious disease, people engulfed in the horror of a cholera epidemic could choose from many possible theories about the genesis and cause of the illness. In some countries, the miasmatic theory of cholera, which pointed to "bad air" emanating from rotting organic compounds, prevailed; in others, people often believed that certain kinds of food and drink made one susceptible. Cholera, among other epidemic diseases, had a particularly "eccentric" character, as many nineteenth-century observers put it—"some houses were spared while neighboring houses were devastated, one side of a street left untouched, another plague-ridden," Asa Briggs writes in a seminal article on social reactions to cholera—that seemed to call out for a commonsense explanation of who fell prey and who remained immune.[3] One pattern, however, did frequently emerge: working-class neighborhoods were often stricken especially hard (due, we now know, to the particularly poor sanitation in those areas).[4] The bourgeoisie often held moral failings of the community in question accountable, blaming the spread of the epidemic on the "drunken, lazy, and immoral habits of the poor,"[5] which weakened them both spiritually and physically, making them especially vulnerable to the disease.[6] Sexual immorality, in particular, was often pointed to as making prostitutes and the dissolute vulnerable to cholera.[7] J. N. Hays writes:

In the second cholera pandemic, many of the people of the propertied classes found the source of dirt to be the poor or the marginal members of society. Perhaps their habits produced the dirt; perhaps their habits reflected their morals, or perhaps their irreligion. . . . In the Europe of 1830 the poor were already widely feared as potential revolutionaries; cholera made them dangerous in another way as well.[8]

These attitudes were often reflected in the public health policies formulated by state and medical authorities, in some cases provoking angry and even violent responses from people who had had little previous contact with medicine and saw no reason to trust it.[9]

Cholera and the Jews

The second global cholera pandemic (ca. 1827–35) was the first to reach Europe, appearing in the Russian Empire in 1829. The contemporaneous report of the German physician Jeremias Lichtenstaedt relates that the Jews of the province of Volhynia were hit hard by the disease, and that in the heavily Jewish town of Berdichev 70 percent of the reported cases in the town (630 out of 900) were among Jews, who over a period of less than two months exhibited an astonishing mortality rate of 97 percent. Lichtenstaedt blamed lack of hygiene and crowded living conditions—"the filthy habits and confined houses of a very numerous body of Jews"—as well as the Jews' refusal to seek medical aid or to cooperate with the authorities.[10] His evaluation of Berdichev Jews' reluctance to heed the authorities is likely fairly accurate, since most Jews of the former Polish lands still viewed the governments under which they lived with considerable suspicion, which was especially true for the regime that had imposed a harsh conscription regime only a few years earlier. Moreover, the Jewish masses harbored considerable ambivalence about modern medicine, in part because it posed a potential threat to traditional forms of healing, often associated with traditional religious observance, and in part because of "the common image of the modern Jewish physician as an *apikoros* [heretic]."[11] Doctors were early on associated in the popular Jewish imagination with the Haskalah and thus, for traditionalists, with the Christian world and potential threats to traditional piety. We know that at least one tsaddik, Tsvi Hirsh of Żydaczów (Zhidachov) explicitly forbade his

followers from turning to physicians for succor during the 1831 epidemic—
and he was probably not alone in doing so.[12] In tragic irony, cholera took his
life and possibly that of his wife as well.[13]

There is fragmentary evidence to suggest that some observers perceived
the living conditions and general sanitary habits of Russian and Polish Jews
to be hospitable to the spread of cholera; there was even suspicion that Jews
were a major vector of the epidemic and that Jewish communities served as
breeding grounds for cholera over the winter. The perception of Polish Jews,
and particularly beggars, as carriers of epidemic goes back to at least the
early eighteenth century, when various German authorities voiced fears of
poor Jews from Poland bringing disease with them.[14] A century later, former
Jewish innkeepers expelled from villages in the Kingdom of Poland and reduced to penury were also viewed as potential carriers of disease, since their
mass migration to Polish town and cities caused overcrowding in Jewish
quarters.[15] In 1831, when, in addition to the scourge of cholera, the Russian-Polish borderlands were also experiencing the upheaval caused by the
November Uprising, at least one Russian government official was convinced
that Jews were responsible for "importing" cholera to the strategically important city of Brest-Litovsk, where it spread among Russian troops garrisoned
there.[16] Many contemporary doctors assumed that all East European Jews
lived in cramped, filthy conditions conducive to the spread of disease.[17] In
later decades, some Russian medical experts on cholera attempted to refute
these accusations, but others continued to reinforce them.[18]

Another tantalizing reference to accusations that Jews were to blame for
the epidemic is found in a newspaper account by the maskil Moshe Lieb
Lilienblum of the cholera's impact on the town of Vilkomir in 1867, which
stated that "some of the Christians blamed the Jews in town, saying that
they had deliberately infected bread and fish with cholera and sold them to
the Christians."[19] In Kiev, the right-wing, Judeophobic newspaper *Kievlianin*
suggested in 1873 that it was no coincidence that cholera epidemics had hit
the city with increasing strength over the past decades, just as Kiev's Jewish
population had surged: the two phenomena were clearly linked.[20]

Even with the dearth of relevant Jewish sources, it is difficult to imagine
that Russian and Polish Jews were unaware that some were accusing them
of playing a role in the spread of cholera epidemics. Is it possible that in

the time of cholera, some ordinary Jews, in turn, blamed the lowliest among them for the evil that had befallen them? Evidence suggests that this may have indeed been the case.

Jewish magical remedies against cholera

EARLY EVIDENCE

Traditional Jewish responses to epidemics, as to any catastrophe, included prayer, fasting, and renewed commitment to pious religious observance, including charity for the poor. We have evidence for the latter from two locales. A set of instructions on strict religious observance issued by a group of Warsaw rabbis as a means to combat the 1831 epidemic that circulated throughout Poland included an admonition on charity that went beyond simple assistance for the needy; it specifically urged Jews to provide for those whom the community had forgotten or neglected.[21] In Pruzhany, a special confraternity established to fight the cholera resolved to direct sums to caring for the destitute who had been stricken by the epidemic. "And we will also open our eyes, God willing, to have mercy upon the poor who are suffering from hunger to whom we have turned a blind eye until this day, and in merit of this may they have mercy on us from heaven to distinguish us for life," it recorded.[22]

In addition, some sought succor in folk cures and magical remedies, the latter often proscribed by religious leaders.[23] In Kotik's account of the 1866 cholera epidemic, palm rings were common in Kamenets Litovsk.[24] In Grodno, red threads were tied to people's necks and wrists; scribes and *ba'alei shem* (shamanistic healers) did a booming trade in amulets.[25] In Congress Poland's Mazovia Province, a rumor in Nowe Miasto nad Pilicą said that local Jews had buried a bell and mill sluice in their cemetery in order to keep the cholera from descending on Jewish homes and to redirect it, as it were, towards their Christian neighbors.[26]

A Hasidic tale about Tsvi Hirsh of Rymanów (1778–1846), the charismatic leader of the eponymous Hasidic dynasty, found in *Be'erot ha-mayim*, a collection of his teachings published in 1888, suggests that the cholera wedding was already in existence during Russia's first cholera pandemic:

In the year 5591 [1831] there was a cholera epidemic, which also came to

Rymanów. And they carried out the known remedy of marrying a poor man to a poor maiden in the cemetery. When they were preparing to bring the groom and bride to the canopy, the bride became ill with that disease, and they told this to the Holy Rabbi Tsvi Ha-Cohen, may his memory endure in the world to come. Then he opened his holy mouth and said, As our tradition teaches, the corpse must be turned aside before the presence of the bride [if the two meet on the road] [*Kayma lan, ma'avirin et ha-met lifnei ha-kalah*] (BT Ketubot 17; also Mishneh Torah Shoftim: Avel 14:8), and she soon recovered from her illness and returned to her previous strength.[27]

The story is terse in the extreme: the epidemic arrives, the remedy—a wedding—is prepared, the bride falls ill and then, presumably thanks to R. Tsvi Hirsh's utterance, recovers. And that is all.

It is noteworthy that the bride and groom in this story are described only as poor people, not as orphans. Moreover, unlike other Hasidic cholera wedding tales, the tsaddik does not explicitly order that the wedding be carried out; rather, R. Tsvi Hirsh only becomes involved when the bride falls ill.[28] His intervention is limited to uttering a Talmudic dictum stating that if a funeral procession encounters a bride on the road, the corpse must give way to the bride. The rebbe pronounces this phrase at a crucial moment in the action: after the cholera bride has been stricken herself. In other words, the putative key to the termination of the epidemic is at risk of being felled by it. An imaginative reading might yield the following, rather broader interpretation: in the context of the epidemic, the force of the dictum is that death, here represented by the synecdoche of the corpse, must yield to the joy of a wedding. Read this way, the narrative thus provides an explicit religious justification for the cholera wedding, even though R. Tsvi Hirsh's association with the ritual itself is minimal, if not absent altogether.

It bears noting that although we can connect this tale with a firm historical episode—the cholera pandemic of 1830–31—that does not necessarily mean that the ritual described here is also based in historic fact. The story may have been retrojected from a later period.

The only other evidence we have of the cholera wedding in the first half of the nineteenth century is a fleeting mention in the memoir of the attorney Wiktor Kopff (1805–89) about the cholera epidemic in Kraków in 1849, which, Kopff maintains, levied a high toll among the city's Jews. "In order to turn away the cholera, the Jews organized a wedding of two poor Jewish couples in the Kraków Jewish cemetery, taking up a collection for the dowry."[29] It may be significant that the only two recorded cases of the cholera wedding in this early period are both from Austrian Galicia; perhaps the ritual emerged here. By the next cholera outbreak, some fifteen years later, it had spread far and wide across the Russian-ruled territories of eastern Europe.

"Upon the arrival in Kraków of a certain Jew of whom rumor told that wherever he appeared, there too would appear the cholera, the Jews gave him gifts and persuaded him to leave the city," Kopff writes. The accuracy of this report is less relevant than the mentalities that may have lain behind it: was this "cholera-bearing Jew" a stereotype of the pestilential, contagious Jew that emerged in the premodern era and persisted into the nineteenth century? If so, this tale suggests that not only were Jews aware of that negative image—and how could they not be?—but may even have taken steps to lessen its harmful repercussions; perhaps, for instance, by trying to persuade Jews arriving from locales where the epidemic had already hit to move on without stopping.

1865–66 AND AFTER

Owing to the emergence of a Jewish press in Odessa in the early 1860s and other sources, such as ethnographic studies, we have much more evidence about Jewish reactions to cholera during the fourth global cholera pandemic, which swept the Russian Empire in 1865–66. Russian and Polish Jews often established cholera committees, akin to sanitary committees or boards of public health, to coordinate care for the sick, undertake burial of the numerous dead, and establish special cholera hospitals.[30] The latter was characteristic of a new approach to cholera across Europe that Peter Baldwin dates to the 1865–66 epidemic, as European countries moved towards "a new variant of quarantinism" based on timely identification of the ill and imposing disinfection and quarantine measures to hinder contagion.[31] Perhaps—though this is no more than conjecture—local elites were motivated to act not only because they wanted to limit the epidemic's damage but also because they were aware of the history of accusations against Jews as carriers of disease.

In addition to sequestering the ill, a variety of prophylactic methods were known and sometimes encouraged by medical experts and even the government. People were urged to drink certain kinds of alcoholic beverages and avoid an array of foodstuffs.[32] Another folk remedy warned people not to eat *kugel* (pudding), *tsimes* (carrot stew), or fish, because the first letters of those words spelled the Hebrew word *ketsef* ("wrath"), a reference to Numbers 1:53: "that there be no wrath upon the congregation of the children of Israel."[33] The link to disease, via the appearance of the same word elsewhere in the book of Numbers (16:46) referring to God's wrath as bringing down a fearsome plague upon the Israelites, would have seemed obvious to all.

Sexual anxiety

As we have seen, it was not uncommon across the Western world for cholera to be accompanied by anxiety about sexual morality. East European Jews, too, paid particular attention to sexual mores during a cholera epidemic. In contradistinction to most other corporate responses to cholera, however, Jews in the Russian Empire did not seem to believe that sinful individuals were at greater risk of contracting the disease, but rather that their actions made the entire community more susceptible to God's anger in the form of an epidemic.[34] In some cases, communal leaders or vigilantes went so far as to identify and punish those individuals in order to halt the plague. The circular issued by the Warsaw rabbinate urging strict observance of certain Jewish ritual and moral precepts, examined above, is an early source that does not specifically require the pinpointing of sexual sinners, but nonetheless reveals angst about sexuality. Six of the document's nineteen sections touch on issues relating to sexuality, including four relating to the *mikveh* (ritual bath), an institution intimately bound up with Judaism's prohibition on sexual relations during and immediately following a woman's period.[35] During the 1866 epidemic, an article in the Yiddish-language *Kol mevaser*, a newspaper established by Jewish progressives, took the rabbis of the southern Ukrainian city of Kremenchug to task for leading ordinary people to believe that the epidemic was caused by such sins as adultery.[36]

Ethnographic works from the period, though problematic in some respects, seem to confirm that religious and communal leaders often looked for a link between sexual misconduct and disease. One such study reported that "in the case of an epidemic, it was the custom to call on all members of the community to report any sin that he or she knew about."[37] In this way, misdeeds, and especially sexual sins—which could call down the wrath of God in the form of an epidemic—could be investigated, a task assigned to the rabbi and a special committee of eighteen prominent men.

There is some evidence that Hasidic Jews were particularly sensitive to the popular belief in the nexus between sexual immorality and disease. Lisa Epstein notes an episode in Uman' during the 1866 cholera epidemic when Hasidim "declared that Jewish women wearing crinolines and earrings were to blame for the epidemic"; some particularly fervent Hasidim then set up an ambush to waylay unsuspecting offenders, tore the crinolines off them, and rained blows on them.[38] In one Hasidic tale collected and anthologized at the turn of the twentieth century, an epidemic breaks out because a certain man has had sexual relations with a married woman.[39] In another, a case of adultery leads to an outbreak of cholera, and only the murder of the sinful couple by the rabbi and ritual slaughterer of the town curbs the epidemic.[40] In another tale anthologized in the late twentieth century, a man and a woman sin—the unspecified nature of the sin makes it more than likely that it is of a sexual nature—and as a result, their children die in an epidemic. After the deaths of the children, the epidemic stops.[41] The quasi-sacrificial nature of the deaths in the latter two tales is suggestive; as we shall see, the cholera wedding ritual also contained an element of the sacrificial.[42]

The cholera wedding: from farce to reality

THE FIRST WAVE: 1865–66

By the time of the epidemic of 1865–66, the cholera wedding was a well-known remedy, employed in at least eight localities across the Pale of Settlement in July, August, and September of 1866: Grodno, Bialystok, Kamenets, Berdichev, Kremenchug, Kherson, Odessa, and Ekaterinoslav.[43] A ninth locale was Bełz, across the border in Austrian Galicia. Another such wedding had been conducted earlier that year in Jerusalem. And a second wedding was conducted in Grodno during another epidemic in 1871.

The basic course of events was as follows: two or more of the poorest and most vulnerable members of the community were matched with each other and married at the cemetery or on the outskirts of town in an uproarious celebration attended by a good proportion of the town's residents. For the seven marriages for which we have information on the bridal couples, two were orphans, one a blind man matched with a "crippled mute girl," one a short, blind man with a long nose coupled with an ugly beggar woman, one a *mamzer* (bastard by Jewish law) paired with "a little child," and the remainder described as poor and "worthless" (*bezuyei ha-am ve-hadlei anashim* or *pehutei-erekh*). Almost all of them took place in the cemetery. At the Kherson and Ekaterinoslav weddings, critical observers—correspondents to maskilic newspapers—reported that the assembled crowd had drunk heavily, and at two others, in Bialystok and Grodno, the crowd was said to have behaved wildly and without restraint. In three instances, observers noted that the organizers of the wedding were local women: in Grodno, a group of women (including elderly women) in 1866 and "the pious women" in 1871; in Kherson, a mother and daughter from among the town's Jewish elite.

Given what we have learned thus far about marginal people in eastern European Jewish society, it should not be surprising that the bride and groom of the cholera weddings were often known not only as "cholera bride" and "cholera groom" but also by such terms as "town son-in-law" and "town daughter-in-law" and *koholishe bokher* and *koholishe moyd* (kahal's young man and kahal's young woman, respectively).[44] These people were often seen as the property of the community, since their very survival was due to the charity of the official Jewish community, to the religious confraternities that operated institutions such as the hekdesh, and to individual almsgivers. If they had a livelihood, it was often thanks to the kahal, as in Apt, where the groom in the 1892 cholera wedding served as bathhouse attendant and the bride worked as a servant in the home of the kahal head. According to that account, found in the Apt yizkor book, one of hundreds of volumes compiled in the decades after World War II to memorialize Jewish communities destroyed in the Holocaust, the bride and groom were "two orphans who in any case [*bemeyle*] already lived on the kahal's support."[45] That *bemeyle* is crucial: since they were already community charity cases, the community was fully justified in using them to help stop the epidemic. Thus, the wedding was not really *their* wedding. As the writer, journalist, and socialist activist Iakov Rombro put it in his description of the fictional cholera bride Khaia in his Russian-language short story "Kholernaia svad'ba" (The Cholera Wedding;

1884): "No one listened or paid any attention to her. And, in truth, wasn't the crux of the matter not her wedding, but rather Minke's [the wedding organizer] desires and the salvation of the town?"[46]

One intriguing aspect of the first major wave of these weddings, during the 1866 pandemic, is the rift they seem to embody between the ordinary Jews of the town and the Jewish establishment: in a number of cases, observers noted conflicts between the organizers of the wedding and the communal and/or religious leadership. In Odessa, *Kol mevaser*'s editor Aleksander Zederbaum claimed, Rabbi Yehiel Zvi Halperin "explicitly forbade" the holding of a wedding in a cemetery, and Zederbaum himself had tried to dissuade the organizers from carrying out their plans.[47] A rabbi in Berdichev barred the wedding from taking place in the cemetery. Communal leaders in Grodno pleaded with the women who intended to hold four weddings—one at each corner of the town—to call off their plans. When their pleas fell on deaf ears, they asked the women to move the weddings to the synagogue courtyard, presumably to minimize the shame that the cholera weddings would bring on the community.[48] And of course the maskilic observers who described the weddings in the pages of *Ha-karmel* and *Kol mevaser* were withering in their scorn for such abominable superstition, though they did not, as far as we know, confront the wedding organizers directly.

That these folk remedies may have been a kind of rebellion of Jewish common folk against the Jewish establishment is not altogether surprising. As we have seen, in a number of European countries, the 1830–31 cholera pandemic witnessed rioting of the masses against the authorities, whom they perceived as using cholera as an excuse for repression.[49] This dynamic set a pattern for the subsequent pandemics: when political and medical authorities sought to impose order on restive populations and bring to bear the latest medical expertise, the masses often reacted distrustfully, preferring folk cures and magical remedies. Such a stance is quite understandable from a twenty-first-century perspective, since the fundamental cause of the disease had not yet been discovered and contemporary medical and sanitary expertise, which was almost entirely guesswork, usually had little impact on the course of the epidemic. The cholera wedding may have been a traditionalist reaction—in the form of a religious ritual perceived as having primordial roots—to Western medical practices imposed by those seen as outsiders or even traitors to established Jewish folkways.

THE SECOND WAVE: 1892–94

In 1884, the German physician and scientist Robert Koch discovered the bacterium that caused cholera, *Vibrio cholera*, also known as the comma bacillus, and the bacteriological nature of the disease gradually came to be recognized over the subsequent years. However, this development did not lead to uniform preventative or control measures across the European continent, and the backward state of public health measures in the Russian Empire in fact allowed the worst pandemic of the century to break out in 1892.[50]

The epidemic triggered mass panic in the hardest-hit areas, leading to riots and violent attacks on medical personnel.[51] While Russian and Polish Jews did not fall upon doctors and nurses with violence, as was the case in other parts of the empire, some of them refused to foreswear magical remedies like the cholera wedding. By now, the objections of communal and religious leaders had faded away; not only we do not encounter such protests in the cholera wedding accounts, but rabbis and communal elders were now taking active part in the custom. In Zambrów, the matrimonial match of Khana Yente, a crippled orphan girl, and Velvl the stuttering beggar was reportedly made by "the notables of the community."[52] The account in the Apt yizkor book claims that the local rabbis determined that a wedding in the cemetery—in this case, the pairing of two orphans, the bathhouse attendant and a servant-woman in the home of a communal elder—was a remedy to halt the epidemic.[53] In Shumsk, it was the kahal elders who made the decision to marry Perets the Fool—blind in one eye, lame in one foot, a stutterer, and a beggar—to a woman who limped a little on her left foot, was paralyzed in her right hand, and was a bit deaf.[54] The Shumsk Jew who authored the memoir account wrote of a local rabbi, "I don't know if Reb Berenyu suggested the remedy, but he certainly gave his assent." During World War I, too, we hear of communal elders taking a leading role; in Kamenets-Podol'sk, the rabbi officiated at the wedding of two young poor people, though against his better judgment.[55] It seems, then, that what emerged at mid-century as an innovative magical ritual dressed up as a hoary folk custom that was rejected as nothing but superstition by both the traditionalist and progressive camps had by the fin de siècle become normalized as an accepted custom, if not by the urbanized, Western-educated Jewish elites, than at least by local rabbis and communal leaders. It bears noting that a generation had passed since the 1866–67 pandemic: a youth in the late 1860s who had witnessed a cholera wedding in his town would, by the early 1890s, have been of an age to take a leadership role in the community.

Some traditionalist rabbis could not find a way to approve of what one rabbi in Elizavetgrad termed "a backward and superstitious custom," but others apparently began to accept it.[56] Some rabbis evidently accepted the explanation, sometimes heard at the time of the wedding itself, that it was the deeply charitable nature of the ritual that made it so religiously efficacious. Apologists explained that the custom had emerged as a way for the community to earn back God's favor by doing a deed of great charity; dowering the needy bride was already an age-old Jewish charitable custom, so how much more would be the reward for bringing to the wedding canopy those members of Jewish society who were otherwise likely never to marry at all. "The rabbis classified facilitating the marriage of dowerless brides as among the highest forms of charity," Salo Baron notes.[57] An 1890 rabbinic work on Jewish customs by Meir Yehiel Lipiets explained: "As it is written, 'Great is charity, for it lengthens life,' and great also is [the commandment of] enabling the poor bride to marry, and especially to marry an orphan boy with a poor orphan girl, and many commandments are included within this [deed], and therefore the whole town participates in this act of charity, and everyone goes to the wedding in the cemetery."[58] Even an 1892 circular from the Warsaw rabbinate forbidding Jews from carrying out magical rituals such as the cholera wedding acknowledged that the wedding, an age-old rite that "in truth contain[s] no abominable idea or alien thought," was ultimately done for the sake of fulfilling a great commandment.[59]

But there was clearly more to the ritual than altruism, not least because at some weddings the brides and grooms were reluctant to participate (in Grodno, a proposed groom was said to have exclaimed, "Because you all want to live, you want to bury me alive!"). Even after several potential grooms had been persuaded to take part, they withdrew their consent once they understood that they would always be known in the town as "cholera grooms." If this was such a tremendously merciful act, one scholar perceptively notes, why was it not carried out during normal times?[60]

There is also evidence that the compassion and humanity to which the cholera wedding was testament—and no one should gainsay that these were indeed present—did not always endure beyond the ritual itself. Moreover, by uniting two outcasts in marriage, the community in effect sentenced their offspring to the same wretched fate. The ugly beggar woman—"fat Perele with the cleft palate"—and her cholera groom, a short, blind man with a long nose became town beggars after their wedding and were soon joined by a little beggar baby, "bringing his suit against all Israel," Avraham Friedberg gibed.[61] The aftermath of the marriage in Zamość of "Leybele the Orphan, a rascal, good-for-nothing, and madman, a bachelor who had done jail time more than once" to the gravedigger's daughter, a blind orphan and old maid, was also unfortunate, a critical local who sketched the sorry story in *Hamelits* noted. For weeks after the wedding, the blind woman demanded that the town elders provide the newlyweds with food and lodging, while the husband found himself a permanent spot in one of pews in the same synagogue. went from one community benefactor to another begging during services, and even slept there at night.[62]

THE THIRD WAVE: 1910–1920

The third and last wave of cholera weddings took place during the pandemic of 1909–10 and then amid the chaos and upheaval that accompanied World War I in eastern Europe. In 1910, the liberal-leaning New York Yiddish daily *Die Wahrheit* (*Di varhayt*) reported that the cholera epidemic, raging across wide swathes of the Russian Empire, was causing a boom in cemetery weddings. "Cripples, idiots, vagabonds, and other wretches [*shlek*] who have never had any hope of getting married may now take a ride to Russia."[63] There, promised the author in a tone dripping with sarcasm, they would be married off with great fanfare and receive many gifts. Such were the measures—marital-magical, rather than sanitary—that Russian Jews took to combat cholera.

This article also claimed that the cholera had driven demand for marginal people so high that, in towns where there were only a few of them, they could now set the terms for their own weddings or threaten to refuse. This peculiar situation highlighted the ambivalent attitude to the worth of marginals: whereas in normal times they were perceived as "wretches," now they were highly valued, though not for their own worth but as magical talismans.

During World War I, the term "cholera wedding" is something of a mis-
nomer, because the epidemics that instigated the rituals were more likely to
be typhus rather than cholera.[64] These weddings, which did not differ significantly from the previous ones, included couples such as the fool Taybele,
an old maid, and the hunchback Zkharye, a poor old bachelor, in Tarnogród;
a paralyzed orphan girl who lived next to the gravedigger's house and an
unknown orphaned beggar boy passing through the town in Luboml; a dim,
deaf old woman and a half-deaf old carrier of corpses with a deformed head
in Siedlce (Shedlits); and a dwarf with deformed legs and an enlarged head
and an old maid who worked as a servant, both of whom were orphaned and
totally impoverished, in Oświęcim (Oshpitsin).[65]

Understanding the cholera wedding

Let us now examine the historical, socio-religious, and anthropological puz-
zle pieces that came together to create the cholera wedding, a ritual that had
no direct antecedents in Jewish tradition—or, for that matter, parallels in
Christian folk practice—but nonetheless had deep roots in Jewish religious
culture and a powerful internal logic, embedded in long-standing attitudes
to social marginals.

THE BEGGAR'S COMEDY REDUX

We return now to the betler-shpil (Beggar's Comedy), the Purim-shpil that
we first encountered in chapter 1. There, we saw that the Beggar's Comedy,
a parody of a marriage between two beggars, is replete with the leitmotifs
associated with marginal people that we have seen in many contexts—ugliness, filth, illness, demons and the world of the dead. The preceding pages of
this chapter allow us to see this Purim-shpil in a different light altogether,
since the cholera wedding was not a theatrical spectacle involving mum-
mers dressed up as beggars but a *real* wedding of *real* people. And yet, the
two types of wedding share many attributes: the mockery of marginals; multiple allusions to the cemetery; and, most significantly, the centrality of the
epidemic. It appears, then, that the cholera wedding did in fact have an ante-
cedent—but a textual one, rather than a historical one, which may have laid
the foundation for the real-life weddings of those people that emerged in the
nineteenth century as a remedy for epidemic cholera.

Let us examine the final scene of the Beggar's Comedy, which takes place under the wedding canopy. The master of ceremonies solemnizes the wedding by stating, "I hereby wed you, you two stains," and wishing a plague on the bride and two plagues on her bridegroom. And then:

At!—

May you both be nipped by the [city name] cat.[66]

(An audience member):

Why the [Odessa] cat?

(Grandfather):

Because it nips better.

Mekudeshes—

Yak sobaka breshesh [Ukr., as a dog lies]

Li—

You should lie in . . . in the poorhouse bed here!

Betabaas—

You should both swell up like a barrel

Kedas moyshe veyisroel—

May you both be punished [*a kapore zolt ir vern*] instead of me and all Israel.[67]

Here, the sacred words of the wedding vow are rhymed with creative curses of various kinds that echo themes associated with marginal people. The theme of filth reemerges here: the grandfather likens the bridal couple to "stains," and plagues are wished upon both of them. Nor are the references to animals incidental, since freaks were frequently associated with the animal world. Most telling is the final couplet, which expresses a wish that the newlyweds serve as a kind of scapegoat for all Jews. We examined the significance of the marginal as scapegoat in chapter 2 and, as we shall soon see, this theme was to become an important pillar of the cholera wedding.

Ignacy Schiper provides reliable evidence for his dating of the text, but like many Purim-shpiln, this farce unquestionably circulated for centuries. That the Beggar's Comedy was still being played in the tsarist period is clear from the reference to "the Odessa cat," since Odessa was not settled by Jews until after the Partitions of Poland.

THE BODY GROTESQUE

Given the intense anxiety about sexuality that often accompanied epidemics, it makes sense that the magical remedy for the cholera be a wedding—and marginal figures were the ideal candidates for such a wedding. Like all unmarried adults in traditional Jewish society, they were sexually suspect, since the only licit outlet for sexuality in Judaism was marriage. Marrying them to each other was the community's way of eliminating any chance of sexual licentiousness—even if this was a remote possibility.

The physical bodies of marginal people, often so different from the norm and thus so alien, were also sites of anxiety. A fascinating exposition of this anxiety is found, again, in Abramovitsh's *Fishke der krumer* (1888), where the description of the cholera wedding and its victims is as follows:

> Fishke [the Lame] was getting on in years. . . . He had even been forgotten during the recruiting of "cholera grooms," that is, when the *kahal* of Glupsk snatched the most hideous cripples, beggars, and vagrants and frantically married them off to each other in the cemetery among the tombstones in order to frighten the epidemic away. The first time this happened, the *kahal* chose not to honor Fishke but the famous cripple Yontl, who had no legs and moved around on his buttocks by pushing himself with two little wooden blocks. He was mated with a well-known beggar woman who had teeth like spades and no lower lip. The cholera epidemic was so terror-stricken by this pair that it wiped out a good part of the population in its fright, after which it took to its heels and fled. The second time, Fishke was again bypassed in favor of Nokhemtshe the village idiot, a well-known fool. Before an assemblage of fine Jews at the cemetery, the fool placed the bridal veil on the head of a girl, a head that had already been covered since childhood because of—pardon the expression—its crown of cankerous sores, and about whom it was rumored that she was a hermaphrodite.[68]

The lofty terms with which Abramovitsh peppers the story—"honor," "famous," "well-known," "assemblage," "crown"—clash violently (and comically, of course) with the actual subjects of the tale, whom he portrays as deformed, freakish characters. He reduces the marginals to their most clownish caricatures: not only is Yontl a cripple, he has no legs at all; as if that were not bad enough, the beggar woman to whom he is married has teeth like shovels and no lower lip to conceal them; and, finally, the bride may not actually be a "bride" at all. (It is hard to avoid the question of gender here: just as the second cholera bride's gender is called into doubt, Yontl's missing legs may be meant to prompt the reader to wonder what other important appendages are missing.) This *reductio ad absurdum* was part of Abramovitsh's stock in trade, especially when it came to portraying the shtetl.[69] But for all the humor and exaggeration of this passage, Abramovitsh was in fact shedding a harsh light on the reality of the cholera wedding, which made the castoffs of Jewish society into a kind of sideshow of the grotesque. Bakhtin's concept of the grotesque body, which he formulated as an analytical tool in his exploration of Rabelais's literary world, is useful in understanding Abramovitsh's discursive strategy (see also discussion in chapter 3). The grotesque body is centered around physical functions that blur the boundaries between the body and the outside world, especially hints about sexual and excretory functions. "The artistic logic of the grotesque image ignores the closed, smooth, and impenetrable surface of the body and retains only its excrescences . . . and orifices."[70] Abramovitsh's cholera brides and grooms are meant to disgust the reader with their bodily protrusions (shovel teeth), repulsive convexities (mouth without a lower lip, cankerous sores), or even an amalgam of the two: Yontl "walks" on his buttocks/anus.[71]

Similar tropes are found in the satirical description of the Grodno cholera wedding in 1871 by the Hebrew writer A. S. Friedberg:

> The pious women found an ugly maiden in the market, a beggar—this was fat Perele with the cleft palate, the very memory of whose appearance was enough to make one vomit. The match they found for her was a blind man, short in the legs and long in the nose [*ha-tsofe penei damesek*; cf. Song of Songs 7:4: "Your nose is like the tower of Lebanon, looking towards Damascus"], and they brought them to the cemetery and married them to each other. And the match was a successful one, since for a number of months the couple was to be seen [begging] at the doorways of houses, she wrapped in rags walking ahead, and the hand of the dwarf husband held aloft and rested on her shoulder from behind, to fulfill the scripture, "And he shall rule over you" [Gen. 3:16].[72]

Like Abramovitsh (whose description of the cholera wedding undoubtedly influenced his own), Friedberg uses elevated language and even biblical intertexts to sharpen his caricature of the lowly couple, with their grotesque and repellent physical features: the abnormal dimensions of the husband's extremities, the malformed nose and mouth of Perele the beggar. The reversal of gender is also an important aspect of the couple's monstrousness: the absurdity of the biblical prooftext only highlights the strangeness of Perele's physical dominance, towering above her husband, walking in front of him and serving as his eyes.

Bakhtin can also help us understand why marrying the grotesque body could have been perceived as an appropriate remedy for cholera. Cholera is a disease that obliterates the boundaries between the interior of the body and the outside world. The classic symptom is severe, watery diarrhea that can last several days. Thus, to tortured onlookers it seems as though all the internal fluids of the patient are draining away through the anus. Given the nature of the epidemic, it is natural that those individuals chosen to help stop it were themselves understood not only as liminal (as we shall soon see) but also as embodying the grotesque body, which celebrates "the lower bodily stratum and its functions and products."[73] Bakhtin argues that "the grotesque body of Rabelais's medieval carnival [is] a comic figure of profound ambivalence: its positive meaning is linked to birth and renewal while its negative meaning lies in decay and death."[74] The epidemic is thus countered by the only entity that can contain both the death and decay that the disease personifies *and* the birth and renewal that a wedding promises: the grotesque body. Or, to add a more recent scholarly approach, the freak's body; as Elizabeth Grosz writes:

> The freak is an object of simultaneous horror and fascination because, in addition to whatever infirmities or abilities he or she exhibits, the freak is an *ambiguous* being whose existence imperils categories and oppositions dominant in social life. Freaks are those human beings who exist outside and in defiance of the structure of binary oppositions that govern our basic concepts and modes of self-definition. . . . They imperil the very definitions we rely on to classify humans, identities, and sexes—our most fundamental categories of self-definition and boundaries dividing self from otherness.[75]

Thus—and here we draw on the work of the anthropologists Arnold van

Gennep, Victor Turner, and Bjørn Thomassen—the body of the marginal person was also liminal. Expanding on van Gennep and Turner's pioneering work, Thomassen suggests a rubric encompassing three dimensions of liminality: subject-based, temporal, and spatial.[76] The cholera wedding fits neatly into all three rubrics simultaneously: a liminal social group (marginals) playing a central role during a liminal moment (epidemic) in a liminal space (cemetery).[77] But, as Abramovitsh and Friedberg's emphases on body parts and openings suggest, the spatial element of liminality was not limited to a geographical place, that is, the cemetery, but arguably could be extended to embrace the very bodies of the cholera bride and groom.

Marginal people were also liminal figures in the symbolic universe of the Jewish town. Frequently referred to as "nonpersons," they usually resided in the poorhouse, which was often located next to the cemetery and sometimes even served as a place to house and purify corpses before burial. Thus, suspended halfway between the living and the dead, marginal people and especially mentally ill people, purportedly possessed by spirits or demons, could easily be perceived as having the power to intercede with the dead on behalf of the living. Also, since marginal people ordinarily did not marry and therefore did not reproduce, they represented a serious aberration from conventional gender norms in Jewish society, as well as a rift in the ordinary order and flow of life (hence also their organic link to the world of death). Marrying them off was vital in order to restore gender to its proper place and to ensure that life continued to flow during a time of epidemic.

A WEDDING AMONG THE GRAVES

Why a wedding at the cemetery, of all places? The most obvious answer is that the cemetery was a natural destination for anyone wishing to pray as efficaciously as possible, since the merit of the righteous dead could be most easily invoked there. Judaism, like Christianity, has a long tradition of praying at the graves of ancestors, and especially of the righteous.[78] The long-standing custom of going to the cemetery on a fast day to pray for rain had a Talmudic foundation (BT Ta'anit 16a), and the Jewish community of medieval Worms would circle the cemetery on fast days, a custom found in other Ashkenazic communities as well.[79] A special prayer written for the Worms burial society asked the dead to pray for the community and the entire House of Israel that God might save them from pestilence and disease and keep the Angel of Death away from their houses.[80] As with other customs of medieval Ashkenazic Jews, these traditions were inherited by the Jews of eastern Europe, who commonly prayed at the cemetery on significant days.[81] It was customary for an orphan bride to visit her parents' grave to invite them to her wedding, since "it was widely believed that the deceased parents could intervene on behalf of the bride."[82]

The cemetery also played a tremendous role in folk magic. Medieval Christian magic recommended the cemetery as a place of great efficacy in the treatment of sickness; churchyard grass and earth were said to have healing properties.[83] There were also magical cures that involved transferring the ailment to the dead, often by means of an object that was secreted in the coffin or thrown into the grave.[84] These practices were not unknown among Jews. In one Hasidic tale, "the sick are healed by means of earth from a grave."[85]

"According to Slavic conceptions, the cemetery as a sacred place has a closed border that protects against demons, pestilence, famine, and other disasters, and nothing impure is permitted to enter," Victoria Mochalova writes of the shared beliefs about the unique potency of the cemetery in both Jewish and Slavic magical traditions. "It is here that magic actions and rituals take place that are meant to heal illness or avert the evil eye, to expel the impure from the village, or attain miraculous wisdom."[86]

That spirits and demons resided in the cemetery was a widespread belief among East European Jews, one that went back to medieval Ashkenazic Jewry.[87] The Austrian-Galician rabbi and folklorist Samuel Rappoport theorized that the cholera wedding was actually a Zoharic-Lurianic ritual meant to counteract the tremendous power of the coupling of the satanic archangel Samael with the demon Lilith and their marriage in a cemetery, understood as the fundamental cause of the epidemic.[88] Since marginal people were often linked to the cemetery, the notion that bringing them to the "holy place" (*heylike ort*, one Yiddish term for graveyard) could help to drive away the demons that had caused the epidemic made a great deal of sense in the logic of folk magic. Naftuli Vaynig, an ethnographer and folklorist associated with YIVO's Ethnographic Commission, took the idea one step further, arguing that "people with deformities were demonized" quite literally: they were seen as demonic, because they looked like demons.[89] And folk magic dictated there was nothing more effective to scare away a demon than the likeness of his own face, just as the basilisk—the mythical snake with a venom of deadly power—can, according to some accounts, only be killed by placing a mirror in front of its face. Thus, argued Vaynig, the ugliness of the cholera bride and groom was quite central to the ritual: it was meant to scare away the epidemic.

In an attempt to locate the roots of the cholera wedding in specific Polish customs, Hanna Węgrzynek points to pre-Christian traditions involving feasts at cemeteries, the most notable of which took place on the night of All Souls' Day (*Dzień Zaduszny*), when locals would gather at the local cemetery and call upon the souls of the dead to join the festivities.[90] Węgrzynek maintains that this custom persisted until the early nineteenth century—which is when we conjecture that the cholera wedding emerged.

A more direct connection between Slavic Christian customs and the cholera wedding is suggested by Yom-Tov Levinski, an Israeli scholar of Jewish customs and folklore, who brings as evidence a Polish chronicle from 1556 relating the story of an epidemic in Lomza fought by exhuming three coffins and bringing them to the church. There, a wedding was carried out in the presence of the corpses.[91] Presumably, this bizarre ritual was intended to contain the fatal power of the epidemic by symbolically enclosing the dead in the redemptory, life-giving space of the church at the moment of a ceremony that embodied the continuation of life—the wedding. Rappoport, harkening back to the biblical story of Aaron standing between the dead and the living to stop a plague (Num. 17:13), argues that the cholera wedding served a similar function; that is, it was intended to draw a clear boundary between the realms of the living and the dead. Echoing this explanation, Levinski writes that the officiant would, quite literally, stand "between the new graves of those cut down by the plague and the couple about to be wed and to enter into life."[92]

Let us try to imagine the tremendous emotional power of celebrating a wedding, among the happiest of life-cycle rituals, in the very place where one had only the day before (or the week or month before) buried beloved family members cut down before their prime, including young adults and children. The juxtaposition is a stark one—and in that very starkness lies its power. The idea must certainly have struck some as a terrifying prospect, yet they went nonetheless—or at least those went who believed, or wished to believe, that the ritual would have some effect on the epidemic. Dancing on the fresh graves, one thumbed one's nose in the face of death. The cholera wedding, then, was an attempt to draw a clear boundary between the realms of the living and the dead by enacting a ritual associated with life and reproduction in the heart of the dominion of death. That boundary was represented by—or, to be more precise, *constituted* by, marginal people—themselves an embodiment of liminality.

"IN ORDER TO BRING JOY TO THE PEOPLE"

Cholera was a horrific disease that struck fear into the hearts of people even before it had arrived for, once it had made its presence known, it could strike a healthy person down within hours. But cholera was terrifying for other reasons, as well. Sufferers who were still clinging to life often exhibited a deathly pallor that could lead to incorrect pronouncements of death, while spasms in the limbs of the recently deceased terrorized onlookers.[93] Public health experts not infrequently warned that fear or malaise could make one more susceptible to cholera or even manifest as the first phase of the disease; hence the Russian government's advice to citizens in 1830 that "a very important means of safety is to repress all tendency to depression and chagrin, and to preserve a cheerfulness and tranquility of mind."[94] This understanding of the significant role that one's mental state played during the epidemic may explain the Mi-Carême carnival revelers masquerading as cholera victims whom Heinrich Heine observed during the 1831 cholera epidemic in Paris, and the "comic songs about the cholera and . . . dances burlesquing the spasmodic movements of the victims" performed in Britain's music halls.[95]

Several accounts of cholera weddings, particularly those from 1866, note that the ceremony was accompanied by carousing and wild celebration. In Bialystok, readers of *Ha-melits* were told, "the rabble ran like wild men through the streets of the town, making a great deal of noise"; the women involved in the organizing of the wedding in Grodno "behaved in an unrestrained manner [*hitholelu*]"; in Kremenchug and Ekaterinoslav, the crowds attending the weddings drank to excess. The 1894 cholera wedding in Działoszyn was described as an uproarious (*tumlidke*) occasion.[96]

While the correspondents to the maskilic press who penned these

descriptions excoriated the benighted Jews who participated in such superstitious revelry, some traditionalists were prepared to defend it on the same
grounds that the Russian authorities recommended "cheerfulness" earlier in
the century. As we have seen, in his book on customs Lipiets cited the great
charitable deed represented by the cholera wedding as a primary reason for
holding one. He added as a second reason, just as significant, the fact that
the wedding in the cemetery was celebrated with "joy and music and much
happiness to arouse happiness in the masses so that they not be sad, which
is a great danger in this matter . . . [so that] they not be afraid, and become
accustomed to the cemetery and not fear death."[97]

It is noteworthy that in the second edition, published five years later,
Lipiets switched the order of the justifications for the custom, now citing the
banishment of fear as the *primary* motivation, albeit with a twist: "[And we
do this] in order to bring joy to the people, for among us Jews it is impossible
to be happy other than through the happiness [brought by the fulfillment]
of commandments, since it is forbidden to go to theaters and circuses."[98]
Clearly, the cholera wedding was also a form of kosher entertainment acceptable for pious Jews.[99]

THE CHOLERA WEDDING AS SACRIFICIAL OFFERING

One of the earliest datings of a plague wedding is that given in a Hasidic
legend collected during the ethnographic expeditions organized by S. An-ski
and the Historical-Ethnographic Society in 1912–14. The legend concerns
a certain Rabbi Liber of Berdichev, considered a holy man in his day. At
the time of an epidemic in 1771, the Jews of Berdichev undertook special
measures that they hoped would bring an end to the outbreak: ordaining
that special prayers be recited, repairing the wall around the cemetery, and
even organizing a "black wedding," as the text has it—clearly some sort of
wedding meant to drive the plague away.[100] Even more fascinating, however,
is how the legend concludes: "When the *tsaddik* R. Liber understood that
everything had been tried and that the end was near for the community, he
called all the leaders of the community together and took it upon himself to
be the communal sacrifice [*korben-eyde*]. That same night he passed away, and
the epidemic subsided the very next morning."[101]

The martyred bridal couple is a related motif. The Historical-Ethnographic

Society's expedition in the Pale of Settlement noted that in some shtetls there were unusual mounds next to the main synagogue; these were the graves of martyred couples said to have been murdered on their way to the wedding canopy by Cossack and Ukrainian followers of Bohdan Khmel'nyts'kyi during a seventeenth-century uprising against the Polish–Lithuanian Commonwealth. In his memoirs of the expedition, Avrom Rechtman recounted the legend of a couple in Nemirov who escaped the initial attack only—at the initiative of the bride—to commit suicide later by drowning rather than fall into the hands of the Cossacks.[102] The Nemirov legend, at least, seems to suggest that these bridal couples were perceived as willing martyrs who, if they did not physically save the community from depredation, served in some way as a spiritual offering on behalf of the community. And indeed, their tombstone—an artifact that the expedition took a rubbing of—read, in part: "The riverbed was too small to contain their dead bodies / They were not slaughtered but drowned as a sacrifice." The first line (*yesod ha-nahal katon me-hakhilah*) hints at a biblical passage (1 Kings 8:64) that relates that the bronze altar in Solomon's Temple was too small to hold the many sacrifices that King Solomon offered during the temple's consecration, while the second line makes plain what the previous line had only implied: the couple's death is to be understood as a sacrifice.[103]

But as noted in the previous chapter, there was another kind of vicarious victim in Jewish society: the marginal figure as scapegoat. We see this most clearly in the Purim shpil farce about the marriage of two beggars. The mock wedding ceremony, during which the officiant again curses the couple with a plague ("or two"), ends with the final pronouncement: "May you both be punished [*a kapore zolt ir vern*] instead of me and all Israel."[104] Whether the force of this curse refers specifically to plague or to any misfortune that might befall the Jewish people is unclear, but there is no question that the beggar couple—perhaps symbolic representatives of the entire marginal caste—are to serve as scapegoats for any heavenly decree that might bring harm to the Jews.

One of Naftuli Vaynig's most persuasive analytical moves about the meaning of the cholera wedding is his argument that the ritual includes an element of the sacrificial. Citing the charge of the prospective cholera groom in Grodno that because the ritual's organizers "all want to live, you want to

bury me alive!" and the crowd's chanting of "From me to you!" to the bridal
couple in Joseph Opatoshu's story "A Wedding in the Cemetery" (on which
see chapter 7), Vaynig suggests that the cholera wedding was a kind of mod-
ern-day human sacrifice in which the community sacrificed the bridal couple
(as a substitute for itself) in order to appease God, the gods, or demons.[105]
(We might add to Vaynig's examples Abramovitsh's use in *Fishke der krumer*
of the term "recruiting" to describe the kahal compelling cholera grooms
to take part in the ritual, a word that evokes the Nicholaevan draft, when
scapegoats were quite literally recruited for the tsar's army.) Vaynig notes in-
triguingly that an ancient Athenian agricultural festival called the Thargēlia
included a ritual in which two people—in some accounts, the ugliest who
could be found; in other accounts, slaves, criminals, or poor people—were
selected as *pharmakoi* (scapegoats), subjected to some sort of denigrating
treatment, and expelled from the city.[106] (Scholars such as Jan Bremmer have
demonstrated that the narratives in which the scapegoats were ritually tortured and killed were mythic, though expulsion amounted, for all intents and
purposes, to communal death for the victim).[107] Bremmer concludes that
"the ritual was performed during the Thargēlia . . . in normal times, but evidently also during extraordinary circumstances such as plague, famine, and
drought."[108] He adds that all the scapegoats had in common that they were
"situated at the margin of Greek society."[109] We may also mention a Hittite
ritual to banish a pestilence from the community that involved sending a
scapegoat (either a woman or an animal) to the land of the enemy, by which
means the disease was to be transferred to the latter.[110]

Despite the enormous chronological and cultural divides, the affinities
between these scapegoat rituals and the cholera wedding are notable. In a
time of great danger to society, marginal people are selected as scapegoats
and put through a degrading ritual that places them, however briefly, at the
center of the community. In the cholera wedding, the bride and groom function as substitute victims for the epidemic, married in the shadow of death in
the cemetery itself, as though the entire community were pleading with the
Destroying Angel: They are already half-dead. Please cast your gaze on them
and not on us.

A final question. Could it be that one of the factors that gave rise to
the cholera wedding were the charges at various junctures throughout the

nineteenth century that Jews were in some way carriers or even deliberate propagators of disease? If Jews sensed that they were being blamed for cholera, might they have sought an alternative scapegoat, whether wittingly or not? We have, of course, no evidence that Jews who organized or participated in cholera weddings ever consciously blamed the cholera bride and groom for the catastrophe, but it bears pondering.

Conclusion

Looking back over almost a century of cholera weddings, we can discern a pattern emerging. After the first two weddings in 1831 and 1849, about which we have very little information—and perhaps there were others that went unrecorded—they came in waves during the great pandemics of the late nineteenth and early twentieth centuries: cholera in 1866 and 1892–93, typhus in 1916–17 (we could perhaps extend this last period to 1920 in the case of Shedlits). Cholera weddings occurred at moments of great national crisis and despair, and then, seemingly, the phenomenon disappeared just as quickly. Weddings of paupers and disabled people did not take place singly for a catastrophe limited to a particular town or region. It seems, then, that intense focus was placed on marginal people precisely at a moment of national *bodily*—not spiritual or political—calamity. When the Jewish body physical was in grave jeopardy, the most inadequate specimens of Jewish physical existence had to be brought to the center of the community and lifted up in a ceremony that was something akin to a restorative ritual. Their normalization by means of marriage would, it was hoped, lead to normalization on the cosmic plane, and the physical aberration caused by the epidemic would dissipate.

Let us also consider the following. In the premodern world, marginal people had had an aura of the fantastical about them, a clear connection to the supernatural. By the late nineteenth century, an age of challenges to traditional belief and piety, that feeling of awe in the presence of the abnormal and the freakish was giving way to disgust. At a crucial moment that both challenged faith in God and seemed to demand higher levels of belief in order for the epidemic to be overcome, the cholera wedding offered a seemingly "age-old" remedy (though in fact it was quite modern!) resonant with echoes of the supernatural. And crucially, marginals, once held in awe, then despised outcasts, and now newly embraced by the community, stood at its center. If they—and by association traditional piety and observance—could be restored to their rightful place in the community and in the collective Jewish consciousness, perhaps all could be made right again.

The modern age, the era that offered such strident challenges to traditional belief, was in some sense a liminal period, an era of transition, as Bjørn Thomassen suggests in his discussion of societal liminality and the collapse of order. The cholera wedding phenomenon emerged at the advent of that period for East European Jewry—the early nineteenth century—and persisted for about a century. It makes perfect sense that a ritual that expressed East European Jews' intense anxiety about modernity was linked to cholera, the quintessentially modern epidemic. In an era of transition from the familiar to an unknown and possibly dangerous future, the innovation that was the cholera wedding offered a moment of putative continuity ("an ancient ritual") centered around the liminal: a moment of "pure liminality" (in Thomassen's words) masquerading, paradoxically, as continuity, consistency, and stability.[111]

CHAPTER 5

A "REPUBLIC OF BEGGARS"?

Charity, Jewish Backwardness, and the Specter of the Jewish Idler

"The very Alms they receive from us are the Wages of Idleness."
 —Sir Andrew Freeport, a fictitious character, in *The Spectator*
 (London), November 26, 1711

"I don't give [street] people money, because most of them make more
than I do."
 —overheard on the street, Portland, Oregon, September 2018

During the crisis of an epidemic, the Jewish community directed an intense
focus on marginal individuals and channeled its collective anxiety about the
modern phenomenon of cholera into the ritual of the cholera wedding. But
the cholera wedding was not the only site of deep disquiet in East European
Jewry's transition to modernity that was linked to marginal people. The question of Jewish economic productivity was central in Jewish progressives' discussions of the future of the Jewish people and its place in European society,
as it was in the deliberations of tsarist officials and debates in the press. And
it was, indeed, a *question*, since many—both Jews and non-Jews—had grave
doubts about the economic basis of Jewish existence in the Russian Empire.
The widespread assumption in official circles that Jews were exploiters of the
peasantry overlapped with another common trope, that of the Jewish idler.
And while Jewish reformers rejected the notion of Jewish exploitation, they
endorsed the idea that it was backward Jewish institutions and customs that

created and nurtured individuals who, rather than contributing to society through hard work, sponged off of it as beggars.

Discussions of charity from the 1860s to the early years of the twentieth century reveal deep ambivalence about and even fear of marginal people. Jewish progressive circles, which included both the figure of the maskil (an amalgam of intellectual and social reformer) and the prosperous, acculturated merchant- or industrialist-cum-communal leader and philanthropist, lambasted traditional charity and charitable institutions such as the hekdesh and the Talmud-Torah (*talmud-toyre*, school for poor boys and orphans) for forming economic and social cripples who were a burden to society. These ostensibly antiquated forms of charity, they argued, did not help recipients achieve self-sufficiency and thus broadly failed to improve the lot of the poor. They also voiced fears that Christians, mistaking the blighted part for the healthy whole, would see all Jews as unproductive, parasitic, idle, even immoral. Now was the time for Jewry to reinvent itself in order to adapt to the modern world and be judged deserving of emancipation, and that reinvention had to include an enlightened system of care for poor, sick, and disabled Jews.[1]

Much of the discussion about rational philanthropy and the question of marginal people was prompted by the ever-worsening economic circumstances of Russian and Polish Jewry due to the impoverishment of large numbers of Jews under Nicholas I as a result of government policies coupled with rapid population growth. The emancipation of the serfs under Alexander II set into motion economic shifts that ultimately worsened the plight of the vast majority of the empire's Jews. The continued existence of the Pale of Settlement meant that most Jews were trapped in a region of the country where there was a glut of typical Jewish economic occupations, to wit, petty commerce and crafts. For many, there was simply no work to be had.[2]

In the large cities of the empire, wealthy, acculturated Jewish merchants and industrialists, intent on showing the authorities and the educated public that Jews were a forward-looking people and a productive element of society, were keen to establish philanthropic institutions that showcased the best of both Jewish compassion and Western scientific methods.[3] European bourgeois values suggested that individual almsgiving actually did a disservice to recipients in the long run by making them dependent on charity and corrupting their natural work ethic.[4] And philanthropy was a particularly modern mode for the expression of Jewish identity.[5] Derek Penslar has traced this idea both to the Sephardim of Amsterdam in the seventeenth century and the Ashkenazic communities of central and western Europe in the late eighteenth century. The latter, "exposed to Enlightenment ideology and the prospect for improvement of their legal and political status . . . sought to rationalize poor care by reducing the number of Jewish vagrants, centralizing the distribution of alms, and forming strict criteria for the receipt thereof."[6] Mutatis mutandis, this was more or less the same situation in which we find the new mercantile and industrial Jewish elite of the Russian Empire in the mid- to late nineteenth century.

Meanwhile, in the market towns that had traditionally been the focus of Jewish settlement in the former Polish lands, still functioning but often creaky traditional communal structures were increasingly challenged by Western-style institutions pioneered by public-minded women and young people.[7] Maskilim often criticized traditional hevrot and other ostensibly antiquated forms of charity as backward, especially since, they argued, such charity provided only short-term assistance and did not help the recipient achieve self-sufficiency, let alone offering any kind of structural reform that would substantially improve the lot of the poor by directing them into productive economic pursuits.[8]

The new Jewish philanthropy frequently followed the expert opinion of Russian government officials and experts in linking poverty and begging with idleness and (the threat of) parasitism, even as social scientists openly questioned whether professional beggary was a phenomenon of any consequence in the Jewish community. This differentiation between the parasite and the truly needy was the modern iteration of the age-old dichotomy of deserving versus undeserving poor. Moreover, one of the motivations for new philanthropic initiatives in the Jewish community was apparently the anxiety that Jewish marginal people, all too visible to the outside world, would come to stand in for Jewry as a whole. That anxiety can be seen clearly in discussions of poverty and charity among Odessa's progressive Jews in the 1860s.

Modern Jewish philanthropy comes to Odessa

The relatively young Jewish community of Odessa—Jews had only begun to settle there in serious numbers in the last years of the eighteenth

century—had by the mid-nineteenth century become known for such progressive institutions as Western-style schools and modernized synagogues.[9]
Prominent Jewish Odessans, who played a significant role in the city council, were concerned about growing poverty, as were local Jewish intellectuals.
Charity and philanthropy as they were currently constituted in the city
seemed unable meet the needs of the poor.[10] "The continued existence of
Jewish begging in the streets, the dilapidated state of the community's hospital, and the large numbers of homeless orphans now seemed an affront to the
Jewish community's leadership," Steven Zipperstein writes.[11]

Crown Rabbi Simon Schwabacher (Rus., Shvabakher), a German-born
and -trained scholar and preacher who was appointed to the position of
official rabbi in 1860, promised to bring new energy to the problem of Jewish need in Odessa.[12] Upon his arrival, Schwabacher immediately set out
to establish the kinds of Western-style philanthropic institutions familiar to
him from his earlier career and that, presumably, many communal leaders in
Odessa—motivated both by Judaism's command to care for the needy and by
their aspiration to the prestige that such institutions bestowed on their pa-
trons—wished to bring to their city.[13] In an article in the newly established
Russian-language journal *Sion*, an organ of the Haskalah, Rabbi Schwabacher
challenged his readers to grasp the superiority of philanthropy—rationally
organized assistance for the benefit of the poor—over traditional charity,
which actually benefited the giver more than the receiver. The most accessible
expression of the new philanthropic methods, he suggested, was an orphanage, since its wards were not "people who had grown old in begging and
idleness" but innocent, guileless children, blank slates "who are capable of as-
similating either good or evil" and whom a good and loving upbringing could
transform into "fruit-bearing trees in the garden of humanity."[14] Painting a
picture of miserable orphans living on the streets, Schwabacher called them
"a terrible reproach"—presumably to the Jewish community—and warned
that that in time they might well mature into adults who were not fully developed either physically or morally.[15] And the nub of the matter: "Insofar as
we turn children to education and good morality [*dobraia nravstvennost'*], we
are narrowing the sphere of the proletariat, that spreading plague of our time,
and increasing the number of members of productive society."[16] Aside from
the succor it would provide, Schwabacher's argument for the establishment

of a Jewish orphanage was, then, that it would benefit both the Jewish community, by averting the discredit that Jewish street urchins would invariably bring down on it, and Russian society at large, by limiting the growing—and menacing—number of proletarians.[17] The latter goal was not dissimilar to that of American Progressive reformers in their approach to the children of the poor: shaping them into useful citizens would not only rescue them from poverty but shield society from the adults they would otherwise become.[18]

The debate about the value of traditional charity and whether it should be replaced by rational philanthropy was part of a larger conversation in Russian imperial society. Schwabacher was, not surprisingly, aligned with the camp that condemned almsgiving for "encouraging begging, idleness, and parasitism," which included many progressives and radicals.[19] The opposing camp, which notably included many Slavophiles, saw charity as rooted in traditional Russian religious culture, stressing "the moral value of helping one's fellow human beings."[20] In a larger European context, Jewish economic elites and progressives in various countries tended to accept the link, in Derek Penslar's words, "between poverty, on the one hand, and unproductivity and immorality, on the other."[21] Russian Jews were so frequently accused of parasitism, idleness, and exploitation that it was only natural for Jewish intellectuals and philanthropists to ask whether such a characterization were in any way accurate.[22] Antisemitism often motivated Jews to question whether there was in fact some truth to the never-ending allegations lobbed at them.[23] As we shall see, Jewish thinkers and opinion leaders may, perhaps subconsciously, have sought out a subgroup within the Jewish community on whom to project the allegations being leveled against the Jews as a collective; Jewish marginal people made a natural target.[24] This kind of displacement would be consistent with social identity theory, which posits that since people naturally prefer to see themselves in a positive light and since a key aspect of individual identity is membership in a social group, members of a given group (an "in-group") are likely to try to distinguish themselves from another group (an "out-group") that they perceive as having a lower status. In our case, that out-group consisted of low-status Jews who truly (as it were) deserved the labels of idlers and parasites.[25]

The ostensibly organic connection between poverty and idleness was one that many maskilim took for granted. Russian Jewish newspapers in the

1860s frequently criticized the foundations of Jewish economic and social existence in the Russian Empire and called on Jews to engage in productive occupations. For example, in 1867 Aleksander Zederbaum, editor of the Yiddish *Kol mevaser*, condemned the institution of early arranged marriages, noting that teenage bridegrooms steeped in Talmud learning lacked practical training to earn a livelihood and thus often became idlers and beggars.[26]

Beggars and begging were thus symptomatic of serious ills in Jewish life, and the mobilization of the terms "idleness" and "idler" on the part of both Zederbaum and Schwabacher was no accident—they had deep roots in Jewish life in the Russian Empire. To understand this, we must turn the clock back several decades to the reign of Nicholas I.

The advent of the Jewish idler

One of the recommendations of the Committee on the Transformation of the Jews, established by Nicholas I in 1841 and headed by his adviser Count P. D. Kisilev, was the division of all Jews under Russian rule into useful and non-useful categories (this plan came to be known by the term *razbor*, or "sorting").[27] Assuming, as most Russian government officials did, that Jews exploited the Slavic peasant population among whom they lived, Kisilev aimed to compel the vast majority of Jews to abandon their middle-man economic niche in the countryside and move into agriculture, crafts, or large-scale commerce. Kisilev's "useful" Jews were to include "all guild merchants, licensed artisans, farmers, and true townspeople with a permanent urban residence"; all others were to be labeled "non-useful."[28] The latter would be expected to move into one of the useful groups within five years or face punishment, including expulsion from villages and the imposition of an even harsher conscription regime than the one imposed in 1827.[29]

The razbor legislation, like so much government policy on the Jews, was driven by the assumption that most Jewish economic activities were harmful, and that Jews therefore had to be compelled to move into productive pursuits. The decree noted that "it is entirely justified that the refractory and disobedient be punished as *idlers* who are a burden to the society of which they are a part."[30] The government in this way proclaimed that it would henceforth classify as idlers those Jews whom it defined as "unproductive." Another term for "non-useful" Jews used in the *razbor* documents was "parasites" (*tuneiadtsy*).

The argument for the razbor centered in part around the question of "settled" (*osedlye*) Jews—those living in towns—versus "unsettled" (*neosedlye*), those living in rural areas or with no fixed domicile. Tsarist officials assumed that unsettled people, like nomads in Russia's eastern borderlands, were lower down on the ladder of civilization and economic productivity.[31]

For various reasons, the *razbor* was never actually carried out, but the idea of the Jew as idler, and the stigma attached to that epithet, persisted for many decades to come. The weighty Russian term *prazdnoshchataiushchiisia* (idler) had such staying power that it even entered Yiddish folk songs wholesale and unmodified, as in this example:

> *A naye gzeyre mit di razryaden,*
> *Lyu-lyu-lyu!*
> *A tsore, a gzeyre mit di razryaden,*
> *Lyu-lyu-lyu!*
> *Loyf tsu Romanovsken,*
> *Zog—du bist a vasertreger*
> *Zog—du bist a holtsenzeger*
> *Zog, zog, ver du bist*
> *Nor nit blayb a prazdnoshchataiushchiisia!*
> A new evil edict: the reclassification,
> Lyu-lyu-lyu!
> What misfortune, what persecution: the reclassification,
> Lyu-lyu-lyu!
> Run to Romanovskii
> Say you are a water-carrier
> Say you are a wood-cutter
> Say, say, whoever you are
> Just don't remain an "idler"![32]

Perhaps more important, the perception that most Jews were parasites on the body economic bored deeply into the worldview of tsarist bureaucrats and decision-makers. For example, a geographical and statistical handbook on Minsk province compiled by the Army General Staff in the 1860s included a long discussion of "settled" and "unsettled"—that is, unproductive—Jews and concluded that "at least half, if not three-quarters" of all Jews could be identified as parasites and idlers (though the author conceded that the situation was a result of the socioeconomic conditions of the Jews and not because of their innate laziness or moral corruption).[33]

As John Klier has shown, this view was eventually carried over from a relatively obscure military handbook to the press. After an article appeared in *Vilenskii vestnik* attributing Jewish poverty to the Pale of Settlement and arguing for its abolition, a response came from A. Korev, a contributor to the General Staff's survey, accusing Russia's Jews of idleness and a contempt for hard work. Some even preferred begging to honest agricultural labor.[34] The discussion of Jewish idleness was not confined to non-Jewish publications. The first issue of *Razsvet*, a pioneering maskilic newspaper, featured an article about the daily life of Jews in the western provinces of the empire by Lev Levanda, an advocate of Jewish modernization and integration:

> As for professional beggars, there are so many here that it is difficult to imagine. . . . Despite the periodic distribution of alms, which during the festivals reaches quite significant numbers, the local resident never has peace from the beggars, who stop him on the street, surround him at the entrance to the synagogue, visit him in his store and at his home, and do not release him from their pestering entreaties even when he sits down to his Sabbath meal. On Sabbath and holidays, in addition to the alms they already receive, each family invites to a meal one or two beggars, who enjoy all the privileges of guests. Although this custom is praiseworthy and even touching, at the same time it actually brings more harm than good to society, because this patriarchal philanthropy cultivates in the poor classes a proclivity towards parasitism and mendicancy, which enjoys many privileges among Jews thanks to their religious teachings and their innate compassion. And, in truth, I noticed among the local beggars many tough, healthy men and women, who, while capable of making a living through hard work, prefer the light beggar's staff to the heavy axe, yoke, and pushcart.[35]

In other words, most Jewish beggars were simply too lazy to work, and Jewish traditions encouraged this "parasitism."[36] The funds now being given to beggars as alms, Levanda suggested, could be better used to fund rational philanthropy and institutions for the poor, including workhouses.

What historians have not pointed out about Levanda's article is that it was founded on a virulent misogyny that blamed Jewish women for many of the ills of Jewish life, including sponging among Jewish men and disability and deformity among Jewish children. Levanda argued that Jewish women had so thoroughly taken over Jewish economic life, and especially commerce, that men had nothing left to occupy their time, while the household was left in the hands of "half-wild, lazy, and unconscientious" servants. "Whatever the Jewish woman has not ruined through her presence in the store, she completes the destruction through her absence from the family hearth."[37] The result was children who grew up in chaos, filth, and illness, leading to more hunchbacked, cross-eyed, crippled, and deformed (*urody*) children than could be found among any people or in any nation. Almost all these wretches owed their disfigurement to their virtual abandonment by their mothers, according to Levanda. This was a natural move for a proponent of a Jewish Enlightenment that generally advocated gender roles for Jewish society that corresponded to bourgeois values of contemporary Europe: men as bread-winners, women as housewives and mothers.[38] Levanda blamed physical defects and deformities on a reversal of gender roles, though he described those disabilities as acquired, rather than congenital.

At around the same time, Moisei Berlin, an advisor on Jewish affairs to government officials, leveled a similar critique at traditional Jewish charity for encouraging mendicancy. In one of the earliest ethnographic works on Russian Jewry, Berlin criticized the large number of beggars in the community, arguing that the custom of charity was now being abused, and that anyone who did not want to work could simply take advantage of it, many of them usually going to large communities where they were sure to be helped.[39] A similar denunciation of Jewish parasitism came from another member of Russian-Jewish maskilic circles, the Yiddish writer Ayzik Meyer Dik, who in a number of fictional works painted an entire array of Jewish beggars and shnorrers in addition to a number of other occupational types who leeched off the Jewish community, such as "pilgrims to the Holy Land, miracles workers (*baley-sheymes*), travelling cantors, match-makers, book peddlers, penitents, mystics in self-imposed exile (*goles-oprikhters*), and grass widows (*agunes*)."[40]

Even those deeply sympathetic to Jewish poverty in Russia condemned what they perceived as widespread charlatanism among Jewish beggars. In the early 1880s, Isaac Rülf, rabbi in the East Prussian city of Memel and an advocate for East European Jewry, crossed the border and traveled through the Pale of Settlement for three days, after which he wrote a booklet entitled *Three Days in Jewish Russia*. Rülf assumed that a goodly number of the many beggars he saw in Vilna were not actually poor; "there are prosperous, even wealthy beggars here," he wrote.[41] To the naïve observer's eye, Jewish beggars were almost all mentally or physically disabled, but only some were truly afflicted; many faked their conditions. Their most successful day was Friday, when they laid claim to their Sabbath support, which was willingly granted by Jews preparing for the holy day. "I would be surprised if the beggar did not bring home a pocket full of kopecks on Friday," Rülf concluded.[42]

The claim that able-bodied Jewish men preferred begging to honest, hard work made its way into a variety of scientific works over the following decades. For example, a multi-volume work exploring the peoples and lands of the Russian Empire's western borderland provinces, an ambitious ethnographic project undertaken by the Imperial Russian Geographical Society in the 1870s, maintained that

> the most important and numerous class [of the Jewish proletariat] are the vagrants [*brodiagi*], beggars by profession, who roam among the Jewish cities and towns in large packs of families. The majority of this class of beggars are healthy young people; they are satisfied with a small handout, but they're audacious and rude in their demands. There are of course quite a few cripples among them, but being crippled is considered a good and advantageous characteristic, since it is considered permissible for a cripple to demand alms.[43]

But the larger problem, the study found, lay with the Jewish community, which, even while viewing such beggars with scorn, never withheld alms from them and refused to acknowledge the harmfulness of such a large mendicant population. Jewish progressives seeking to reform East European Jewry's communal structures agreed that existing charitable institutions were deficient; to remedy the situation, they offered Western-style philanthropic solutions.

A modest proposal

Given the link that many saw between Jewish impoverishment and Jewish parasitism, it was only natural that some acculturated Jewish leaders felt that any solution to the problem of Jewish need in the Russian Empire would also have to address the question of sloth and idleness in the Jewish community. A proposal submitted to the tsarist authorities in the early 1860s by a group of communal leaders in Odessa with Rabbi Schwabacher at its head did just that.[44] Apparently, Schwabacher had served as the head of a Special Commission charged with investigating the current state of Jewish charitable institutions and making recommendations on their reform. His proposal formulated a vision for a set of institutions that were explicitly intended to serve as a model for Russian Jewry as a whole and to set in motion a far-reaching transformation of Jewish institutional charity.[45]

Among the projected institutions were those intended for marginal types: the chronically ill, the disabled and deformed, and the insane. The writers envisioned every large hospital having a hospice-poorhouse (bogadel'nia) to house individuals with chronic illnesses and deformities who were unable to support themselves either because they were unable to work or because their condition inspired disgust in others (the example given was that of a person missing a nose). The hospice was to accept only local residents who had to be "truly indigent" (sovershenno bednye) to gain admission; thus, itinerant beggars were ineligible.[46] There was also a workhouse aspect to the institution, as the proposal stated that "those maintained in the hospice-poorhouse may be put to work in various ways in the service of Jewish philanthropic institutions."[47] Those hospitals that had the resources to do so were encouraged to build a ward for the insane.[48] The description of the ward conforms to the contours of European insane asylums in the "golden age" of psychiatry: isolation of the insane, a "highly structured internal order," and the "subordination of the patients" to medical personnel.[49] At a time when psychiatry in the Russian Empire was only beginning to come into its own as a profession and the medicalization of insane asylums was in its early stages—the first of the reformed provincial lunatic asylums, in Kazan, was completed in 1869, several years after this proposal—Russian Jews were apparently at the vanguard of this movement.[50] It is understandable that a man such as Schwabacher would have played a central role here, since psychiatry was much more developed in central Europe.

It is interesting to consider Schwabacher's proposal in the light of Foucault's Great Confinement. This was the name that the French social theorist gave to the establishment by the early modern French state of hundreds of asylums for madmen and madwomen, as well as disabled people, paupers, and other deviants. The Great Confinement brought to an end a quasi-idyllic period in the Middle Ages when mad people were free to roam from town to town, Foucault asserts. Since they were officially excluded from mainstream society, that society did not have to fear frequent encounters with them, encounters that resonated powerfully in the cultural production of the day.[51] A crucial element to Foucault's argument is that at the root of the Great Confinement was economic policy masquerading as morality: in Gary Gutting's words, it was "an economic policy meant to deal with problems of poverty, particularly begging and unemployment. It was a way of getting a large class of idle, potentially disruptive people off the streets and putting them to work in a controlled environment."[52] While the periodization is different, it may be that the earliest impulse to institutionalization among East European Jews, an example of which we see in Schwabacher's proposal, was indeed tied up with anxiety about accusations of Jewish sloth and parasitism.

Sholem Yankev Abramovitsh found much to poke fun at—and to criticize—in the new scientific philanthropy. In *Fishke der krumer*, the eponymous hero says:

> Finally we came to the city of A———. . . . A cavalry was stationed in that city—the field beggars with their vans. A revolution had just taken place there. The richer young men [*balebeslekh*] of the town had just started something new. They decided that it wouldn't hurt the beggars to work for their daily bread—except for the old and sick and crippled. There was no reasons for healthy young men and women to live on alms and charity. The foolish Jewish spirit of charity causes only trouble, they claimed. That's why, they said, there are so many lazy loafers among the Jews—who suck other people's blood like bedbugs. The rich young men set up a sort of factory where the beggars were put to work making ropes and sewing sacks and, in return, were given food. Beggars began to turn up much less often in the town.
>
> The field beggars that we met there were up in arms against this new custom. "Gvald!" they cried. "What's happening to the world? Where is Jewish charity? Jewishness is dead!" [*Gevald! S'iz shoyn gor keyn velt nisht. Vu iz dos yidishe rakhmones? Oys yidishkayt, kh'lebn!*][53]

Abramovitsh understood very well that the Jewish haute-bourgeoisie was prepared to replicate the antisemitic accusation about the Jewish parasite in its own critique of the Jewish poor. In Abramovitsh's fictional Jewish town, the wealthy Jewish young men take rational philanthropy to its most extreme conclusion: the workhouse (which, in reality, never made an appearance on the Russian or Polish Jewish street). The response of the beggars is one that could have been uttered by any poor Jew confronted with this newfangled and rather alien variety of charity: "Where is Jewish charity?" Their next step, however, is to take this lament to its most absurd conclusion: "Jewishness is dead!" Abramovitsh thus slyly condemns the most extreme tendencies of both prosperous and underprivileged Jews—including their inclination to accuse the other group of the worst faults imaginable: unqualified sloth ("It's time for a change—let the rich try to work a bit!" cries Fayvesh) and the murder of authentic *yidishkayt*.

Orphans and the Talmud-Torah

Central to the proposal submitted to the authorities by the Odessa Jewish reformers was an orphanage. Schwabacher took up the subject of orphan care immediately after his arrival in Odessa, and it remained a predominant element of the Jewish philanthropic scene in the city. And no wonder. For progressives and acculturated communal leaders, orphans presented both glaring signs of the backwardness of Jewish society and were also a potent symbol of the growing impoverishment and despair of Russian and Polish Jewry, as more and more parents—especially mothers—abandoned children whom they could not care for. The rise in the number of illegitimate children may have been a product of changing sexual mores (a phenomenon that the organized Jewish community was loath to discuss) and, more generally, the far-reaching upheaval in traditional Jewish ways of life caused by urbanization and other transformations that accompanied modernity.[54] Without the premodern household or community around her to assist in the raising of children, a widowed or deserted mother might simply decide to leave a child (or children) in the hands of those whom she thought might be better prepared to raise them than she.[55] We know that, owing to an array of complex factors, Jews married later than members of other religious groups.[56] More fundamentally, there were simply more children among Jews than among the general population; 52 percent versus 48.5 percent for the empire as a whole.[57]

Like the hekdesh, the Talmud-Torah—a community-funded religious school for orphans and poor boys whose parents could not afford to send them to heder—was a ubiquitous charity institution among the Jews of eastern Europe.[58] It was also notorious for its poor conditions, as illustrated by this memoir of a graduate of the Talmud-Torah in Pruzhany (Pruzhene), who attended the school in the 1870s:

> Hard times fell on my family, and my father could no longer afford the tuition for Efroym-Yoysl the *melamed* [children's teacher]. I started going to the Talmud-Torah and studying with Kalmen the melamed in the Tailors' *beys-medresh* [house of study].[59] The air in there was not very good, because Yankl the Blind, Mordkhe the Cripple, and Mikhoel "Kalb" [the Calf] had their quarters there. . . . Kalmen der melamed was a bitter man, and was mean to his pupils. We received many slaps. . . . Every few days, pairs of pupils with *pushkes* [charity collection boxes] in hand would go around to pious women to beg for candles to learn by. Whoever did not have a candle had to throw a couple coins in the pushke. . . . The pupils were also taken to mothers who had just given birth to say *Kriyes-shma* [the Shema prayer] and to recite Psalms by the bedside of the very ill. These all yielded extra income for the melamdim of the Talmud-Torah.[60]

In addition to laying bare the arduous lives of Talmud-Torah boys, Lev's description is striking for the clear linkages that he draws between those boys and other marginal people such as disabled individuals. The custom of having the boys recite the *Shema* prayer in the homes of new mothers (a folk remedy to ward off evil) and Psalms by the bedsides of the very ill was widespread, as was the practice of requiring them to walk in front of the coffin in funeral processions, especially those of notable or charitable Jews.[61] All three of these customs were appropriate for marginal types, since they involved liminal rituals or states that related to moments of great vulnerability: birth, illness/dying, and death.

Maskilim waged battle with the institution of the Talmud-Torah for its ostensible devastation of an army of young souls. S. Y. Abramovitsh's first

Yiddish story, a novella-cum-parable entitled "The Little Man" (*Dos kleyne mentshele*, 1864), features an orphan, Isaac Abraham, who, after suffering an abysmal childhood replete with slaps, blows, and bullying, achieves prosperity by virtue of his unethical and immoral behavior. Olga Litvak has noted that "the motif of the 'little man' symbolized the inherent potential for moral degeneration and conveyed the urgency of the enlightenment project: the child was a blank slate, easily corruptible . . . by bad influences."[62] In his will, Isaac Abraham asks the rabbi to use the sizable sum that he is bequeathing to the Jewish community to implement two projects that any maskil would have been proud of: improve the local Talmud-Torah and establish a vocational school to train orphans and poor children as artisans so that they won't have to become the kind of maltreated apprentice that he was. "Many orphans who become apprentices, poor things, spoil their health and are left crippled, with bruises all over their bodies. Why doesn't anyone think about such unfortunate children?"[63] Here, as in Levanda's 1860 article, it is the degenerate Jewish environment that creates the deformed Jewish child.

In 1880, the Russian-Jewish newspaper *Russkii evrei* called for the transformation of the Talmud-Torah, since in its present state the institution was of no use, producing graduates who were fit only for hospitals and poorhouses rather than training orphans and poor boys to make a living.[64] Three years later, *Russkii evrei* again complained bitterly about the state of the Talmud-Torah, pointing to numerous reports from throughout the Pale:

> Almost everywhere the Talmud-Torah is a dirty hovel or a damp basement, where a number of ragged kiddies languish under the severe and ignorant direction of an antediluvian pedagogue. . . . Neither food nor clothing nor shoes are the boys given; no one looks after them; they shiver from cold, exhausted, pale from hunger and deprivation, assimilate all kinds of bad habits and enter life sickly, without knowledge/skills [*znaniia*], without any virtues.[65]

"Fate itself, as it were, condemns the poor orphans to fall into the very dregs of society," the editorial noted, and it called for modern-style assistance to orphans on the model of the St. Petersburg Jewish orphanage, whose annual report was reproduced in the same issue of the newspaper.

A few years earlier, in the same newspaper, a former Talmud-Torah

teacher from the central Ukrainian town of Kremenchug (Poltava province) described the pitiful state of the filthy and chaotic school where he had
worked and recommended that it be transformed into a vocational school.
"This Talmud-Torah can only disfigure [the pupils] intellectually, morally,
and physically, and increase the abundant number of parasites." The writer
also accused the trustees of the school of not providing for the poorest pupils,
who were forced "to live half-starving or to go from house to house, begging
for dinner."[66] And again we note the allegation that the traditional Jewish
milieu, rather than forming Jewish children, actually deformed them.

Despite these very serious accusations, there is no reason not to think
that many of those active in establishing and supporting Talmud-Torahs
did so out of purely charitable motives; the regulations of the religious
confraternities that supported the schools often evinced compassion and
kindheartedness towards their wards. For example, the pinkas of the Talmud-
Torah society of the Ukrainian town of Ostropol, Volhyn province, insisted
that orphans and boys whose parents could not care for them due to illness
or because they were away from the town took precedence over boys who
were being cared for properly; that the trustees (*gaba'im*) had to collect donations to help boys who could not walk to school in winter because they
lacked proper clothing or footwear; and that the trustees were further to
watch over the boys carefully and take immediate action if they discovered
that any of them were being maltreated by a teacher.[67] Yekhezkel Kotik's
memory of the Talmud-Torah in Kamenets Litovsk around the midpoint
of the nineteenth century depicts an orderly institution housed in a decent
building, schooling pupils who were well dressed, "never short of food," and
taught by skilled *melamdim*.

As in other areas of communal concern, education for the poor was a
problem of ever greater disquiet to Jewish communal leaders, philanthropists,
and social entrepreneurs in the waning decades of the nineteenth century
and the first decades of the twentieth, since Jewish impoverishment continued apace and tsarist restrictions on Jewish economic and physical mobility
in the Pale of Settlement grew ever tighter. It is likely that it was precisely
the Talmud-Torah's visible stagnation that made it the most obvious target
for renewal and, indeed, around the turn of the century many communities
undertook to modernize their Talmud-Torahs and other aspects of orphan

care. (The modern schools and orphanages that were the products of this development, mostly in urban centers, often grew up side by side with other new institutions: Western-style hospitals, clinics, child-care facilities, and old-age homes.)[68] In Vilna, one sign of the modernization of the Talmud-Torah was the ending of the age-old custom of having male pupils participate in funeral processions, which a correspondent to Russian-language Jewish weekly *Nedelnaia khronika Voskhoda* referred to as "a form of exploitation . . . frequently tearing them away from their lessons and generally having a demoralizing effect on them."[69] The practice, explained the article, was arousing dissatisfaction among the high-minded (*zdravomysliashchaia*) segment of society as well as among officials responsible for education. The challenge for the Talmud-Torah was that it would have to look for an alternative source of income, since the boys' involvement in the processions brought in several hundred rubles a year, a significant sum.

The archives of the Jewish Colonization Association (JCA) contain correspondence between it and social welfare activists in Bialystok, who envisioned establishing a modern Talmud-Torah and vocational school for three hundred children, including fifty orphans. The extensive facility would consist of two stone buildings housing classrooms, workshops, offices, and a residence for the orphans.[70] According to the 1905 charter of the Society for the Care of Poor and Shelterless Children of Bialystok, the organization would institute a guardianship system (*popechitelstvo*) in which volunteer social welfare workers would assess individual families and children for their level of need. Guardians were to keep track of the poor in their respective districts—including keeping "detailed lists of the needy"—and to provide them with the appropriate aid.[71] And in Warsaw, Yekhezkel Kotik, whose memoir (cited in these pages) recalled specific details about the life of the poor in his hometown of Kamenets Litovsk, established an orphan aid organization called Ezras yesoymim (Ezrat yetomim) that would soon grow to be one of the largest of its kind in eastern Europe.[72]

It may be, however, that it was easier to transform orphan aid in cities like Warsaw and Bialystok than in provincial towns. In many shtetls, there was seemingly little change over the decades, and orphans were still seen as potential delinquents. For example, the archive of the Inspectorate of Public Schools reveals that in 1905 the authorities closed the Talmud-Torah in

FIGURE 5.1. Photograph from the 1912–14 ethnographic expedition organized by
S. An-ski (location unknown). Note on verso reads, "Orphanage. Children at work."
Central Archives for the History of the Jewish People.

Chernobyl due to its filthy and unhygienic state and its staff of unauthorized
teachers of the traditional type (*melamdim*). Six years later, the Inspectorate received a request to reopen the school because the orphans and poor
children who had previously studied there now could be found roaming the
streets during the day, exposing them to bad influences and possibly even
leading them to become "harmful and criminal members of society."[73] The
school was reopened, but later closed again because of its terrible conditions.[74] In some towns, such as in Krasnopol'e, an attempt at reforming the
Talmud-Torah was begun but then abandoned for lack of interest.[75] And
many Talmud-Torahs in the northwestern provinces of the Pale of Settlement operated in a grey zone, according to a sweeping survey of Jewish
economic circumstances in the Russian Empire conducted by the JCA in
1898–99, since they were not officially registered with the authorities.[76]

Schools for poor girls were a rarity, but they did exist.[77] In the late 1850s,
an initiative to establish a girls' shelter (*devichii priiut*) in Vilna was initiated

FIGURE 5.2. Photograph of children in a Jewish orphanage taken during the 1912–14 ethnographic expedition organized by S. An-ski (location unknown). The photograph is labeled "Work." Central Archives for the History of the Jewish People.

by the wealthy Romm family, famous for their Hebrew printing house, after the death of Yosef Re'uven Romm. The bequest stipulated that the institution be called "Talmud-Torah," suggesting that the Romms envisioned a school for poor girls paralleling the existing Talmud-Torahs for boys.[78] Eliyana Adler has shown that similar schools were established in Mogilev in 1858 and in St. Petersburg in 1866, and a long-term effort starting in the late 1860s on the part of a group of Jewish women in Odessa eventually led to the founding of a vocational school for Jewish girls in that city in 1881.[79]

Another interesting example of such a school could be found in Vilna. The same correspondent who had written to *Nedel'naia khronika Voskhoda* about the changes in the Talmud-Torah there also reported on an initiative of "several female representatives of our *beau-monde*" to establish a school for poor and orphaned girls, who up until that point had no schooling options at all, leaving them with only the path "leading to beggary and debauchery" (i.e., prostitution).[80] (Across Europe, it was widely assumed in middle-class circles that adolescent girls and young women who became paupers would sooner or later end up as prostitutes; the link between poverty and a debauched life was implicit but understood by all.) The women petitioned the local Talmud-Torah to establish a branch of the institution for girls for which they would shoulder all fund-raising responsibilities.

By the turn of the century, schools for Jewish girls were emerging across the Pale of Settlement and the Russian-ruled kingdom of Poland and were often described as far superior to what was available for boys. In Łomża, for example, a new school where poor Jewish girls studied Hebrew, Russian, and handicrafts was described by a local not only as an institution run in an orderly fashion but also as "unique and exciting."[81]

Social science and the question of urban beggary

With the rise of Jewish social science in the 1880s and 1890s, which mobilized demographics and sociology as well as criminology and psychology to understand the peculiar circumstances of the Jews in Europe and elsewhere, scholars and social reformers turned to the question of beggars.[82] Would their observations confirm the widespread assumption that many Jewish beggars were idlers who chose a life of mendicancy over a productive existence? Memoir accounts spanning the turn of the century to the interwar period seem to substantiate Isaac Rülf's assessment that not all Jewish beggars were simply down on their luck, and that successful panhandling often involved a con game. Reconstructing his childhood years in the Polish shtetl of Kutno, for example, Yekhiel Trunk wrote that professional beggars who lived in the back alleys of town weren't actually so badly off. However, on Fridays, a "begging day,"

> all the beggars surfaced. They made a point of dressing in tattered clothes and displaying piteous bodily deformations to arouse compassion. On Friday various imitation and phoney cripples came out in force, cripples with bandaged necks and faces and hands, cripples on crutches, and beggarly cripples who crawled on the ground. The women made themselves look old, ugly, and frail. Working en masse, they engulfed the Jewish houses and shops. They did not beg but, standing still and morose, demanded pennies. And woe to anyone who tried to refuse! They howled and swore. Eerie curses reminiscent of the world beyond echoed from the mouths in the bandaged faces of the dirty and ragged beggars.[83]

Experts, however, tended to downplay the existence of professional mendicancy among East European Jews. The sweeping statement of the American Jewish anthropologist Maurice Fishberg from his magnum opus, *The Jews: A Study of Race and Environment*, sums up the consensus of the camp: "There are comparatively few vagrants and paupers among Jews, considering a pauper one who is able-bodied, but has lost all ambition to work for himself and his own. Among the Jews there are many poor, but they mainly consist of the sickly, the infirm, and the defective."[84] In the Russian Empire, three important works published around the turn of the century investigated different aspects of Jewish economic conditions and poverty in the Pale of Settlement; all three authors painted brutally stark pictures of Jewish poverty without, however, blaming the poor for their fate, and all concluded, like Fishberg, that most Jewish beggars turned to begging as an absolute last resort.

In 1887, the economist Andrei Pavlovich Subbotin undertook an expedition through the western provinces of the empire and published his observations, together with pertinent statistics and economic data. In what amounted to the first serious attempt at an economic analysis of Jewish existence in the Russian Empire, Subbotin paid particular attention to Jewish poverty and the dire living conditions of impoverished Jews. Commenting on Jewish begging in the Lithuanian city of Kovno, he observed that begging in that city was nowhere near as lucrative as in St. Petersburg, Moscow and other urban centers in the interior of the empire and noted that there were very few Jews among the relatively small number of professional beggars in Kovno. "In general," he remarked, "begging among Jews is not an independent trade as it is among us [Russians] but rather a result of a truly hopeless situation, usually incapacity to work."[85]

Subbotin acknowledged that Jewish beggars were quite pushy but explained that the terrible poverty in Kovno province was due in large measure to the impact of the 1863 Polish Uprising (after which the tsarist government emancipated the Polish peasantry), and emphasized that the alms that Jewish beggars received were so paltry that no one could possible live on them:

> In recent years, with the decline of trade and the displacement of Jews
> from villages, the number of Jewish beggars in Kovno has grown visibly. . . .
> [But] there is neither an orphanage nor an old-age home here. Hence, many

decrepit Jews are forced to beg for alms on the street, and there are also many child beggars; in this respect Kovno differs from other large cities. On Thursdays and Fridays, and also on holiday eves and the first of each month (Rosch-Cheidesch) whole groups of Jewish beggars roam the streets . . . seeing themselves on these days as having the right to demand aid quite insistently. They are given sums that are entirely homeopathic: more prosperous Jews give a kopeck to each beggar, and others, of more ordinary means, give a half- or quarter-kopeck, often one kopeck to an entire gang of five or ten men. If a would-be donor does not have enough money, he gives in bread or potatoes.[86]

Subbotin described Jewish children heading directly from their studies at school to beg on the streets in order to bring home a few coins for their destitute families to buy food.

About fifteen years later, in an overview of Jewish philanthropy in the Russian Empire that appeared in *Trudovaia pomoshch'* (Work Relief), a journal published by the state-created Guardianship of Houses of Industry and Workhouses (*Popechitel'stvo o domakh trudoliubiia i rabotnikh domakh*), Samuil Ianovskii wrote, "Neither love for idleness nor ill will propels the Jewish pauper to the path of beggary. As long as he has some possibility for work, and with his work to earn even a portion of his necessary livelihood, he will not turn to alms-collecting; and will only do so once broken down by backbreaking labor, aged before his time and having lost all ability to work."[87]

Reviewing figures on Jewish poverty in Ekaterinoslav from a recent annual report of that city's Society for Aid to Poor Jews, Ianovskii argued that only a small segment of paupers who sought aid from the society were registered as having "no specific occupation," that is, were totally reliant on communal philanthropy. (Neither the report nor Ianovskii assumed that these people were beggars per se, but they were clearly without any means of support.) That "small segment" amounted to 1,019 people, or just over one-fifth of all recipients of aid from the Society, not an insignificant proportion.[88]

The third publication, *Evreiskaia nishcheta v Odesse* (Jewish Poverty in Odessa), reported on a study undertaken by the Commission for the Distribution of Aid to the Poor Jews of Odessa. The house-to-house survey counted 8,435 needy families for a total of 45,549 people, or 32 percent of

Odessa's Jewish population of approximately 150,000. The author of the study, Isidor Brodovskii, a staff writer at local newspaper *Odesskie novosti* (Odessa News), emphasized that these families lived in extreme privation and horrific conditions—a step down from ordinary poverty.[89] In addition to day laborers, petty traders (mostly women, walking the streets with baskets of half-rotten fruit, "making thirty, twenty, and ten kopecks a day"),[90] handcart pushers, and factory workers, the student-volunteers working as canvassers found seventy-nine beggars. Conceding that this number seemed quite low, Brodovskii stressed that such people did not want to be seen or counted, and most must have hidden themselves so well that the students did not find them. Those who were included in the survey lived mostly in the poor outskirts of the city and received their donations from the impoverished residents of those neighborhoods. Brodovskii made a point of explaining their circumstances and noting their fundamental humanity:

> We would like to call attention to the generally accepted term "professional beggar." This usually refers to a person who is ill-willed, lazy, a parasite unwilling to provide for himself by means of his own labor, preferring rather to live off of society in an easier fashion. Our legislation holds the same view of beggars, perceiving mendicancy as a criminal offence. A person comes to exactly the opposite conclusion when encountering beggars in real life, attempting through personal conversations to understand the circumstances that led them to this last path. In almost all cases, these are people who are totally incapable of any kind of work: elderly men and women, sick people, cripples, blind, idiots, and the like.[91]

Brodovskii added that the beggars had all once been young, strong, and healthy, and had never shunned or feared work. Once a life of hard work ruined their health and made them unfit to work, however, society did not help them but instead cast them out as unworthy of help or even hauled them into the local police precinct. (In his commentary on the beggars uncovered by the survey, Brodovskii related exclusively to the elderly among them; for some reason nothing more is said about the physically or developmentally disabled mentioned in his initial description.)

Some social scientists, however, maintained that professional beggary did exist in the Jewish community, sustained by archaic charitable structures such

FIGURE 5.3. Hekdesh in Annopol'. Photograph from the 1912–14 ethnographic expedition organized by S. An-ski. Central Archives for the History of the Jewish People.

as the hekdesh. The authors of the JCA survey, for example, condemned the hekdesh in its current state for maintaining professional beggars rather than aiding the genuine needy—men who were wandering from place to place in search of honest labor to support themselves and their families. The JCA experts recommended that all poorhouses institute compulsory labor for anyone seeking shelter in a hekdesh.[92] The perception that the hekdesh fostered professional mendicancy persisted well into the twentieth century, to judge by a remark of Isaac Levitats, a Jewish scholar and educator active in the United States in the mid-twentieth century and the author of two important surveys of Jewish communal life in the Russian Empire. Charity "frequently went to the wrong people and for the wrong causes," Levitats writes. "It is obvious that the Hekdesh and the methods of poor relief tended to breed pauperism and to encourage professional beggary and vagrancy.[93] Those "wrong people" were, of course, the infamous idlers, siphoning off charitable funds that should by right have gone to those more deserving.

Transforming the hekdesh

Perhaps unbeknownst to the authors of the JCA survey, a transformation of the hekdesh was already underway, part of the larger reform and professionalization of Jewish health care that began in the Russian Empire in the late nineteenth century.[94] In some locales, the poor sick were now taken care of by modernized societies for visiting the sick (Bikur Holim), which were transformed from religious confraternities to committees—often composed of bourgeois Jewish women—that were "devoted to aiding the indigent sick."[95] These committees cared for the sick not by putting them in the hekdesh but by providing the services of a local doctor or a *feldsher* (akin to a physician's assistant). Moreover, the seriously and chronically ill were increasingly likely to be sent to hospitals for treatment, thus rendering obsolete the medical function of the hekdesh. In some places, as in Bialystok, for example, the hekdesh itself was almost entirely rebuilt as a small hospital for the poor and insane, complete with state-of-the-art equipment.[96] Even hekdeshim that still functioned as poorhouses could apparently be modernized, to judge from a survey of communal welfare in Volhyn province carried out by a liberal newspaper in Kiev. Praising Jewish social care institutions, *Zaria* reported that Jewish shelters for the poor compared very favorably to Christian ones. At a hekdesh in the town of Aleksandriia, for example, indigent people spent 2–3 nights and received food, clothing, medicine, and even monetary aid (up to 20 kopecks per person).[97] As François Guesnet notes, by the last decades of the nineteenth century, despite its continued existence, many contemporaries in Congress Poland viewed the traditional hekdesh as a relic of a past era.[98]

But making a hekdesh over into a hospital meant that the beggars who had previously sheltered in the hekdesh, as bad it was, now had nowhere to turn. And indeed, contemporary reports paint a dire picture of urban poverty, despite the best efforts of urban Jewish philanthropists and reformers. Newspapers reported on mobs of insane people wandering the streets, with packs of Jewish child beggars roaming the streets of Odessa. In Warsaw as elsewhere, there were regular reports of "abandoned, orphaned, and missing [Jewish] children."[99]

In some cities the hekdesh persisted. In 1880s-era Kovno, there was both a modern hospital with beds for six hundred and an old-fashioned hekdesh where a few poor sick Jews lay side by side with beggars.[100] In Vilna, by the late nineteenth-century there was a hekdesh (called *bogadel'nia* in its Russian-language materials) for the elderly that also housed chronically and mentally ill people and served as a hospice for the dying.[101] The institution's 1908 annual report begged for donations, saying,

> We are witnesses every day to terrible, heart-wrenching sights: elderly men and women, blind people and cripples in their dozens throng at the door of the old-age home, and in hot tears they plead to be admitted into the home, but only a few are so fortunate; the remaining 90 percent are abandoned and alone in the world, with no one to care for them and to save them from the shame of hunger and cold.[102]

According to the JCA survey, a similar situation was found in Kremenchug in the central Ukrainian province of Poltava, where in 1897 the Jewish old-age home, home to about 450 elderly Jews, also provided temporary shelter to many more itinerant paupers—about 3,800 annually.[103] Clearly, even if a community could boast that it did not have a hekdesh, institutions for the destitute were still sorely needed.

The Jewish vagrant

The statistic from Kremenchug is also significant for its reference to wandering Jewish beggars, a marginal type we know existed but about whom we know frustratingly little. In his memoir of turn-of-the-century Poland, Yekhiel Trunk described this type as well:

> These were the beggars wandering over the fields and villages of Jewish communities. These were the so-called mendicant Jewish country walkers [*medine-geyer, medine-vanderer*]. . . . In *Fishke the Lame*, S. Y. Abramovitsh [Mendele Moykher-Sforim] describes such itinerant Volhynia paupers. But they existed in Poland too and lived like gypsies. . . . [They] trekked from one village to another in dilapidated cloth-covered wagons drawn by sick, crippled, and half-blind horses. The carts, packed with whole families of the wandering poor, barely made it over the Polish roads. The people slowly lumbered from village to village, stopping over at night with Jewish dairymen and saloon keepers and in barns and on haystacks. They hung about cow-

sheds among the cows and begged a little milk and freshly baked country bread from the village Jews. On Sabbaths, they descended on the wealthier farmers. . . . They waited out the cold months in the poorhouses found near the graveyards of the Jewish towns. . . . As a rule, these poor people were profoundly silent. Their ragged clothes reeked of the fields and of the sun. . . . The hordes also contained grotesque cripples, the lame, the deformed, the blind, and people who were covered with boils.[104]

One of the keys to understanding this passage is Trunk's reference to the vagrants described in Abramovitsh's *Fishke der krumer*, as if that novel were an ethnographic study of the Jews of the Volhynia region of the Ukrainian-Belorussian-Polish borderlands.[105] While it is generally accepted that Abramovitsh had gained familiarity with itinerant Jewish beggars in his teenage years as he wandered through the provinces of the Pale with a beggar by the name of Avreyml, his portrayal of "field beggars" or "Jewish gypsies"— as we have seen in previous chapters—was far from being either journalistic reportage or scientific inquiry.[106] While there is no doubt that *medine-geyer* existed, Trunk's description, like Abramovitsh's, is stylized for the larger purposes of the memoir.[107] His vagrants are "ragged," "laconic," "silent"—but do not harass or harangue people as do their urban cousins. Their clothing "reeks of the fields and the sun," but there is no mention of the stench of poverty or filth. This is a romantic vision of the Jewish beggar, seen through a lens misty with nostalgia.

The impact of Abramovitsh's literary portrayal of Jewish vagrants extended to social science literature. In a survey of Jewish social care in eastern Europe published in the Zionist monthly *Der Jude*, Leo Rosenberg calculated three distinct classes of itinerant poor, each with its own form of accommodation in the average shtetl; the "lower beggar class" lodged in the hekdesh, while the two superior classes—that is, those with an ulterior motive for collecting alms (preachers, emissaries of charitable institution, fire victims, householders who had fallen on hard times, and the like)—were housed the guesthouse run by the local Hakhnasat Orhim society or in private homes.[108] Rosenberg signaled that in recent years, the institution of Jewish vagrancy had threatened to become "a true national plague of degenerate beggars going door to door [*ausartenden Häuserbettelei*]," and local committees had been

FIGURE 5.4. Hekdesh in Shepetovka. Photograph from the 1912–14 ethnographic
expedition organized by S. An-ski. Central Archives for the History of the Jewish
People.

established in many places that, in a manner reminiscent of Jewish philanthropic organizations in western and central Europe, gave wandering beggars
a lump sum that was collected centrally, rather than allow them to go from
door to door. Here, too, the image of *Fishke* was summoned up: "since Mendele portrayed this republic of beggars of East European Jewry [*Ostjüdische
Bettlerrepublik*] in his at once funny and tearful manner," wrote Rosenberg,
"nothing has changed." When it came to beggars, it seemed, the wheels of
history remained frozen in time, and the itinerant beggars endured—exactly as they had been (fictionally) portrayed a quarter-century earlier. No
more authentic description of the *medine-geyer* seems possible. The vagrants
themselves left no records, and almost every description of them defaults to
Abramovitsh's.

It makes sense that the author of an article that referred to a nascent
"national plague of degenerate beggars" was a German Jew, since it was in
central rather than eastern Europe that the beggar loomed large as a threat
to the well-being and respectability of "ordinary" Jews. Between 1800 and

1860, Britain, France, the Netherlands, Germany, and the Austrian Empire all saw the creation of centralized Jewish poor care commissions that, in one way or another, attempted to categorize the destitute as worthy or unworthy. Those who saw the very needy as unproductive and immoral tended, of course, to the latter view. The foreign poor, often itinerant beggars originally from Russia and Poland, were frequently given lowest priority or rejected outright for aid. The Deutsch-Israelitischer Gemeindebund, the first national German-Jewish organization, was established in 1869 in large measure to deal with the problem of Jewish beggars from eastern Europe. At the organization's first meeting, the members resolved that "the highways of Europe will be cleared of the already proverbial Jewish schnorrers."[109] Although "the problem of the vagrant poor" was one of German society as a whole, German Jews tended to see it as a particularly Jewish issue, given the antisemitic tropes that it invoked: the *Ostjude*, the wandering Jew, the Jewish rapscallion playing on honest people's compassion.[110] Jack Wertheimer points out that East European Jews in Germany were often called "Polnische Schnorrer," and that "the very term 'Polish Jew' became synonymous with '*Schnorrer*'"— "cartoonists merely had to sketch a beggar garbed in black to evoke an image of the Eastern Jew."[111] Bourgeois German Jews tended to worry that they would be associated in the eyes of German society with the negative characteristics of the *Betteljuden*; eventually, some would go so far as to argue that the stanching of Jewish migration from across the eastern border would solve the so-called Jewish question altogether.[112] Government officials, too, tended to associate East European Jewish immigrants with beggars, and thus with disease and epidemics.[113]

With the onset of the Russian-Jewish emigration crisis in 1881, Jewish aid organizations in the west resolved not to assist disabled and "unemployable" Jews who sought to leave the Russian Empire, and ultimately the Immigration Act of 1891 barred "paupers and invalids" from entry to the United States.[114] In the years just before World War I, the problem of wandering Jewish beggars in Germany had become so serious in the eyes of some German Jews that it led to the establishment in 1910 of a separate organization, the Zentralstelle fur jüdische Wanderarmenfürsorge (Central Welfare Office for the Jewish Vagrant Poor), under the combined international oversight of several national Jewish defense organizations.[115] An observer attending the 1914 conference of the organization commented in the Yiddish press that while the stated goal was to provide aid to truly needy itinerant beggars and mendicants, the real aim was to combat beggary by the undeserving (*shnoreray*).[116] In that vein, one Polish-Jewish attendee urged German Jews not to assist itinerant beggars from eastern Europe, since they were parasites and had given a bad name to Russian and Polish Jews, who were now often seen as one mass of beggars.[117]

In contrast to German Jews' efforts to combat the challenge posed by itinerant beggars, there was no equivalent effort among Russian or Polish Jews to establish a national organization to combat begging, as they did in the realms of education and health.[118] Despite the putative damage that Jewish vagrants posed to the image of Jewry as a whole, Jewish poverty was endemic in eastern Europe, and a few additional poor Jews wandering from place to place and begging for alms was not particular noteworthy. It was not until 1935 that Vilna, for example, saw the establishment of a "Jewish Committee to Support Poor Folk and Combat Beggary," whose leaflet asked merchants and petty traders, "Do you want to be rid of the beggars who are banging on your doors and disturbing your work? Then become a member of this committee."[119]

Conclusion

What drove Jewish philanthropy in the Russian Empire? Although nineteenth-century European philanthropy tended strongly to social control and moralizing, it is fairly clear that the primary goal of Jewish philanthropic institutions was not the moral improvement of the poor, as was frequently the case with their non-Jewish counterparts.[120] But they *were* extremely concerned with respectability, the more so because Jews were generally assumed to be lacking that trait. Moreover, there was genuine fear that if they did not try to solve the problem of the growing masses of Jewish outcasts in the streets of the empire's cities, the part would be mistaken for the whole—in the eyes of outsiders, marginals would come to represent all Jews.

Then as now, there was no dearth of skepticism about the true motivations of wealthy and acculturated Jews when it came to the philanthropy that many of them supported so passionately. Intellectuals and social reformers often questioned their sincerity and accused them of indifference, especially because Jewish philanthropists—like so many do-gooders—generally condescended to the poor and assumed that they knew what was best for them. Even today, it is not unusual for a scholar to write a sentence such as the following: "Many wealthy Jews increasingly distanced themselves from the poor by putting philanthropic institutions between them and the destitute, and taking the path of assimilation."[121] The first part of that statement holds more than a kernel of truth, as many of us living in the early twenty-first century can affirm: isn't it easier to click a "donate" button on a website or in an email than it would be to ask a homeless person on the street about his or her life and how one might best help? Therefore, who are we to judge the motives of those who claimed a sincere desire to help their destitute and marginalized coreligionists? As for assimilation, while there is no doubt that many Jewish philanthropists were more acculturated than were poor Jews, it was in many cases philanthropy itself that maintained and even strengthened their connection to the Jewish collective and to Jewish identity.

Our survey of Jewish philanthropic attitudes and undertakings has exposed the deep ambivalence about and even fear of marginal people that we have seen running through so many of our sources. Were orphans the future of the Jewish people—or its potential downfall? Were beggars honest workers who had fallen on hard times—or scheming parasites who threatened to stain the good reputation of hard-working Jews with the epithet of "idler"? Much was riding on philanthropy, for it could determine which of the two possible outcomes came about. But the entire enterprise in fact rested on how one understood the origins of these problems. Perhaps marginals were the inevitable products of the miserable conditions in which East European Jewry as a whole found itself, in which case ameliorating individual people's circumstances was only one part of the solution, the other being political emancipation or self-emancipation. Or perhaps it was Jewish society—its neglectful mothers, its abysmal Talmud-Torahs, its abusive artisan masters—that created its monsters. In that case, the only remedy was a thoroughgoing overhaul of Jewry itself.

CHAPTER 6

MADNESS AND THE MAD

From Family Burden to National Affliction

"I pray that my wife be healed from the strong and terrible malady that has afflicted her for nine months, which has taken away her senses and her sense."

—petition to Rabbi Eliyahu Guttmacher
from Binyomin ben Toybe of Dobrzyń

As was true of many societies, East European Jews struggled to make sense of people who did not fit into conventional categories of behavior, livelihood, and family structure. This chapter explores the world of mentally ill and developmentally disabled people in two distinct socio-geographic contexts: the town and the city. We uncover the former through requests that family members sent to an illustrious rabbi for healing and medical advice. These petitions reveal a realm of pain, humiliation, uncertainty, and doubt, the stuff of matters so private and shameful that even now, almost a century and a half later, one archivist has qualms about allowing them to be digitized because of the dishonor that they might, it is argued, inflict on the descendants of their authors. With few exceptions, it was also the shtetl that was home to the so-called town fool, apparently a ubiquitous real-life character found in many towns and even some cities who was either a harmless "idiot" (i.e., developmentally disabled?) or a "madman" (i.e., mentally ill?). Both a figure of fun and an object of compassion, and always somehow integrated into the shtetl community and daily life, at first blush the town fool seems to be life imitating art. Could the village idiot of conversational cliché have been a real person? Evidence suggests that the answer is yes—though who precisely the town fool or local madman or madwoman was, and what a contemporary diagnosis of his or her condition might be, is difficult to ascertain. Fiction like I. L. Peretz's compelling portrait of a madman in "The Mad Talmudist" perhaps offers more insight into the question than do the extant journalistic or memoiristic accounts.

Cities were the sites of insane asylums, which resolved the challenge presented by cognitive disorders by removing the psychologically deviant from mainstream society to a place where they could receive what was deemed appropriate treatment. Scientific experts and social activists proclaimed that the problem that the mentally ill posed for East European Jewish society existed on the plane not just of the family or the individual town or city but of the nation—and that it posed an imminent threat to East European Jewry as a whole because of that group's putative predisposition to neurosis, psychosis, and other kinds of mental illness. Thus madness was not just a concern of individual families but a national threat.

Madmen and madwomen

In the eighteenth century, the Russian state began to segregate the mentally ill in madhouses. Psychiatric care advanced in the nineteenth century, providing a medical model of mental illness. "In the nineteenth century the rise of specialized medical practitioners, and specialized medical vocabulary, caused holy fools and lunatics to be 'recategorized' as pathological," Angela Brintlinger and Ilya Vinitsky observe.[1] Nonetheless, eastern European societies generally lagged behind their western counterparts when it came to institutionalizing the mentally ill. In 1860, the Russian Empire had forty-three madhouses, with a total population of just over 2,000. By contrast, at the end of the tsarist period, there were 160 insane asylums housing 42,489 inmates.[2]

Other than occasionally housing the mad in the hekdesh, Jews in eastern Europe did not move to begin segregating the psychologically disturbed until the late nineteenth century. And in all probability, the vast majority of mentally ill Jews were never institutionalized anywhere, whether in the shtetl hekdesh or the psychiatric wards that were eventually established at big Jewish hospitals in Warsaw and other cities. With few exceptions, East European Jews were generally unwilling to give their sick over to the care of general charitable medical and psychiatric institutions, which were typically Christian. Most of the evidence at our disposal barely mentions either of these kinds of institution, assuming the family's central role in caring for the mentally ill.

Mental illness among East European Jews:
the evidence of the Guttmacher *kvitlekh*

Did the understanding of mental illness among ordinary Jews in eastern Europe begin to change with the rise of psychiatry across nineteenth-century Europe and the more widespread introduction of insane asylums in the mid-century Great Reform era? A remarkable source base provides tremendous insight into this shift, and more generally into how Jews across eastern Europe viewed and experienced the impact of mental illness. These are the Guttmacher kvitlekh, a collection of about six thousand hand-written petitions submitted in person or sent to the "wonderworker" rabbi and kabbalist Eliyahu Guttmacher of Grätz (today, Grodzisk Wielkopolski), in Prussian Poland, in the 1860s and 1870s.[3] The collection was discovered in the 1930s and divided between the YIVO Institute, a research center for East European Jewish studies in Vilna, and the Hebrew University in Jerusalem; during World War II, the Vilna collection was looted by the Nazis and subsequently restored to YIVO by the U.S. Army.[4] The authors of the petitions ask Guttmacher for blessings, advice, and remedies and amulets for a wide variety of problems: economic difficulties, marital issues, infertility, sexual dysfunction, and illnesses and diseases of all kinds—including mental illness and insanity.[5] It is worth noting that, in the case of petitions that were sent by mail or emissary, almost none of Guttmacher's written replies have survived; for the most part, we have only one side of this remarkable correspondence.

Now, we are speaking of course of the modern era, not the sixteenth or seventeenth centuries. The science of psychiatry had arrived in Russia in the early nineteenth century, so understanding insanity as an illness was not an altogether novel idea in the years when the kvitlekh were composed, and their authors were far from disengaged from the modern world and the advances of modern medicine.[6] The Guttmacher corpus paints a picture of a traditional society that was on the cusp of change: Jews living in the rhythm of time-honored observance and piety, yet aware of a modern world—including advances in medicine and psychiatry—and sometimes even engaged with it and ready to take advantage of its blessings. Many, however, were still deeply suspicious of that world, and not necessarily ready to welcome it in.[7]

The fact that most of the authors of the petitions that we shall examine described abnormal states of consciousness as illness betrays the influence of modernity; many of the references to madness or mental illness refer to confusion of mind (*bilbul ha-da'at* or *bilbul ha-sekhel*), which seem to imply that observers understood that something was amiss in the mind of the sufferer. Some were even willing to take a chance with modern medicine, and Guttmacher himself was known for his quasi-medical knowledge, including homeopathic remedies. But ultimately they were writing to him because of his reputation as a holy man, a kabbalist, a worthy intercessor for the unworthy. Sometimes they wrote to ask Guttmacher for *segulot* (remedies, charms, and amulets, several of which are extant in the collections); sometimes they asked him if they should consult modern doctors; and a few kvitlekh even mention unspecified psychiatric treatments by doctors at hospitals. But most petitioners wrote to Guttmacher because they had more faith in him than in whatever modern science and medicine had to offer.

Language and perceptions of mental illness

Part of the challenge in using these documents to chart the history of madness among East European Jews is that they do not speak in the psychiatric language that we are familiar with today. The vast majority of the petitions were written in Hebrew of wildly varying literary quality; a much smaller number are in Yiddish. These documents use Hebrew or sometimes German terms to describe symptoms and illnesses that were undoubtedly articulated orally in Yiddish, since most of the petitions were likely dictated to a scribe/translator hired for the task. So, for example, when a mother writes that her son began suffering from epilepsy (*holi nikhpah*), and that he then became lame in one leg, an idiot or madman (*shoteh*), and rebellious (*sorer u-moreh*)—all terms derived from biblical and rabbinic texts—what are we to make of her description?[8] Or when a father described his daughter using the phrase *nitbalbelah be-sikhlah*—she became confused of mind—what does this mean? And what exactly is *hasar da'at*, literally, "lacking in sense"?[9] Normally it would refer to a madman or a fool, but in this petition the daughter is described as having been *haserat da'at* for some years, but is now healthy again, or at least on the mend.

While our first instinct may be to translate these documents into twenty-first-century psychiatric terminology, that may not be a fruitful path. Rather, we must try to understand what is being described on its own terms. In other words, how did those people, at that time, perceive these different and often frightening states of consciousness?[10]

This is especially true for those petitions that use phrases redolent of traditional concepts of madness. For example, Moshe Zindl ben Miryam wrote the following about his daughter Bluma, who suffered from insomnia accompanied by weeping and certain symptoms reminiscent of obsessive-compulsive disorder such as clapping her hands together until her fingers bled: "an evil spirit has emerged within her" (*alah bah ruah ra'ah*).[11] This phrase has a history of being used to refer to the soul of a deceased sinner who possesses someone in order to achieve expiation for his sin (the sinner in question was almost always male), also known as a *dybbuk*.[12] Another petition makes even clearer the sense of *ruah ra'ah* as an evil spirit; this letter, from a couple in Opoczno, asked for Guttmacher to pray for their son Mendel Yankev: "Sometimes he is like a regular person [*ke-ehad ha-adam*] and other times an evil spirit enters into him and then he cannot bless, pray, or don *tefillin* [prayer boxes for the head and arm]."[13]

In a few cases the kvitlekh allow us to hear the voices of the afflicted persons themselves. Ester Malke bas Feyge, who had been ill for three years, reported that sometimes her heart gave her pain, sometimes the rest of her organs, including her nose, and sometimes she felt that something was moving inside of her and she would curse it to leave her alone. Then, continued the kvitl writer, Ester Malke would say that because of the pain, she would say yes (i.e., to the thing inside of her). The doctors had diagnosed her with nervous illness ("weakness of the nerves"), perhaps not that surprising when we learn that after her daughter's death she had taken in her eight grandchildren and was also raising her niece's five children.[14]

One clear sign of the lasting power of medieval medicinal theories was the widespread use in the kvitlekh of the term *marah shehorah* (*mare-shkhoyre*)—often rendered today as "depression," but literally translated as "melancholy" (from Greek, *melan chole*, or black bile—hence the Hebrew/

Yiddish term)—a clear reference to the medieval theory of the humors. Of
course, it is impossible to know the exact connotation that the writers of the
kvitlekh had in mind when they used the phrase. On the other hand, melancholy had wide currency in the nineteenth century as a medico-scientific
diagnosis of a specific kind of mental illness, and a popular Hebrew-language
medical handbook (which was actually a translation of a late-eighteenth century German publication) listed it—translated as *marah shehorah*—as one of
five types of mental disturbance.[15]

The fact that some kvitlekh writers referred to evil spirits while others
cast the afflictions in medical terms is evidence of a contemporaneous shift
mapped by the Guttmacher corpus. What Foucault writes of the change that
the Classical Age wrought in the disposition of madness is applicable, mutatis mutandi, to this historical context: "The animal in man no longer has any
value as the sign of a Beyond; it has become his madness, without relation to
anything but itself: his madness in the state of nature."[16]

Guttmacher at the nexus of traditional healing and modern medicine

Since Guttmacher was known not only as a wonderworking rabbi, a holy
man, and a kabbalist, but also as a medical expert, he may have unwittingly
made modern medicine more accessible and, in some way, permissible for
many of the petitioners. After all, the same Hebrew term—*segulah*, "remedy"—was used to refer to both his herbal pharmacopeia and amulets. Some
petitioners made clear that they had already consulted doctors; however, but
were writing to Guttmacher because medical advice and treatment had not
been effective, or had not produced the results they were hoping for. Others
asked the rabbi if they should consult modern doctors. Several even mention unspecified psychiatric treatments by doctors at hospitals. A number of
petitioners clearly had more faith in Guttmacher than in whatever modern
science and medicine had to offer. One writer from Berlin reported that a
sick man who had taken an herbal remedy prescribed by Guttmacher was
feeling better, and the rabbi had even come to him in a dream. But, the author continued, "in my opinion the prayer of the great Rabbi is better [than]
human medicine because God harkens to the prayers of holy men."[17] We recall that the person writing on behalf of Ester Malke bas Feyge reported that

"the doctors" had diagnosed the woman with nervous illness, but apparently had not been able to help her.

But others displayed more ambivalence about traditional approaches, mingled with tentative openness to modern medicine. Yankev Shloyme ha-Cohen ben Golde from Działoszyn (Zolshin) wrote a series of petitions about his daughter, Riva Reyzl, stricken with madness. His first appeal was answered with an amulet that, as he wrote in a subsequent note, had not helped. In another correspondence, he asked whether the rabbi thought that he should travel to his court or consult with the doctors in Warsaw, Breslau, or Berlin. Despite his lack of means, wrote Yankev Shloyme, "if you command it, I will carry out your word with all my means and strength." A last petition referred to the hospital in Warsaw—probably the Jewish hospital, which had a psychiatric ward.

Yankev Shloyme was engaged in a complex dance between tradition and modernity. If Guttmacher's kabbalistic amulet did not work, why did he not just give up and find a way to consult with psychiatric experts in a major city? Breslau, about a hundred miles away, offered one of the largest Jewish hospitals in Germany. But he persisted in his communication with Guttmacher, in the process voicing some of his own questions about the rabbi's traditional approach to the crisis he was experiencing. Remarkably, Yankev Shloyme had the temerity to ask Guttmacher himself whether, if he was going to make a journey that would require a considerable investment on his part, he should travel to Guttmacher's court or to a doctor. Was this tantamount to challenging the rabbi to confirm that his mystical remedies would, eventually, heal Riva Reyzl (Guttmacher apparently had no herbal remedies for madness)? Or—we recall his words, "If you command it . . . "—was he suggesting that a trip to the doctor would have an essentially religious nature because it would have been ordered by the holy rabbi himself? On the other hand, if Guttmacher were to advise him that he should head for Breslau or Warsaw instead of Grätz, home to the rabbi's court, then presumably Guttmacher himself would be communicating something about the ultimate victory of modernity over traditional piety.

Other petitioners who had already sought out modern methods of healing may have written to Guttmacher in frustration that those techniques were proving unsuccessful. A petitioner from Dobrzyń (Dobrin) asked for healing for his wife "from the strong and terrible malady that has afflicted her for nine months which has taken away her senses and her sense"; among other symptoms were hallucinations ("visions") in which she saw angels.[18] In an earlier era, such visions might have been taken as evidence of a connection to the supernatural, or at least possession of some kind. No longer. At the time he wrote, she was already being treated in the psychiatric wing of the Warsaw Jewish hospital. Shmuel Zalmen ben Rokhel Leah of Warsaw, wrote a relative, had already been in the insane asylum for nine years "and he is still insane, and there is no cure for him." At one point he had been released when it seemed that he was doing better, but for reasons that are unclear from the text of the petition, he was compelled to return to the asylum.[19] And the stepfather of the young woman in Dobrzyń suffering from depression told Guttmacher that he had "consulted several expert doctors about her, and they prescribed medicine that did not work."[20]

These documents suggest that there was considerable ambivalence among traditional Jews about modern medicine. Many were willing make use of it, but felt compelled to consult a rabbi such as Guttmacher first; others sought medical treatment first and only later asked Guttmacher whether it was worth continuing that treatment. And some Jews were probably just hedging their bets: it certainly couldn't hurt to try everything in the hope that *something* might work.

This ambivalence is corroborated by two ethnographic studies on the Jews of the Russia Empire carried out in the 1860s (i.e., more or less contemporaneous with the kvitlekh). Both studies found that quite a few diseases and disorders, including insanity and epilepsy, were still commonly ascribed by Jews to evil spirits, and the recourse was usually to the local Tatar healer, a *ba'al shem*, or a Hasidic tsaddik.[21] Moisei Berlin, a Russian-Jewish historian and ethnographer active in the mid-nineteenth century, described "psychic or nervous diseases" among Jews as including insanity or madness (*sumassh-estviia*), epilepsy, fits (*spazmy*), and children's convulsions.[22] (This list gives us a sense of what "experts" of the day might have considered to be psychiatric conditions.) Jews continued to go to ba'alei shem, shamanistic folk healers who employed kabbalistic amulets, magical remedies, and folk medicine to seek treatment for madness and other mental illnesses, and in this they did not differ significantly from their Christian neighbors, Berlin claimed.[23] Folk medicine called for bringing the mentally ill patient to a healer, often a Tatar, sometimes a magician or a ba'al shem (this last was of course specific to Jewish society), who would variously smoke herbs, cast spells, draw magic circles, and the like to heal the patient. Berlin hinted that rabbis were usually opposed to these folk healers, but if they were successful in treating patients, the rabbis were unable to limit their influence. An ethnographic expedition in the Russian Empire's southwest provinces in the 1860s found that while Jews were more likely than their neighbors to consult a doctor and/or a pharmacist, this was true "especially in cases of adult illnesses." Children, on the other hand, were protected from sickness with charms and amulets, and if young ones fell ill, these were also used to treat them. They might also be brought to the local *babka*, or elderly woman folk healer.[24] Indeed, in one kvitl Shmuel ben Ester Khaye wrote that, in the case of his daughter Sheyna Rivka's insanity, he had consulted not only *tsadikei ha-dor* (the great rabbis of the generation) but also *mekhashfim*—clearly a reference to witch doctors or folk healers of some kind.[25]

In his memoir *Profiles of a Lost World*, Hirsz Abramowicz notes that recourse to Tatar healers was still common in Lithuania at the turn of the twentieth century. Jews would take their mentally ill family members to towns with Tatar populations such as Butrymantsy (Yid., Butrimants; Pol., Butrymańce; Lith., Butrimonys), where, "for a small fee, the patient would be left in the home of some poor folks, who were responsible for feeding the patient and taking him to the Tatars for the 'cure.'"[26]

Madness and gender

One striking pattern that emerges from the kvitlekh relating to mental illness or insanity among children is the gendered nature of the conditions. The representative sample is small, but the pattern is significant. Out of twelve cases of children suffering from mental illness—seven girls and five boys—six of the girls are described as either suffering from "bilbul ha-sekhel" (some sort of insanity) or from a kind of depression or mania, including self-harming.[27] Of the five boys, on the other hand, three of them are described as *shoteh* or *mehusar sekhel* ("idiots" or "imbeciles"). Others were said to suffer from epilepsy. This pattern conforms to the contemporary belief that women

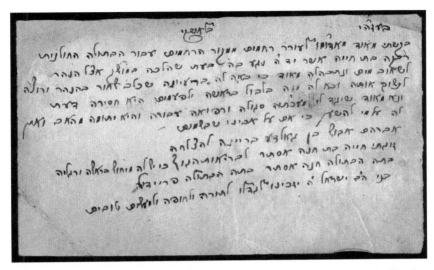

FIGURE 6.1. Petition from Avraham Abush ben Golde of Blaszki to Rabbi Eliyahu
Guttmacher, 1870s. Archives of the YIVO Institute for Jewish Research, New York.
Source: YIVO Archive RG 27, box 2, folder 1.

and girls were more susceptible to certain kinds of mental illness (hysteria,
for example) than were men.

An interesting and poignant case is that of Rivke bas Khaye, whose
stepfather reported to Guttmacher that she had gone "down to the river on
Saturday night to draw water and took great fright, for she hallucinated [ba'
ah lah be-ra'ayonah] that there was a black dog in the river that wanted to bite
her, and because of this she became confused of mind, and sometimes she is
insane [haserah da'at]."[28]

It is also noteworthy that two of the girls suffering from insanity were
having trouble menstruating. Ester Khaye Bluma of Zakroczym, aged
sixteen, had been ill—"like one who is mad"—for over three years, and
her father wrote that "many say that this was caused because she never
began to have her period."[29] Ele, stepdaughter of Oyzer ben Toybe of Do-
brzyn, who apparently had a speech defect (she was described as "heavy
of speech and tongue"), suffered from such melancholy that she had lost
her period. Furthermore, "all her limbs are heavy," and she engaged in

self-harming behaviors—"she always scratches the flesh . . . of her arms and legs."[30]

Some of the kvitlekh note that a young woman suffering from insanity was soon to be married or had recently wed. As Rachel Elior has argued, one way for young women to express their opposition to arranged marriages within a patriarchal society was to succumb to illness, "a step that . . . used the power of physical and mental weakness to gain a degree of distance and liberation from the expected order."[31] Elior focuses specifically on the phenomenon of the dybbuk, but her larger argument holds true for the kind of mental or emotional disturbance that Bluma and young women like her were suffering. "In the absence of any other way to resist the forces of the hegemonic power structure, the dybbuk allowed for the expression of such resistance, represented by the loss of control over one's mind and body," Elior writes. It is significant that the authors of the kvitlekh did not identify such loss of control as caused by a dybbuk; as we noted in chapter 1, the decoupling of madness and spirit possession began in the late eighteenth century and was more or less complete by the 1870s, when the kvitlekh were written (though Yoram Bilu documents a few eastern European cases in the nineteenth century, many of them apparently based on Hasidic tales).[32]

Bluma, who clapped her hands until they bled, was engaged to be married, and her father, Moshe Zindl, feared that her fiancé would tear up the *tnoim* (terms of engagement) if he discovered her madness. "Please pray for her," he wrote, "that God may return her to her former strength so that she may marry."[33] A more dramatic case was that of Rekhil bas Malye Leah, a thirty-year-old woman who had only recently married—three months earlier, to be precise. Soon after the wedding, while still a virgin, she had become insane.[34] Again, there is no mention of a possessing spirit, but the proximity to a potentially anxiety-producing marriage is very clear. The fact that this bride was so old (in relative terms) helps explain why she might have suffered such crippling anxiety—if that is what we are dealing with here—before the marriage was consummated.

Economic dependence, whether on the family or on the community, was a consistent hallmark of social marginality. Disability and chronic illness were often structurally linked to destitution and social marginality, since those who could not work depended for their survival on their families—provided those families were in a position to support them for decades on end—or the Jewish community. Also, sickness and disability were frequently impediments to marriage, which in and of itself was a necessary foundation for economic survival, since both husbands and wives tended to contribute to the family income.[35] Especially relevant is the fact that Jewish law banned insane people from marrying, because marriage was a legal contract that required conscious consent and the insane were not responsible for their actions.[36]

These conditions help to explain the anxiety that many of the petitioners expressed about their children's future. Nosen ben Ester and his wife Khayke bas Gutke of Godlewo asked Guttmacher to pray for a good match for their only daughter, Sore Rivke, who for several years had not been in her right mind. They pleaded, "May the honorable *admor* [Hebrew acronym for "our master, our teacher, and our rabbi"] take pity on her."[37] And Elyakim Getsil ben Rivke of Ozorków wrote of his daughter Rivke Glikel, who seems to have suffered from a developmental or intellectual disability caused by a childhood illness:

> May God help us, for from the time that she fell ill when she was a child she has never returned to the level of intelligence that would befit her age [*le-da'atah ha-re'uyah lefi shenoteha*], and I suffer a great deal over her, because many people wonder why I do not provide a husband for her, but I know that her intelligence is lower than it would rightfully be for one of her age [*da'atah katsrah lefi shenoteha*].[38]

In this case, the father was not even trying to make a match: barring a miracle, marriage was now out of the question, a clear sign of Rivke Glikel's permanently marginal status in the Jewish community. We don't know what became of Rivke Glikel, but given her father's obvious concern, we may assume that she remained in her parents' home for most of her adult life. Never fully integrated into the current of Jewish life, she would probably also not have been completely segregated from it, as would have been the case had she been institutionalized. In all likelihood, such cases of family concern and care made up the majority of the instances of mental illness or developmental disability in Jewish society.[39]

As we might expect, the parents of afflicted sons hoped that they would recover and be able to observe the commandments and study Torah, as traditional Jewish society expected of them. Mikhoel Getsl ben Dvoyre and Rivke bas Khaye Sore of Brześć Kujawski (Brisk de-kuya) asked Guttmacher to pray for healing for their eldest son that he might come to his right mind in order "to study in understanding and with diligence." Similarly, Shlomo Avraham ben Tsharne of Praga asked that God help his twelve-year-old son Shimen Mordekhai to be able to pray, which he could not do because he was blind in one eye, had a very serious speech impediment, and had a very poor memory. Indeed, his *melamed* had remarked that no sooner did he teach something to Shimen that the boy forgot it.[40] This petition likely conveys the pain and concern felt by many parents of developmentally disabled sons as the latter approached Jewish adulthood.

Caring for the insane

The heavy financial and emotional burden that caring for a mentally ill relative placed on a family will come as no surprise to those of us familiar with such cases in our own day and age. The kvitlekh suggest the kind of burden that a mentally ill or disabled child placed on his or her parents, not only emotionally but also financially and in other ways. The search for a cure took much time and energy. Shmuel, the father of sixteen-year-old Ester Khaye Bluma, who had never menstruated and was mentally confused, had sought help for her from tsaddikim, folk healers, and doctors, but nothing had helped, and he had lost much of his property in the process, he noted. In fact, he had had to turn his business over (i.e., sell?) to a Christian, presumably in order to get the money that he needed to pay for expensive journeys and cures.

In a petition that seems to have been handed to Guttmacher in person (perhaps before the petitioner went in for a personal audience with the rabbi), Shraga Fayvl ben Gitl ha-Levi, a storekeeper in Żuromin, told the rabbi about his son Tsvi Chaim ben Hinde.[41] The boy was handicapped (*ba'al mum*) and an idiot (*mehusar sekhel*), and had to be fed by others. To make things worse, the author's second wife—whom he had married only two months earlier—was "unable to bear the heavy burden" of caring for Tsvi Chaim, and the boy's grandmother (apparently freshly widowed, though the exact circumstance is unclear) therefore had to take him in and care for him.

Shraga Fayvl, the author of the petition, was having difficulty with his livelihood and very high rent, and therefore was considering moving to another
town. This was clearly a difficult decision to make, given that he would be
leaving behind his own mother and disabled son, who might well need financial assistance from him in order to get by. No wonder that Shraga Fayvl
traveled the two hundred miles from Zhuromin to Grätz "to hear the holy
advice of the admor." The case also provides evidence of alternatives to institutionalization: if the immediate family could not care for the child, another
relative might be willing to take him or her in. But at what cost?

If family members could not—or would not—care for a person with
mental illness, an even more difficult life awaited. We have already seen the
dreadful conditions of many hekdeshim. One terse petition to Guttmacher
asks the rabbi to bless "Taybe Leah bas Sore Sheyndil for healing, for she has
been mad for six years now in the hekdesh in her town."[42] No more information is provided, though we know from other sources that it was usually
a source of great shame to have a family member taken into the hekdesh.
("Other people's fool is a joke, but one's own fool is an embarrassment" [*A
fremder nar iz a gelekhter, an eygener iz a shand*], a Yiddish commonplace ran;
"A fool brings constant woe" [*Mit a nar, iz an eybiger tsar*], another bromide
complained, while a third lamented: "A fool is an evil decree from heaven" [*A
nar iz a gzar*].)[43]

For some families, especially prosperous ones, institutionalization was a
possibility, but before the establishment of Jewish insane asylums, the family
had to be willing to give the care of their loved one over to a state or even
a Christian institution. There was a tradition of rabbinic legal authorities
deeming insanity to be a life-threatening condition, and therefore permit-
ting measures that would otherwise be considered potentially dangerous to
traditional Jewish observance.[44] Such was the case with a woman who was
brought to the mental illness ward of the Infant Jesus Hospital in Warsaw
in the late 1880s, as a writer recounted in the pages of the Hebrew newspaper *Ha-yom*.[45] In some cities, it was apparently fairly common for family
members to bring loved ones to the municipal hospital; in 1871, for example,
about half of the Jewish patients committed to the Odessa City Hospital
(like most Jewish hospitals in the Russian Empire, the city's Jewish Hospital lacked a psychiatric clinic) were brought in by spouses, siblings, or other

family members, while seven were brought in by the police.[46] Fourteen of the thirty-two committed were listed as teachers, an astounding statistic; whether this was an anomaly for this particular year or part of a larger pattern will have to be ascertained by further research.

What of those who could not afford to pay for hospital treatment? A series of petitions dating to the turn of the twentieth century unearthed in the former Soviet archives by ChaeRan Freeze show that individuals could request that the authorities require the institutionalization of a mentally ill individual—at no cost to themselves—if circumstances demanded that the person be treated. Thus, Mordukh [Mordecai] Baskin, a relative of Meer Ginzburg, requested in 1902 that the governor of Vil'na province order that Ginzburg be "admitted for treatment in the section for the mentally ill at the [Vil'na] Jewish Hospital," because when Baskin had brought Ginzburg to the hospital for evaluation without such an order, the hospital authorities told him that he would have to pay for his relative's care.[47]

A petition submitted by Enta Pushner of Vilna on April 5, 1895, requesting that her mother, Dvoira Zlotoiabko, be hospitalized for mental illness provides some insight into the challenges that family members of a mentally ill person could face. Pushner, who was illiterate, dictated the following:

> My mother, Dvoira Zlotoiabko, has gone mad. She breaks everything, hits, causes arguments, so that it is impossible to keep her in the apartment where I have my own small children who are scared to death. I keep my mother in a cold storeroom in my house where she could catch some other dangerous disease. She will not accept my request to place her in the section [of a hospital] for the mentally ill.[48]

The petition further revealed that Pushner kept Zlotoiabko locked up because she "wanders about town and conducts herself indecently, provoking street urchins to throw rocks at her." Several weeks later, Pushner submitted another petition, complaining that for some unknown reason her mother had not been admitted to a hospital, and that the situation was now deteriorating, with Zlotoiabko having "severely beat[en] up two [people]" and now grabbing "a knife in her hand with the intention of stabbing everyone."[49] Zlotoiabko was apparently admitted to the Jewish Hospital some time afterwards, for the hospital authorities reported to the provincial authorities on

July 23 that she had died on May 29 of pneumonia—perhaps brought on by the difficult conditions in which she had been housed?[50]

In some cases, as another petition reveals, townspeople might request that the authorities take action against a mentally ill person who was perceived as posing a threat to public safety. In 1902, a group of Oshmiany residents asked the police to hospitalize "the violent and insane Rivka Arliuk," who "beats passers-by and neighbors, throws stones at people, and tries to set fire to the house where she lives. She has bitten several people."[51] After her admittance to the Vilna Jewish Hospital, she was described as being in "an excited mental state," chatty and lively, though sometimes belligerent. The diagnosis was mania.[52]

Town fools

As we have seen, rabbinic law excluded the *shoteh* from full participation in the religious Jewish community because of his inability to partake of Jewish learning and ritual with full cognition and right intent. Paradoxically, however, he was also perceived as being capable of serving as a conduit for God's word; a rabbinic adage had it that with the destruction of the Temple, "prophecy had been taken from prophets and given to young children [*tinokot*] and fools [*shotim*]."[53] Judith Abrams remarks that "*shotim* can function as God's mouthpiece because they are unaware of the consequences of their words and are thus trustworthy; they have no stake in their utterances."[54] In one of the hagiographical tales about the Ba'al Shem Tov, for example, a madwoman possessed by a spirit tells every person "his sins and his virtues" (*to'avotav ve-tovotav*).[55] This image of the madman or fool found its continuation in Jewish folklore in the motif of the fool who is actually a wise man, a theme with parallels in Russian and many other cultures. In Jewish folklore, as S. An-ski noted, the end of the story always has him teaching great insights from Torah.[56]

Yaffa Eliach has argued that the insane had particular and unique insight into social and communal life because they stood both inside and outside of the bounds of normal existence. The insane of the shtetl were an integral part of town life, each of them reflecting the particular segment of Jewish society where he or she had originated, a reflection distorted, however, by madness, as in a funhouse mirror. And yet, just as a funhouse mirror often shows us, by bending and stretching our features, aspects of ourselves that we know to be true but would rather not ponder, "it was understood that in their craziness was skewed lucidity; thus many of their sayings were held up as pearls of wisdom." This was to some extent true, Eliach maintains, in the city as well.[57]

There is some evidence that the urban Jewish intelligentsia—if not the ordinary folk who were the neighbors of the shtetl's insane—began at the turn of the twentieth century to see mad people as the modern equivalent of the holy fool who possessed hidden wisdom, inner vision, even the power of prophecy. Many anecdotes about the mad have them using their prophetic faculty to call their coreligionists to account for their sins. In the 1890s, the Yiddish author and critic Kalman Marmor recalled, Vilna's sole town fool (*shtot-meshugener*) would give sermons on the Sabbath in the courtyard of the Great Synagogue enumerating the sins of the Jewish elite, mocking the large crowd that gathered to hear him, or making fun of the customs of putatively "sane" people.[58] That same courtyard played host to madmen and madwomen in the interwar period; one of them was a certain "Rabbi" Isserson who would preach in front of the Great Synagogue on the eve of festivals, attack storekeepers who traded on the Sabbath, and hurl Polish curses at Polish students he encountered in the street.[59] One madman in Lwów claimed to be the messiah, the Yiddish daily *Haynt* reported: "He speaks only Hebrew, recites Psalms, and shouts that Jews are sinful. On his head he wears a paper crown with a Star of David and asks for alms."[60] Just how fine the line was between libel and madness is illustrated by Moshe Engelshtern, one of the Vilna "characters" described by Israel Klausner in his magnum opus about that city's Jewish community, who constantly published leaflets and brochures condemning and slandering the communal leadership. "Some of his actions bordered on the insane," Klausner maintains.[61]

The post–World War II testimony of *yizker-bikher* (more about which in chapter 7) reveals a different kind of contrary madman who went against the norms of his community: the *apikoyres* (heretic). In Bobruisk, in Soviet Belorussia, Meir Kalte Vaser, so called because he sold mugs of water from a barrel, experienced periodic fits when he would tear Torah scrolls and pour salt on mezuzot.[62] In Slutsk, about seventy miles west of Bobruisk, Yudel, the town fool, ate pork in public because he claimed that Moses had given him permission to do so; seen praying to a crucifix on the street, Crazy Dovid, another fool, said that perhaps the old man was not listening, so he would try praying to the young man.[63]

More often, however, town fools were usually seen not as prophets but as figures of fun and sources of entertainment. Yosele, the town idiot of Skałat in southwestern Poland, was often chased by the children of the town, who threw stones at him and called him names.[64] In the Polish town of Radomsko (Yid., Radomsk), Leybele the Fool, an androgynous man with a high-pitched voice who could not grow a beard, was chased by youngsters, who would scream, "Leybele the Fool, Leybele the Maiden [*Leybele moyd*], you want a bride?"[65] In the Galician town of Leżajsk (Yid., Lizhensk), Mottele the town fool, a rag-clad orphan who slept in the House of Study and wandered aimlessly around the town, was "a source of constant amusement" for the local children, who teased him and played tricks on him.[66] The description of Mottele ("his head lolled like a large ox, his mouth uttering moans of terror interspersed with the smile of a lunatic; he paid no attention to our mocking") suggests that he was severely developmentally disabled. In other cases, as with Leybele, the "fool" was not actually intellectually disabled but just peculiar or different in some way. (It is noteworthy, however, that the Lizhensk memorial volume also relates that among the various people in the town who cared for Mottele was one Reb Yossel, a teacher, who not only looked after the youth in various ways but also provided him with a bar mitzvah.)

In some cases—and these descriptions ring true for own day and age as well—the "crazy" people were invisible to the townspeople. As the Będzin (Yid., Bendin) yizkor book puts it, "Bendin simply did not have the time to pay attention to the unfortunates—they just dragged themselves around the streets, without a roof over their heads. They spent the night in the 'hekdesh,' in the anteroom of the study house, or in a corner of a stairwell." The same volume tells the story of Crazy Sore, a local madwoman who, it was said, had gone mad after the death of her daughter; Sore met a tragic end during a severely cold winter in 1928, when one morning she was found to have frozen to death on the street during the night.[67]

"A corpse! That's me, yes, yes! . . . And yet: who am I?"

"The Mad Talmudist" (*Der meshugener batlen*) is one of three stories in I. L. Peretz's first book, *Bakante bilder* ("Familiar Scenes") (1890). In the story, Peretz recreates the inner monologue of a classic marginal figure: orphan,

FIGURE 6.2. Postcard studio portrait of a *shtot meshugener* (town fool) with a Russian-language newspaper (Vilna, before World War I). Archives of the YIVO Institute for Jewish Research, New York.

madman, *batlen* (Talmud-recluse), cipher/enigma. Berel queries himself over and over again about his very identity: "Who am I?" What does his name actually represent? As he puts it, what is the store under the sign? How does the signifier relate to the signified?

> In Tzachnovka everyone knows who Berel is; but in America? Suppose someone in America were suddenly to say, "Berel Chantsia's." Would anyone know he meant me? Here it's different. They smile, shake their heads, make wry faces. "A familiar creature [*a bakante zakh*], this Berel."[68]

Only in the shtetl is there something to attach the name to, but that something is provided by other people. Berel is a known quantity, but only to others, not to himself, and only in terms of the labels that others provide; and even then not necessarily as a human being, but as a creature or thing—*a bakante zakh*, as the townspeople say knowingly, part affectionately, part condescendingly. Berel is known variously as a *batlen* (idler, Talmud-recluse); a madman; an enigma ("*kh'veys vos*"—"who knows?"); an orphan; and someone named after his uncle.

Once this marginal figure leaves the shtetl for the anonymous city, he loses his unique, externally imposed identity as the mad, orphaned Berel Chantsia's. "America" stands in here for any place that is not Tzachnovka, any place where everyone does not know everyone else. Presumably, Berel would be nameless there, one madman among many, one orphan among many, as he says a bit later: "But there are many *batlonim*, madmen, and orphans in the world, perhaps of such men as myself—somewhat fewer; but there are, maybe in another city, maybe in America. But are they all alike? No, God forbid, each is different."[69] When Berel considers the possibility that there are many people like him elsewhere in the world, he immediately wonders what distinguishes them from one another; perhaps they are all alike. Perhaps no one will recognize him for who he is as a unique person. And even the realization that they are, in fact, distinctive human beings ("No, God forbid, each is different") does not entirely comfort him, because it leads him back to his original problem: "In that case, who the devil am I?"[70]

Berel questions his own identity unceasingly, comparing himself to others in Tzachnovka, even other former *batlonim*, who have stable, fixed identities. "They're human beings. I too want to be a human being!"[71] The instability of his identity applies to gender as well: "I'm a man . . . all human creatures that aren't female are men. But they're not all Berel Chantsia's, are they?"[72] He knows he's not female, so he must be male. But is even that true? Even it can, in Berel's unstable mind, be called into question. Another sign of this insecurity is his use of the image of a little dove (*taybele*), which is also a Yiddish female name, to describe himself: "Berel Chantsia's is a little dove, a little bird."[73]

Towards the end of the story, Berel looks at himself in the mirror and sees "a corpse, an utter corpse." "A corpse! That's me, yes, yes! That's Berel the batlen, Berel the orphan, Berel the madman! That's it! And yet: who am I?"[74] His realization that he is dead—that he does not really exist—is transformative, because it finally allows him to claim an identity that is truly his own. And perhaps not only the identity of a corpse, but also the other identities that have been imposed upon him, since the labels attached to the name "Berel" that follow are both descriptors and actual names. Shtetl residents were often known by nicknames that corresponded to their occupation, a personality trait, or a physical feature. So "Berel yosem" is both "Berel the orphan" and "Orphan Berel"; "Berel meshuge" is "Berel the madman" and "Madman Berel." He is no longer just "the orphan" or "the madman," as earlier in the story; now the labels are integrated into his name and his identity. "That's it!" But ultimately the instability of his identity gains the upper hand, and he is back to his original and most fundamental question: "Who am I?"

In the larger context of marginal people in East European Jewish culture, Berel's journey towards seeing himself as dead, a corpse, a being without a soul, is a logical one. As we know, marginal figures were often associated with the world of the dead, and madmen and madwomen in particular with spirits from the other world such as the dybbuk. Typical of this perception was a feuilleton-style piece on a mental hospital in rural Poland in the Yiddish newspaper *Nayer haynt* in which the writer called the institution "the kingdom of living death" and likened the head doctor who gave him his tour of the asylum to Virgil in the Inferno.[75]

Later in the 1890s, Peretz would return to the theme of madness in his *Fun dul-hoyz* ("From the Madhouse") cycle, where he explored the inner life of the mad with much greater intensity and artistic daring (see chapter 7).

"The situation is desperate": insane asylums and the threat of mental illness

Disabled Jews or their families were often drawn to big cities because of the medical institutions there and the treatments they offered; others went to the city because they had become vagrants and the city promised abundant alms. It is possible, however, that some mentally ill and developmentally disabled people were better off in a small-town environment, where they could rely on the safety net provided by family or an informal communal network. In the city, they were often on their own.

On the other hand, one must take with a grain of salt the hysterical pitch of news stories at the turn of the century that described hordes of lunatics descending upon cities. As Scott Ury has written on the Yiddish press in Warsaw, the chaos and violence of modern urban life seemed to defy authority and public order.[76] In 1913, for example, *Haynt* informed its readers that a new charitable society was being established in Novo-Vileisk, just outside of Vilna, to care for the hundreds of mentally ill people roaming the streets there. A resident of the town wrote to *Der shtern* to express his amazement at the *Haynt* article, since, he reported, patients accepted to the hospital were admitted the very moment they arrived in the town; he had never seen so much as a single insane person wandering the town.[77]

In the 1920s, *Haynt* raised a similar alarm about the situation in Lwów (Lviv), which was "experiencing an invasion of madmen." The paper confided to its readers that no fewer than six hundred insane people had been let out of a nearby asylum because of overcrowding and government funding issues and were "roaming the city and inspiring fear."[78] "Whatever the actual story," the author continued, "it is a fact that there are more madmen roaming free in the city than ever. Not a day goes by without scandals involving the mentally ill." (The article portrayed some of the lunatics as "dangerous," but the specific cases it described would be better categorized as nuisances—this was not the kind of attempt to link mental illness with true criminality that could be found in eugenicist writings, social scientific studies, and even public policy across Europe in this period.)

Throughout the nineteenth century, as David Wright argues, "the concern for public order which had been heightened by urbanization and migration prompted the construction of local institutions for 'lunatics'" across Europe.[79]

In the early years of the twentieth century, Western-style institutional care for the mentally ill advanced rapidly in East European Jewish society. By 1908, there were three Jewish psychiatric wards in the Russian Empire, each one a unit of the Jewish Hospital of its respective city: Warsaw, Vilna, and Minsk.[80] That year was also the date of the founding of the first Jewish Psychiatric Hospital, in Otwock, a resort and sanitarium town outside Warsaw, by the newly established Jewish Organization for the Indigent Nervous and Mentally Ill. A few years later, Jews began to plan a mental hospital in Łódź as well.[81] These initiatives were responses, not merely to the problem of mental illness that existed among Jews, just as it did among other ethnic groups, but to what was generally perceived—by both Jews and Christians—as a specifically Jewish issue that was a growing threat to normal life in the urban centers of eastern Europe.[82]

In a speech delivered in June 1906 to a gathering at his home of experts and supporters, Dr. Adam Wizel, director of the mental health ward at Warsaw's Jewish Hospital and founder of the Jewish Organization for the Indigent Nervous and Mentally Ill, pointed to a mental health crisis among Polish Jewry. Of the estimated 3,900 Polish Jews suffering from mental illness (3 in 1,000 of Russian Poland's 1.3-million Jews), only 315, or 8 percent, were currently receiving inpatient treatment, "an appallingly low proportion," especially when compared with similar statistics in Western European countries.[83] "As we can see," Wizel concluded, "the situation here is simply desperate." At the Warsaw Jewish Hospital, he continued—as the Warsaw Yiddish daily *Der veg* reported several weeks later—dozens of families requested that a mentally ill family member be admitted, and were turned away for lack of space. (The ward for the mentally ill, built for 100 patients, was now seriously overcrowded at 150.) Though care for the insane was one of the most important marks of a civilized society, all too often Jews looked cold-heartedly at the mentally ill, as ordinary folk made fun of "idiots and the insane in the streets," without understanding how tragic and sad the lives of these victims were.[84] Wizel also noted that mentally ill people were also placed at two asylums for incurable patients, one housed in Warsaw's main Jewish elderly home and the other located in Łódź. There were about a hundred Jewish patients in Christian institutions, such as that in Tworki, just outside of Warsaw, the Brothers Hospitallers' Psychiatric Hospital in

Kalwaria Zebrzydowska, and a hospital in Góra Kalwaria, he added, but Christian institutions took in Jews only reluctantly, "and Jews also have little desire to go there because of the poor treatment Jews receive there." (It was not only in Russian Poland that the lack of space in Jewish institutions was compelling Jews to bring their mentally ill to state psychiatric hospitals; this was also the case in the Pale of Settlement, as evidenced by the example of the regional hospital in the Vilna suburb of Novo-Vileisk [Novaia Vileika], one of five regional psychiatric hospitals established in provinces that did not have the zemstvo form of local government.)[85]

According to the account in *Der veg*—though this part of the speech was not reproduced in the society's own publication—Wizel continued in a vein particularly appropriate to the revolutionary moment in which the meeting had been called. Apparently, his aim was to prod his listeners, who were likely Jewish professionals sympathetic to the revolutionary cause, to extend their concern for workers to others oppressed by the current social structure. Did not the proletariat have the right to ask why the comfortable and well-off did not care about the most unfortunate? How could one sympathize with the working class and then allow an insane person to suffer, along with his family?

This rhetorical move was a significant one. Most people in eastern Europe, and indeed throughout the West, were used to seeing the mentally ill as unfortunates worthy of condescension and pity, or worse, an entertaining spectacle or annoying disturbance. But Wizel cast the situation in a new light, one more consonant with a twenty-first-century approach: mentally ill people were, like the proletariat, an oppressed and persecuted class.

Just as significant, though in this case not unique, was Wizel's characterization of mental illness as a pathology of the environment, which was typical of contemporary psychiatry. Wizel repeated assumptions about mental disorders among Jews that were widespread among both experts and laypeople: that Jews were particularly susceptible to mental illness and especially to neurosis; that the persecution and poverty that dogged East European Jews made them even more prone to those illnesses; and that the current era of revolution and upheaval made the situation even more delicate. "The growing poverty, the constant fear, the murders in the streets, the explosions—all of this is terribly unnerving [*dos alts denervirt shreklekh*] for people and is making [mental] illness very widespread." To the extent that all Jews in the Russian Empire suffered from persecution and rightlessness, mental illness was only an extreme manifestation of the phenomenon. The insane person was thus in some sense a synecdoche of the suffering nation.

Jewish madness or neurosis as a product of persecution was a common trope in the literature of the day, both scientific and general, and the theories about the prevalence of mental illness among Jews that we hear in Wizel's speech were characteristic of the era. John Efron and Sander Gilman have written about doctors or self-appointed experts, many of them trained in Germany, who wrote about the high rates of neurosis and mental illness among East European Jews.[86] These men drew universal conclusions about the state of East European Jewry from its psychopathology. Some pointed to low ethical standards and deviant sexual behavior, others to the difficult economic circumstances of many East European Jews and the persecution that they suffered, others still to certain aspects of traditional religious life or even the Yiddish language. The starting assumption, in all these cases, was that the Jews of eastern Europe had higher rates of varying forms of neurosis and psychosis—which, ironically, statistical evaluations by respected Jewish social scientists showed was not, in fact, the case.[87]

An early expression of these ideas was offered by the physician Samuel Gruzenberg (1854–1909) in a series of articles that appeared in the Jewish journal *Evreiskoe obozrenie* in the 1880s in which he argued that "a hypersensitive nervous system . . . made Jews more vulnerable to mental illnesses and numerous physical disabilities."[88] The classic formulation is found in the anthropologist Maurice Fishberg's 1911 study of Jews' racial and social characteristics: "Nearly all physicians who have practiced among the Jews agree that derangements of the nervous system are very frequently met with among them" (Fishberg's article on nervous diseases in the 1913 *Jewish Encyclopedia* subsequently canonized this view). Referring to the French neurologist Fulgence Raymond's 1888 study of neurological conditions in Russia, *L'Étude des maladies du système nerveux en Russie*, Fishberg emphasized the prevalence of hysteria, in particular, among both Jewish men and women.[89] Indeed, Efron (following Sander Gilman) argues that the tendency to see Jews as chronically unhealthy was based in the understanding that the male Jewish body displayed many female characteristics, a perception that goes back to medieval myths about Jewish men menstruating and persistent Christian anxiety about circumcision.[90] Gilman has argued that similar evaluations of madness on the part of non-Jewish experts were often linked to long-standing antisemitic tropes—insanity as a result of the inbreeding and incest that was ostensibly endemic in the Jewish community.[91] These are, of course, stereotypes of Jewish insanity that fall well outside the bounds of reality; a social history of mental illness—a "people's history of madness," as it were—must take a very different approach to understanding how insanity was experienced and perceived by the people closest to it.

A significant trend in the social science of the day across Europe (and in North America as well) was the attempt to engineer stronger and healthier societies through demographic and medical interventions: eugenics.[92] Experts, policymakers, and thought leaders voiced fears that without immediate action, a given society would face biological and social degeneration and come out the loser in the fierce competition for survival against its rivals that social Darwinism insisted was the fate of all nations. And the steady stream of government statistics emanating from new statistics bureaus highlighted the declining fertility rates of the middle class, while suggesting "a dramatic increase in the numbers of disabled individuals, those deemed the least 'fit' of society."[93]

Generally, one did not hear such discussions within Jewish social scientific circles, but one expert, the psychiatrist Raphael Becker, suggested that the Jewish community embark on a eugenicist plan to lower the number of mentally and physically ill. He called "for the implementation of a program of negative eugenics, insisting on the need for Jewish society to self-regulate unhealthy marriages among the mentally and physically ill, or between cousins."[94] This does not necessarily mean that Becker saw Jewry, or part of it, as degenerate per se, but it seems to suggest that Jews faced the same kind of biological danger that other Western societies understood themselves to be encountering. The question of degeneracy was picked up by some Zionists in their writings about the sorry state of the Jewish nation and the need for national regeneration (about which more in the next chapter).

Conclusion

While some Jews in the middle decades of the nineteenth century still consulted folk healers for madness, a condition they associated with evil spirits, others were already open to modern explanations of mental illness. By the turn of the century, psychology was an established science in the Russian Empire and those explanations became more widely accepted. Psychiatric treatment of mentally ill people was now much more accessible than before. At the same time, however, an apparent crisis of Jewish mental illness was emerging in the city, a condition that was now no longer the product of evil spirits but of the evil of antisemitic persecution.

Paradoxically, just as Adam Wizel was advocating for greater availability of inpatient treatment for Jews, a number of Russian psychiatrists began promoting deinstitutionalization, known in contemporary European psychiatric circles as "boarding-out" or "family patronage" (*patronage familial*). One scholar describes this new approach as "a community-based program of foster care for chronic patients who were judged to pose little threat to the community."[95] Among Jews, this was practiced in agricultural colonies near Vilna such as Deksznie, where in the late nineteenth century colonists started taking in stable mentally ill (or perhaps developmentally disabled) people as a supplemental form of income. The number of such fostered patients grew from about twenty in 1900 to two hundred in 1914.[96]

Some Russian psychiatrists who favored boarding-out envisioned it as a way encourage traditional Russian values by placing insane people in peasant homes. The idea was to remove the patient from the city, from the noisy industrial environment—in other words, from the modern world—and to settle him or her in a traditional rural setting. Presumably, this was meant to help not only the patient but also, in some sense, the host family: "The longer the peasants participated in the program, its supporters proclaimed, the more caring and generous they became."[97] For Jews, that most urban of people, the rural environs would presumably have an even more therapeutic effect; as Sander Gilman writes, many Jewish psychiatric experts agreed that "the cause of the Jews' illnesses is their confinement in the city, the source of all degeneracy; the cure is 'land, air, light.'"[98]

But in one telling incident among Russian Orthodox boarding-out patients in Voronezh, "a female patient was returned to the hospital after it was discovered that she had been telling fortunes and 'healing' the sick. She had set up shop in her foster home and was making quite a profit at her business."[99] This sounds strangely similar to what madmen and madwomen were frequently known for in the pre-psychiatric world; and clearly here both the madwoman, her host family, and the village had reverted to those traditional patterns (if, indeed, any of them had ever departed from them in the interim).

The medicalization of madness, then, could not erase the age-old nexus between madness and the supernatural—a connection between insanity and great vision and insight. As the next chapter will show, in his developing vision of the meaning of madness, I. L. Peretz saw in the mad a truth that could not be found elsewhere in human society.

CHAPTER 7

"WE SINGING JEWS, WE JEWS POSSESSED"

The Jewish Outcast as National Icon

Leah: (Opens her eyes) I know the spirits, and I am not afraid of them.
They are not evil.

—S. An-ski, *The Dybbuk, or, Between Two Worlds*

From the last years of the nineteenth century to the years immediately following the end of World War I, Jewish philanthropic and welfare practice,
political thought, and cultural production embraced the Jewish outcast as a
potent symbol. Whereas an earlier generation of philanthropists had spoken
of their wards as "unfortunates" to be assisted, mostly with a view to making
them productive members of imperial society in pursuit of the far-off, eventual goal of social and economic integration of Jews, the nationalist-minded
social welfare institutions and networks that emerged during this period saw
the marginal as bearing the scars and hopes of the entire Jewish nation, as
did folklorists, writers, and political leaders.

Even before the turning point of World War I, the lines between the core
of the normative community and its outcasts had become blurry. This was
truest in the big cities, where growing numbers of marginal people seemed
to overwhelm any reasonable capacity to care for or contain them.[1] The new
anthropological approach to defining and diagnosing the collective Jewish
body also drew attention to the collective physical and psychiatric weaknesses of that body. Mentally ill people no longer necessarily seemed outside
the norm, but more like organic manifestations of a much larger malady.
Indeed, in a natural extrapolation of Scott Ury's argument about life in the
big city, the neurological science of the day asserted that the pressures of

the metropolitan lifestyle made ever growing numbers of Jews susceptible to mental breakdown.[2] For most Jewish practitioners of what Marina Mogilner calls "medical materialism"—a scientific discourse in which "the language of race played an important role in connecting concerns about the Jewish collective body with debates about modernity"—such maladies were cultural in origin, and could thus be cured by normalizing the circumstances in which Jews lived.[3] That was exactly the kind of normalization proffered by Jewish nationalists of various stripes in the early decades of the twentieth century.[4]

Indeed, Zionist thinkers saw in the dispossessed and the vulnerable troubling icons of a nation weakened by degeneration, though also capable of transformation. For some—like Aharon Appelfeld's editor in the account that opened this book ("We came to Israel to forget Bertha. You are taking a retarded girl as the hero of the story? What are you going to learn from such a story? How will this story help us build a new nation of new people?")—the true sign of the national renaissance would be the disappearance of such people altogether and, by extension, of the stereotypical "ghetto Jew" of eastern Europe whom they denoted.

By contrast, the emerging fields of Jewish folklore and ethnography saw marginal folk as embodying something unique and otherworldly in traditional Jewish culture that modernity threatened to erase. Along similar lines, modernist literature posited that rather than being a loathsome and abhorrent aspect of human existence that had to be expunged, the "ugliness" of the marginal was simply an amplified reflection of a world that was itself ugly, deformed, and full of fear, but in whose truth beauty could be found.

After the expulsions and massacres of World War I and its aftermath created hundreds of thousands of Jewish refugees and orphans, many of them with serious physical and mental injuries, figures that had previously been seen as outcasts now represented the mainstream of Jewish society. Moreover, the colossal Jewish relief effort of wartime brought an entire generation of political activists into the sphere of welfare work.[5] In independent Poland, prewar philanthropic initiatives often initiated by the haute bourgeoisie were now transformed into large-scale welfare initiatives (the orphan-care organization CENTOS, for example, or the Bund-affiliated Medem Sanatorium) seen as a national duty.[6] This shift was accompanied by a much more sympathetic attitude to the most vulnerable of the nation.

Folklore discovers the Jewish marginal

At the beginning of the twentieth century, Jewish folklore was emerging as a distinct discipline and legitimate field of inquiry. Figures such as S. Anski, I. L. Peretz, and Noach Pryłucki (Noyekh Prilutski) fused a passion for creating a new, secular Jewish culture with an interest in Jewish folklore, including the oral culture of the lowest classes and the underworld.[7] Among the hundreds of songs Peysakh Marek and Shaul Ginsburg collected for their "Jewish Folksongs in Russia," for example, were three specimens of beggar's laments, including "The Orphan Girl's Lament" ("Give alms to a poor child / Whose mother is dead! / Miserable is she and blind, / Give alms, give some money / To a poor orphan girl who cannot see the world!").[8] Similar songs were included in a collection of Jewish folksongs published in the Polish ethnography journal *Wisła* by the pioneering folklorist Regina Lilientalowa.[9] There was as yet no clear theoretical framework for understanding marginality, but these works seem to mark a dawning realization among collectors and scholars of folklore that their definition of "the folk" needed to be expansive in order to be fully comprehensive. The very fact that Jewish folksongs spoke of the experiences of the marginalized meant that they had to be included in the oeuvre of Jewish folklore.

The ethnographer and writer S. Z. Rappoport, who published under the pseudonym "S. An-ski," sought to gather ethnographic material by journeying through the Pale of Settlement between 1912 and 1914, and documents that survive from those expeditions reveal an emerging awareness of marginal characters as well. The longest extant questionnaire from such an expedition, "The Jewish Ethnographic Program," or simply "The [Jewish] Person," was structured around the cycle of life, from birth to death, with a few questions probing the realm of the socially marginal or deviant: "Does the *Hakhnoses Kale* society [which provided dowries for poor brides], or private individuals, invariably make an effort to arrange a marriage for an old maid, even if she is a cripple?"; "Is there a poorhouse [*hekdesh*] in your community? If there was . . . in the past, describe what the conduct in it was like"; "Would it ever happen that in order to stop an epidemic, a marriage ceremony would be held at the cemetery?"[10] The questionnaire's hypothetical respondent had full access to and knowledge of all aspects of that society, including its margins. Of course, such an approach to gathering folklore was by its very nature limited, since rather than seeking out the marginals themselves, the investigator sought information *about* them. Still, it was an important first step.

A. Litvin (Shmuel Hurvits, 1862–1943) was a journalist, folklorist, and activist who also took an interest in marginal people. Litvin traveled through Jewish communities in Lithuania, Poland, and Galicia in the early years of the twentieth century and collected material for his folkloristic miscellany *Yudishe neshomes* ("Jewish Souls"), which offered sketches of the overlooked characters of the Jewish street who Litvin felt held significance for Jewish self-understanding. Madmen, for example, "are representatives of a better world, a beat-up world, a mutilated [*tsukalietshete*] world, but a more beautiful one all the same, because there everything is possible, and the supernatural is natural; because there everything is fantasy that has overcome the bitterest, the most frightening reality, fleeing into the unbounded space that knows nothing either of past or future."[11]

Litvin also argued—as did most contemporary psychiatrists—that Jewish madmen were a living symbol of the oppression of the Jewish people in eastern Europe: "Jewish madness is a product of the Jew's abnormal political and social situation in Russia, of his terrible rightlessness." He even contended that the First Russian Revolution (in 1905), with its promise of liberation and of an end to despair, had begun to lessen the numbers of idiots and insane people among Jews.[12] Litvin's valorization of the marginal figure was the beginning of a trend in Jewish society of calling attention to marginal people, not because they represented the backward nature of that society, but just the opposite: because they embodied something special and otherworldly that had the potential to lift up and redeem the ordinary and workaday.

Abraham Samuel Herschberg (1858–1943) took a similar approach in his monumental *Pinkes byalistok*, a communal history and ethnography of Bialystok that he wrote during the interwar period and was published posthumously after the war (Herschberg perished in Auschwitz). Commenting on the role of the hekdesh in the Jewish community, Herschberg argued that

> The Hebrew word *hekdesh* is used to call anything that has been set apart from our profane, worldly sphere, that which we might enjoy, and transferred into an unworldly, sacred sphere from which one cannot draw enjoyment. Those who live in the hekdesh have also been set apart from our world of

utility and enjoyment. . . . In the hekdesh are people who have been thrown out of life, who have no relevance to actual life. They have been hopelessly neglected by their close ones, to whom they have become a burden. In biblical language, they are called "afflicted and stricken by God," "a punishment from God." Thus in a certain sense they can also be called *kdoyshim*: they serve as a portent [*onzog*] from God to healthy, normal people.[13]

Herschberg's point is that *hekdesh-layt* are more than mere unfortunate castoffs. On the symbolic plane, they represent all that ordinary people seek to avoid or ignore in daily life: suffering, wretchedness, neglect. But by calling them *kdoyshim*—which has the dual meaning of "holy people" and "martyrs"—he also attempts to link their status etymologically to the term *hekdesh* and to suggest that they have somehow been set apart, or perhaps even sacrificed, for the greater psychological and spiritual good of the community. Herschberg seems to be warning us that we ignore the portent embodied by the people of the hekdesh at our peril.

Thus, in some way marginal people offered something that ordinary people were in need of. Indeed, Litvin argued, every Jewish community needed a madman: "One cannot imagine a Jewish community without a madman, just as it is impossible to imagine it without a rabbi, a *mikveh* and a policeman. . . . The masses think of him as 'one of us' [*an eygener mensh*], a member of the household [*a shtub-mensh*]. . . . And simple, less developed workers pass the time with him: they laugh at his ideas, songs, jokes."[14]

Another of Litvin's "souls" was Aaron Gaburin (1864/65–1900), known as the Young Man or Bachelor (*bokher*) of Beyki, because he never married. Gaburin, paralyzed in both legs as a youth, became a beloved and venerated rabbi known for his learned advice. Maskilic sources closer to the chronological dates of his life such as the Hebrew newspaper *Hatsefirah* painted him as an autodidact, sickly from his early youth, who was deeply knowledgeable in both Jewish and secular studies and gave erudite counsel in commercial and business affairs.[15] Litvin, however, portrayed him as a curiosity, "perhaps the most curious of all rebbes [*gute yidn*]"; indeed, a tragedy so profound and so remarkable that "no artist and no historian has yet been born" capable of describing it.[16] The reader was to understand, then, that only the folklorist—inhabiting the space between art and history, perhaps?—was capable of communicating the full picture of the Bokher's life.

Litvin expanded upon what the correspondents to Ha-tsefirah had written about the Bokher's erudition, contending that he was learned in medicine, astronomy, and mathematics, and knew many European languages. Lawyers and generals sought his advice; he had visitors from as far away as Africa and America, and even the illustrious Slonimer Rebbe wrote letters to him.[17] Astonishingly, Gaburin achieved this status despite being severely disabled. According to Litvin, the young Gaburin, full of youthful energy, used to love to climb trees, but one of those climbs ended in a fall that left him a lifelong cripple. Thereafter, he channeled his natural vitality into learning; he would study all night long, keeping his feet in cold water (presumably to keep himself awake). "In this manner," Litvin continues,

> he caught a chill and became just a shadow of a person, a living skeleton, with a large head, deep, wonderful eyes, and just a few hairs on his head. Those eyes shone strangely and gave his entire figure something unearthly [*epis nit erdishes*]. Whoever saw the Beykier Bokher even once could never forget him.
>
> With twisted feet and two humps, from front and from back. . . . He could not move from his spot. He could not even sit. He lay in a sitting pose, bolstered by two pillows in front and behind. He lived his childhood and youth thus; studied Mishnah and *poskim* [Jewish legal decisors] and various secular sciences and languages, and received religious and secular books, refusing eat and drink.[18]

Litvin thus transforms an ordinary paralytic into a genius who has mastered both Jewish and secular knowledge, a living skeleton who speaks almost all European languages—in other words, a freak who sacrificed ordinary life and its pleasures for knowledge, which he shared freely with others. Indeed, no Hasidic rebbe was as idolized as he in Grodno province. Litvin's remarkable claims were expanded upon even further decades later in the Slonim yizkor book, which described Gaburin as a prophet, a wonderworker, and a healer (*ba'al shem*) who was not only known for his sage advice but also for the amulets and incantations (*lehishot*) that he dispensed to visitors.[19]

There was also a voyeuristic aspect to this kind of literature. Like Litvin's

folksy sketches, innumerable articles in the Yiddish press portrayed oddi-
ties like the Bokhur of Beyki and Warsaw's Jewish underworld for ordinary
Jews.[20] Even putatively highbrow pieces highlighting achievements in the
philanthropic arena took detours into the gutter to ensure that readers and
would-be donors understood the serious nature of the poverty and depravity that social welfare workers were battling.[21] In 1911, the Warsaw Yiddish
daily *Haynt* ran a profile of the *Ezras yesoymim* orphans' aid society that
included colorfully drawn vignettes such as "A Prostitute for a Sister." In
this sketch, Tutke comes to the organization's door, begging for help for her
younger sister: "'Let not the younger sister become what the older has! We
are both orphans. . . . Nothing more can help me in my fallen state [*Meyle,
ikh ferfalen* . . .], but she—no, I don't want this . . . Have mercy . . . ' And she
falls silent, weeping. Ezras yesoymim took the innocent dove into its nest."[22]

When writers such as I. L. Peretz turned to folklore as the repository of
the richness of Jewish culture—"the stories, songs, and sayings of ordinary
Jews that were as important to the creative life of a people as the formal
works of their writers"—they discovered, willy-nilly, the marginal types
embedded in those folk materials.[23] In a study of Peretz's role in Jewish folkloristics, Mark Kiel outlines the symbolic role of marginal people such as the
blind beggar in the emerging folklore of Congress Poland, and their role in
the transmission and recreation of Jewish culture. Kiel describes the fascinating role played by the marginal Jew as symbol in "the secular ritualization
of folklore research in its stylized celebration at the annual Purim ball in
fin-de-siècle Warsaw. . . . The high point of the evening came as the guests
watched the scene of the blind beggar being led dutifully about the hall by
a girl as they sang and collected folk songs from the guests."[24] Kiel specu-
lates that the beggar represents "the simple man of the folk who touches the
heart of the more 'civilized' people with his sad songs," while the girl stood
for an unworldly servant or seamstress from the provinces who served as
"the proverbial source for the folklorist."[25] Paradoxically, her journey (and
the beggar's too?) to the city epitomized the end of traditional folk culture,
which was usually seen as rooted in shtetl life.

The scene at the Purim ball represented a further shift in the perception
of the marginal type, who was now unmistakably valorized as a repository
of communal and national memory. The blind beggar did not just perform

folk songs for the crowd of intellectuals and literati; he and his companion also *elicited* songs from the guests, as if to remind them that, underneath their sophisticated, urbane mien, they too were members of "the folk," with an organic connection to the authentic culture of the people. The marginal individual was thus not only a performer, a relic, a curiosity to be gazed upon, but an important actor with a key role to play in catalyzing the revival of "authentic" culture. If modernity offered or even at times compelled standardization and assimilation, marginal people might offer the antidote.[26]

This notion of the idealized marginal Jew in eastern Europe corresponded to the romanticized, misty vision of the *Ostjude* that we find in the writings of Central European Jews such as Arnold Zweig. Zweig's *Das ostjüdische Antlitz* (*The Face of East European Jewry*) (1920) depicts the Jew of eastern Europe as "the more authentic, primal Jew"—noble, sincere, and pure—over and against the assimilated western Jew, compromised by modernity.[27] The idolization of the Ostjude was often more easily practiced from a distance, but some German Jews could even see an appealing authentic Judaism in itinerant Jewish beggars from Poland who had come to Germany to collect alms, even though such Betteljuden normally aroused feelings of embarrassment rather than pride.[28] The German Jewish poet Jakob Löwenberg recalled feeling ashamed that his Christian friends should know that the filthy, rag-clad beggars in his village were Jews, but his father helped him see another side to these men. "On the Sabbath my father would invite them for Friday night dinner and would discuss Talmud with them, and it then became clear that the Polish Jews had great spiritual qualities."[29]

Nationalist discourse and marginals

Just as modernist writers such as Peretz began invoking the trope of the marginal, the emerging nationalist ideologies of Jewish eastern Europe also mobilized the marginals for their own ends—usually to cast the entire Jewish people as dispossessed outcasts of society. A classic example is this excerpt from a Bundist leaflet published in 1903 by the Kovno Social Democratic Committee:

> The Zionists kowtow and lick the hand of the slaughterers of the whole
> Jewish people, the tsarist autocracy, the atrocious, thieving tsarist autocracy

that has made paupers, beggars, sick, weak, and feeble wretches out of the Jews. . . . You tell us to hide in a corner so that, God forbid, no one should notice and trample on us; keep our heads bowed as low as possible, so we should not catch anyone's eye; speak quietly, like a beggar at the door; beg for mercy and kindness.[30]

The Zionist movement, too, often portrayed *Ostjudentum* synecdochically as the "one big pauper" depicted in Abramovitsh's *Fishke der krumer*. Thus, Herzl's *Altneuland* featured a beggar boy from a family of East European Jewish migrants to Vienna who ardently desires to settle in Palestine; later in the novel we meet him again, now a prosperous resident of Haifa—the consummate "new Jewish man."[31] Hayyim Nahman Bialik's "Masa nemirov," a poetic response to the Kishinev pogrom of 1903, disdainfully apostrophized pusillanimous diaspora Jews, declaring, "Just as you have always been beggars, you always will be beggars."[32]

The episode of the "Kishinev orphans"—children orphaned by the 1903 pogrom and subsequently sent to Palestine to be settled at a proposed agricultural school—is another illustration of Zionist activists' use of marginal figures to demonstrate the movement's ostensible ability to transform pathetic victims of history into productive members of society. Critics charged that they were nothing more than pawns in the Zionist movement's drive for popularity and funds.[33] Zionist activists also established several orphanages on Zionist principles. The first members and activists of Warsaw's Ezras-yesoymim [Aid to Orphans] Society, it was later remembered, had hailed from Lithuanian Zionist circles.[34] This is consistent with Tara Zahra's argument about the role of nationalist organizations in promoting children's welfare in the Bohemian lands, which "transformed imagined boundaries between public and private" inasmuch as they claimed the children whom they educated and cared for in schools, shelters, orphanages, and day-care centers as belonging to the nation as a whole.[35]

Zionist-style productivity was even more promoted in the interwar period. As the leaders of the Kishinev Jewish Orphanage put it in an anniversary volume celebrating the thirty-fifth year of the institution's founding, published only a few years after the orphanage had been taken over by Zionists, "the weak little orphans . . . have been given over to us . . . to make into healthy, prepared [*shtandfehige*], and honorable members of society."[36] The only solution for the orphans' future was to give them a Jewish national orientation and to prepare them for "a healthy and productive life in the Land of Israel," working the land.[37]

The marginal as literary protagonist

In their quest to fashion a modern Jewish identity on the foundation of traditional Jewish culture and lifeways, several great Yiddish writers drew on and transformed marginal types—madmen, beggars, cripples, orphans—into literary heroes. Dovid Bergelson's "Der toyber" ("The Deaf Man") (1906) is a good example of the new interest in exploring the inner world of the marginal figure.[38] Madness, in particular, was a common theme in modern Hebrew fiction, often because the mad protagonist was effectively an extension of the writer—an outsider misunderstood and ostracized by his community.[39] A representative selection of such works is discussed below.

PERETZ'S MADMEN (1895–1900)

"The Mad Talmudist" (1890) was Peretz's first story on the theme of madness. Later in the 1890s, Peretz took up this theme again. His Yiddish-language "Fun dul-hoyz" ("From the Madhouse") was published in 1895 in *Yontev-bletlekh*, a radical journal that he had founded the year before, and a Hebrew-language version, "Be-agaf ha-meshuga'im" ("In the Insane Wing"), followed in 1896 in the Hebrew daily *He-tsefirah*. In a series of vignettes, the narrator guides us through an insane asylum—"a world unto itself"[40]—introducing us to various inmates, letting them speak in their own words.

Ken Frieden suggests that "From the Madhouse" was likely influenced by Chekhov's "Ward 6," published in 1892.[41] There is certainly some similarity between Ragin, a doctor who begins to pay visits to the mental ward and eventually becomes a patient himself, and Peretz's narrator, whose possible identity as the doctor of the ward is suggested by the title of the first vignette: "Doctor or Patient?" From the outset, Peretz suggests strongly that the two worlds—that of the sane and that of the insane—may not be as neatly separated as we might wish, a supposition confirmed by the narrator: "It's no wonder that sometimes I ask myself: 'What am I? A doctor or a patient? And perhaps the entire hospital never was, and I have made the whole thing up? What's the difference, in the end? [*Lemai nafka mina?*] We are all mad or we are all sane!'"[42] If in some sense we are all mad, then what is reality? What is the boundary between reality and fiction, between reality and madness? (It turns out that one of the inmates knows the answer: there is no such thing as madness. "Leib the Philosopher says that there is no truth and falsehood in the world, and a fortiori there is no madness or madmen.")

The multiplication of fences, borders, and regulations in the asylum only highlights the tenuousness and porousness of those limits: "everyone acknowledges that the guarding is not sufficient or good enough to keep things inside those boundaries."[43] An extra paragraph in the Yiddish version extends boundary-crossing to gender: the male patients ponder what would happen if the wall between their section and the women's ward were to be broken down: "within two or three generations we would multiply so greatly that there would be more of us than the sane, and we would put them into hospitals."[44] It is soon made clear, when we meet the bearded, husky-voiced storekeeper Yentl, that the wall separating the sexes—or at least the genders—has already been broken through. In fact, because "there is nothing to distinguish her from a man" (*hi gever le-khol davar*), the guards allow her to come and go as she pleases among the men.[45] Policing the boundaries of a world gone mad is an exercise in futility.

HOLY FOOL, MAD SAINT

Another theme running through "From the Madhouse" is the madman as a holy figure with a mysterious connection to the divine and the hereafter, including the dead. As he would do frequently throughout his oeuvre, Peretz here drew on traditional folk archetypes, both Jewish (the madman with a supernatural link to the world of spirits) and Russian (the holy fool).[46] One might also say that he was playing with the idea of the madman's liminality; since he is neither fully one thing nor another, he has the power to move easily between worlds. In the second vignette, "A Conversation with the Vapor Man" (Yid., "A shmues mit gazeman"; Heb., "Siah va-sig im ba'al ha-edim"), the eponymous madman—who is keeping a terrible secret: that the vapors collecting in the bowels of the earth will at some point cause the earth to split open and swallow everyone—describes a conversation with a dead man. Fleeing from a gang of hooligan boys, he tripped over a stone and found himself in a graveyard. "The tombstones move to and fro, and the dead rise up from their graves."[47] One of them, a dignified old corpse, approaches the Vapor Man and begins to talk to him. Once the clock struck midnight, they all set out for the synagogue for prayers (the dead praying in the synagogue at midnight was a well-known trope in East European Jewish folklore). Elsewhere in the story, we learn that the mad have access to the 310 worlds of the hereafter.[48]

The Saint is another inmate with a special connection to the unearthly, for he has "a lot of influence in heaven, a great deal to say, but here in the hospital—nothing!"[49] Unlike tsaddikim, wonderworkers who carry keys to the treasures of heaven, keys that "that open up people's hearts and pockets," he has turned his back on earthly needs, becoming "just an eternal assistant to God in his war—his holy war with Satan—which does not earn him even one penny."[50] Hence he was locked up in the asylum. Here again the question is posed: what is madness? Why is one man who claims to have a special connection to supernal realms declared a raving lunatic while another is proclaimed a miracle-worker and a saintly rabbi?

"CREATED ON SABBATH EVE"

The folkloristic nexus between madness and the realm of demons is reaffirmed in the next vignette, "The Fire and Again the Fire," which reveals just how elemental and indeed primordial madness is. "The madhouse is old, very old . . ." One inmate dates the madhouse to the time of Haman, another to before the giving of the Torah, a third to the eve of the very first Sabbath. "The Saint believed that it dated from the Six Days of Creation . . . that it was created on Sabbath Eve at dusk along with the demons and devils."[51] But note: it was not *madness* that was created in the last moments of Creation but the *madhouse*, which, together with demons and devils, will prove to be an eternal thorn in the side of humankind. The madhouse segregates the saints, visionaries, and prophets from ordinary ("sane") people and muffles their words of wisdom.

And then, an unexpected development (or is it?): on Christmas Eve—according to East European Jewish folkloric tradition, an auspicious time for demonic activity[52]—the Saint sets the madhouse on fire in his own auto-da-fé:

> And the Saint? The Saint stands at the peak of the roof, stands ready, as if he is
>   leaning on the Pillar of Cloud, tongues of fire lap at his shanks like serpents,
>   like seraphim . . .
> And he stands—his palms spread out, his eyes shining and gazing heavenwards,
>   and his voice pierces the heart as an awl:
> 'Hear O Israel! Hear O Israel!'
> And then no more, for the roof caves in underneath him.[53]

The Saint has a corporeal connection, as it were, to the Pillar of Cloud, the physical manifestation of God's glory on earth; at his feet are additional reminders of the Israelites' wandering in the desert and, by extension, of the primordial quality of madness: the magical serpents (Num. 21). But it seems that the very preternatural nature of the madhouse and the madman means that neither of them can have a true existence in the material world—they are fated to be consumed in (holy?) fire.

THE MEANING OF MADNESS

Is "In the Mental Ward" about madness? Or are the inmates signifiers of something else altogether? To what extent is Peretz actually exploring the mind of the madman, or rather presenting the madman as the consummate societal outsider (much like the artist himself) who has special insight into the nature of existence?[54] Since they are unconstrained by the niceties and formalities of society, madmen have a freedom that the sane do not enjoy. Both "brave travelers" (in the Hebrew version of the story) and "trailblazers" (in the Yiddish) "who venture onto unpaved roads to discover new lands in the world of the spirit," they can explore new paths, reveal new territories and worlds, even the worlds that sane people may only gain access to after death, and then only if the latter are among the righteous.[55] They can observe the world from above, like "free birds," without the strictures of sanity.

In his evaluation of madness motifs in Peretz's writing, the American critic Perets Tsunzer contended that the great writer was not interested in psychology per se but rather in the contradiction between the "normal" and the "abnormal" in daily life. The "normal" ones, he wrote, are those who toe the line and live their lives in accordance with the ethics and norms of the day. The "insane" are "the proud, the defiant, those who leap over the fence, all those who do not want to live in the way they are called on to live."[56] But even if Peretz's goal was not to explore insanity as a phenomenon, it is significant that in exploring the world of the person who stands apart, who does not move with the masses and does not answer the call of the ordinary, he chose the persona of the madman. In this, he may have been a pioneer in the realm of Jewish literature, but he was treading a well-worn path in the larger world of letters. In the Russian cultural context, madness was frequently understood as a malady not only of the individual but of the body social and political as well.[57] But, as we have seen in the case of town fools-cum-prophets, the converse could also be true: the insane, it seems, could be particularly sensitive to the defects of society; or, at the very least, had no inhibitions to prevent them from saying what was on their minds.

Peretz's writings on madmen, his attempts to deconstruct madness and the concept of and need for a madhouse, were an attempt to reclaim madness for the realm of culture and perhaps even morality in the age of the medicalization of insanity: after his banishment by modernity to the realm of the pathological, the madman had to be restored to his rightful place, his words and deeds given back their true meaning. In the premodern world, the madman and madwoman, integrated into an everyday life suffused with faith and magic, had held an important place in the religious and cultural landscape, but over the course of the nineteenth century, modern scientific and medical approaches had transformed them into a problem to be dealt with by isolation and treatment. As David Ingleby argues, "When the patient's experience and behavior are regarded as symptoms of physical illness, they are completely emptied out of moral significance: whereas in an earlier time they might have been ascribed to the agency of the devil, or a possessing spirit, they are now not seen as intelligible at all."[58] Peretz seemingly rejects the segregation of the mad from the "world of reason" in "In the Mental Ward" and insists that we accompany him into the insane asylum and into the very mind of the madman. Living in the insane asylum, Peretz's narrator comes to appreciate their worth, deep insight, and clairvoyance. Thus, he breaks down the artificial barriers between the realms of "sanity" and "insanity," insisting on the moral significance and relevance of the visions (at times even in the prophetic sense) of the mad.

This literary move was a natural one for Peretz, who dedicated much of his life's work to recovering foundational elements of premodern and traditional Jewish culture—especially folk culture—for an emerging modern Jewish culture. (David Roskies maintains that Peretz began his project of cultural reclamation in 1899–1900 with the creation of his first "credible hasidic storyteller," but his earlier foray into madness may have been a prelude to that initiative.)[59] For an artist seeking an authentic Jewish culture and way of being in the world, the figure of the madman was appealing, since the mad are arguably more authentic than the sane: their inner selves resemble what lies on the outside.[60]

S. An-ski's *The Dybbuk*, or, *Between Two Worlds* (1913–16)

The *YIVO Encyclopedia of Jews in Eastern Europe* calls *The Dybbuk* "the most celebrated play in the history of both Yiddish and Hebrew theater." No wonder that it has been analyzed from multiple perspectives in a wide array of languages.[61] The beggars, paupers, and cripples who populate the stage in several scenes of *The Dybbuk* play a very different role than the freaks and misfits that usually appeared on the Yiddish stage for comic effect; these included, among many others, Avrom Goldfadn's *Tsvey kuni-lemls*, with its half-blind, lame, stammering protagonist, expressly designed—along with the plot and slapstick laugh lines—to send the audience into hysterics, and Dovid Pinski's *Cripples*, a comedy about beggars fighting for a place at the entrance to a church.[62] Jacob Gordin, whom contemporaries hailed as transforming the Yiddish theater from *shund* ("trash," i.e., popular theater) to serious in his attempt "to mirror contemporary social reality," had already introduced a new approach to marginal Jews in his *Khasye di yesoyme* (Khasye the Orphan).[63] Unlike her outcast predecessors, Khasye was not meant to be laughed at or pitied; here was a fully developed protagonist for whom the audience was meant to feel true pathos.[64] S. An-ski's marginal people were minor characters (albeit with speaking roles), but their presence was meant to infuse the setting with ethnographic realism. This makes sense, given An-ski's dedication to his larger ethnographic project, which aimed to understand "the experiences of Jews, especially the most traditional and poorest," in the words of his biographer Gabriella Safran.[65] A play that was, in the words of one critic, "an ethnographic museum"[66]—a collection of various aspects of traditional folklife and magic that An-ski encountered on his ethnographic expeditions—could not exclude the colorful characters at the lowest rung of the social ladder who figured so heavily in folklore, religious tales, and ethnographic and travel accounts. But *The Dybbuk* is more than just a folkloristic miscellany; it is a work of high art, of transcendent beauty in which An-ski brought together many of the strands of marginality that he had uncovered in Jewish folk culture—a topic that he was well aware was intimately interwoven with perceptions of the dead, the supernatural, and the sacred (the play's Russian and Yiddish titles are "Between Two Worlds").

Conflating the Russian- and Yiddish-language versions of the cast of characters (the wording differs slightly), we have a poor hunchback, a beggar on crutches, three disabled elderly beggar women—a crippled woman, a woman missing a hand, and a blind woman—and two young beggar women, one carrying a child.[67] This makes seven in total, a number that Ans-ski was without question aware had general symbolic value in Judaism and a very specific relationship to the seven beggars in R. Nahman's Tales. Act II opens on a scene in the fictional shtetl of Brinnitz: on the left, the synagogue; on the right, the house of R. Sender, the prosperous father of the play's heroine, Leah; in the distance, the bathhouse and poorhouse, and beyond that the cemetery.[68] The physical layout seems to signal that the Jewish religious and social establishment lies at the center of the drama, while the realms of the poor and the dead, which were usually on the outskirts of town, are of little direct significance. However, there are additional details suggesting that the world of the dead/poor that lies at the edge of—or perhaps hidden under—ours actually encroaches upon it and intrudes into it. Next to the synagogue lies the grave of a bride and groom martyred during the Khmel'nyts'kyi uprising of 1648—an extension, as it were, of the cemetery into the very heart of the town—while Sender's courtyard and the square itself are filled with long tables at which are seated beggars, cripples, children, and old people, gobbling down the paupers' feast that has been provided for them, as was customary at Jewish weddings hosted by prosperous families. The poorhouse in the distance has, it seems, disgorged its denizens into the town square.[69]

Early in the act, Meyer, the shammes of the synagogue, a wedding guest, and one of the three *batlonim* remark on the lavishness of the feast.

Second Batlen: Leave it to Sender—he knows what he's doing. If one isn't too generous to an invited guest, there's no great harm in it. At the worst he will grumble and pout. But if one fails to do one's duty by the poor, the danger is great indeed. Who knows? The person in rags may really be a beggar or someone else entirely—a holy man or even one of the thirty-six righteous for whom the world is preserved.

Meyer: Perhaps even Elijah the Prophet. He always comes disguised as a pauper.[70]

Echoing the play's ever-present motif of hidden/revealed or, to be more specific, a mystical world hidden under the visible world, the conversation makes clear that a beggar may be just a beggar—or he may be a holy or righteous man, perchance Elijah the Prophet himself.

Later in Act II, the paupers clamor to dance with Leah, a half-orphan with a special connection to the world of the dead. Although about to wed Menashe in an arranged marriage, she is still in love with Khonon, who has died in his attempt to use kabbalistic magic to make Leah his bride. Leah is also inexplicably drawn to the story of the martyred bride and groom. In the pre-wedding festivities, dancing "with one poor old woman after another," Leah is spun in dizzying circles by the pauper women.[71] Her nurse Frade and friend Bassia express concern on this count:

Frade: (Uneasy) Oh my, oh my! Is Leah'le still dancing with the poor folks? She's sure to get dizzy. Girls, bring her here. . . .

Bassia: Your poor head must be spinning.[72]

Leah is then pulled once again into a dance, this time by the Half-Blind Old Woman, who refuses to let the bride go once she has her spinning. The scene becomes frantic, the old woman screaming in something approaching a mad frenzy until she is gasping for breath, "More! More! More! More!"

Leah then sits down, "eyes closed, head thrown back, [and] speaks as if in a trance":

They held me, they surrounded me, they pressed themselves against me and pushed their cold dry fingers into my flesh. My head was spinning, I grew faint. And then someone lifted me high into the air and carried me away—far, far away. . . . [73]

Is she speaking of the beggars—or something else? An-ski purposefully obscures the object of Leah's dreamlike monologue; at first it seems obvious that she is talking about the paupers with whom she has been dancing, but ultimately we learn that she is referring to "the spirits"—"the souls of people who have died before their time."[74] There is an organic nexus, it seems, between the pauper folk represented by the beggars and cripples who dance with Leah and the spirits who linger in this world because their work here is not yet done. Moreover, there are erotic overtones to the interaction between those spirits and Leah. The Dance of the Beggars, then, foreshadows the promiscuous mingling of the worlds of the living and of the dead that enables Khonon's soul to enter Leah as a dybbuk and climaxes in the final act of the play with the union of the lovers' souls.[75]

In Evgenii Vakhtangov's 1922 staging of *The Dybbuk* for the Habimah Hebrew-language company in Moscow, which the troupe would use in touring over the next several decades, the dance of the beggars was made a central feature of Act II.[76] Here, the beggarfolk help Leah's deceased *bashert*, Khonon, to win back his love by whirling around Leah "in an ecstatic, violent dance, weakening her body and spirit."[77] We need not rely upon the rather forced Marxist interpretation of Vakhtangov's Dance of the Beggars as found in Soviet analysis of the production, which posits that the poor folk aim to assist Khonon and Leah to rebel against "the heartless world of the rich," to argue that the beggars play a key role in the Habimah production, as they do already in the play as written.[78] They serve as a kind of bridge between Leah and Khonon, between the worlds of the living and the dead.

Contemporary observers were struck by the dark, hellish vision of the beggars' dance. Writing in 1922, the theater critic Nikolai Volkov wrote that Vakhtangov's ugly, grotesque beggars were "people-monsters" characterized by "monstrous faces, deformed bodies and contorted movements."[79] Another contemporary described the beggars as "phantoms, the tormented progeny of hell."[80] Viewing the piece in Paris in 1926, the ballet critic André Levinson described the scene as a "nightmarish vision [of] the meeting place of all human miseries."[81]

FIGURE 7.1. "Dance of the Beggars" in the 1922 Habima production of *The Dybbuk*. Courtesy The Israeli Center for the Documentation of the Performing Arts, Tel Aviv University. Reprinted with permission.

But there was more to Vakhtangov's modernist, symbolist vision of the paupers than just horror and darkness. Rather than elicit pity or pathos in the viewer, Vakhtangov's beggarfolk revealed the hidden, repressed side of human existence: animalistic, instinctive, automatic: the id expressed in dance. Indeed, in rehearsing the dance, each actor chose a different animal to inspire his character's temperament and movements: a monkey, a fox, a frog.[82] The ambiguity of category—is this a hunchbacked man or a fox?—prompted further anxiety in the viewer, as Elizabeth Grosz argues in explaining the horror and fascination provoked by the freak, "an *ambiguous* being whose existence imperils categories and oppositions dominant in social life."[83] Even as they circle around Leah, ostensibly the focus of the paupers' gaze and therefore the viewers', the marginal types, limbs akimbo, repeating movements mechanically, themselves become the center of the action. Their heavily stylized deformity and ugliness were not, of course, meant to mirror reality but were rather an artistic interpretation. Nor was that stylization

limited to the choreography; the *New York Times* theater critic J. Brooks Atkinson described the makeup and set design as "grotesque," "off-center," and
"angular."[84] In other words, the entire production was painted in exagger-
ated, grotesque artistic techniques. As Vladislav Ivanov argues, the Dance
of the Beggars was one significant focal point of an entire production in
which Vakhtangov "created a new picture of the world." In their contorted
movements, the beggars were only extraordinary because they were a heightened version of the world around them, a world that had become the world
of the marginals: all crooked angles, deformity, ugliness. Their "expressive
deformity" and "ritualistic repetition of changing movement," Ivanov contends, brought a kind of otherworldly terror to the stage, similar perhaps
to Nijinsky's 1913 *Rite of Spring*.[85] Here, ugliness "bursts out into new and
unexpected forms of beauty—beauty on the far side of possible."[86]

In his 1937 film version, Michał Waszyński staged the dance in similar fashion; the beggars—while perhaps not appearing as monstrous as in
Vakhtangov's interpretation—nonetheless dance wildly in seemingly random
ways, flailing their arms. A "crippled" man dances in the middle, holding
up a crutch.[87] Beggars also seem to dance in Chaim Grade's impressionistic
depiction of a begging day in 1930s-era Vilna, a virtual assault by a horde of
filthy beggars descending on the shopkeepers of his mother's street:

> One man strides seemingly without moving, as if he were not actually walk-
> ing but simply letting the floor slide away from under him. Another, who is
> lame, is so twisted over his crippled leg that he almost touches the floor; he
> waves his hands about, winglike, as though seeking something to hold onto
> so as not to sink into the ground. The body of third is totally rigid, while his
> head and neck writhe in convulsions.[88]

Vakhtangov's aesthetic approach was very much of its day, a period in which
symbolism was on the rise—"the new aesthetics of expressing the moods
and emotions of the inner man and not the external reality."[89] But it was
also a faithful interpretation of An-ski's text, which exploded the realm of
the dead and the poor onto the plane of the ordinary. *The Dybbuk* challenged
the boundaries between visible reality and the invisible world that lies just
beyond, whether that world is the realm of the spirits, of the marginal people,
or of ugliness.

World War I and the emergence of national social welfare

World War I and its aftereffects brought unprecedented upheaval and destruction to East European Jewry, and with them also a new understanding of
society's outcasts. Wartime expulsions and pogroms, and the genocidal massacres that took place in the Ukrainian lands during the Russian Civil War,
left—in addition to tens, perhaps hundreds of thousands of dead—hundreds
of thousands of Jewish refugees and orphans, many of them with serious
physical and mental injuries. Terms such as "charity cases," "the homeless,"
and "madmen" now took on entirely new resonances and required radically
different approaches.[90] In many ways figures that had previously been seen as
outcasts now represented the mainstream of Jewish society. A 1923 image in
New York's *Jewish Daily Forward* captured the tragedy by showing a barefoot
beggar woman in the unlikely environs of a photograph studio. The caption
read, "Her husband died of starvation, a son was killed in the war, while one
of her daughters is reputed to have become a camp mistress of the German
soldiers."[91] The subtext was that this could have been any Jewish woman in
eastern Europe—her family torn apart by war, her menfolk killed by gunfire
or starvation, her daughter sexually abused and humiliated.

In this context, the definition of marginal people took on starkly different
dimensions. Leyb Yakhnovitsh, a stringer for New York's *Forverts*, reported
in 1922 on a wedding of two couples in Odessa's Jewish cemetery as a measure against an epidemic, apparently one of the very last instances of the
cholera wedding. One of the couples consisted of two refugees from the massacres of the previous years, an ordinary young man and a beautiful young
woman. Why had they been chosen as cholera bride and groom? The man
was "not fully of sound mind" because he had been forced by bandits to bury
his father alive, while the woman had been raped and infected with venereal
disease. The second couple were a veteran who could no longer speak thanks
to a wound sustained in combat, and who did not want to go back to his
hometown because he did not want his parents to see him as a mute, and a
woman from a small town who had had one of her eyes gouged out by po-
gromists. In Yakhnovitsh's words, she was also—presumably like the others
married in the ceremony—"a half-person."[92]

At one point, Yakhnovitsh mentions that the wedding party is standing
on a grave—which we soon learn is the grave of a victim of the 1905 Odessa

FIGURE 7.2. Studio portrait of a beggar woman
in Vilna, *Forverts*, December 16, 1923. The English
caption reads, "A WAR VICTIM. Her husband
died of starvation, a son was killed in the war, while
one of her daughters is reputed to have become a
camp mistress of the German soldiers." Archives of
the YIVO Institute for Jewish Research, New York.

pogrom. The author's unnamed interlocutor uses the term "martyr," signaling
that brides and grooms who have experienced unspeakable horrors are to be
seen in the same light, or almost: they are suspended somewhere between
life and death, between full personhood and nonexistence. Surely there were
now countless such "half-persons" throughout eastern Europe. This was a totally new category of marginal individual. Unlike in previous generations,
the plight of such marginal people was not due to an accident of birth or
a mishap but to large-scale persecution of the Jewish people. Their horrific

suffering and trauma has thus been experienced on behalf of all Jews. There could be no more fitting candidate for the cholera wedding, whose bride and groom are meant to bear the burden of suffering on behalf of the entire community.

During the war, Russian and Polish Jewish communal leaders and activists had leaped to the aid of their coreligionists, infusing new funds and energies into the few existing national relief organizations—primarily OZE (the Society for the Protection of the Health of the Jewish Population) and ORT (the Society for Handicraft and Agricultural Work among the Jews of Russia)—and establishing an array of new relief organizations such as Ekopo (the Jewish Committee for the Relief of War Victims) and Evobshchestkom (the Jewish Public Committee for Assisting Victims of War and Pogroms).[93] After the war, the shift to widespread relief organized on the national level continued in newly independent Poland, where the interwar period saw rapid growth in Jewish welfare organizations such as CENTOS (the Federation of Orphan Care Societies). There, nationalist-minded social welfare professionals laboring in the fields of education and orphan and refugee aid sought self-consciously to shape a new kind of aid, one that would be light-years away from the old "charity." As one activist put it in a 1927 article on the subject, "Compassion [rakhmones] is a noble emotion, but it is appropriate to charity, not to systematic, goal-oriented aid."[94]

The first state-sponsored social welfare systems in western, central, and northern Europe had emerged in the decades immediately prior to World War I, and the war and the many social problems it engendered made necessary an expansion of those systems, which advanced economies could afford.[95] Newly independent Poland, by contrast, had neither the wherewithal to care for all its citizens nor the proclivity to provide aid for a religious and ethnic minority whom many Poles—including Polish political leaders—perceived as an alien group. The network of Jewish welfare organizations that emerged on the Polish lands during and immediately after the war, then, might in another context have served as partial foundation for a true welfare state. But nationalism dictated another path, and the politicized educational and child welfare systems among Jews in interwar Poland was part of a larger trend in east-central Europe of nationalizing social care, as Tara Zahra shows in the case of the Bohemian lands. Indeed, Zahra's observation that "[n]ationalist movements flourished by focusing their attention precisely on children and families, and by defining social issues as questions of national survival" could apply directly to the Jewish situation in Poland.[96]

That impulse also existed among Jewish communal leaders in Soviet Russia, where although relief efforts were regulated by the state, funds (primarily from the American Jewish Joint Distribution Committee) and projects were routed through Evobshchestkom (now known also as Yidgezkom), which brought together organizations such as ORT and OZE.[97] However, attempts in the early 1920s to create social welfare institutions and networks, even with concerted support from the JDC, went nowhere once the Soviet state made the fateful decision to nationalize Jewish institutions and close down all organizations with links to nationalist movements.[98]

Back in Poland, it was not only the new national organizations that revealed a fresh approach to traditional charity. As an article in the memorial volume for Oświęcim (Oshpitsin) recalls, the town's Talmud Torah Society had existed for many years, but "its first successful activities began with the outbreak of World War I, when the city became host to refugees fleeing the front lines and isolated settlements. . . . Children wandered the streets like unattended sheep without anyone to care for them."[99] Organizers took the initiative to raise funds and hire teachers so that no child would go without schooling, and in the subsequent years the institution expanded rapidly.

But the new social welfare system sometimes had its own cost. In a memoir of interwar Prużany, Mendeleh and Rive-Zisl are two marginal individuals brought together in a match arranged by the town pranksters.[100] After taking up residence in the hekdesh, the couple have three children in quick succession, after which Mendeleh passes away suddenly. Thus far we have a fairly typical tale of shtetl marginal folk. What is different here, however, is that a Jewish welfare network intervenes to assist Rive-Zisl's children, who are rescued from the cold poorhouse where they sleep on a straw sack on the floor and placed in a "very well organized" Jewish orphanage in town. There the children are well cared for and educated while their mother is employed as an aide so that she can be near them. The story ends on a note of triumph: the good-looking, intelligent eldest son, Nochim, graduates from the Hebraist Tarbut gymnasium. Thus, a tale that began with all the classic marks of marginality ends on a note of redemption: modern philanthropy has, it seems, ended the cycle of marginality. But at what cost? Rive-Zisl, now employed as a "helper" in the orphanage, is near her children, but she surely cannot function as a normal mother if her children are in the care of an institution. Thus, in order for the children to thrive, she must endure the severing of the mother-child relationship. Nor is the legacy of marginality completely erased: the last thing that the memoirist tells us about the family is that Nochim's younger siblings, who go unnamed in her account, are developmentally disabled ("retarded"). We hear nothing more. Is the lesson here that, no matter the good intentions of the Jewish community to aid its outcasts—here rewarded by the happy case of Nochim—marginality will always breed marginality?

"Ovadiah the Cripple" (1921)

S. Y. Agnon offered a more optimistic statement about the new national Jewish welfare and its transformative impact on Jewish marginals in a short story published soon after the war. A marginal character is the protagonist of Agnon's story "Ovadiah the Cripple." Compare this to Abramovitsh's *Fishke the Lame*, for example: while one might argue that Fishke is the protagonist, he is not really the hero of his own story. Abramovitsh attempted to make Fishke a full person with a true interior life, but ultimately Fishke remains secondary to the Mendele frame story.[101] By contrast, the character Ovadiah is drawn with great attention to his inner life and psyche; indeed, much of the story unfolds there.

A cripple and a hunchback, Ovadiah Halbleyb ("Half-life") earns his living as a water carrier. The story begins in this way: "Ovadiah the water carrier never complained about his lot [lit., against heaven]; to the contrary, he found a reason to give praise for his deformity, for if he had been like all other men, would he have gotten engaged to a young woman who was gossiped about?"[102]

His name is fitting. Its meaning is "servant of God," but is this a servant in its secular sense? In other words, is Ovadiah a peer of his fiancée, the servant Sheyne Serl? Or is his being called a servant of God a suggestion that his true nature places him far above most of the other residents of his town? Agnon ironically dubs him *ba'al mum*, "the cripple," an allusion to the physical defects that make a priest ineligible to offer sacrifices (Lev.

21:17–20), which in the traditional sense would exclude him from divine service—whereas his given name suggests him to be *more* worthy of serving God, rather than less. Still, there is no denying the fact that Ovadiah is stricken with at least two of the bodily defects that Leviticus lists: he is lame (*pise'ah*) and a hunchback (*giben*). We shall soon see that the last defect in the list—*meroah ashekh*, crushed testicles—may also apply, if only symbolically. Moreover, with only one chapter, Obadiah is the shortest book in the Bible, perhaps an oblique reference to Ovadiah's marginal status in the town.

From the start, we are given to understand that Sheyne Serl deserves to be the subject of gossip, since she is a shameless and rather dissolute young woman who is happy to flirt with other men even after she becomes engaged to Ovadiah. The expression Agnon uses to describe her is *shifhah harufah*, a Talmudic term referring to a strange situation suggested by a phrase in Leviticus 19:20: a woman who is a half-slave. The situation arises because she has two masters, one of whom has freed her, while the other has not. Thus, a Hebrew slave may marry her, but is technically only marrying the half of her that is free. The term can also mean, more simply, a female slave who has been given in marriage to another of her master's slaves.

The use of the term *shifhah harufah* shows Agnon's mastery of irony in his use of biblical and rabbinic allusions. The early chapters of the story make it clear that Ovadiah will only ever be marrying half of Sheyne Serl at most, since she is so clearly interested in dallying with other men. This circumstance makes the fact that his name means "servant" even more significant. Also, since Sheyne Serl ends up having an affair with Reuben, a servant in the same household, the term in its second meaning turns out to be quite prescient.

Early on in the story, Ovadiah acknowledges Sheyne Serl's questionable moral reputation to himself, but he comes to terms with the situation by placing the two of them on similarly low positions: "Right now I am only an insubstantial and inferior creature and she is a *shifhah harufah*," but when they marry he will be transformed into a householder, an independent man, the master of his own house (*ba'al bayit*), and she will become the mistress of the house (*ba'alat bayit*).[103] However, the narrator immediately intervenes and begs to differ, informing the reader in somewhat crass terms that Sheyne Serl may not be so easily transformed from the *shifhah harufah* that she is now into a proper wife: "As soon as a man gets himself a bed, he also gets himself fleas. So it was with Ovadiah: he got himself a bride, and everyone else got her too [*zakhah kalah, zakhu bah aherim*]."[104] Thus Ovadiah is seemingly destined to be a cuckold from the start, an important building block for Agnon's shaping of the role of gender in the story.

There follows a wrenching scene that takes place in the town dance hall. After having hesitated for some time about whether or not to go to the hall and tell Sheyne Serl that he no longer wants her to frequent the place, Ovadiah finally picks up the courage to enter, despite the fact that he senses that he may be bullied. Aware that he looks like a pauper—even with clothing and shoes, he is described as "naked" and "barefoot"—he nonetheless summons enough self-confidence and gumption to ask himself, "Should I be ashamed in front of those beggars?"[105] (And indeed, the reader wonders: who is worthy of scorn in this scene—the marginal person, or those who treat him as less than human?) After he has delivered his message to Sheyne Serl, who promptly turns her back on him, the lads in the dance hall "gathered around him, mocking and taunting him, and knocked his crutch from his hands. He leaned over to pick it up, and as he leaned, he almost lost his balance and fell over." Then it is the girls' turn to taunt him by mock-arguing over which of them will win him as a dance partner, one pulling him this way and another that way.[106] Singing a ditty ridiculing him, the young men then hoist him up on his crutch. Ovadiah flails about and is finally let down, only to have Reuben grab his crutch, attempt unsuccessfully to break it, and then throw it into the fire. Ovadiah thrashes "like a drowning man," collapses, and is taken to the hospital. Here as elsewhere in the story, Agnon contrasts the moral ugliness of the shtetl with the innocence and purity, perhaps even childlike nature, of the marginal hero; we shall see this contrast again in the fiction of Joseph Opatoshu and Israel Joshua Singer.

This shocking incident is nothing less than Ovadiah's public symbolic emasculation, perhaps even castration. Having been publicly scorned by his fiancée, he is violently made to lose hold of his crutch—a clear phallic symbol, as Gershon Shaked points out—and is later made a figure of fun as he is forced to keep his balance while sitting astride the crutch.[107] It would seem, then, that the biblical defect of crushed testicles does, in fact, apply to Ovadiah, at least from the point of view of the townspeople. Moreover, while it is

Sheyne Serl who becomes pregnant and gives birth, Ovadiah is described in similar terms: in the hospital, he lies "like a woman giving birth." And later, after Ovadiah is released from the hospital, a man whom he encounters in the town tells him, "You disappeared all of a sudden. We were sure that you had gone to Brody and found employment as a wet nurse."[108] The reader is left to wonder if Ovadiah's hope to be the master of his household can ever actually be realized. Is he even a real man? Agnon deliberately leaves the definition of masculinity in question all the way until the very end of the story.

Established by a young Zionist doctor who was appointed chief doctor of the decrepit institution after the death of his senior colleague, the hospital to which Ovadiah is taken is a successor to the hekdesh and the so-called hospital for the poor that we saw in chapter 3. The young doctor instituted so many far-reaching changes that it eventually became a new thing altogether—a modern hospital that "became a blessing for the town." Here, treated with kindness, Ovadiah marvels at the expert medical care, the food, the clean sheets, and the clothing.

It is modern philanthropy in a nationalist key, then, that lifts the marginal figure up and restores his humanity to him. Upon arrival, he is convinced that the Christian nurse who speaks compassionately to him has mistaken him for someone else because he is not dressed in his usual rags, and that the next day she will realize her error and reproach him. "She had glanced at the chair, surely intending to look at his clothing, for she would be able to judge his character from his clothing."[109] But the staff's empathy is real and unceasing—indeed, "not a day passes without their doing him a kindness."[110] During his long stay in the hospital, which Agnon describes in great detail, Ovadiah's body undergoes changes that diminish some of the unattractive physical aspects that denoted his marginal status: toothpaste whitens his teeth and freshens his breath; the cream he is given softens his hands, smooths his wrinkles, and makes his sores fade away; his new rubber-tipped crutch makes no noise when he walks; and "even his hunch did not weigh so heavily on his back and did not pull him downwards, as if the tip of it had been lopped off and a bit of had been tossed away."[111] If we see this as a symbolic circumcision, Ovadiah has, in effect, undergone a rebirth. Just before his release from the hospital, he goes for a walk, and while he still limps, "his gait now was not like it had been before. Before he entered the hospital, he would move jerkily and creep [*zohel*] like a cripple [*ke-va'al mum*], but now he walked like a refined person [*ke-istenis*]."[112] At one point, the doctor pats him on the back—his back, the site of his disfigurement!—and says, "Today you have become a man, Ovadiah."[113] Perhaps being treated like a human being has also restored the masculinity that was so cruelly taken from him through his abuse at the hands of the townspeople.

After he finally and somewhat reluctantly leaves the hospital, Ovadiah seeks out Sheyne Serl, not knowing of course that while he has been in the compassionate hands of the doctors and nurses at the hospital, her lot has worsened considerably. He finds her sitting on a stoop, having been thrown out of the house where she served. In her arms is a newborn baby, the result of her affair with Reuben: "She pushed her nipple into the baby's mouth and screamed, 'Here you go, bastard, suck and choke!'"[114] Afraid to give Sheyne Serl candies he has bought for her, Ovadiah bends down and puts them in the baby's hand—not only balm for Sheyne Serl's constant rage but, no less important, a symbol of his own readiness to care for a child that is not his own. Ovadiah thus becomes the embodiment of compassion, grace, mercy, love—all gifts showered upon him during his stay in the hospital, which immersed him in the humanistic ethos at the heart of its mission. Even more important, Agnon suggests, all those traits are part of the complex admixture that is Ovadiah's masculinity—yes, together with fearfulness, hesitancy, and timidity.[115]

Ovadiah is still a cripple and a hunchback, but perhaps not *ba'al mum* in the same way as before—he sees himself differently now, and others (or at least some others) do too. This is the true regeneration, Agnon suggests, not the erasure of all bodily weaknesses and flaws promoted by some strands of Zionist ideology but the lifting up of the individual and his self-esteem. Nor does this renewal demand conventional bourgeois masculinity, but rather an expression of gender that crosses traditional boundaries. On the national plane, this corresponds to a restoration that is not a total remaking of the nation but a reconciliation with weakness and infirmity—both physical and psychic—until the point is reached where, while the nation's flaws do not define it, they are not denied either.

Ironically, the Zionism that endorsed the kind of transformation that Ovadiah undergoes in this story as the key to the regeneration of the Jewish people often ended up reproducing in its discourse of transformation the stereotypes that it sought to overcome. The diaspora Jew deformed by centuries of unnatural living, the neurotic Jew sickened by persecution and self-hatred, the weak ghetto Jew estranged from the land, the effeminate Jew alienated from true masculinity—all these images of degeneration were reified in arguments like the one that Max Nordau made so famously in his "Muskeljudentum" speech at the Second Zionist Congress in 1898 and that Max Mandel'shtam, a prominent ophthalmologist and Zionist leader in Kiev, made (somewhat less famously) at the Fourth Zionist Congress two years later.[116] A suitable foil for Nordau's call for physical regeneration, Mandel'shtam's speech described at length the bodily degeneration from which East European Jewry suffered: Jews' bodies were less developed and more susceptible to disease, and their overdeveloped brains predisposed to neurosis and mental illness.[117] "The muscle Jew was a paradoxical figure of regeneration," Todd Presner writes. "It epitomized the rebirth of the strong Jew as drawn from Jewish history and mythology; but, at the same time, many of the anti-Semitic stereotypes of Jewish degeneracy were internalized in its conceptualization."[118] Would the Zionist movement place the same emphasis on internal, emotional rehabilitation that accompanies Ovadiah's physical regeneration? And what if Ovadiah had exited the hospital renewed spiritually but unchanged physically? Would that have been sufficient or satisfying for Agnon's readers?

New interest in Jewish marginals at home and abroad

Historians also began to take an interest in the margins of Jewish society.[119] Veteran historians such Majer Bałaban and Ignacy (Yitskhok) Schiper included the hekdesh, paupers, and beggars in their studies, while younger scholars, many of them fervent socialists, were often dedicated to understanding the experience of the poor Jewish masses in history.[120] Emanuel Ringelblum was particularly interested in bringing to light "the Jewish dregs," to quote the title of one of his sketches of little-known episodes and figures in Polish Jewish history.[121] His short study of Jewish beggars, which attempted to understand the roots of the widespread problem of Jewish beggary and destitution in late eighteenth-century Poland, was one of the first works of Jewish history to approach the subject of the socially marginalized in a systematic way and to begin a full exploration of the topic and its relationship to larger questions of Jewish history.[122] Unlike some Zionist ideologues and writers, historians like Ringelblum did not seek to transform or expunge the "deformed" aspect of Jewry, but rather to resurrect it in order to gain a fuller understanding of the Jewish experience in eastern Europe.

The interwar years also registered a new emphasis on marginal figures in the work of Jewish writers and folklorists. Interwar-era folklorists expanded their understanding of "the folk" to include such outcasts as criminals and prostitutes, most notably in the miscellany *Bay undz yidn* (1923), but also in a number of other collections of folklore, including collections of songs.[123] A YIVO handbook for its *zamlers* (lay or amateur folklorists) included just such types in its taxonomy of groups in Jewish society whom the amateur ethnographer could interview and describe.[124] Those groups included thieves, prostitutes, and other *dek-mentshn* (people at the bottom, or "the lowest of the low"), wandering organ-grinders, beggars, and swindlers. Professional photographers might also have "interesting types" sit for portraits for artistic reasons, as Avraham Rotenberg of Staszów apparently did in the 1930s. (Rotenberg perished during the war, but his son Simcha, who had worked with his father in the studio, survived and managed to save many of the latter's photographs by giving them to a Christian for safekeeping.)[125]

A sympathetic attitude to misfits, freaks, and outcasts was consonant with Jewish ideological currents in the Second Polish Republic, since such people could be seen as the salt of the earth and an embodiment of the true spirit of the Jewish nation. By contrast, the ideological strictures of Soviet scholarship did not provide much scope for Jewish folklorists to investigate shtetl society, let alone marginal people or deviance. As Deborah Yalen has shown, that line of inquiry was at odds with state policy that aimed to rid society of "unproductive" elements.[126] Despite the appearance of pamphlets such as *Research Your Shtetl!* (published in 1928 by the Social-Economic Commission and Bureau for Regional Studies of the Jewish Section of the Institute for Belorussian Culture), all too soon academics toeing the Stalinist ideological line branded scholars who conducted ethnographic studies of shtetl society as "scholarship for scholarship's sake" as bourgeois. "Henceforward, local studies (Yiddish: *kantkentnish*) would devote itself to the task of socialist construction . . . [a] strictly utilitarian approach to the collection of socioeconomic data.[127]

FIGURE 7.3. "The Beggar," Staszów, Kielce Province, Poland (1930s). Studio photo: Abraham J. Rotenberg. © Museum of the Jewish People at Beit Hatfutsot, Oster Visual Documentation Center, Courtesy of M. Carmi, Israel.

A folkloristic interest in the Other of Jewish society in eastern Europe emerged in the immigrant community in North America as it looked back on its towns of origin, which from afar and in comparison with modern American life often seemed strange and exotic. One strain of cultural production in this vein was the travelogue-ethnography created by émigrés returning to visit their native towns. In the portrait of his hometown Nowogródek (Yid., Navaredok) that he wrote after his journey back to Poland in 1920 as a representative of the Naveradoker Aid Committee in New York, the Yiddish linguist and writer Alexander Harkavy described several "curious personages" who had lived in the town during his youth in the 1870s. One was the much-beloved Yisroel the madman, the town's jester-prankster. Yisroel was not really crazy, Harkavy wrote, but fundamentally a lazy person who pretended to be a fool so he would not have to work at a constant job. Instead, he was supported by the community and earned some money from odd jobs, one of which was as a stretcher-bearer transporting corpses for purification before burial.[128] Another was Binye the water-carrier, a man of great strength and few words, which made him seem mysterious to the townsfolk. Children imagined that he would enter the synagogue after midnight to be called up to the Torah by the dead.[129] Like so many marginal people, Yisroel and Binye were connected to the realm of death and the afterworld.

New media such as photography and film also played an important role in creating the image of the outcast of Jewish eastern Europe, often stylized and presented as part of the authenticity of this "native" culture. Travelers less cerebral than Harkavy also documented the underclass, including beggars and town fools in their photographs and 16-millimeter amateur films of their hometowns.[130] Ethnographic postcards of Polish and Lithuanian street scenes and interesting "types" produced during World War I frequently included beggars, suggesting that it was already accepted practice to highlight marginal people as quaint or eccentric aspects of the tourist landscape.[131] In 1923, the Yiddish-language *Jewish Daily Forward* (*Forverts*) launched a new rotogravure section, which often featured photographic essays on the Old Country entitled "Pictures of Jewish Life and Characters."[132] "Like other tabloids of the era, the *Jewish Daily Forward* . . . combined photographs of middle-class life in New York with pictures of poverty rendered exotic by their distant locales," Roberta

FIGURE 7.4. Portrait of Kalman the Fool of Staszów, *Forverts*, April 27, 1924, 19. The English caption reads, "Kalman, the town 'idiot' of Stashev, Poland." Archives of the YIVO Institute for Jewish Research, New York.

Newman notes.[133] The section introduced readers to characters such as "Kalman, the town 'idiot' of Stashev, Poland"; Motele, the town fool of Zwolen ("every town must have its town fool . . . He's probably enjoying the fact that the city can't do without him"); and "'Motke' the town fool [of Siedlce] and his pretty, young wife. His main source of income is to dance and make merry at weddings."[134] Nor were village idiots the only marginal types to appear in these pages; the *Forward* also highlighted beggars such as a beggar woman in Opatów photographed going to sleep in the cemetery and "Itshe" of Sokolowa, "son of the well-known Rabbi Mendel," who "wanders through the streets of the shtetl"—though these figures were portrayed without the tongue-in-cheek humor that the paper sometimes applied to the town fools. Itshe's portrait was presented alongside those of other beggars and homeless people under the heading "Curious Characters in European Shtetls." This could hardly be called journalism; it was, rather, sensationalized entertainment to satisfy a kind of prurient curiosity about life in the Old Country, now become somewhat alien.

FIGURE 7.5. The *shtot meshugener* (town fool) eating a bowl of noodles on a staircase in Płock (undated photograph). Archives of the YIVO Institute for Jewish Research, New York.

FIGURE 7.6. Photograph of a beggar woman, location unknown, *Forverts*, August 3, 1924. The English caption reads, "This Jewish beggar woman has established lodgings in the Jewish cemetery." Archives of the YIVO Institute for Jewish Research, New York.

Thus, in some sense the idea of the Jewish town fool or the village idiot as a phenomenon of journalistic interest emerged from the American Jewish immigrant milieu as it looked back on the world it had left behind. And even then, such curiosities were only made interesting by their existence; other than brief captions, no narrative accompanied the photographs of the town fool or beggar. The press was interested in stories, not ethnography, and for the most part the marginal people of the shtetl and city did not offer any discrete stories. Thus, while the *Forward* featured an array of photographs of town fools over the years, a search of the term "town fool" (*shtot-meshugener*) in interwar Yiddish newspapers published in Europe turns up almost no results.[135]

Yizker-bikher and the shtetl's ubiquitous Other

By contrast, the mad, town fools, and homeless beggars crowd the shtetl landscapes of the post–World War II yizkor volumes that memorialize the destroyed Jewish communities of Poland, Lithuania, and the Soviet Union.

FIGURE 7.7. Studio photograph of a beggar man,
Forverts, April 8, 1923. At left a hand can be seen dropping a coin into the man's hand, whether to heighten
the photo's authenticity or perhaps its comic value. The
English caption reads, "Itshele of Ostrow, Poland. All
his relatives are in the United States." Archives of the
YIVO Institute for Jewish Research, New York.

The memoiristic-ethnographic genre of the yizkor book allows for the inclusion of short sketches and vignettes in which a former resident of a town describes a peculiar individual or set of individuals, including anecdotes about inconsequential events or traditions that would never have made it into the pages of a prewar newspaper.[136]

In their attempts in the wake of the total destruction of the Holocaust to resurrect the lost universe of the shtetl down to its last detail, many of the memorial books include recollections and anecdotal accounts of the outcasts. There is sometimes a nostalgic cast to these sketches, and others are meant to be humorous, while a handful are bitingly harsh in their descriptions of the poor treatment of marginal people at the hands of the townspeople. In her study of the "Others" in yizkor books, Rivka Parciak argues that editors chose to include sketches of such people as foils for the otherwise normal life and residents of the small town, which must be "depicted and preserved in the collective memory as beautiful and untarnished."[137] This is possible. More likely is the desire of many editors and contributors to try to resurrect the destroyed shtetl, as it were, on the page, by remembering and writing down every detail, however trivial, grotesque, or even ugly.[138] Each yizkor book editor or writer had his or her own vision of the shtetl, however, and many left out or ignored whole swathes of their hometowns' religious or political life.[139] As with the *Forward*'s rotogravure section, the distance from one's hometown—in this case not only geographic but also chronological—made the mundane noteworthy and the nonconforming downright peculiar.

Unlike the othering gaze of many yizkor book accounts, artistic representations of East European Jewry and its marginal people in the interwar period tended to be sympathetic, depicting marginal characters as real people. Some were created outside of eastern Europe, like the work of the artist and photographer Moï Ver (Moshe Raviv-Vorobeichic), who included a photomontage of "Gedalke the Cantor," one of the four "crazy" people who lived in Vilna's *shul-hoyf*, in his photographic portrait of the Jewish community of that city.[140] Vorobeichic focused on the mundane and the shabby—petty traders, day laborers, and street urchins—rather than on Vilna's fabled Jewish past and storied religious institutions. Gedalke was not an exotic Other in his panorama of poverty and the commonplace. He was just another subject,

FIGURE 7.8. "Gedalke the Cantor." From M. Vorobeichic, *Rehov ha-yehudim be-vilnah: 65 temunot = Ein Ghetto im Osten—Wilna: 65 Bilder* (1931). Photo: Moshe Vorobeichic-Raviv- Moï Ver. Courtesy the Raviv family and archives in Israel. Reprinted with permission.

presented with the same keen eye for light and shadow, for the melding of humanity and the built landscape that Vorobeichic cast on all his subjects.[141]

The cholera wedding redux: Literary and cinematic representations of the cholera wedding in the interwar period

The era of the cholera wedding now belonged to the past, albeit a very recent one, the last having taken place in 1922. And it was precisely that past that writers such as Joseph Opatoshu and Israel Joshua Singer were now mining for material for their fiction. To some extent, the eclipse of the cholera wedding signaled the end, facilitated by new social welfare networks, of the cruel and degrading treatment of marginals that the ritual embodied. Or-phans, disabled people, and other marginals were now increasingly likely to find support from a local branch of CENTOS or TOZ, the national Jewish health-care network in Poland, or from a newly established or revivified local institution. Even the hekdesh was on the wane: by the 1920s, the traditional poorhouse had mostly disappeared from cities and large towns, thanks to the institutionalization and professionalization of welfare services in the Jewish community, which had taken on a more urgent pace during and immediately after World War I.[142]

But as Opatoshu and Singer must have known, "medieval" attitudes persisted, especially in provincial towns. One could still find a traditional hekdesh in many *shtetlekh*: in some locales newspaper reports portrayed an institution that differed little, at least in some places, from its prewar variant. In towns and cities across Poland, beggars and "idiots" wandered the streets, frequently pitied and given a coin or two, often laughed at, and sometimes (as in Chaim Grade's portrait of beggar-bandits in Vilna in *My Mother's Sabbath Days*) feared. Gifted artists used historical material to explore the meaning of history itself—"turning history inside out and telling us what's under the skin," in Hilary Mantel's words[143]—but also to reveal troubling aspects of contemporary Jewish society. Opatoshu sought to recreate the dynamism and vitality of previous eras of Jewish history; his first historical novel, *In poylishe velder* (In Polish Woods, 1921), featured the unforgettable Bare-foot Israel, a madman and prophet.[144] Singer also wove historical themes, as well as contemporary concerns, into novels that delved deeply into the Jewish condition in eastern Europe. S. Y. Abramovitsh, who first wrote about the cholera wedding only a few years after the first wave in the mid-1860s, never fundamentally changed his position as a middle-class writer taking his educated, middle-class audience on a journey into the underclass that, although edifying, was both humorous and risqué (sans the risk, of course), but there was no element of "slumming" in Opatoshu's and Singer's treat-ment of the cholera wedding. They insisted on immersing the reader in the harsh environment in which the cholera wedding was possible. Paradoxically, however, they achieved the immediacy that infuses their narratives—and the inspired and insightful analyses of the inner meaning of the folk ritual—by putting critical distance between themselves and their subjects; and not only the distance afforded by a historical subject. Opatoshu had been living in America since 1907, and Singer would emigrate to the United States in 1934, several years after the publication of *Yoshe Kalb*, the novel discussed below. He was, however, as Anita Norich writes, already "looking to a new location"—America.[145]

JOSEPH OPATOSHU'S "A WEDDING IN THE CEMETERY" (1929)

Opatoshu opens his story in a town struck by an epidemic. Families are shuttered in their homes, listening for the sound of stretchers being carried through the streets. No house has been untouched by sickness. Corpses lie unprepared for days because the members of the burial society are worn out from washing and burying so many bodies. The religious and communal leadership huddle together night after night to consult about what is to be done. Finally, the town learns of their decision: Shloyme *batlen*, a hunchback, will marry Brokhe, Berl the melamed's daughter, the developmentally delayed (*nisht-derbakene*, lit., unbaked) maiden, in the old cemetery. A wave of relief washes over the townspeople. Dressed in their finery, men and women, young and old, Jews and Christians, stream in their hundreds—no, in their thousands—away from town, towards the cemetery. "In their dark faces, in their saddened eyes, it was more a funeral than a wedding."[146]

> The bridegroom was so skinny, so tall . . . and on top of that, a hunchback. The hunch under his silk *kapote* [robe] looked like an appendage, because tall people have no hunch. His wide face, confused, bony, with red patches of beard, was deeply pockmarked, looking like a cemetery with dug-open graves, where the dead have run away. The bride was thin, drawn, with reddened cheeks and lips as if they had been painted, with two and a half hairs on her head, on which a white paper flower had been stuck. The right hand shorter than the left, withered, with a little fist, like a three-year-old child.

They are led first to the gravedigger's house for the ritual of seating the bride. Then the master of ceremonies announces: "Wedding gifts!" All look around, afraid to be the first to set their gifts on the empty tables. Then "a woman in tattered clothes, a beggar, stepped forward." She limps and is "disheveled, like a witch."[147] The wealthy Jews cannot believe that she will be permitted to be the first—but yes, she is called forward.

The beggar woman jumped up, and while hobbling forward pulled a new tin spoon out of her beggar's sack. She lifted the spoon over her head, spun it over her head once, then twice, as one does with *kapores*, then laid it on the table, crying, "It should be away from me and stay with you! [*S'zol avek fun mir un blaybn bay dir!*] From me to you!"[148]

As the crowd begins to put their gifts on the table, everyone utters the same phrase, "From me to you!" The setting down of gifts goes on for an hour, then a second hour. The air becomes saturated with tears. "'From me to you!' 'From me to you!'"[149]

The primary narrative is then broken by a bizarre episode. The town engineer, a Christian, is photographing the scene. The crowd asks him not to take pictures, and an argument breaks out. A Jew rips away his camera and throws it in the air; another spectator, a Christian, catches it and throws it again. It shatters into pieces. Policemen standing nearby, pretending not to see, mutter, "Break his bones, the son of a bitch, then he'll know what it means to serve the Devil!"[150]

The attendees dance their way joyously to the wedding canopy, erected next to the *ohel* (structure erected around the grave) of a local tsaddik. Then the bride is led under the canopy, looks around, and takes fright.

She pulled the groom's hands away from his face and looked at him as a child looks at a doll she has just received and began shifting backwards. "It's Shloymele? Shloymele batlen, my bridegroom? No, no, no!" Her shriek became a thin, sharp cry, floated up over the thousands of bowed heads, and rent the blazing sky.[151]

The story is rich with the symbolism of the cholera wedding and of the marginals of the East European Jewish world. The groom is physically deformed, the bride cognitively disabled, childlike, and physically repulsive. The bridal couple's connection to the world of the dead is clear: his face looks "like a cemetery with dug-open graves, where the dead have run away"; she undergoes the ritual of "seating the bride" in the gravedigger's house. There is also a suggestion of gender reversal, since we later learn that the face that is covered under the wedding canopy is not the bride's, as would normally be the case, but Shloyme's, who is covering his face with his hands. The lame beggar woman, another marginal, is a central figure, and Opatoshu hints at her link to the world of the supernatural in comparing her to a witch and having her be the first to utter the signal phrase—or, perhaps more accurately, incantation: "From me to you!" That phrase begins its life as a longer sentence: "Let it away from me and stay with you!" But what is her meaning? Clearly it is not just a reference to her gift of a tin spoon but rather to the plague itself, and perhaps to the evil that brought it: may it be removed from me and rest upon you. The bride and groom are, then, scapegoats in the true sense of the term: that which is repellent to the community is transferred to their heads. And thus it emerges that the tin spoon actually holds great significance after all, for it is that spoon that the beggar woman waves above her head as if she is doing the ritual of *kapores,* transferring one's sins to a symbolic scapegoat. Ironically, it is only another marginal person who truly understands what the community is doing to its outcasts; and only after the beggar woman has made this clear through her words—"From me to you!"—does everyone else take up the cry, recognizing in it their deepest desire for what the cholera wedding is meant to achieve.

The town engineer who attempts to photograph the wedding may be read as Opatoshu himself, inserting himself into the story. In his profession and avocation (as photographer) a symbol of modernity and the outside world, he separates himself from the members of the assembled crowd—who, while spectators in one sense, are active participants in the ritual in another—by seeking to record the spectacle on film. He thus becomes a voyeur, peering in on the "medieval" scene from the outside. The crowd will have none of it; his camera is smashed, and even the Christian policemen curse him; ironically, it is he, a fellow Christian, whom they call a servant of the Devil, rather than disparaging the magical Jewish ritual that they are overseeing. Modern medicine has not checked the plague, and thus the townspeople fall back on the security of "tradition"; the camera, an artifact of the modern world, must not be permitted to disturb the sanctity of the ritual.

The iniquity of the community's treatment of Shloyme and Brokhe (their names, in another irony, mean "peace" and "blessing") is most vividly evident in the poignant last lines of the story, when the bride realizes—she only now understands—whom she is about to marry. In the only intimation of redemption in the story, Brokhe, who hitherto has spoken not a word, suddenly gains the self-assurance to communicate her pain to those gathered around her and to the entire world, a pain embodied in a "No!" so full of agony that it rips through the heavens themselves. But it's too late. This is the end of the story, and we must assume that her cry of anguish has had no impact on the townspeople. No one will come to the aid of Brokhe and Shloyme; the only hint of the modern world has been smashed; ignorance, depravity, and venality rule the day, just as the epidemic reigns in the town. There is, ultimately, no salvation in the story.

I. J. SINGER, *YOSHE KALB* (1932)

The protagonist of *Yoshe Kalb* is actually two characters: Nokhem, a rabbi's son and member of the Hasidic elite who flees his town after an affair with his mother-in-law that ends in tragedy, and his alter ego—the person he becomes upon beginning his wanderings—Yoshe Kalb, an unlearned itinerant beggar. In his wanderings, Yoshe arrives in the town of Bialogura and settles into a beggar's life; we are then introduced to another marginal figure in town, Tsivye the prostitute. In the end Nokhem/Yoshe is revealed to be a *gilgl*, or transmigrated soul, showing once again the enduring connection between the marginal figure, ever a liminal character, and the world of the dead. And Tsivye lives with her father the beadle in the *taare-shtibl*, the house for the purification of the dead.[152]

When an epidemic strikes Bialogura, the Jewish community is swept up in a frenzy of newfound piety and suspicion. Reb Meir'l, the town rabbi, is convinced that the epidemic can be traced to the sins—likely sexual sins—of one of the town's Jews. That sinner is soon uncovered: in attempting to grope her, as he has fondled so many local women, Abish the butcher discovers that the unmarried Tsivye is pregnant. (Of course, it is Tsivye, not Abish, who is the licentious one in this traditional setting as depicted by Singer.) The scene that follows makes the blood run cold:

> Four butchers lifted her up, each one throwing a hand or leg over his shoulder, as if she were a slaughtered animal.[153] Screaming and struggling, she was carried in procession towards the house of Reb Meir'l, the Rabbi. Women and children, hearing the wild yelling in the street, came running out and

joined. . . . Workers joined them. . . . Water-carriers . . . ran with their burdens. In front ran Abish the butcher, like a marshal.

"We've caught her," he roared to every side. "Zivyah [Tsivye], Reb
Kanah's daughter. We're taking her to the Rabbi."

There were some men who laughed, but the women, with hatred in
their blazing faces, shook their fists toward the struggling, panting girl, and
screamed:

"Stone her, the whore! For the sake of our little ones, stone her!"[154]

When Tsivye's father, the beadle, accuses Yoshe of having "ruined" his daughter, the mob makes for the synagogue, and a similar scene ensues. Yoshe is
beaten, tied, and hoisted up exactly as Tsivye was. "He looked, in fact, like a
slaughtered animal." And again, calls come from all sides to stone the sinner.[155] After much consultation, the rabbinic leaders of the town determine
that Yoshe and Tsivye must be married—in a cholera wedding. The biblical
punishment of stoning called for by the townspeople is not carried out, of
course; but is this apotropaic ritual so much less primitive? Their callousness
and vulgarity are made clear during their deliberations when one of the rabbinic judges remarks, "They're a well-matched pair, too. She's an imbecilic
cow [*beheyme*], and he's a calf [*kalb*]."[156] Even the putative sources of communal morality find Yoshe and Tsivye nothing more than a joke.

Though the species are different, Singer could hardly have made clearer
the image of the outcast as sacrificial lamb. For the townspeople, Yoshe and
Tsivye are animalistic, inhuman, wholly Other. Singer also plays on the
traditional association of plague with sexual sin. As we know, the historical cholera wedding was motivated in part by sexual anxiety, for which the
cholera bride and groom stood in as proxies. But in Singer's cholera wedding,
in the eyes of the town the bride and groom have unambiguously committed an act of sexual licentiousness, the proof of which is Tsivye's swelling
belly. To deepen the irony, for Yoshe, the cholera groom, life has led him to
this particular state of affairs because of one act of passionate adultery in his
previous existence as Nokhem, which one might even say has come to define
his entire life.

The first literary rendering of the cholera wedding, that of Abramovitsh
in *Fishke der krumer* (see chapter 4), is a caricature in which the brides and

grooms figure not as full-fledged characters but as grotesque creatures, note-worthy only for their repellent physical appearance (though of course two of the novel's main protagonists—Fishke and Beyle, both sympathetic charac-ters—are marginals). Opatoshu and Singer, in contrast, draw portraits of the cholera bridal couple that are both fuller and, crucially, more sympathetic. In "A Wedding at the Cemetery," the pathos is palpable: Shloyme and Brokhe barely know what is happening to them; the crowd gathered around them on the wedding day is indifferent, even heartless. And by presenting his readers with a character who, in his split personality, is in one dispensation firmly part of the Jewish establishment and in another on the margins of Jewish society, Singer suggests—as did Abramovitsh before him—that the two can-not be separated. The center and the margins are part of one collectivity, and, as in "A Wedding at the Cemetery," it is the former's appalling treatment of the latter that shows the reader just how low traditional society has sunk. Seeing that society through the eyes of writers like Opatoshu and Singer, the observer is in no doubt about which characters are the true monsters. "There is, then, no source of meaning on the social or individual level," Norich com-ments. "The remnants of what may once have been an ideologically coherent world are rendered in this novel as a symbolic system from which the indi-vidual must struggle to break free. Only the signs of religious authority and meaning are left, transfigured into corruptions and superstitions."[157]

FISHKE DER KRUMER (THE LIGHT AHEAD, 1939)

The apotheosis of the marginal figure as sympathetic protagonist—and, cor-respondingly, of representatives of traditional Jewish society as repulsive villains—is reached in *Fishke der Krumer* (titled *The Light Ahead* in English), a 1939 Yiddish-language film directed by Edward Ulmer from a screenplay by Chaver-Paver (Gershon Einbinder). Loosely based on Abramovitsh's novel, the film features as its two heroes marginal figures—a cripple and his blind love interest—and the shtetl and its traditional leadership are painted as both physically and morally repellent. Whereas the lead actors David Opatoshu ("Fishke") and Helen Beverly ("Hodel") are illuminated in close-ups that give them "a distinctive glow," the rabbinical and communal worthies of the town are portrayed as uncaring louts who only pay the couple any mind when they need them for a cholera wedding that they hope will bring to an end the epidemic that has struck the town.[158] Thanks to a scene in which the town fathers reject allocating any money to build a hospital or clean the polluted river that flows through the town, preferring instead to fund traditional prayer societies, the film makes clear that the shtetl's ill health can be attributed to the backward mind-set of the traditionalists. But it is Fishke and Hodel who have the last laugh—twice over, in fact. First, Fishke is delighted to discover that the elders want to marry him off to Hodel in the cholera wedding, for he is already in love with her (Hodel, on the other hand, despite her love for Fishke, is despondent at the prospect of a wedding steeped in shame). And more triumphantly, at the height of the wedding revelry the couple escape from the clutches of the shtetl folk ("Where did they go? Where did they go?" ask the townspeople hysterically), bound for new horizons, free from oppression.

The viewer is compelled to identify with Fishke and Hodel, despite—or perhaps because of—their disabilities. The pair's physical beauty is such that one is drawn to them ineluctably. "Beverly and Opatoshu are perhaps the most beautiful couple in the history of Yiddish cinema, and their scenes have a poignant erotic chemistry," J. Hoberman writes."[159] Hodel and Fishke represent the Jewish future, somewhere out there beyond the shtetl, which, as in Vakhtangov's staging of *The Dybbuk*, was designed to look dark, contorted, and cramped, all "crazy angles and skewed lampposts."[160] Unlike the visual representation of Jewish marginality found in the pages of the *Forward* in the same period, *Fishke der Krumer* does not exoticize the cripple and the blind woman but instead makes them appealing figures in some sense representatives of the nation as a whole.[161] It is also crucial that Fishke and Hodel are a loving, gender-stable, heterosexual couple, since almost all of the cholera wedding narratives we have reviewed included some element of gender reversal, and to incorporate that here would have risked alienating the audience utterly. Indeed, both the plot and the film's visual language insist on the emancipation of the marginal character from all of its traditional symbolic connections; the couple escape from the cemetery rather than allowing themselves to be chained to its symbolic nexus—they refuse to be the scapegoats of Opatoshu's story.[162] On the other hand, one could argue that *Fishke* is a quintessentially American story, and that—unlike Opatoshu's and Singer's cholera couples—Fishke and Hodel are in fact American film heroes with little relationship to the actual marginal people of Jewish eastern Europe.

FIGURE 7.9. Publicity still, Helen Beverly and David Opatoshu as Hodel and Fishke in *The Light Ahead* (1939). Courtesy the National Center for Jewish Film. Reprinted with permission.

Conclusion

In 1938, the New York-based Committee for the Medem Sanitarium, a facility outside of Warsaw established to care for and cure sickly Jewish children and affiliated with the Bund, sent a letter to the American Jewish Joint Distribution Committee requesting funds for urgent needs. "Among the basic problems of Jewish life," the letter opened, "that of the destitute, the physically weak and sick Jewish child is one of the most important. Of the 550,000 Jewish children of school age in Poland, more than half, due to the frightful conditions under which they live, are suffering from malnutrition[,] are physically malformed and mentally retarded."[163]

Two decades after the end of World War I, social care activists continued to describe a suffering Jewish nation using the same tropes that had been used to portray the victims of expulsions and massacres. The threats remained the same: widespread poverty, antisemitism, and the specter of violence—and the fear that they struck into the hearts of Jewish children, which was leading to an increasing incidence of "nervous disorder and psychic disarrangement." The sanitarium undertook the demanding work of rebuilding children "both physically and mentally," but funding was needed not only for this particular institution but to establish additional sanitaria in order to rescue all Polish Jewish children "from destruction or physical collapse." In fact, the many Jewish sanatoria, orphanages, and insane asylums of the Second Polish Republic could care for only a fraction of the countless needy. As Opatoshua and Singer made clear in their work, there would be no easy redemption for Polish Jewry's most vulnerable. If they were not sentenced to a life of misery and physical degeneracy by the Christian environment, steeped as it was in antisemitism, they would fall victim to the retrograde (at least in the eyes of modernists and modernizers) traditional Jewish milieu. They were no longer the scapegoats of yore, and yet . . . Opatoshu and Singer seem to suggest that Jewish society had not given up on its need for an Other to blame for its troubles. Even Zionism singled out the marginal as the most visible manifestation of the Jewish nation's degenerate state.

The great Polish Jewish poet Julian Tuwim's *Słowa we krwi* (Words in Blood; 1936) includes a short poem entitled "Little Jew-Boy" (*Żydek*):

> He sings in the courtyard, the poor little lad
> Wrapped up in rags, a Jew-boy gone mad.
> God unbalanced his mind and he's driven around,
> Ages and exile for his queer speech account.
> He wriggles and dances, outstretching his hands,
> and sobbing and singing his lot he laments.
> The gentleman from the first floor looks down on the boy:
> Look, my poor brother, at the one without joy!
> Where has fate carried us, where have we strayed

FIGURE 7.10. "Two brothers who are beggars on the streets of Warsaw" (1920). American Jewish Joint Distribution Committee Archives NY_04425. Reprinted with permission.

in an alien world, unloved and afraid?

Gentleman from the first floor—your brother's insane,

dancing across the globe, his poor head aflame.

The gentleman from the first floor, who's a poet, alas!

will wrap up his heart like a coin and thus

throw it through the window and on to the street

to be trampled upon till it ceases it to beat.

Thereafter we'll go on our different ways,

each one on his own through sad and mad days.

We'll never find peace and a haven of rest,

we singing Jews, we Jews possessed.[164]

There were indeed singing beggar boys in the courtyards of the teeming Jewish neighborhoods of Poland's cities, cities like Łódź, where Tuwim spent his childhood. And the gentleman from the first floor is none other than the poet himself, gazing down upon the spectacle below. Instead of throwing a coin down, as was the common practice when street singers and musicians played in a courtyard, he throws down his heart, for his lot and the lot of the Jew-boy are in fact one, as the last line makes clear: "we singing Jews, we Jews possessed." In Tuwim's vision, the polonized, bourgeois Jew embraces the street urchin as a brother, rather than rejecting him because he reflects negatively on himself, as might have been the case in earlier eras. In an echo of Abramovitsh and Peretz, Tuwim's poem "Żydek" embodies a renunciation of a Jewish self-hatred that replicates antisemitic stereotypes. Moreover, Peretz had insisted on the relevance of the madman's vision as counterpart to the hollow promises of nationalist, scientist modernity. Now, it seemed, insanity was to be the condition of the entire nation. In a world gone mad—and true madness had not yet even arrived—the mad were the only truly rational ones.[165]

EPILOGUE

Poland, 2017. The orphaned streets of Vilna, Warsaw, Sejny, and Łęczna bear no trace of the beggars, fools, cripples, and orphans we have encountered in these pages.[1] The grounds of the former Jewish psychiatric hospital in Otwock, near Warsaw, are abandoned and desolate. The visitor approaches on a rutted road; the sturdy main building, while structurally intact, is a hulking ruin, overhanging boughs grazing the peeling stuccoed walls swathed in graffiti. It is said to be haunted. In another Polish town not far away, stalls in the picturesque market square offer *żydki*, Jewish figurines, including bearded rabbis holding coins, peddlers, musicians—and hunchbacks. They are said to bring good luck.[2]

The gulf between 1939 and the present day is vast, almost unbridgeable. A yawning chasm has swallowed up the entire world with which this book has occupied itself. And yet, our subject lives on beyond the Nazi invasion of Poland, and even—in a sense—beyond the peak killing years of 1941 and 1942.

Shoah/Khurbm

Over the course of this study, we have seen that East European Jews, German Jews, and antisemites were prepared, for various reasons, to substitute the marginal people of East European Jewry for the whole. As it did with everything else, Nazi antisemitism took this trend to its most radical conclusion; in

FIGURE E.I. Former Zofiówka Jewish Psychiatric Hospital, Otwock, Poland (2018). Its buildings have stood derelict for many years. Photograph by the author.

Nazi propaganda, "the Jew" could be the dirty Jewish beggar, the deformed, physically repulsive Jewish subhuman, or the devilish, deranged-looking banker seeking to undermine Western civilization and take over the world. The poster for Fritz Hippler's film *Der Ewige Jude* (*The Eternal Jew*; 1940), for example, pictured a Jewish man with distorted body including sloping shoulders, suggesting hunchback, and with his outstretched hand holding coins—clearly a beggar, a reference to the film's insistence that Jews are "a race of parasites."[3] Like the figure in the poster, the film also portrayed Jews as dirty ("In plain language, Jewish dwellings are filthy and neglected" [2:37]). This image was by no means a new one, and indeed the Nazis drew upon a ready stable of stereotypes, especially those that pictured the *Ostjude*—and by extension German Jews as well, since they were of the same racial stock—as rapacious and parasitical beggars.[4] In late 1941, the SS official newspaper *Das Schwarze Korps* described the Jews as having sunk to "the status of pauperized parasites and criminals" (in Ian Kershaw's paraphrase).[5] Nazi

FIGURE E.2. Jan Malik, "Jew with hunchback" figurine (1970s). From the collection of Leszek Macak. Photograph by Grzegorz Mart. Reprinted with permission.

persecution ultimately sought to turn all Jews into the social outcasts that propaganda had imagined them to be; amid the filth, starvation rations, and unsanitary conditions of the ghetto, once proud, self-sufficient, and healthy people were frequently reduced to begging, chronic illness, and even insanity.

The beggar figure in the ghetto now stood for all Jews, then, not only symbolically but in reality. In Khane Khaytin's poem "On a Begging Walk" (1942), the Lithuanian Jewish songwriter told the tale of the Jewish beggar in the ghetto:

> I stride with quick, with speedy steps,
> A full beggar's bag along with me I drag,
> And my legs are bending out of fatigue
> And the water is seeping through my shoes.[6]

The beggar makes his or her way through the ghetto, collecting potatoes, barley, meat, and bread. After bribing the guard, the beggar returns to a house of sickly children, who, as the food goes into the pot, forget their troubles for the moment. And Khaytin's last verse reveals the true meaning of the song:

> Beggars we have become today. . . .
> Because we are Jews, we are hated,
> Forever we shall sing the same song:
> Oh how awful and bitter to be a Jew.[7]

It is not only the singer of these lines who is the beggar, but all Jews in the ghetto. Nazi rule has transformed the marginal figure into the norm.

Along similar lines, one scholar hypothesizes that one reason marginal folk appear in almost every yizkor book is because survivors of the Holocaust came to identify with them, as in the case of a contributor who compared his starving wartime self, thirsting for every last drop of soup, to the plight of his town's madwoman in the prewar years.[8]

The scourge of orphanhood that Polish Jewish social welfare activists had worked so hard to eliminate now returned with greater and more tragic force than ever before. The frequent breakdown of family, the breaking up of families due to flight, the chaos of war, premature death, and deportation—there were now so many orphans as a result that it was impossible for existing social welfare agencies to care for them all. Many ended up on the street, where conditions were too arduous for them to survive for long. In winter, their frozen corpses were collected by ghetto undertakers on a daily basis.[9] Of the Warsaw Ghetto, Emanuel Ringelblum wrote, "Little children with bare feet, bare knees, and torn clothing, stand dumbly in the street weeping. . . . Early October, when the first snows fell, some seventy children were found frozen to death on the steps of ruined houses. Frozen children are becoming a general phenomenon."[10]

Given the circumstances—dire beyond imagining, with hundreds dying on a daily basis of disease and starvation in the largest ghettos and rumors of worse to come—it was natural that the cholera wedding made a comeback during the Holocaust. In Żelechów, a typhus epidemic prompted the towns-people to organize a wedding in the cemetery of Motele Beygers and Khavale Yudkes, a woman in her fifties.[11] In the same year, Adam Czerniaków, head of the Warsaw Judenrat, wrote the following in his diary on October 27:

> Alarming rumors about the fate of the Jews in Warsaw next spring. I received the following written request from the rabbis: "Because the epidemic raging in our city is spreading from day to day, we propose to organize at public expense as a propitiating religious rite at the cemetery, a marriage ceremony between a bachelor and a spinster, both of them poor people, immediately af-ter the approaching Day of Atonement. This rite has been studied and tested and with God's help will certainly be effective in arresting the epidemic." This resolution was agreed upon at the meeting of the Rabbis' Council on September 28, 1941.[12]

Whether the ritual was actually held is unknown, but the fact that Czerni-aków chose to juxtapose the "alarming rumors" about what the future held in store for Warsaw's Jews and the wedding is eerily prescient. In eras past, the cholera wedding had been revived whenever the Jews as a collectivity were in grave physical danger. Here, the danger was not only the obvious—the typhus epidemic—but the unknown, the rumored, the imagined—even the worst of which would pale in comparison with the reality to come. The Nazis revived the old canard that Ostjuden, and especially beggars, spread disease; one propaganda poster in German and Polish ("The Path of Horror") de-picted an elderly Jewish beggar woman who had, it was claimed, infected forty-two people with typhus along her wanderings.[13]

In a postwar memoir, Manus Iadushlivyi recalled a wedding in 1942 in the village of Bazaliia in the Teofipol'skii district of Khmel'nitskii region. No epidemic is mentioned, and in fact the motivation seems to have been not disease but the Nazi persecution itself, which "one of the old men" advised had been caused by the Jews' having fallen away from religion and angered God. A "former rabbi" (this territory had been Soviet since the early 1920s) suggested organizing a wedding at the cemetery, inviting the dead, and asking them to save their young relatives and with them all the Jews of the town.[14]

After the Flood

After the war, in addition to contributors to yizkor books who wrote about the marginal characters of the shtetl, frequently portraying them as pica-resque characters of a bygone world rather than as historical actors with their own motivations and complex societal contexts, Yiddish writers attempting to reconstruct the lost world of East European Jewry often highlighted mar-ginal people in their fiction. In his memoir of interwar Vilna, Chaim Grade offered an extended description of the city's underworld in a chapter entitled "The Day of the Beggars." In Grade's vivid, stark portrayal, an army of beg-gars overwhelms the streets and courtyards of the old Jewish quarter in an almost military assault on the denizens of the neighborhood.[15] Hatzkel the grocer, whose shop is located in the same courtyard where Grade's mother Vella sells apples from a basket, is overwhelmed by the surging crowd of beggars. Though "a good-natured soul," as the beggars approach, he "feels a stabbing pain in his heart, a tightness in his chest, a choking in his throat, as though all these invalids and cripples were tearing him apart, piece by piece." As his shop is overrun with the destitute, it empties of customers.

> Hatzkel looks forlornly about him. Not one customer remains in his shop—there is only the line of paupers twisting and turning like a snake, with no beginning or end. It is no longer just a single line; now the beggars come in pairs . . . three abreast . . . four abreast. The ice has melted and the Wilja is overflowing its banks! A swarm of locusts has descended upon him! Woe, woe—all the beggars of the Synagogue Courtyard are coming, all the in-mates of the poorhouses, all the wretched hostels of the poor, all the decaying back alleys are on the march . . .

"Help!" Hatzkel tears at his hair. "Help me, good people! They'll ruin me. I myself will have to throw a sack over my shoulders and go begging from door to door."

In despair, he seizes the pile of copper coins and runs out to stand at the entrance of his shop.

"Quickly! Quickly!" Hurrying the far-stretching line of beggars along, he distributes his coins. "I see you have plenty of time, just as if this were afternoon Sabbath after the cholent. Father in Heaven, the line is as long as our Jewish Exile. Exile, when will you end?"

The line of paupers, it seems to Hatzkel, is never-ending, multiplying before his eyes from a single line to a double and then three and four abreast; the bowels of the city have vomited up their wretched, and they are legion. But this army of the abject is not only menacing in its size and abhorrence; it also threatens to overwhelm and engulf ordinary Jews like Hatzkel. And in some sense, as Hatzkel's exhortation intimates, it represents, metonymically, the Jewish people as a whole. Here Grade returns us to the familiar slippage between "normal," everyday Jews and the destitute, the maimed, the repugnant. Is there really so much difference between "us" and "them"? Do they not, in fact, represent the dire plight of the entire Jewish people in its exilic state?

However, while the storekeepers view the beggars with fear and loathing, Grade's mother Vella, often portrayed in the book as a font of self-effacing wisdom, muses at the chapter's close, "A beggar, too, is a human being. When someone shames him, he, too, will stand up to fight for his dignity."[16]

When Grade returns to Vilna at the end of the war and finds only the ruins of the thriving community he had fled as a refugee in 1941, he wanders the empty streets of the former Jewish quarter, almost paralyzed with grief. In a haunting passage that reminds one of the modernist, stylized shtetls of Vakhtangov and Ulmer, he is shadowed by various elements of desolate houses and shops just as Vilna's shopkeepers were once besieged by marginal people: "I drag myself along the dark streets, followed by houses with windows that have no panes, by empty walls and smoke-blackened chimneys, by crooked roofs and maimed dwelling-places—a throng of cripples, a host of blind beggars who feel their way with their hands."[17] Barely a remnant of the physical presence of Jews survives—not even the street people are left. All that is left to represent the absence of the Jews are the buildings themselves, which now come to life, animated, it seems, by the absolute void that inhabits them.

One finds a similar absence at the conclusion of the short story "Shibele's Lottery Ticket," one of many stories written in Yiddish by Avrom Karpinowitz, a Vilna native who settled in Israel after the war, that offer earthy portrayals of Vilna between the wars. Shibele the Conductor and his friend Zerdel are vagabonds who while away their days in the city's courtyards and sleep in "the garret over the public bath."[18] On Thursdays, they line up at Probe's bakery with the other beggars to receive a coin. The story is a tragic one: Zerdel dies alone of an untreated pulmonary disease, and Shibele disappears after he loses a winning lottery ticket. "No trace remained of Shibele," the narrator muses. On the other hand, "Shibele is gone, but from time to time his dream of wealth springs up in one of the other little courtyard synagogues."[19] Similarly, no trace remains of the Jews, rich and poor, who once walked the streets of Vilna and eastern Europe's other cities and towns, but their dreams—perhaps embodied in stories such as Karpinowitz's?—can live again, if only for a moment.

Gimpel's hekdesh; or, The marginal Jew comes to America

The titular hero of Isaac Bashevis Singer's "Gimpel the Fool" is a classic marginal figure in the historical context of East European Jewish society. An orphan who is known as the fool of Frampol and is the butt of everyone's jokes in the town, Gimpel is married off to another orphan—the dissipated Elka who walks with a limp and passes her bastard son off as her younger brother—in a cholera wedding (though the specific epidemic in question is dysentery). Eventually, he leaves Frampol, becomes a wandering beggar, and ends up in a hekdesh. What could be a more typical marginal story? But in Yiddish, as Joseph Landis astutely noted, the hero of "Gimpel the Fool," despite the fact that others call him *nar*, is not actually a fool at all—he is *Gimpel tam*, Gimpel the simple, the gullible, the naïve. "The failure to use the word 'simple' has led almost all who discuss the story into misreading it," Landis argues. "Though childishly simple, he is nevertheless far from being a fool," and ultimately he journeys from naïveté to "an intellectual determination to believe as a way of life, a willed affirmation of faith as the only alternative to a world of lies, deception, chicanery, humiliation."[20] For Gimpel differs from previous schlemiels in that he *"chooses* to be fooled, to be used, to forsake his dignity," much like holy fools in the Russian tradition who chose a life of idiocy and poverty.[21]

Much in the same way, rather than having it thrust upon him, as would have usually been the case, Gimpel chooses a life as wandering beggar; indeed, it is vital to the narrative strategy that Gimpel not remain in Frampol but instead, after making his fortune, decide to give away his wealth and wander the world as a beggar. In other words, he deliberately chooses to live the life of a marginal Jew, thus harmonizing his inner self—which has never departed from its essential "fool-ness," naïveté, purity—with his newly wealthy and thus ostensibly changed external identity. Like the wandering beggars so beloved of *zamlers* and folklorists because of their earthy familiarity with the true life of the folk, Gimpel tells stories; but these are "yarns—improbable things that could never have happened—about devils, magicians, windmills, and the like." So what of the monologue that we hearing from him now, as he lies on his pallet of straw in the hekdesh? Yet another yarn? Are we being hoodwinked by him, who had once been the most gullible of all? Only Gimpel knows the truth.

And although Gimpel's hekdesh clearly lies at the outskirts of some unnamed Polish shtetl, his audience lies across the Atlantic; the story was published in 1945, when almost all the denizens of that shtetl and all the others were already dead. Thus, although Gimpel himself, it is to be presumed, never set foot outside eastern Europe, he becomes, as David Roskies argues, following Sidra DeKoven Ezrahi, "the cultural ambassador of East European Jewry."[22] In this, arguably the best known of all Yiddish-language representations of the vanished world of East European Jews in the Anglophone world (where "Singer's schlemiel-hero occupies center stage," Roskies observes),[23] it is—irony of ironies—the marginal Jew who survives, as it were, to tell the tale of the one upright and honest person in a cruel, corrupted, and uncouth world. Why? "In the eyes of Bashevis," Dan Miron writes, "Gimpel is the archetypical Jew, just as he is the embodiment of the Yiddish language . . . the language of the weak, the victims."[24] Miron contends that, contra the overwhelming impulse of modern Jewish culture and politics, which strove to overturn what they perceived as "the passivity, weakness, inertia, and stagnation" of East European Jewish society, Bashevis Singer harbored "a deep distrust in human will power and absolute aversion for both the Nietzschean 'will to power' and the liberal faith in 'progress.'"[25]

Gimpel's monologue—for that is what the story boils down to, though one is surprised to see it so described—captures within it the entire world of Yiddish-speaking Jewry. "Bashevis created an idealized transcript of Yiddish folk speech, a reincarnated speech act. One voice successfully orchestrated multiple utterances: communal and individual, male and female, natural and supernatural."[26] How far we have come from Abramovich's Fishke, whose speech is so muddled that Mendele must reconstruct his narrative, that is, serve as his mouthpiece. Now it is the marginal figure who contains multitudes, speaking not only for himself but also for the entire world that has oppressed and taunted him.[27]

CONCLUSION

Jewish Intersectionality at the European Fin-de-Siècle

The 1910 article in New York's Yiddish daily *Die Wahrheit* poking fun at East European Jews' fondness for cholera weddings that we saw in chapter 4 offered the following astute observation. The pious women who instigated the weddings did so because "they could never stand by when various idiots and all kinds of cripples wander about God's earth without any purpose [*takhles*]." It was surely not lost on any readers that that the *takhles* implied was a sexual one which also (by extension) embraced gender.

Eastern Europe's marginal Jews served as troubling, destabilizing reminders of the Jews' fundamental inability to fit in, to become ordinary. Rachel Adams writes:

> If identity formation, whether individual or collective, involves a dual gesture of incorporation and repudiation, freaks remind us of the unbearable excess that has been shed to confer entry into the realm of normalcy. . . . The assumption of identity always entails the acquisition of desired attributes and the refusal of the intolerable abject. Freaks embody this cast off refuse, reminding the viewer of the costs of normality, but also stirring doubts about whether she really belongs there.[1]

In other words, Jewish marginals constantly served as a decentering reminder to ordinary Jews trying to acculturate or integrate their inescapable otherness into the gentile world. Marginals' bodily othernesses were reminders of the

Jew's physical difference, a difference often inflected by gender: the legacy of medieval anxiety about circumcision's putative emasculation or even castration; the common image of the weak, effeminate Jewish man; the stereotype of the masculine, overbearing Jewish woman. Insane people were icons of Jewish neurosis and hysteria, conditions also frequently inflected by gender. Jewish beggars exemplified the stereotype of the Jew as parasite and idler; Jewish vagrants evoked the legendary Wandering Jew. Jews were a disabled body struggling to be seen as able-bodied in a Western civilization with compulsory able-bodiedness at its core, and to hazard another metaphor, a queer body striving to integrate against the grain of compulsory heterosexuality. "Jewish 'queerness,' then, is a symptom of Jewish modernity as cultural mismatch, category crisis, incomplete integration, and colonial mimicry," Naomi Seidman writes.[2]

In this light, Lev Levanda's 1860 condemnation of premodern Jewish gender roles that had women handling the family's business affairs makes perfect sense. It was the hypermasculine Jewish woman who, in Levanda's eyes, gave birth (figuratively speaking) to the disabled and deformed Jewish child. Part of the problem was that women left their households in the hands of "half-wild" servants, a term that suggested Levanda's equation of the traditional order with the savage colonial subject and, by contrast, the civilizing nature of bourgeois Western society.[3] It is not too much of a stretch to restate his logic as follows: the queer Jewish woman will inevitably give birth to the disabled Jewish child.

In traditional Jewish society, itinerant beggars had been associated with sexual deviance, a trait that was probably linked conceptually to the porousness of the border between vagrants and the gentile world. Recall that Jewish beggars—who also often had anomalous bodies—sometimes attached themselves to the (mostly Christian) unbound people (*ludzie luźni*) in early modern Poland. The marginal figure, then, was not only liminal and frequently disabled but also, in some sense, queer—and this conception had deep roots in Jewish sociocultural consciousness.[4] In the modern period, those roots generated literature that often conflated the disabled body and the queer body. At Abramovitsh's cholera wedding, we encounter legless Yontl and his bride, a suspected hermaphrodite. In Peretz's insane asylum, we meet the deep-voiced, bearded storekeeper Yentl, with "nothing to distinguish her from a man," and elsewhere Peretz introduces us to the madman Berel Chantsia's, unsure of whether he is male or female. Agnon's shtetl is home to a crippled and hunchbacked man who is compared to a woman giving birth and a wet nurse. And then there is the cholera wedding, a historical phenomenon that in some ways became inseparable from its literary renderings.

The cholera wedding, a Jewish ritual that emerged under the pressure of modernity, both reified marginal difference by setting it apart as spectacle, in a very literal performance of marginal identity, and attempted to suppress at least one aspect of it—the reproductive barrenness of marginals—by "correcting" it through marriage. Moreover, the wedding, especially when it was revived in later pandemics of cholera and subsequently typhus, underscored Jewish queerness by maintaining a peculiar (though invented) ritual that was uniquely Jewish and that also identified the larger corporate body of Jews with the queer body of the Jewish marginal, even while the rite served simultaneously to distance the one from the other. As Rachel Adams explains it with respect to the psychoanalytic understanding of the subject's self-definition in relation to others, the spectator sees himself (or an aspect of himself) in the other—in the case the freak or marginal person—and simultaneously disavows that aspect of himself.[5] In this case, it is the Jew as perpetual Other, as parasite, as lowlife, as freak.

Despite protestations by its practitioners to the contrary, the cholera wedding was a consummately *modern* phenomenon, since it was an expression of the anxiety about marginality and the queer/disabled Jewish body generated by the Jewish encounter with modernity. As Seidman writes—and here I take the liberty of substituting "cholera wedding" for "drag," the subject of her discussion, "[the cholera wedding] is produced in Yiddish cultural expressions not as a symptom of incomplete modernization . . . but rather as the enactment of modernization as ambivalent desire, with Ashkenaz as cultural agent."[6] The cholera wedding reenacted both the traditional integration of the marginal figure into the community and the modern demonization and (at times) expulsion of that figure from the collectivity striving for integration. At the risk of moving too far in the direction of postcolonial theory, is it possible to posit the marginal figure as a doubly colonized subject? East European Jews, themselves frequently cast by the surrounding society as uncivilized, immoral, ugly, and savage, created an Other based on those very characteristics.

We have seen that an important shift came with World War I, when the marginal figure's ugliness, physical difference, or cognitive disability could be embraced or at least accepted as central elements of the Jewish people's experience in modernity. Cultural modernism was interested in the inner life of the madman and the symbolism of the beggar; modern social welfare sought to cure and transform the suffering orphan and the chronically ill; the new Jewish studies—folklore, ethnography, history—strove to limn the experience of the *dek-mentshn*, the "dregs" of society; and Zionism used the symbol of the wretched and lowly to explain the need for the regeneration of Jewry. But once marginality came to define a significant portion of the Jewish nation, or even the nation as a whole, was there room for "real" marginal individuals: beggars, disabled people, the mentally ill? What happened to society's outcasts once their traits were appropriated by the majority? For his 1937 film adaptation of Anski's *Der dibek*, Michał Waszynski recruited real beggars in his staging of the Dance of the Beggars, making them stars for a day, as it were, and at the same time objectifying them, as Zehavit Stern argues, "through the grotesque design of the beggars and the poor, including images such as a lame beggar hopping on one leg and waving one of his crutches in the air."[7]

The challenge in studying this topic is to balance the study of marginality as a category of analysis with attentiveness to the people who lived lives shaped by that marginality. On the other hand, as the disability studies scholar Simi Linton warns, there is also a danger of shifting focus to "the individual as deviant subject, rather than on the social structures that label difference as deviance and pathology."[8] We must find a way to use marginality as an analytical tool without reifying bodily, cognitive, and other differences as primary categories of identity.

And here we return to the thorny challenge we started with: the problem of the sources. How was the voice of a beggar, a poor orphan, or a disabled person to enter into the historical record? The Guttmacher kvitlekh offer some of those voices, though fragmentary, and other archival collections surely hold additional stories; when we find them, they are almost always second-hand, told to a relative, a rabbi, a police officer, a judge. Literature reconstructs the voices we seek, sometimes in extraordinary ways, but ultimately it has its limitations. And so we must resign ourselves to the fact that while much in history can be found and thus hopefully known, more—perhaps much more—will not.

NOTES

Abbreviations Used in the Notes

ARCHIVES AND SOURCES

CAHJP	Central Archives for the History of the Jewish People, Jerusalem (CAHJP)
DAKO	State Archive of Kiev Oblast', Kiev
JDC	American Jewish Joint Distribution Committee Archives, New York
LVIA	Lithuanian State Historical Archives, Vilnius
NBUV IR	Vernadsky National Library of Ukraine, Manuscript Division, Judaica Section
NLI-DM	National Library of Israel, Department of Manuscripts
RGIA	Russian State Historical Archive, St. Petersburg
TsDIAU	Central State Historical Archive of Ukraine, Kyiv
YIVO	YIVO Institute for Jewish Research, New York

ARCHIVAL CITATIONS

R = Russian; U = Ukrainian

ark.	*arkush, arkushi* (folio, folios) (U)
d.	*delo* (file) (R)
f.	*fond* (collection) (R, U)

1. (ll.)	*list, listy* (folio, folios) (R)
od. zb.	*odynytsya zberezhennya* (storage unit or file) (U)
op.	*opis'* (inventory) (R, U)
ob.	*oborot* (verso) (R)
RG	record group
spr.	*sprava* (file) (U)
t.	*tom* (R, U)
zv.	*zvorotnyi bik* (verso) (U)

Introduction

1. David Samuels, "A Last Conversation with Aharon Appelfeld," *Tablet*, January 5, 2018, www.tabletmag.com/jewish-arts-and-culture/books/228475/last-conversation-aharon-appelfeld (accessed December 2, 2019). For the story, see Aharon Appelfeld, "Bertha," in *Truth and Lamentation: Stories and Poems on the Holocaust*, ed. Milton Teichman and Sharon Leder (Urbana: University of Illinois Press, 1994), 149–59.

2. Aharon Appelfeld, "Ba-derech el atsmi," *Moznyaim* 22 (June–November 1966): 364–65, cited in Shachar Pinsker, "The Language That Was Lost on the Roads: Discovering Hebrew through Yiddish in Aharon Appelfeld's Fiction," *Journal of Jewish Identities* 7, no. 1 (2014): 132. Trans. modified.

3. Henri-Jacques Stiker, *A History of Disability*, trans. William Sayers (Ann Arbor: University of Michigan Press, 1999), 10.

4. Benjamin Nathans, *Beyond the Pale: The Jewish Encounter with Late Imperial Russia* (Berkeley: University of California Press, 2002), 45–79.

5. Catherine J. Kudlick, "Disability History: Why We Need Another 'Other,'" *American Historical Review* 108, no. 3 (June 2003): 766.

6. Dan Miron, "Sh. Y. Abramovitsh and His 'Mendele,'" in id., *The Image of the Shtetl and Other Studies of Modern Jewish Literary Imagination* (Syracuse, NY: Syracuse University Press, 2000), 106.

7. See Timothy B. Smith, "Marginal People," in *Encyclopedia of European Social History from 1350 to 2000*, ed. Peter N. Stearns (New York: Scribner, 2001), 3: 175, and Wolfgang von Hippel, *Armut, Unterschichten, Randgruppen in der frühen Neuzeit* (Munich: Oldenbourg, 1995), 5, 14–15, who stresses poor people's lack of social esteem (*soziale "Ehre"*).

8. Richard J. Evans, "Introduction: The 'Dangerous Classes' in Germany from the Middle Ages to the Twentieth Century," in *The German Underworld: Deviants and Outcasts in German History*, ed. Richard J. Evans (London: Routledge, 1988), 1. See also Hippel, *Armut, Unterschichten, Randgruppen*, 4–7.

9. Fernand Vanhemelryck, *Marginalen in de geschiedenis: over beulen, joden, hoeren, zigeuners en andere zondebokken* (Leuven: Davidsfonds, 2004), 9. As the title suggests,

the study embraces executioners, Jews, prostitutes, and gypsies in addition to witches and heretics.

10. Ephraim Shoham-Steiner, *On the Margins of a Minority: Leprosy, Madness, and Disability among the Jews of Medieval Europe*, trans. Haim Watzman (Detroit: Wayne State University Press, 2014), 9.

11. Evans, "Introduction: The 'Dangerous Classes,'" 1–2. In his study of early modern German society, Evans includes not only pariahs like vagrants, itinerants, and practitioners of despised occupations, such as tanners and executioners, but Jews and Roma among the underworld's marginalized "dishonorable people" (*unerhliche Leute*).

12. Peter N. Stearns, *European Society in Upheaval: Social History since 1750* (Toronto: Maxwell Macmillan Canada, 1992), 81.

13. For another interesting conceptual approach to marginal people, see Susan A. Ashley, *"Misfits" in Fin-de-Siècle France and Italy: Anatomies of Difference* (London: Bloomsbury Academic, 2017). Ashley discusses two categories of "misfit": mental misfits, including geniuses, lunatics, and neurotics, and social misfits, including vagabonds, criminals, and sexual deviants.

14. On the role of shame in defining marginality, see Smith, "Marginal People," 3: 180.

15. Elizabeth Grosz, "Intolerable Ambiguity: Freaks as/at the Limit," in *Freakery: Cultural Spectacles of the Extraordinary Body*, ed. Rosemarie Garland-Thomson (New York: New York University Press, 1996), 10.

16. YIVO Archive RG 27 (Papers of Eliyahu Guttmacher), ser. 1, boxes 1–17.

17. Jacob Katz, *Tradition and Crisis: Jewish Society at the End of the Middle Ages* (New York: New York University Press, 1993), 59.

18. Ibid.,123. On patterns of courtship and marriage among East European Jews, see Shaul Stampfer, "Love and Family," in id., *Families, Rabbis and Education: Traditional Jewish Society in Nineteenth-Century Eastern Europe* (Oxford: Littman Library of Jewish Civilization, 2010), 26–55; ChaeRan Y. Freeze, *Jewish Marriage and Divorce in Imperial Russia* (Hanover, NH: Brandeis University Press and University Press of New England, 2002), 11–72.

19. Katz, *Tradition and Crisis*, 118.

20. See Shaul Stampfer, "Remarriage among Jews and Christians," in id., *Families, Rabbis, and Education*, 56–85.

21. Katz, *Tradition and Crisis*, 123. On *agunot*, see Bluma Goldstein, *Enforced Marginality: Jewish Narratives on Abandoned Wives* (Berkeley: University of California Press, 2007); Haim Sperber, "Agunot, 1851–1914. An Introduction," *Annales de démographie historique* 136, no. 2 (2018): 107–35.

22. See Bjørn Thomassen, "The Uses and Meanings of Liminality," *International Political Anthropology* 2, no. 1 (2009): 5–28.

23. Victor W. Turner, "Betwixt and Between: The Liminal Period in *Rites de Pas-*

sage," in *The Forest of Symbols: Aspects of Ndembu Ritual* (Ithaca, NY: Cornell University Press, 1967), 95–97.

24. Mary Douglas, *Purity and Danger: An Analysis of the Concepts of Pollution and Taboo* (London: Ark, 1984), 38–41; Turner, "Betwixt and Between," 98.

Chapter 1

1. Derek J. Penslar, *Shylock's Children: Economics and Jewish Identity in Modern Europe* (Berkeley: University of California Press, 2001), 90–92. This approach was predominant among historians in mandatory Palestine and the early state period who wrote Jewish history in a nationalist key.

2. Aryeh Tartakower, "Al ofi ha-oni ha-yehudi veha-tsedakah ha-yehudit," in *Kelal yisra'el: perakim ba-sotsyologyah shel ha-am ha-yehudi*, ed. Ben Zion Dinur, Aryeh Tartakower, and Jacob Lestschinsky (Jerusalem: Mosad Bialik, 1954), 434–35, 437.

3. Ibid., 434. For other examples of this approach, see Yehuda Bergmann, *Ha-tsedakah be-yisra'el: toldoteha u-mosdoteha* (Jerusalem, 1944), 91, and Salo Baron, *The Jewish Community: Its History and Structure to the American Revolution* (Philadelphia: Jewish Publication Society of America, 1942), 2: 320.

4. Jacob R. Marcus, *Communal Sick-Care in the German Ghetto* (Cincinnati: Hebrew Union College Press, 1947), 171. Tartakower argues something similar for the modern period. Tartakower, "Al ofi ha-oni ha-yehudi," 438.

5. Elimelekh [Elliot] Horowitz, "Va-yihyu aniyim (hagunim) benei veitekha: tsedakah, aniyim u-fiku'ah hevrati be-kehilot yehudei eiropa ben yemei ha-veinayim le-reishit ha-et ha-hadasha," in *Dat ve-khalkalah: yahasei gomlin*, ed. Menahem Ben-Sasson (Jerusalem: Merkaz zalman shazar le-toldot yisra'el, 1995), 213.

6. Ibid.

7. Isaac Levitats, *The Jewish Community in Russia, 1772–1844* (New York: Octagon Books, 1970), 248. On the other hand, it could be argued that the *pinkas* is only one way of understanding the activities of the members of those societies, and that their actions may in fact speak rather louder than their (written) words.

8. On conjunctural and structural poverty, see Michel Mollat, *The Poor in the Middle Ages: An Essay in Social History* (New Haven, CT: Yale University Press, 1986), 26. For examples from the Jewish world, see Mark R. Cohen, *The Voice of the Poor in the Middle Ages: An Anthology of Documents from the Cairo Geniza* (Princeton, NJ: Princeton University Press, 2013), 32–33; Horowitz, "Va-yihyu aniyim (hagunim) benei veitekha," 227; Penslar, *Shylock's Children*, 93. On poor relief in early modern Europe, see Marco H. D. Van Leeuwen, "Logic of Charity: Poor Relief in Preindustrial Europe," *Journal of Interdisciplinary History* 24, no. 4 (1994): 589–613.

9. Smith, "Marginal People," in *Encyclopedia of European Social History*, 3: 179. See also the examples from literature offered in Bronisław Geremek, *The Margins of Society in Late Medieval Paris* (Cambridge: Cambridge University Press, 1987), 197.

10. Mollat, *Poor in the Middle Ages*, 5. I am indebted to Ephraim Shoham-Steiner for this reference. See Shoham-Steiner, *On the Margins of a Minority*, 8–9.

11. Penslar, *Shylock's Children*, 93, 95–96.

12. Tirtsah Levie Bernfeld, *Poverty and Welfare among the Portuguese Jews in Early Modern Amsterdam* (Oxford: Littman Library of Jewish Civilization, 2012), 80.

13. Ibid., 86.

14. Ibid., 118.

15. Ibid., 230.

16. Penslar, *Shylock's Children*, 19–20; Yacov Guggenheim, "Meeting on the Road: Encounters between German Jews and Christians on the Margins of Society," in *In and Out of the Ghetto: Jewish-Gentile Relations in Late Medieval and Early Modern Germany*, ed. R. Po-chia Hsia and Hartmut Lehmann (Cambridge: Cambridge University Press, 1995), 127.

17. There is a growing literature on beggars, vagabonds, and other categories of marginal people in the early modern period. The advances in research have been most noticeable in the field of French social history, followed by studies of early modern England. See, e.g., Robert Forster and Orest A. Ranum, eds., *Deviants and the Abandoned in French Society: Selections from the Annales, Économies, Sociétés, Civilisations*, vol. 4 (Baltimore: Johns Hopkins University Press, 1978); Pierre Dancoine, *Mendiants, vagabonds et prostituées dans le nord au XVIIIème siècle* (Steenvoorde: Foyer culturel de l'Houtland, 1996); André Gueslin, *D'ailleurs et de nulle part: mendiants, vagabonds, clochards, SDF en France depuis le Moyen Âge* (Paris: Fayard, 2013); David Hitchcock, *Vagrancy in English Culture and Society, 1650–1750* (London: Bloomsbury Academic, 2016); Bohdan Baranowski, *Ludzie gościńca w XVII–XVIII w.* (Łódź: Wydawn. Łódzkie, 1986).

18. Guggenheim, "Meeting on the Road," 127 n. 6.

19. Yacov Guggenheim, "Von den Schalantjuden zu den Betteljuden: jüdische Armut in Mitteleuropa in der Frühen Neuzeit," in *Juden und Armut in Mittel- und Osteuropa*, ed. Stefi Jersch-Wenzel et al. (Cologne: Böhlau, 2000), 65. Limiting non-local beggars' stay in a given locale became a common practice for some Christian municipalities in the Germanic lands; see Bronisław Geremek, *Poverty: A History* (Oxford: Blackwell, 1994), 46–47.

20. Guggenheim, "Von den Schalantjuden zu den Betteljuden," 59.

21. Penslar, *Shylock's Children*, 19. See also Mordechai Breuer and Michael Graetz, *Tradition and Enlightenment, 1600–1780*, trans. William Templer, vol. 1 of *German-Jewish History in Modern Times*, ed. Michael A. Meyer and Michael Brenner (New York: Columbia University Press, 1996), 247; Moses A. Shulvass, *From East to West: The Westward Migration of Jews from Eastern Europe during the Seventeenth and Eighteenth Centuries* (Detroit: Wayne State University Press, 1971), 25–50; Rudolf Glanz, *Geschichte des niederen jüdischen Volkes in Deutschland; eine Studie über historisches Gaunertum, Bettelwesen und Vagantentum* (New York: n.p., 1968), 133–47; Fritz Backhaus, "Im Heckhuß

die Lahmen, Blinden, Hungerleider . . .': Die sozialen Institutionen in der Frankfurter Judengasse," in Jersch-Wenzel, *Juden und Armut*, 42–45.

22. Penslar, *Shylock's Children*, 94.

23. Baron, *Jewish Community*, 2: 322–3.

24. Guggenheim, "Von den Schalantjuden zu den Betteljuden," 60; Penslar, *Shylock's Children*, 94. The *Pletten* system had its parallel in the Christian world in the form of tokens used to keep track of alms distributed to the poor. See Geremek, *Poverty*, 37–38.

25. Guggenheim, "Von den Schalantjuden zu den Betteljuden," 60.

26. Shulvass, *From East to West*, 98.

27. Ibid., 101.

28. Antony Polonsky, *The Jews in Poland and Russia* (Oxford: Littman Library of Jewish Civilization, 2010), 1: 64; Baron, *Jewish Community*, 2: 323–4. On *hezkat ha-yishuv*, see Baron, *Jewish Community*, 2: 5–17; Katz, *Tradition and Crisis*, 88–89. On Jewish beggars more generally in pre-Partition Poland, see Jakub Goldberg, "Armut unter den Juden im alten Polen," in Jersch-Wenzel, *Juden und Armut*, 83–86.

29. Gershon David Hundert, *Jews in Poland-Lithuania in the Eighteenth Century: A Genealogy of Modernity* (Berkeley: University of California Press, 2004), 86–87; Polonsky, *Jews in Poland and Russia*, 1: 58–67.

30. Simon Dubnow, ed., *Pinkas ha-medinah o pinkas va'ad ha-kehilot ha-rashiyot be-medinat lita* (Berlin: Ayanot, 1925), 17.

31. Baron, *Jewish Community*, 2: 323.

32. Horowitz, "Va-yihyu aniyim (hagunim) benei veitekha," 225.

33. Penslar, *Shylock's Children*, 94.

34. Translation based on Baron, *Jewish Community*, 2: 323–4. Compare a contemporary Moravian regulation referring to "vagabonds, worthless people, robbers, and cutthroats who endanger the entire Jewish community"; such people faced expulsion or handing over to the authorities. Penslar, *Shylock's Children*, 94. Rather remarkably, some time after this ban on aiding beggars was enacted, the Council decreed in an undated ordinance, which one scholar has dated to 1628: "Whoever eats at his father or father-in-law's table more often than was promised to him at the time of his marriage is obligated to host poor beggars in his home on Sabbath [by means of] *pitka'ot*." Perhaps this is a remnant of an earlier, gentler attitude? Israel Halpern, "Tosafot u-milu'im le-pinkas medinat lita (hotsa'at dubnov)," *Horev* 2, no. 1 (1935): 70.

35. Baron, *Jewish Community*, 2: 324.

36. Ibid., 325; Horowitz, "Va-yihyu aniyim (hagunim) benei veitekha," 213; Anna Michałowska, *The Jewish Community: Authority and Social Control in Poznań and Swarzędz, 1650–1793*, trans. Alicja Adamowicz (Warsaw: Wydawn. Uniwersytetu Wrocławskiego, 2008), 43.

37. Michałowska, *Jewish Community*, 221.

38. For specifics, see Guggenheim, "Armut," 58–59. See also Teller, "Jüdische Unterschichten."

39. Sh. Trunk, "A yidishe kehile in poyln baym sof XVIII yorhundert, kutne," *Bleter far geshikhte* 1 (1934): 121.

40. Gershon Hundert also acknowledges in his study of the Jews in a Polish noble-owned town that it is nearly impossible to include the itinerant poor in any demographic study, because they rarely paid taxes. "Those at the very bottom of the social scale, the itinerant poor . . . have left virtually no record in the sources connected with Opatów." Hundert, *The Jews in a Polish Private Town* (Baltimore: Johns Hopkins University Press, 1992), 71–72.

41. François Guesnet, "Jüdische Armut und ihre Bekämpfung im Königreich Polen: Grundzüge und Entwicklungen im 19. Jahrhundert," in Jersch-Wenzel, *Juden und Armut in Mittel- und Osteuropa*, 188–89.

42. Goldberg, "Armut unter den Juden," 81–82.

43. Ibid., 83–84. See also Baranowski, *Ludzie gościńca w XVII–XVIII w.*; Mirosław Frančić, *Ludzie luźni w osiemnastowiecznym Krakowie* (Wrocław: Zakład Narodowy im. Ossolińskich, 1967).

44. Goldberg, "Armut unter den Juden," 83–84.

45. Guggenheim, "Meeting on the Road," 132.

46. Breuer and Graetz, *Tradition and Enlightenment*, 247, 250.

47. Emanuel Ringelblum, "Shnorers in poyln in di amolike tsaytn," in *Kapitlen geshikhte fun amolikn yidishn lebn in poyln*, ed. Jacob Shatzky (Buenos Aires: Tsentralfarband fun poylishe yidn in argentine, 1953), 172.

48. Yitskhok Shiper, *Geshikhte fun yidisher teater-kunst un drame: fun di eltste tsaytn biz 1750* (Warsaw: Kultur-lige, 1927), 62.

49. Ibid., 63–64.

50. Schiper, however, argues that her bad housekeeping is due to her being lovesick. Ibid., 66–67.

51. Ibid., 64–65.

52. Ignatz Bernstein, *Yudishe shprikhverter un redensarten: folshtendige groyse oysgabe* (Warsaw: Universal, 1912), 22.

53. Shiper, *Geshikhte fun yidisher teater-kunst un drame*, 65–66.

54. Sander L. Gilman, "Jews and Mental Illness: Medical Metaphors, Anti-semitism, and the Jewish Response," *Journal of the History of the Behavioral Sciences* 20, no. 2 (1984): 151

55. Marcus, *Communal Sick-Care in the German Ghetto*, 160.

56. Ibid., 161. For a fuller excursus on the origin and use of the term *hekdesh* in the Middle Ages, see ibid., 164–65 and 274–75. See also Ephraim Frisch, *An Historical Survey of Jewish Philanthropy* (New York: Cooper Square Publishers, 1969), 147–50; Mark

R. Cohen, *Poverty and Charity in the Jewish Community of Medieval Egypt* (Princeton, NJ: Princeton University Press, 2005), 200–204.

57. *Jewish Encyclopedia*, s.v. "Charity and Charitable Institutions."

58. Bergmann, *Ha-tsedakah be-yisra'el*, 56; Marcus, *Communal Sick-Care in the German Ghetto*, 161.

59. Shoham-Steiner, *On the Margins of a Minority*, 55. The medieval Christian "hospital," like its Jewish counterpart, often housed "a changing, and poorly defined, clientele of the sick, the aged, and the disabled." David Wright, "Developmental and Physical Disabilities: The 'Blind,' 'Deaf and Dumb,' and 'Idiot,'" in *Encyclopedia of European Social History from 1350 to 2000*, ed. Peter N. Stearns (New York: Scribner, 2001), 3: 508.

60. For the argument that the hekdesh was mostly for alien Jews, see Marcus, *Communal Sick-Care in the German Ghetto*, 169, 172–73. See also the study of the hekdesh in Frankfurt am Main in Backhaus, "'Im Heckhuß die Lahmen, Blinden, Hungerleider . . .,'" 33–39. On the other hand, in the case of early modern Germany, the hekdesh existed mainly to serve the local elderly and sick, according to Breuer and Graetz, *Tradition and Enlightenment*, 246.

61. Breuer and Graetz, *Tradition and Enlightenment*, 246.

62. For scholarship on the hekdesh in early modern Poland, see, e.g., Majer Bałaban, *Dzieje Żydów w Krakowie i na Kazimierzu (1304–1868)* (Kraków, 1912), 1: 285–287; id., "Obyczajowość i życie prywatne Żydów w dawnej Rzeczypospolitej," in *Żydzi w Polsce odrodzonej: Działalność społeczna, gospodarcza, oświatowa i kulturalna*, ed. Ignacy Schiper (Warsaw: Wyd-wo "Żydzi w Polsce Odrodzonej," ca. 1932), 1: 348.

63. Mollat, *Poor in the Middle Ages*, 5.

64. Klaus-Peter Horn and Bianca Frohne, "On the Fluidity of 'Disability' in Medieval and Early Modern Societies: Opportunities and Strategies in a New Field of Research," in *The Imperfect Historian: Disability Histories in Europe*, ed. Sebastian Barsch, Anne Klein, and Pieter Verstraete (Frankfurt a/M.: Peter Lang, 2013), 23.

65. Shoham-Steiner, *On the Margins of a Minority*, 8.

66. Władysław Roczniak, "Preserving the Poor: Pre-Modern Polish Hospitals, Twelfth to Eighteenth Century" (Ph.D. diss., City University of New York, 2004), 3, 12.

67. Ibid., 282–83.

68. Judith Abrams, *Judaism and Disability: Portrayals in Ancient Texts from the Tanach through the Bavli* (Washington, DC: Gallaudet University Press, 1998), 127.

69. Ibid., 133.

70. David M. Feldman, "Deafness and Jewish Law and Tradition," in *The Deaf Jew in the Modern World*, ed. Jerome D. Schein and Lester J. Waldman (New York: Ktav Publishing House for the New York Society for the Deaf, 1986), 12. Halakhic authorities differed on whether the rabbinic definition of deafness was categorical or functional, i.e., whether the restrictions on the deaf person's participation in Jewish life

were unconditional or could be alleviated if he achieved the ability to communicate (ibid., 13–16).

71. See Shoham-Steiner, *On the Margins of a Minority*, 151.

72. Abrams, *Judaism and Disability*, 87–91, 95 (quote on 95). See also Ephraim Shoham-Steiner, *On the Margins of a Minority*, 141–44.

73. Ibid., 97–99.

74. Ibid., 76–78. For a contrasting analysis of the relationship between disability and sin in ancient Judaism, see Stiker, *History of Disability*, 23–33.

75. Shoham-Steiner, *On the Margins of a Minority*, 141.

76. Ibid., 147–48.

77. Ibid., 148.

78. Ibid., 160.

79. Tzvi Marx, *Disability in Jewish Law* (London: Routledge, 2002), 17. See also Shoham-Steiner, *On the Margins of a Minority*, 160.

80. Shoham-Steiner, *On the Margins of a Minority*, 153; Joshua Trachtenberg, *The Devil and the Jews: The Medieval Conception of the Jew and Its Relation to Modern Antisemitism* (Philadelphia: Jewish Publication Society, 1993), 44–52; Alexandra Cuffel, *Gendering Disgust in Medieval Religious Polemic* (Notre Dame, IN: University of Notre Dame Press, 2007), 160–75.

81. Shoham-Steiner, *On the Margins of a Minority*, 15.

82. Herbert C. Covey, *Social Perceptions of People with Disabilities in History* (Springfield, IL: Charles C. Thomas, 1998), 123.

83. Shoham-Steiner, *On the Margins of a Minority*, 81.

84. Ibid., 79, 121; Covey, *Social Perceptions of People with Disabilities*, 133–34. Jewish madwomen, even if they did not pose a threat to others, had to be kept within private, family space in order to protect them from being preyed upon. Female begging was also viewed as "a threat to public order" (Shoham-Steiner, *On the Margins of a Minority*, 119–21).

85. Roy Porter, *A Social History of Madness: The World through the Eyes of the Insane* (New York: Weidenfeld & Nicolson, 1988), 13–14.

86. H. C. Erik Midelfort, *A History of Madness in Sixteenth-Century Germany* (Stanford: Stanford University Press, 1999), 70–71.

87. Porter, *Social History of Madness*, 14.

88. Sergey A. Ivanov, *Holy Fools in Byzantium and Beyond* (New York: Oxford University Press, 2006), 262–69. Not all holy fools were truly mentally ill; on this, see Harriet Murav, *Holy Foolishness: Dostoevsky's Novels and the Poetics of Cultural Critique* (Stanford: Stanford University Press, 1992), 3–5.

89. Ivanov, *Holy Fools*, 285–310.

90. Julie V. Brown, "Societal Responses to Mental Disorders in Prerevolutionary Russia," in *The Disabled in the Soviet Union: Past and Present, Theory and Practice*, ed.

William O. McCagg and Lewis H. Siegelbaum (Pittsburgh: University of Pittsburgh Press, 1989), 14.

91. Zvi Mark, "Dybbuk and Devekut in the *Shivhe Ha-Besht*: Towards a Phenomenology of Madness in Early Hasidism," in *Spirit Possession in Judaism: Cases and Contexts from the Middle Ages to the Present*, ed. Matt Goldish (Detroit: Wayne State University Press, 2003), 258. For analyses of the phenomenon of the dybbuk, see Jeffrey Howard Chajes, *Between Worlds: Dybbuks, Exorcists, and Early Modern Judaism* (Philadelphia: University of Pennsylvania Press, 2003); Yoram Bilu, "The Taming of the Deviants and Beyond: An Analysis of Dybbuk Possession and Exorcism in Judaism," in *Spirit Possession in Judaism*, ed. Goldish, 27–40; Rachel Elior, *Dybbuks and Jewish Women in Social History, Mysticism and Folklore* (Jerusalem: Urim Publications, 2008).

92. Mark, "Dybbuk and Devekut," 259–60. There is a kind of parallel here to Foucault's conception of Christianity in the Classical Age regarding as obsolete the idea of holy madness: "Christian unreason was relegated by Christians themselves into the margins of a reason that had become identical with the wisdom of God incarnate." Michel Foucault, *Madness and Civilization: A History of Insanity in the Age of Reason*, trans. Richard Howard (London: Routledge, 2001), 74.

93. Angela Brintlinger, "Introduction: Approaching Russian Madness," in *Madness and the Mad in Russian Culture*, ed. Angela Brintlinger and Ilya Vinitsky (Toronto: University of Toronto Press, 2007), 8; Brown, "Societal Responses," 16–17.

94. Porter, *Social History of Madness*, 16–17. Foucault, who famously dubbed this phenomenon "the Great Confinement," linked it to the growing power of the absolute state and the bourgeois impulse of Enlightenment rationality to impose its version of morality—especially in relation to work and the absence of work, i.e., idleness—upon all of society. Foucault, *Madness and Civilization*, 35–60.

95. Brintlinger, "Introduction: Approaching Russian Madness," 8.

96. Brown, "Societal Responses," 14–15.

97. Julie V. Brown, "A Sociohistorical Perspective on Deinstitutionalization: The Case of Late Imperial Russia," *Research in Law, Deviance & Social Control* 7 (1985): 18–19.

98. Ibid., 19.

99. Ellie R. Schainker, *Confessions of the Shtetl: Converts from Judaism in Imperial Russia, 1817–1906* (Stanford: Stanford University Press, 2017), 37–38. In 1820, when he was 36, Moshe converted to Christianity. See David Assaf, *Untold Tales of the Hasidim: Crisis and Discontent in the History of Hasidism*, trans. Dena Ordan (Waltham, MA: Brandeis University Press and University Press of New England, 2010), 29–96.

100. An interesting comparison is offered by early modern Amsterdam, where prosperous Portuguese Jewish families sometimes paid working-class Ashkenazi Jews to care for their intellectually disabled relatives. Levie Bernfeld, *Poverty and Welfare*, 196–97.

101. Wright, "Developmental and Physical Disabilities," in *Encyclopedia of European Social History from 1350 to 2000*, ed. Stearns, 3: 508; Lia Iangoulova, "The *Osvidetel'stvovanie* and *Ispytanie* of Insanity: Psychiatry in Tsarist Russia," in *Madness and the Mad in Russian Culture*, ed. Brintlinger and Vinitsky, 56–57.

102. See, e.g., Baron, *Jewish Community*, 2: 362, 364.

103. Ibid., 330–32.

104. See, e.g., a case from Poznan in 1724 in Dov Avron, *Pinkas ha-kesherim shel kehilat Pozna (Acta electorum communitatis Judaeorum Posnaniensium, 1621–1835)* (Jerusalem: Memorial Foundation for Jewish Culture, 1966), 288–89. In this case, the wording of the entry in the *pinkas* suggests that this was a custom that had fallen out of use by the eighteenth century, so we cannot be sure of the extent of its application in early modern Poland.

105. Katz, *Tradition and Crisis*, 126.

106. *Encyclopaedia Judaica*, 2nd ed., s.v. "Orphan, orphanage"; Baron, *Jewish Community*, 2: 175.

107. ChaeRan Y. Freeze, "Family," in the *YIVO Encyclopedia of Jews in Eastern Europe*, ed. Gershon Hundert (New Haven, CT: Yale University Press, 2008), 1: 494–500.

108. "Talmud-tora," *Evreiskaia entsiklopediia: svod znanii o evreistve i ego kulture v proshlom i nastoiashchem* (St. Petersburg: Brokgauz-Efron, 1906–13), 14: cols. 723–25; Simon Dubnow, *History of the Jews in Russia and Poland* (Philadelphia: Jewish Publication Society of America, 1916), 1: 114.

109. "The professional itinerant, the miserable individual who finds in wandering a way of life, fractures the structures of social life and threatens established society. . . . The individual outside of established social attachments, familial and neighborhood connections [is rendered] disturbing or dangerous for society." Bronisław Geremek, *Truands et misérables dans l'Europe moderne (1350–1600): inutiles au monde* (Paris: Julliard, 1980), 71, 84.

110. Keith Thomas, *Religion and the Decline of Magic: Studies in Popular Beliefs in Sixteenth and Seventeenth Century England* (London: Weidenfeld & Nicolson, 1971), 568.

111. Smith, "Marginal People," 178–79.

112. Rachel Adams, *Sideshow U.S.A.: Freaks and the American Cultural Imagination* (Chicago: University of Chicago Press, 2001), 9.

113. Mark, "Dybbuk and Devekut," 260.

114. Bernstein, *Yudishe shprikhverter un redensarten*, 173.

115. Mark, "Dybbuk and Devekut," 261.

116. Elior, *Dybbuks and Jewish Women*, 94. See, e.g., the story in *Shivhe ha-besht* (In Praise of the Ba'al Shem Tov) of the madwoman possessed by an evil spirit who was able to tell each person both his shortcomings and virtues (*to'avotav ve-tovotav*). Dov Baer ben Samuel, *Sefer shivhe ha-besht*, ed. Samuel A. Horodezky (Berlin: Aya-

not, 1922), 22–23. Elior demonstrates that "the forces of life and death associated with a woman's body" because of the religious and cultural resonances of menstrual blood made the link between a possessed woman and the "untamed, impure, chaotic world of the dead" especially apposite. Elior, *Dybbuks and Jewish Women*, 70, 90. I am grateful to my student Stephanie Elliott for pointing me to this reference.

117. Bilu, "Taming of the Deviants and Beyond," in *Spirit Possession in Judaism*, ed. Goldish, 42; see also Elior, *Dybbuks and Jewish Women*, 60. On dybbuks, see also Yoram Bilu, "Ha-dibuk ba-yahadut: hafra'ah nafshit ke-mash'av tarbuti," *Jerusalem Studies in Jewish Thought* 2, no. 4 (1983): 529–63; id., "Dybbuk and Maggid: Two Cultural Patterns of Altered Consciousness in Judaism," *AJS Review* 21, no. 2 (1996): 341–66.

118. *Pinkas* of Kiev Hevra Kadisha (5553/1793), folio 29 verso, in Israel Nahum Darewski, *Le-korot ha-yehudim be-kiyov* (Berdichev, 1902), 110.

119. Israel M. Ta-Shma, *Minhag ashkenaz ha-kadmon: heker ve-iyun* (Jerusalem: The Magnes Press, 1999), 307. I am grateful to Ephraim Shoham-Steiner for this reference.

120. E. E. Levkievskaia, "Sirota," in *Slavianskaia mifologiia: entsiklopedicheskii slovar*, ed. S. M. Tolstaia (Moscow: Mezhdunarodnye otnosheniia, 2002), 433, quoted in Viktoriia Mochalova, "Istselenie, spasenie, izbavlenie v evreiskoi traditsii i magicheskaia praktika (evreiskii obriad kladbishchenskoi svad'by i ego slavianskie paralleli)," in *Narodnaia meditsina i magiia v slavianskoi i evreiskoi kul'turnoi traditsii: sbornik statei*, ed. O. V. Belova (Moscow: Tsentr nauchnykh rabotnikov i prepodavatelei iudaiki v vuzakh "Sefer" and Institut slavianovedeniia Rossiiskoi Akademii Nauk, 2007), 94.

121. Stiker, *History of Disability*, 8, argues that disability is intrinsically tied to death because of humans' instinctual desire to eliminate the abnormal, which we can see clearly in the ancient practice of allowing babies with deformities or disabilities to die.

122. Rosemarie Garland-Thomson, "Introduction: From Wonder to Error—A Genealogy of Freak Discourse in Modernity," in *Freakery*, ed. id., 3.

Chapter 2

1. Adele Lindenmeyr, *Poverty Is Not a Vice: Charity, Society, and the State in Imperial Russia* (Princeton, NJ: Princeton University Press, 1996), 9–10.

2. Ibid., 10.

3. Iu. G. Galai, *Nishchenstvo i brodiazhnichestvo v dorevoliutsionnoi Rossii: zakonodatel'nye i prakticheskie problemy* (Nizhnii Novgorod: Nizhegorodskaia pravovaia akademiia, 2012), 11–12.

4. Ibid., 14.

5. Lindenmeyr, *Poverty Is Not a Vice*, 11.

6. Ibid., 18–19.

7. Joseph Bradley, *Muzhik and Muscovite: Urbanization in Late Imperial Russia* (Berkeley: University of California Press, 1985), 252–56, quote on 256.

8. Among other attributes, liminality is associated with anonymity, absence of property, absence of status, unselfishness, sacredness, and simplicity—all qualities associated with, or imputed to, the life of a wandering beggar, according to Victor W. Turner, "Liminality and Communitas," in *The Ritual Process: Structure and Anti-Structure* (Chicago: Aldine, 1969), 106–7.

9. Lindenmeyr, *Poverty Is Not a Vice*, 19. See also "Kaliki ili kaleki perekhozkhie," *Entsiklopedicheskii slovar' Brokgauza i Efrona* (St. Petersburg, 1890–1907), 14: 27–28; Faith Wigzell, "Folklore and Russian Literature," in *The Routledge Companion to Russian Literature*, ed. Neil Cornwell (London: Routledge, 2001), 44.

10. Piotr Grochowski, *Dziady: rzecz o wędrownych żebrakach i ich pieśniach* (Toruń, Poland: Wydawn. Naukowe Uniwersytetu Mikołaja Kopernika, 2009), 19–92.

11. Ibid., 93–94.

12. Galai interprets this shift as a response to the chaos of the Time of Troubles and peasant uprisings. Galai, *Nishchenstvo i brodiazhnichestvo*, 21.

13. Lindenmeyr, *Poverty Is Not a Vice*, 31. See also Galai, *Nishchenstvo i brodiazhnichestvo*, 22, 38.

14. Lindenmeyr, *Poverty Is Not a Vice*, 33–34.

15. Ibid., 37.

16. Ibid., 39–41.

17. The hidden righteous man (*lamed-vavnik*), one of thirty-six such people believed to be present in the world at any given moment, often assumed a disguise as a lowly person. Gershom Scholem, "The Tradition of the Thirty-Six Hidden Just Men," in *The Messianic Idea in Judaism and Other Essays on Jewish Spirituality* (New York: Schocken Books, 1995), 251–56.

18. Some of the most important works among the vast literature on Nahman's tales are Joseph Dan, *Ha-sipur ha-hasidi* (Jerusalem: Keter yerushalayim, 1975), chap. 3; Nahman of Bratslav, *The Tales*, trans. Arnold J. Band (New York: Paulist Press, 1978), introduction and commentaries; David G. Roskies, *A Bridge of Longing: The Lost Art of Yiddish Storytelling* (Cambridge, MA: Harvard University Press, 1995), chap. 2; Ora Wiskind-Elper, *Tradition and Fantasy in the Tales of Reb Nahman of Bratslav* (Albany: State University of New York Press, 1998); Marianne Schleicher, *Intertextuality in the Tales of Rabbi Nahman of Bratslav: A Close Reading of Sippurey Ma'asiyot* (Boston: Brill, 2007).

19. Roskies, *Bridge of Longing*, 55.

20. Ibid., 267.

21. Wiskind-Elper, *Tradition and Fantasy*, 143.

22. Nahman of Bratslav, *Tales*, 323. See also Wiskind-Elper, *Tradition and Fantasy*, 171.

23. Wiskind-Elper, *Tradition and Fantasy*, 35. It may also be significant, given Nahman's own messianic claims, that one way of referring to the Messiah in Yiddish was

as "the younger beggar." Nahum Stutchkoff, *Der oytser fun der yidisher shprakh*, ed. Max Weinreich (New York: Yidisher Visnshaftlekher Institut–YIVO, 1950), § 607 (*malkhes shomayim*).

24. See, e.g., Moses Gaster, ed., *Ma'aseh Book*, vol. 2 (Philadelphia: Jewish Publication Society of America, 1934), 326–27, 468, 473–78; Beatrice Weinreich, ed., *Yiddish Folktales* (New York: Pantheon Books, 2007), 77–79, 85–88. These motifs fall under L412 (rich man made poor to punish pride) and L419.2 (king becomes beggar) in Stith Thompson, *Motif-Index of Folk-Literature: A Classification of Narrative Elements in Folk-Tales, Ballads, Myths, Fables, Mediaeval Romances, Exempla, Fabliaux, Jest-Books, and Local Legends*, rev. and enl. ed., (Bloomington: Indiana University Press, 1955).

25. Rabbi Leib Sores was known for being "in secret contact with the hidden just men." Scholem, "Tradition of the Thirty-Six Hidden Just Men," 255.

26. Gedalyah Nigal, *Ha-"aher" ba-sipur ha-hasidi* (Jerusalem: Ha-makhon le-heker ha-sifrut ha-hasidit, 767), 108–12; Gedalyah Nigal, *The Hasidic Tale* (Oxford: Littman Library of Jewish Civilization, 2008), 103.

27. Iulii Gessen, *Istoriia evreiskogo naroda v Rossii* (Leningrad: n.p., 1925; repr. Moscow: Evreiiskii universitet, 1993), 2: 63.

28. John Klier, *Russia Gathers Her Jews: The Origins of the "Jewish Question" in Russia, 1772–1825* (DeKalb: Northern Illinois University Press, 1986), 150–51; Glenn Dynner, *Yankel's Tavern: Jews, Liquor, and Life in the Kingdom of Poland* (New York: Oxford University Press, 2014), 55.

29. See Dubnow, *History of the Jews in Russia and Poland*, 1: 407, 2: 20, 32; Polonsky, *Jews in Poland and Russia*, 1: 354. On the expulsion of Jews living within fifty versts of the western border, see Michael Stanislawski, *Tsar Nicholas I and the Jews: The Transformation of Jewish Society in Russia, 1825–1855* (Philadelphia: Jewish Publication Society of America, 1983), 175.

30. Tsvi Hirsh Lifshits Kolp, *Sefer mi-dor le-dor* (Warsaw: N. Sokolov, 1901), 55. Kolp's reference to 1844 is puzzling, since the last expulsion from villages took place in 1830.

31. Dynner, *Yankel's Tavern*, 57.

32. Polonsky, *Jews in Poland and Russia*, 1: 291.

33. Stanislawski, *Tsar Nicholas I and the Jews*, 170–82; Polonsky, *Jews in Poland and Russia*, 1: 386–88.

34. LCVIA f. 620, op. 1, d. 21 ("O kollektivnom ob"iazatel'stve chlenov [Vilenskoi] obshchiny vydelit' sredstva na obuchenie evreiskikh sirot" [1804]), l. 172, microfilm at CAHJP HM2/9825.3.

35. Dubnow, *History of the Jews in Russia and Poland*, 1: 351; Klier, *Russia Gathers Her Jews*, 146–50, 161.

36. LCVIA f. 620, op., 1, d. 15 (Kagal Vil'no [1828]), microfilm at CAHJP HM2/9821.2, contains correspondence from the Vilna kahal to the Russian authorities

about the increased tax burden that "many poor people, infirm, cripples, and orphans without any means to support themselves"—many of them recent newcomers to the city—placed on the more prosperous members of the Jewish community.

37. Lindenmeyr, *Poverty Is Not a Vice*, 32–38.

38. Mordechai Zalkin, "'Ha-ketsavim de-po parku ol': me'afyenim u-megamot be-fe'ilut ma'arekhet ha-revahah be-kehilat vilnah be-reshit ha-me'ah ha-tesha esreh," in *Mi-vilnah le-yerushalayim: mehkarim be-toldotehem uve-tarbutam shel yehude mizrah eiropah mugashim le-profesor shemu'el verses*, ed. David Assaf et al. (Jerusalem: Magnes Press, 2002), 25–42.

39. Israel Klausner, *Vilnah, yerushalayim de-lita: dorot rishonim, 1495–1881* (Lohame ha-geta'ot: Beit lohame ha-geta'ot, 1988), 154; Gessen, *Istoriia evreiskogo naroda v Rossii*, 2:69.

40. Israel Klausner, *Toldot ha-kehilah ha-ivrit be-vilnah* (Jerusalem: n.p., 1938), 120.

41. Ibid., 121. See also Israel Cohen, *Vilna* (Philadelphia: Jewish Publication Society of America, 1943), 129. In Balta, the hekdesh was also run by the society for visiting the sick. NBUV IR Iudaika f. 321 (*Pinkasim* Collection), op. 1, od. zb. 1 ("Pinkas leha-havurah Bikur Holim de-po k"k Balta" [1821]), ark. 18 (entry dated 1833).

42. Kolp, *Sefer mi-dor le-dor*, 49.

43. Ibid., 49.

44. E. Tsherikover, "Der arkhiv fun shimen dubnov," *Historishe shriftn*, 1 (1929): 578.

45. Iakov Brafman, *Kniga kagala* (St. Petersburg, 1875), 2: 164–66. *Kniga kagala* was a collection of Jewish communal documents published by the convert Iakov Brafman in an attempt to reveal the putative avarice and corruption of the organized Jewish community. Brafman did forge some documents, but there is no reason to suspect that this particular excerpt from the Minsk *pinkas* has been corrupted or falsified.

46. Brafman, *Kniga kagala*, 2: 166.

47. Ibid., 2: 167, §14.

48. Isaac Levitats, *The Jewish Community in Russia, 1772–1844* (New York: Octagon Books, 1970), 59.

49. Brafman, *Kniga kagala*, 2: 327. "[In the cities] the custom was to give a quarter-kopeck as charity. . . . to three beggars, and thus one kopeck was enough for twelve beggars. . . . but in the small towns . . . they would make pieces of tin, or print pieces of paper marked specially for distribution as charity, and each one was worth one-third of a quarter-kopeck and was given to three beggars. Thus one kopeck covered thirty-six beggars. The beggars would bring these 'coins' to the householders and exchange them for real coins." Kolp, *Sefer mi-dor le-dor*, 50.

50. It was possible to buy one's way out of hosting the poor for meals; the Minsk regulations for the "*Pletten*-teller" clarify that those who were able to afford this were, however, required to participate in the system on festivals, the New Year, and the Day of Atonement. Brafman, *Kniga kagala*, 2: 215.

51. Brown, "Sociohistorical Perspective," 180. See also Lindenmeyr, *Poverty Is Not a Vice*, 53.

52. Lindenmeyr, *Poverty Is Not a Vice*, 44. Lindenmeyr notes that at least one historian considers the 73,000 figure to be "greatly underestimated."

53. Brafman, *Kniga kagala*, 2:167.

54. Ibid., 2: 168.

55. Robert Pinkerton, *Russia, or, Miscellaneous Observations on the Past and Present State of That Country and Its Inhabitants* (London: Seeley & Sons, 1833), 90; Levitats, *The Jewish Community in Russia, 1772–1844*, 258.

56. Pinkerton, *Russia*, 113.

57. Levitats, *Jewish Community in Russia, 1772–1844*, 258–59. These regulations probably date from the early nineteenth century.

58. Dubnow, *History of the Jews in Russia and Poland*, 2: 13–29; Gessen, *Istoriia evreiskogo naroda v Rossii*, 2: 31–36, 58–61; Yohanan Petrovsky-Shtern, *Jews in the Russian Army, 1827–1917: Drafted into Modernity* (New York: Cambridge University Press, 2009), 24–60; Iokhanan Petrovskii-Shtern, *Evrei v russkoi armii: 1827–1914*, Historia Rossica (Moscow: Novoe literaturnoe obozrenie, 2003), 21–70. For the long-term impact of conscription on Russian-Jewish culture, see Olga Litvak, *Conscription and the Search for Modern Russian Jewry* (Bloomington: Indiana University Press, 2006).

59. Gessen, *Istoriia evreiskogo naroda v Rossii*, 2: 60; Stanislawski, *Tsar Nicholas I and the Jews*, 20.

60. Stanislawski, *Tsar Nicholas I and the Jews*, 20, 28.

61. RGIA f. 1286, op. 4–1828, d. 461 ("Po pros'bam evreev Mogileva, Shklova i Grodno o dozvolenii otdavat' bespoleznykh chlenov obshchestva . . . ," 1828), l. 20b, microfilm in CAHJP RU1111; Gessen, *Istoriia evreiskogo naroda v Rossii*, 2: 60–61.

62. *Neterpimye [v obshchestve] za besporiadki*, a vague phrase, is difficult to translate. Other renderings are "violators of community discipline" or "those of dubious reputation or behavior or with an unacceptable way of thinking." Immanuel Etkes, *Rabbi Israel Salanter and the Mussar Movement: Seeking the Torah of Truth* (Philadelphia: Jewish Publication Society, 1993), 154–55 (for the former); Petrovsky-Shtern, *Jews in the Russian Army*, 55 (for the latter). Portraying the Nicholaevan draft as a cosmic religious drama, at least one prominent religious leader, Dov-Ber b. Shneur Zalman (1773–1827), the second rebbe of Habad-Lubavich, cast the recruits as "impure and wicked" Jews who had to be weeded out as part of the process of redemption. Eli Lederhendler, *The Road to Modern Jewish Politics: Political Tradition and Political Reconstruction in the Jewish Community of Tsarist Russia* (New York: Oxford University Press, 1989), 65–66. See also the reference to "parasites" as ideal recruits in an 1854 petition from wealthy Jewish merchants to the Jewish Committee in Nathans, *Beyond the Pale*, 45.

63. RGIA f. 1286, op. 4–1828, d. 461, l. 20b.

64. Ibid., l. 7; Stanislawski, *Tsar Nicholas I and the Jews*, 29.

65. Ibid., ll. 3, 5–50b, 7–8. Petrovskii-Shtern mentions the entreaties to the authorities regarding religious practice in his overview of the Nicholaevan conscription. Yohanan Petrovsky-Shtern, "Military Service in Russia," in the *YIVO Encyclopedia of Jews in Eastern Europe*, 2: 1172.

66. Correspondence cited in n. 37 above.

67. The phrase is from Stanislawski, *Tsar Nicholas I and the Jews*, 20.

68. Ibid., 28.

69. Shoyl Ginsburg, *Historishe verk*, ed. Isaac Rivkind (New York: Shoyl ginzburg 70-yohriger yubiley komitet, 1937), 3: 18.

70. Stanislawski, *Tsar Nicholas I and the Jews*, 28.

71. TsDIAU f. 442, op. 141, spr. 196 ("O zloupotrebleniiakh pri sostavleniia ocherednykh rekrutskikh knig dlia Berdichevskogo evreiskogo obshchestva," 1834), ark. 21.

72. Ginsburg, *Historishe verk*, 3: 27.

73. Stanislawski, *Tsar Nicholas I and the Jews*, 28–29.

74. Ginsburg, *Historishe verk*, 3:24.

75. Ibid., 27.

76. Levitats, *Jewish Community in Russia, 1772–1844*, 63.

77. Stanislawski, *Tsar Nicholas I and the Jews*, 28; Petrovsky-Shtern, *Jews in the Russian Army*, 55.

78. YIVO Archives RG 12 (Minsk Jewish Community Council Records), folder 6, no. 165 (Delo po prosheniiu Berki i brata ego Itski Khaikelevykh Klotsov ob uvol'nenii poslednego k naimu sebia v Rekruty za Semeistvo Gertsa Slepiaka, November 12, 1840), l. 1. I thank Nila Fridberg for assistance in translating a particularly thorny Russian term in this passage.

79. YIVO Archives RG 12, folder 6, no. 164 ("Po prosheniiu brat'ev Peisakha i Girsha Abramovichev Chertovykh ob uvol'nenii poslednego dlia naima sebia v Rekruty za semeistva Mendelia Margolina," 1840).

80. Ibid., no. 160 ("Po prosheniiu vdovy Ovseevoi i syna ee Aby Moshikovykh ob Uvol'nenii poslednego dlia naima sebia v Rekruty za Semeistvo Moshki Batki," 1840).

81. Ibid., l. 1.

82. H. Aleksandrov, "Fun minsker arkhivn," *Tsaytshrift far yidisher geshikhte, demografye un ekonomik, literatur-forshung, shprakhvisnshaft un etnografye (Institut far vaysruslendisher kultur, yidisher sektor)* 2–3 (1928): col. 770.

83. Levitats, *Jewish Community in Russia, 1772–1844*, 64.

84. Aleksandrov, "Fun minsker arkhivn": col. 769.

85. E.g., petitions from the widow Keila Lipinskaia protesting the conscription of her only son by the Belaia Tserkov' kahal in 1831, from Nukhim Kushnir objecting to the conscription of his only son by the Torgovitsa kahal in 1840, and from "Jewish poor folk" in Chichelnik in 1853. TsDIAU f. 533, op. 3., spr. 1091 (1831); DAKO f. 2, op. 1, spr. 13676 (1840); O. Margolis, *Geshikhte fun yidn in rusland: etyudn un dokumentn*

(Moscow: Tsentraler felker-farlag fun F.S.S.R., 1930), 353–56. For additional cases, see Stanislawski, *Tsar Nicholas I and the Jews*, 129–30. See also Petrovsky-Shtern, *Jews in the Russian Army*, 55–56.

86. YIVO Archives RG 12, folder 8 (Corruption, Jewish Conscription, 1841), no. 160, ll. 37–370b.

87. See, e.g., Stanislawski, *Tsar Nicholas I and the Jews*, 127–33; Lederhendler, *Road to Modern Jewish Politics*, 66–68; Polonsky, *Jews in Poland and Russia*, 1: 361–62.

88. The conscription statute directed the Russian military to allow Jewish soldiers full religious freedom, but in practice this varied considerably; "while Jewish soldiers could legally perform their rituals, they were punished if their observance contravened army discipline." Petrovsky-Shtern, *Jews in the Russian Army*, 65.

89. N. Tsukerman, "Pinkes fun der pruzhener kehile," in *Pinkes fun der shtot Pruzhene* (Pruzhene: Pinkos, 1930), 35. "With dominion and fear" is a phrase from Job 25:2, but its exact meaning here is unclear.

90. Saul M. Ginsburg and P. S. Marek, eds., *Evreiskie narodnye pesni v Rossii* (St. Petersburg: Redaktsiia "Voskhoda," 1901), 51–52. For English translations, see Ruth Rubin, *Voices of a People: The Story of Yiddish Folk Song* (Philadelphia: Jewish Publication Society, 1979), 211–12.

91. For a critical evaluation of Ginsburg and Marek's project, see Roskies, *Bridge of Longing*, 11–13.

92. Alexander Harkavy, *English-Yidisher verterbukh* = *English-Yiddish Dictionary* (New York: Hebrew Publishing Company, 1910), 178.

93. Meyer Viner, ed., *Folklor-lider: naye materyaln-zamlung* (Moscow: Emes, 1936), 2: 241. Rubin translates three stanzas in *Voices of a People*, 212–13.

94. Viner, *Folklor-lider*, 2: 243.

95. Guggenheim, "Meeting on the Road," 129.

96. Shiper, *Geshikhte fun yidisher teater-kunst un drame*, 65–66.

97. E. Sidney Hartland, "The Sin-Eater," *Folklore* 3, no. 2 (1892): 147–48.

Chapter 3

1. Yekhezkel Kotik, *Journey to a Nineteenth-Century Shtetl: The Memoirs of Yekhezkel Kotik*, trans. David Assaf (Detroit: Wayne State University Press in cooperation with the Diaspora Research Institute, Tel Aviv University, 2002), 153; original: Yekhezkel Kotik, *Mayne zikhroynes*, vol. 2 (Berlin: Klal-farlag, 1922), 62.

2. Ephraim Deinard, *Zikhronot bat ami: le-korot ha-yehudim veha-yahadut be-rusiyah be-meshekh karov le-shiv'im shanah* (St. Louis, MO: Moineshter, 1920), 1: 64.

3. François Guesnet, *Polnische Juden im 19. Jahrhundert: Lebensbedingungen, Rechtsnormen und Organisation im Wandel* (Cologne: Böhlau, 1998), 57.

4. A. P. Subbotin, *V cherte evreiskoi osedlosti: otryvki iz ekonomicheskikh izsledovanii v Zapadnoi i IUgo-zapadnoi Rossii za leto 1887 g.* (St. Petersburg, 1888), 1: 133 n. 28.

5. François Guesnet, "Jüdische Armut und ihre Bekämpfung im Königreich Polen: Grundzüge und Entwicklungen im 19. Jahrhundert," in Jersch-Wenzel, *Juden und Armut* (Cologne: Böhlau, 2000), 202. On the abolition of the kahal in Poland, see Polonsky, *Jews in Poland and Russia*, 1: 292–93.

6. Dubnow, *History of the Jews in Russia and Poland*, 2: 102; Guesnet, *Polnische Juden im 19. Jahrhundert*, 51–52.

7. See Shaul Stampfer, "Scientific Welfare and Lonely Old People: The Development of Old Age Homes among Jews in Eastern Europe," in id., *Families, Rabbis and Education*, 92. On the functioning of kahal institutions after 1844, see Azriel Shochat, "Ha-hanhagah be-kehilot rusyah im bitul ha-kahal," *Tsiyon* 42 (1977): 143–233.

8. Jewish Colonization Association, *Recueil de matériaux sur la situation économique des Israélites de Russie, d'après l'enquête de la Jewish Colonization Association* (Paris: F. Alcan, 1906), 246.

9. NBUV IR f. 321, op. 1, od. zb. 1 (*Pinkas le-havurah bikur holim* (5581 [1821]); Imperatorskoe russkoe geograficheskoe obshchestvo, *Trudy Etnografichesko-statisticheskoi ekspeditsii v Zapadno-Russkii krai snariazhennoi Imperatorskim Russkim geograficheskim obshchestvom (IUgo-Zapadnyi otdel): materialy i izsledovaniia*, ed. Pavel Chubinskii (St. Petersburg: 1872–78), 7: 105. The eclecticism and lack of transparency in the management of the hekdesh goes back to the Middle Ages. A hekdesh was always founded by a community or burial society, but "it is difficult to determine who established, controlled, and supported the hospital in each specific community" (Marcus, *Communal Sick-Care in the German Ghetto*, 173).

10. Jewish Colonization Association, *Recueil de matériaux*, 2: 246–47.

11. See, e.g., L. Rokhlin, *Mestechko Krasnopol'e Mogilevskoi gub.: opyt statistiko-ekonomicheskago opisaniia tipichnago mestechka cherty evreiskoi osedlosti* (St. Petersburg: Sever, 1909), 76; Kotik, *Journey to a Nineteenth-Century Shtetl*, 212.

12. Mordechai Zalkin, "Charity," in the *YIVO Encyclopedia of Jews in Eastern Europe*, 1: 307.

13. Jewish Colonization Association, *Recueil*, 2: 246; Gershon Levin, "Dos bukh fun mayn leben: frihlings-yohren in lublin," *Haynt*, December 8, 1933.

14. Kolp, *Sefer mi-dor le-dor*, 86. See also Leo Rosenberg, "Armenwesen und Soziale Fürsorge im Ostjudentum," *Der Jude* 1, no. 11 (February 1917): 333–34.

15. Kotik, *Mayne zikhroynes*, 1: 67; translation based on Kotik, *Journey to a Nineteenth-Century Shtetl*, 153.

16. Levin, "Dos bukh fun mayn leben."

17. Lisa Epstein, "Caring for the Soul's House: The Jews of Russia and Health Care, 1860–1914" (Ph.D. diss., Yale University, 1995), 179.

18. Moyshe-Arn Shatskes, *Der yudisher far-peysakh order minhag yisroel* (Warsaw, 1881), 61–62, quoted in Isaac Rivkind, *Yidishe gelt in lebenshteyger, kultur-geshikhte un folkor* [sic]: *leksikologishe shtudye* (New York: American Academy for Jewish Research, 1959), 78.

19. Ben Sholem, "A shreklikher hekdesh," *Folkstsaytung*, December 4, 1906, 2.

20. Stutchkoff, *Oytser*, § 416 (*umreynkayt*).

21. Levin, "Dos bukh fun mayn leben."

22. Stutchkoff, *Oytser*, § 243 (*toyt, mes*).

23. Kotik, *Journey to a Nineteenth-Century Shtetl*, 253.

24. Kolp, *Sefer mi-dor le-dor*, 50.

25. "Tramps, Mediæval and Modern," *Westminster Review* 129, no. 5 (May 1888): 587 (review of C. J. Ribton-Turner, *A History of Vagrants and Vagrancy, and Beggars and Begging* [London: Chapman & Hall, 1887]).

26. Stutchkoff, *Oytser*, § 215 (*raybung*). Similarly, to describe a filthy environment, one might say, "Lice like on a beggar" (*layz vi bay a betler*) (§ 416, *umreynkayt*).

27. See Roy Porter, "Foucault's Great Confinement," *History of the Human Sciences* 3, no. 1 (1990): 47.

28. The hospitals at Haina and Merxhausen housed the elderly, the sick and disabled, and the insane, in addition to growing numbers of orphans. Midelfort, *History of Madness*, 330–42.

29. See, e.g., Hundert, *Jews in a Polish Private Town*, 71–72.

30. Marcus, *Communal Sick-Care in the German Ghetto*, 177. There are many examples of hekdeshim located in or next to cemeteries; see, e.g., Rokhlin, *Mestechko Krasnopol'e Mogilevskoi gub.*, 72.

31. Marcus, *Communal Sick-Care in the German Ghetto*, 177. The practice continues today in some societies, albeit in different fashion. In 2018, local councils in the United Kingdom gave homeless people one-way tickets "to return to areas where they ha[d] family and support networks." In London, one-third of the tickets were for destinations in eastern Europe. Patrick Greenfield and Sarah Marsh, "Revealed: Homeless People Given One-Way Tickets to Other Areas," *Guardian*, December 28, 2018.

32. On the cemetery as liminal space in East European Jewish culture, see Gadi Sagiv, "Hasidism and Cemetery Inauguration Ceremonies: Authority, Magic, and Performance of Charismatic Leadership," *Jewish Quarterly Review* 103, no. 3 (2013): 328–51.

33. Avriel Bar-Levav, "We Are Where We Are Not: The Cemetery in Jewish Culture," *Jewish Studies*, no. 41 (2002): 22.

34. BT Hagigah 3b.

35. Stutchkoff, *Oytser*, § 523 (*naketkayt*).

36. Samuel Max Melamed, "The Hekdesh and Its People," *American Jewish Chronicle*, April 6, 1917, 2, no. 22 edition, 708. See also A. S. Herschberg, *Pinkes Byalistok: grunt-materyaln tsu der geshikhte fun di yidn in byalistok biz nokh der ershter velt-milkhome*, ed. Yudel Mark (New York, 1949), 2: 163; Levin, "Dos bukh fun mayn leben"; Epstein, "Caring for the Soul's House," 173.

37. Avidav Lipsker, "Ha-kalah ve-shiv'at ha-kabtsanim—le-she'elat mekorotav shel

sipur-hamisgeret shel 'mayse meha-7 betlirs,'" *Jerusalem Studies in Jewish Folklore* 13–14 (1992): 235–38. Lipsker contends that this polarity stems from the two types of poor people in traditional Jewish culture: the poor people in the town who were integrated into communal life, and the alien poor who came to the community as guests, even guests in one's home or at a family celebration such as a wedding.

38. Ayzik M. Dik, *Di nakht fun tes-vav kislev* (Vilna, 1867), 38.

39. Kolp, *Sefer midor ledor*, 49. The maxim is based on BT Avodah Zarah 5a. For an incisive analysis of the use of *ani hashuv kamet* in the context of a medieval Jewish tale, the *Mayse fun vorms*, which also features characters who live in the poorhouse, see Jeremy Dauber, *In the Demon's Bedroom: Yiddish Literature and the Early Modern* (New Haven, CT: Yale University Press, 2010), 155–58.

40. Brafman, *Kniga kagala*, 2: 167.

41. The shtetl's most important communal institutions were the synagogue, cemetery, and bathhouse, according to Dan Miron ("The Literary Image of the Shtetl," in id., *Image of the Shtetl*, 39).

42. See ibid., 37–38. On the magical role of the bathhouse in Russian culture, see William F. Ryan, *The Bathhouse at Midnight: An Historical Survey of Magic and Divination in Russia* (University Park: Pennsylvania State University Press, 1999), 51–52; E. J. W. Barber, *The Dancing Goddesses: Folklore, Archaeology, and the Origins of European Dance* (New York: Norton, 2013), 122.

43. This was apparently also true in earlier periods. See Stanislaw Gajerski, "Szpitale żydowskie na Rusi Czerwonej w XVI–XVIII w.," *Biuletyn Żydowskiego Instytutu Historycznego*, no. 4 (1979): 29–30; Marcus, *Communal Sick-Care in the German Ghetto*, 160, 162; Ephraim Frisch, *An Historical Survey of Jewish Philanthropy* (New York: Cooper Square Publishers, 1969), 143–46.

44. Timothy B. Smith, "Charity and Poor Relief: The Modern Period," in *Encyclopedia of European Social History from 1350 to 2000*, ed. Peter N. Stearns (New York: Scribner, 2001), 3: 458.

45. Levin, "Dos bukh fun mayn leben."

46. Foucault, *Madness and Civilization*, 64.

47. Ibid., 65.

48. Chaim Shevah, "Ha-dibuk," in *Piesk ve-most: sefer yizkor* ([Tel Aviv:] Irgun yots'e pyesk u-most be-yisra'el veha-tefutsot, 1975), 150–52. The folktale is reproduced without source or date in the memorial volume for the communities of Piesk and Most (Pol. Piaski and Masty), but it was presumably known and retold during the interwar years, since most of the contributors to *yizker-bikher* were Holocaust survivors who had come of age in independent Poland. See Jack Kugelmass and Jonathan Boyarin, "Yizker Bikher and the Problem of Historical Veracity: An Anthropological Approach," in *The Jews of Poland Between Two World Wars*, ed. Israel Gutman et al. (Hanover, NH: Brandeis University Press and University Press of New England, 1989), 532.

49. Miron, "Literary Image," esp. 32–39.

50. Elior, *Dybbuks and Jewish Women*, 76–77.

51. Dan Miron, "Abramovitsh, Sholem Yankev," in the *YIVO Encyclopedia of Jews in Eastern Europe*, 1: 3; Yekhiel Hirshhoyt, "Mendele Moykher-Sforim (Sholem-Yankev Abramovitsh)," in *Leksikon fun der nayer yidisher literatur* (New York: Congress for Jewish Culture, 1956), trans. Joshua Fogel (2017), http://yleksikon.blogspot.com/2017/11/mendele-moykher-sforim-sholem-yankev.html (accessed December 5, 2019).

52. Miron, "Abramovitsh, Sholem Yankev."

53. Ruth R. Wisse, "Peretz, Yitskhok Leybush," in the *YIVO Encyclopedia of Jews in Eastern Europe*, 2: 1340.

54. Litvak, *Conscription and the Search for Modern Russian Jewry*, 128.

55. S. Y. Abramovitsh [Mendele Moykher-Sforim], "Fishke the Lame," in *Selected Works of Mendele Moykher-Sforim*, ed. Marvin S. Zuckerman, Gerald Stillman, and Marion Herbst, trans. Gerald Stillman (Malibu, CA: Joseph Simon / Pangloss Press, 1991), 239; id., "Fishke der krumer," in *Geklibene verk* (New York: IKUF Farlag, 1947), 3: 82.

56. David G. Roskies, "Ayzik-Meyer Dik and the Rise of Yiddish Popular Literature" (Ph.D. diss., Brandeis University, 1975), 208–9; id., *Bridge of Longing*, 87; Joseph Bradley, *Muzhik and Muscovite: Urbanization in Late Imperial Russia* (Berkeley: University of California Press, 1985), 254–56.

57. I. L. Peretz, "Be-agaf ha-meshuga'im," *Ha-tsefira* 23, no. 195 (September 2, 1896): 948.

58. Abramovitsh, "Fishke the Lame," 248.

59. Translation (with some modifications) from ibid., 256–57. Yiddish: Abramovitsh, "Fishke der krumer," 3: 101–3; Hebrew: S. A. Abramovitsh [Mendele Mokher Sefarim], "Sefer ha-kabtsanim," in *Kol kitvei mendele mokher sefarim* (Tel-Aviv: Dvir, 1947), 121–22.

60. On candle-making and its associated odor, see Anja-Silvia Goeing, "Chandling the Scholar," H-Ideas, May 28, 2018, https://networks.h-net.org/node/6873/blog/premodern-universities/1871241/chandling-scholar (accessed December 3, 2019). I am grateful to Joan Petit for this reference.

61. Mikhail Bakhtin, *Rabelais and His World*, trans. Hélène Iswolsky (Cambridge, MA: MIT Press, 1968), 318.

62. Abramovitsh, "Fishke the Lame," 256; id., "Fishke der krumer," 101.

63. Bakhtin, *Rabelais and His World*, 318.

64. Abramovitsh, "Sefer ha-kabtsanim," 122.

65. BT Megillah 12b. See also Leila Leah Bronner, "Esther Revisited: An Aggadic Approach," in *A Feminist Companion to Esther, Judith and Susanna*, ed. Athalya Brenner (Sheffield, England: Sheffield Academic Press, 1995), 189; Rachel Adelman, "'Passing Strange'—Reading Transgender across Genre: Rabbinic Midrash and Feminist

Hermeneutics on Esther," *Journal of Feminist Studies in Religion* 30, no. 2 (September 25, 2014): 85.

66. Sigmund Freud, *The Uncanny*, trans. David McLintock (New York: Penguin Books, 2003), 123, 148.

67. Stavroula Constantinou, "Grotesque Bodies in Hagiographical Tales: The Monstrous and the Uncanny in Byzantine Collections of Miracle Stories," *Dumbarton Oaks Papers* 64 (2010): 46.

68. Gershon Shaked, "Dickens' *Oliver Twist* and Mendele's *The Book of Beggars*," in id., *The New Tradition: Essays on Modern Hebrew Literature* (Cincinnati: Hebrew Union College Press, 2006), 174.

69. *Novoe Vremya*, August 29, 1888, cited in Emile Joseph Dillon, *The Jews in Russia* ([London], 1890), 26.

70. Shaked, "Dickens' *Oliver Twist*," 174.

71. Ibid., 181.

72. Gershon Shaked, "Three Kalikes: A Comparative Study of Mendele, Agnon, and Bashevis," in id., *New Tradition*, 185.

73. Gershon Shaked, "A Groan from a Broken Heart: Mendele's *Fishke the Lame* as a Demand for Responsibility," in id., *New Tradition*, 205.

74. Ibid., 206–7.

75. Gershon Shaked, *Bein sehok le-dema: iyunim be-yetsirato shel mendele mokher-sefarim* (Tel-Aviv: Agudat ha-sofrim be-yisra'el le-yad hotsa'at masadah, 1965), 107.

76. Dror Mishani, "'Kol yisrael kabtsan hu'—huts meha-soharim, ba'alei ha-bayit vekha-yotse ba-eileh: he'arot le-shihzur ha-dibur ha-ma'amadi be-'sefer kabtsanim,'" in *Sifrut u-ma'amad: likrat historiografiyah politit shel ha-sifrut ha-ivrit ha-hadashah*, ed. Amir Benbaji and Hannan Hever (Jerusalem: Van Leer Institute and Ha-kibbutz ha-meuhad, 2014), 105.

77. Ibid., 108. Mishani unfortunately undermines his own argument by citing historical works on Jewish socialist movements that are almost four decades old and unrepresentative of more recent trends in the historical scholarship.

78. Abramovitsh, "Fishke the Lame," 237; id., "Fishke der krumer," 82.

79. Translation based on S. Y. Abramovitsh, "Fishke the Lame: A Book of Jewish Poorfolk," in *Tales of Mendele the Book Peddler: Fishke the Lame and Benjamin the Third*, ed. Dan Miron and Ken Frieden, trans. Ted Gorelick (New York: Schocken Books, 1996), 154.

80. Abramovitsh, "Fishke the Lame," 238–39.

81. Shmuel Yosef Agnon, "Ovadiah ba'al mum," in id., *Kol sipurav shel shemu'el yosef agnon* (Jerusalem: Schocken, 1967), 2: 413.

82. BT Sanhedrin 75a, William Davidson digital edition of the Koren Noé Talmud, with commentary by Rabbi Adin Even-Israel Steinsaltz, "Sefaria," www.sefaria. org/Sanhedrin.75a?lang=bi (accessed December 6, 2019).

83. Agnon, "Ovadiah ba'al mum," in id., *Kol sipurav shel shemu'el yosef agnon*, 2: 413.

84. Job 26:2–4, assuming as many scholars do that these words are actually addressed to Job by Bildad; 26:11 contains the phrase "The pillars of heaven tremble."

85. Agnon, "Ovadiah ba'al mum," in id., *Kol sipurav shel shemu'el yosef agnon*, 2: 413.

Chapter 4

1. J. N. Hays, *Epidemics and Pandemics: Their Impacts on Human History* (Santa Barbara, CA: ABC-CLIO, 2005), 272.

2. Ibid., 194. The literature on cholera is vast. Among the most important works are Louis Chevalier, ed., *Le choléra, la première épidémie du XIXe siècle* (La Roche-sur-Yon: Impr. centrale de l'Ouest, 1958); Charles E. Rosenberg, *The Cholera Years: The United States in 1832, 1849, and 1866* (Chicago: University of Chicago Press, 1962); Roderick McGrew, *Russia and the Cholera, 1823–1832* (Madison: University of Wisconsin Press, 1965); R. J. Morris, *Cholera, 1832: The Social Response to an Epidemic* (New York: Holmes & Meier, 1976); Michael Durey, *The Return of the Plague: British Society and the Cholera, 1831–2* (Dublin: Gill & Macmillan; New York: Humanities Press, 1979); François Delaporte, *Disease and Civilization: The Cholera in Paris, 1832* (Cambridge, MA: MIT Press, 1986); Richard J. Evans, *Death in Hamburg: Society and Politics in the Cholera Years, 1830–1910* (Oxford: Clarendon Press, 1987); Frank M. Snowden, *Naples in the Time of Cholera, 1884–1911* (New York: Cambridge University Press, 1995); Elisabeth Mühlauer, *Welch' ein Unheimlicher Gast: Die Cholera-Epidemie 1854 in München* (Münster: Waxmann, 1996); Pamela K. Gilbert, *Cholera and Nation: Doctoring the Social Body in Victorian England* (Albany: State University of New York Press, 2008); and Christopher Hamlin, *Cholera: The Biography* (Oxford: Oxford University Press, 2009).

3. Asa Briggs, "Cholera and Society in the Nineteenth Century," *Past & Present*, no. 19 (April 1, 1961): 79.

4. See, e.g., Nancy M. Frieden, "The Russian Cholera Epidemic, 1892–93, and Medical Professionalization," *Journal of Social History* 10, no. 4 (1977): 546.

5. Richard J. Evans, "Review Article: Blue Funk and Yellow Peril: Cholera and Society in Nineteenth-Century France," *European History Quarterly* 20, no. 1 (January 1, 1990): 120; Gilbert, *Cholera and Nation*, 18.

6. See, e.g., Stephen Halliday, "Death and Miasma in Victorian London: An Obstinate Belief," *BMJ: British Medical Journal* 323, no. 7327 (December 22, 2001): 1469–71.

7. Donald F. Stevens, "Eating, Drinking, and Being Married: Epidemic Cholera and the Celebration of Marriage in Montreal and Mexico City, 1832–1833," *Catholic Historical Review* 92, no. 1 (January 1, 2006): 78.

8. Hays, *Epidemics and Pandemics*, 217.

9. Durey, *Return of the Plague*, 164–70, 184; McGrew, *Russia and the Cholera, 1823–1832*, 109–11.

10. David Craigie, "On the Progress of Cholera through the West of Russia to

Poland," *Supplement to the Edinburgh Medical and Surgical Journal* 37 (February 1832): cxxxiii; Jeremias Lichtenstaedt, *Die asiatische Cholera in Russland in Jahren 1830 und 1831* (Berlin, 1831), pp. 123–24, cited in McGrew, *Russia and the Cholera, 1823–1832*, 99–100.

11. Epstein, "Caring for the Soul's House," 34, 106.

12. Raphael Mahler, *Hasidism and the Jewish Enlightenment: Their Confrontation in Galicia and Poland in the First Half of the Nineteenth Century* (Philadelphia: Jewish Publication Society of America, 1985), 15–16; Epstein, "Caring for the Soul's House," 113–14.

13. Raya Haran, "Zhidachov-Komarno Hasidic Dynasty," in the *YIVO Encyclopedia of Jews in Eastern Europe*, 2: 2121.

14. Guggenheim, "Von den Schalantjuden zu den Betteljuden," 59.

15. Mahler, *Hasidism and the Jewish Enlightenment*, 183, 185–86.

16. "Report of the Circle Physician Dr Schnur, on the Propagation of Cholera in the Kingdom of Poland, Dated the 12th May 1831," in Craigie, "On the Progress of Cholera," cxxxv.

17. Eberhard Wolff, "Juden als Verkörperung von Armut und Unsauberkeit in ärztlichen Berichten über die Choleraepidemie in Osteuropa 1830/31," in Jersch-Wenzel, *Juden und Armut*, 127, 141.

18. For the former, see Grigorii Ivanovich Arkhangel'skii, *Kholernyia epidemii v Evropeiskoi Rossii* (St. Petersburg, 1874), 339–40. For the latter, see L. Pavlovskaia, *Kholernye gody v Rossii: istoricheskii ocherk* (St. Petersburg, 1893), 28, 45, which claims that Jews were "the primary factor in the primary factor in the transfer, propagation, and culturing [*kul'tivirovka*] of cholera" (50).

19. Moshe Leib Herlikhstzohn [Lilienblum], "Vilkomir," *Ha-karmel*, no. 23 (26 Heshvan 5627 [October 23, 1866]): 177–78. Lilienblum lived in Vilkomir from 1856 to 1869.

20. *Kievlianin* no. 40, April 3, 1873: 1. See Natan M. Meir, *Kiev, Jewish Metropolis: A History, 1859–1914* (Bloomington: Indiana University Press, 2010), 36.

21. Shoyl Ginsburg, "Vi unzere elter-zeydes hoben kemft gegen der kholere-mageyfe," in id., *Historishe verk*, edited by Isaac Rivkind, 1: 233 (New York: Shoyl ginzburg 70-yohriger yubiley komitet, 1937).

22. G. Urinski, "A dokument vegn der kholere in pruzhene," in *Pinkes fun der shtot pruzhene* (Pruzhene: Pinkos, 1930), 40.

23. See, e.g., Joshua Trachtenberg, *Jewish Magic and Superstition: A Study in Folk Religion* (Philadelphia: University of Pennsylvania Press, 2004), 146.

24. Kotik, *Journey to a Nineteenth-Century Shtetl*, 384.

25. Regina Lilientalowa, "Wierzenia, przesady i praktyki ludu żydowskiego," *Wisła* 19, no. 2 (March–April 1905): 176; A. S. Friedberg, *Sefer ha-zikhronot* (Warsaw, 1899), 2: 76.

26. Ol'ga Belova, "Narodnaia magiia v regionakh etnokul'turnykh kontaktov slavian i evreev," in Belova, *Narodnaia meditsina i magiia*, 126.

27. Tsvi Hirsh Rymanower, *Sefer be'erot ha-mayim* (Przemyśl, 1894), 174.

28. For other tales, see Avraham Hayim Simhah Bunem Michelsohn, *Ohel Elimelekh* (Przemyśl, 1915), no. 153, 66; Justin Jaron Lewis, *Imagining Holiness: Classic Hasidic Tales in Modern Times* (Montreal: McGill–Queen's University Press, 2009), 185.

29. Wiktor Kopff, *Wspomnienia z ostatnich lat Rzeczypospolitej Krakowskiej* (Kraków: Druk. "Czasu," 1906), 138.

30. Epstein, "Caring for the Soul's House," 199. On hospitals, see Friedberg, *Sefer ha-zikhronot*, 76; M.H., "Kishinov," *Ha-melits*, June 28, 1866, cols. 448–49; "Bialystok," *Ha-karmel*, September 9, 1866, 154–55; M.M.A., "Letter from Grodno," *Ha-karmel*, August 26, 1866, 147.

31. Peter Baldwin, *Contagion and the State in Europe, 1830–1930* (New York: Cambridge University Press, 1999), 139.

32. Friedberg, *Sefer ha-zikhronot*, 2: 76.

33. M.M.A., "Letter from Grodno."

34. Pamela Gilbert notes that Anglican clergy during the 1832 epidemic faced the dilemma of mediating between two discourses of sinfulness, one blaming the individual victim and the other impugning the sinfulness of the nation as a whole. Gilbert, *Cholera and Nation*, 18–23.

35. Ginsburg, "Vi unzere elter-zeydes hoben gekemft," 231–34.

36. Menakhem Nakhum b' ha-rov Yerakhmiel, "Misterei (di geheymnise) krementshug," *Kol mevaser*, July 26, 1866, 416.

37. M. Berlin, *Ocherk etnografii evreiskago narodonaseleniia* (St. Petersburg, 1861), 32. See also A. S. Dembovetskii, *Opyt opisaniia Mogilevskoi gubernii v istoricheskom, fiziko-geograficheskom, etnograficheskom . . . otnosheniiakh* (Mogilev, 1882), 1: 768

38. "Naye mittel gegen der kholera," *Kol mevaser*, no. 25 (June 30, 1866): 385; Epstein, "Caring for the Soul's House," 114–15. For background on the Hasidic ban on crinolines, see "On Crinoline: The Memoirs of Abraham Paperna," in *Everyday Jewish Life in Imperial Russia: Select Documents, 1772–1914*, ed. ChaeRan Y. Freeze and Jay Michael Harris (Waltham, MA: Brandeis University Press, 2013), 303–4.

39. *Ma'aseh ha-kedoshim* (Lemberg, 1894), no. 9, cited in Gedalyah Nigal, *The Hasidic Tale* (Oxford: Littman Library of Jewish Civilization, 2008), 169.

40. Avraham Hayim Simhah Bunem Michelsohn, *Shemen ha-tov* (Piotrków Trybunalski, Poland: N. N. Kranenberg, 1905), "Stories," § 129, cited in Nigal, *Hasidic Tale*, 144.

41. Raphael Nahman Cohen, *Shemu'ot ve-sipurim* (1972), 230–31, cited in Gedalyah Nigal, *Leksikon ha-sipur ha-hasidi* (Jerusalem: Ha-makhon le-heker ha-sifrut ha-hasidit, 2005), 85. Nigal places this tale in the category of "sexual licentiousness" (*zenut*).

42. In his novel *Yoshe Kalb*, I. J. Singer portrays the fictional town of Bialogura during an epidemic, its residents obsessed with the sexual depravity that might have caused the pestilence: prostitution, immodesty, married women's failure to rigorously keep the laws of

menstrual purity and the custom of their shaving and totally covering their heads. Israel Joshua Singer, *Yoshe Kalb*, trans. Maurice Samuel (New York: Schocken Books, 1988), 146–48. The cholera wedding episode in the novel is examined in chapter 7.

43. Menakhem Nakhum b' ha-rov Yerakhmiel, "Misterei (di geheymnise) krement-shug," 416–20; Shimon Yehuda Stanislavski, "Letter from Ekaterinoslav," *Ha-karmel*, August 3, 1866: 123; M.M.A., "Letter from Grodno"; Nahum Friedwald, "Kol todah," *Ha-melits*, September 6, 1866: 512–13 (editor's note); Friedberg, *Sefer ha-zikhronot*, 2: 75; Kotik, *Journey to a Nineteenth-Century Shtetl*, 383–84.

44. Lewis, *Imagining Holiness*, 27; Tsukerovich, "Kalat ha-ir"; Peretz, *Ver es vil nisht, shtarbt nisht*, 48.

45. Pinye Taytl, "A 'shvartse' khasene in apt," in *Apt (Opatow); sefer zikaron le-ir va-em be-yisrael*, ed. Z. Yasheev (Tel Aviv: Apt Organizations in Israel, U.S.A., Canada, and Brazil, 1966), 106–7.

46. Ia. Rombro, "Kholernaia svad'ba," *Voskhod* 4, no. 6 (June 1884): 38.

47. Menakhem Nakhum b' ha-rov Yerakhmiel, "Misterei (di geheymnise) Krement-shug," 419.

48. M.M.A., "Letter from Grodno."

49. See, e.g., Anna Afanasyeva's work on Russian imperial policies on cholera in Central Asia in "Quarantines and Copper Amulets: The Struggle against Cholera in the Kazakh Steppe in the Nineteenth Century," *Jahrbücher für Geschichte Osteuropas* 61, no. 4 (2013): 489–90.

50. Baldwin, *Contagion and the State in Europe, 1830–1930*, 123; Frieden, "Russian Cholera Epidemic," 542; Charlotte Henze, *Disease, Health Care and Government in Late Imperial Russia: Life and Death on the Volga, 1823–1914* (Hoboken, NJ: Taylor & Francis, 2010), 23.

51. Frieden, "Russian Cholera Epidemic," 544–45.

52. Tsukerovich, "Kalat ha-ir," 14.

53. Taytl, "A 'shvartse' khasene in apt."

54. M. Khazen, "A khupe ofn beys-oylem," in *Shumsk: sefer zikaron le-kedoshe Shumsk she-nispu be-sho' at ha-natsim bi-shenat 1942*, ed. Chaim Rabin (Tel-Aviv: n.p., 1968), 384.

55. Yisrael Garmi (Grimtlikht), "Ha-hupah ha-shehorah," in *Sefer yizkor le-kehilat luboml*, ed. Berl Kagan (Tel Aviv: Mofet, 1974), 89–90; Leon S. Blatman, "The Wedding at the Cemetery," in *Kamenetz-Podolsk: A Memorial to a Jewish Community Annihilated by the Nazis in 1941*, ed. Leon S. Blatman (New York; n.p., 1966), 86.

56. Avraham Matityahu Halfan, *Tal orot* (Odessa, 1890), § 44. For an example of a rabbinic responsum that does not reject the cholera wedding outright, see Shmuel Glick, *Or nagah alehem: ha-zikah she-ben minhagei nisu' in le-minhagei avelut be-masoret yisra' el* (Efrat: Keren Ori, 1997), 176. I am grateful to Haim Sperber for alerting me to these references.

57. Baron, *Jewish Community*, 2: 332.

58. Meir Yehiel Lipiets, *Sefer ha-mat'amim* (Warsaw, 1890), 73. For another rabbinic handbook of customs that mentions the cholera wedding, see Abraham Eliezer Hirshovitz, *Otsar kol minhagei yeshurun* (St. Louis, MO: n.p., 1919), 97.

59. Peretz, *Ver es vil nisht, shtarbt nisht*, 51.

60. N. Vaynig, "Mageyfe-khasenes," *Sotsyale meditsin* 10, no. 9–10 (1937): 30.

61. Friedberg, *Sefer ha-zikhronot*, 2: 75.

62. David Shifman, "Ma'asim be-khol yom: zamoshtsh," *Ha-melits*, April 8, 1894, 4. I am grateful to Haim Sperber for alerting me to this reference.

63. "Az men vil zikher zayn fun kholera—makht men khasene kalikes," *Di varhayt*, November 3, 1910, 8. Thanks again to Haim Sperber for this reference. Another wedding of outcasts is described in "A khasene fun mishegoyim," *Der moment*, November 25, 1910.

64. On epidemics in the Russian Empire during World War I, see John F. Hutchinson, *Politics and Public Health in Revolutionary Russia, 1890–1918* (Baltimore: Johns Hopkins University Press, 1990), 119–32; John P. Davis, "The Struggle with Cholera in Tsarist Russia and the Soviet Union, 1892–1927" (Ph.D diss., University of Kentucky, 2012), 214–56.

65. Nokhem Krumerkop, "Der yidisher yishev in tarnogrod," in *Yizker-bukh: nokh der khorev-gevorener yidisher kehile tarnogrod*, ed. Shimon Kanc (Tel Aviv: Tarnogroder landslayt in yisroel, 1966), 51–118; Garmi (Grimtlikht), "Ha-hupah ha-shehorah"; Y. Kaspi, "3 hatunot-mitsvah be-shedlits," *Reshumot*, n.s., 2 (1946): 101–2; "Ayarati," in *Sefer oshpitsin: oshviyents'im-oshvits*, ed. Hayim Wolnerman et al. (Jerusalem: Irgun yots'ei oshpitsin be-yisra'el, 1977), 371–76.

66. Schiper notes here that each local variant provided the appropriate toponym, e.g. "Odessa," "Kiev," etc.

67. Shiper, *Geshikhte fun yidisher teater-kunst un drame*, 65–66.

68. Translation (with some modifications) from Abramovitsh, "Fishke the Lame," in id., *Selected Works*, ed. Zuckerman, Stillman, and Herbst, 193. Yiddish, Abramovitsh, "Fishke der krumer," in id., *Geklibene verk*, 3: 36.

69. Miron, "Introduction," in Miron and Frieden, *Tales of Mendele the Book Peddler*, lii.

70. Bakhtin, *Rabelais and His World*, 318.

71. Ibid., 317–18.

72. Friedberg, *Sefer ha-zikhronot*, 2: 75.

73. Constantinou, "Grotesque Bodies in Hagiographical Tales," 46.

74. Felicity Collins, "Brazen Brides, Grotesque Daughters, Treacherous Mothers: Women's Funny Business in Australian Cinema from *Sweetie* to *Holy Smoke*," Senses of Cinema (December 2002), http://sensesofcinema.com/2002/feature-articles/women_funny_oz (accessed December 3, 2019).

75. Elizabeth Grosz, "Intolerable Ambiguity: Freaks as/at the Limit," in *Freakery: Cultural Spectacles of the Extraordinary Body*, ed. Rosemarie Garland-Thomson (New York: New York University Press, 1996), 57.

76. Bjørn Thomassen, "The Uses and Meanings of Liminality," *International Political Anthropology* 2, no. 1 (2009): 16.

77. Thomassen defines a liminal moment in the context of society as "a whole society facing a sudden event (sudden invasion, natural disaster, a plague) where social distinctions and normal hierarchy disappear" (ibid., 17).

78. On the origins of, and Jewish legal complexities associated with, visiting the graves of the righteous, see Israel M. Ta-Shma, "'Tsadikim einam metam'in'—al halakhah ve-agadah," *JSIJ —Jewish Studies, an Internet Journal* 1 (2002): 45–53. See also Elliott S. Horowitz, "Speaking to the Dead: Cemetery Prayer in Medieval and Early Modern Jewry," *Journal of Jewish Thought & Philosophy* 8, no. 2 (1999): 303–17; Ephraim Shoham-Steiner, "'For a prayer in that place would be most welcome': Jews, Holy Shrines, and Miracles: A New Approach," *Viator* 37 (2006): 369–95.

79. Daniel Sperber, *Minhagei yisra'el: mekorot ve-toldot*, 8 vols. (Jerusalem: Mossad Harav Kook, 1994), 3: 118–19; Sylvie Anne Goldberg, *Crossing the Jabbok: Illness and Death in Ashkenazi Judaism in Sixteenth- through Nineteenth-Century Prague* (Berkeley: University of California Press, 1996), 139–41; Bar-Levav, "We Are Where We Are Not," 44–45; Jousep Schammes, *Minhagim de-k.k. vermaisa* (Jerusalem, 1648), 2: 103 n. 11, 127, 143, 172; Sagiv, "Hasidism and Cemetery Inauguration Ceremonies," 332.

80. Schammes, *Minhagim de-k.k. vermaisa*, 2: 267–68.

81. See, e.g., S. Ans-ki's reference to Jews praying at the cemetery during the Mstislavl blood libel in "Iz legend o mstislavskom dele," *Perezhitoe* 2 (1910), cited in Mochalova, "Istselenie, spasenie, izbavlenie," 92.

82. Hanna Węgrzynek, "Shvartze Khasene: Black Weddings among Polish Jews," in *Holy Dissent: Jewish and Christian Mystics in Eastern Europe*, ed. Glenn Dynner (Detroit: Wayne State University Press, 2011), 63.

83. George Lyman Kittredge, *Witchcraft in Old and New England* (New York: Russell & Russell, 1956), 141–43.

84. Carly Seyfarth, *Aberglaube und Zauberei in der Volksmedizin Sachsens: ein Beitrag zur Volkskunde des Königreichs Sachsen* (Leipzig: Heims, 1913), 209–16.

85. Ya'akov Kaidaner, *Sipurim nor'aim*, ed. Gedalyah Nigal (Jerusalem: Karmel [1992]), para. 40, cited in Nigal, *Hasidic Tale*, 194.

86. Mochalova, "Istselenie, spasenie, izbavlenie," 91.

87. See Schammes, *Minhagim*, 2: 106 n. 12.

88. Samuel Rappoport, "Seuchenhochzeit (mageyfe-khasene)," *Jüdisches Jahrbuch für Österreich* 1932–33, 185–87. For the kabbalistic background, see Gershom Scholem, *On the Kabbalah and Its Symbolism* (London: Routledge and K. Paul, 1965), 153–57.

89. Vaynig, "Mageyfe-khasenes," 30. For a short biographical sketch of Vaynig, see

Itzik Nakhmen Gottesman, *Defining the Yiddish Nation: The Jewish Folklorists of Poland* (Detroit: Wayne State University Press, 2003), 166–69.

90. Węgrzynek, "Shvartze Khasene," 59–60.

91. Yomtov Levinski, "'Hatunot mageifah' be-minhagei ashkenaz," *Mahanayim*, no. 83 (1963): 62.

92. Ibid., 60.

93. Frieden, "Russian Cholera Epidemic," 545.

94. Hamlin, *Cholera*, 66, 68. See also Baldwin, *Contagion and the State in Europe, 1830–1930*, 56.

95. "One could even see maskers, who, in caricatures of the livid colour and sickly mien, mocked the fear of the cholera and the disease itself." Heinrich Heine, *The Works of Heinrich Heine*, trans. Charles Godfrey Leland (New York: Croscup & Sterling, 1892), 14: 166; Gilbert, *Cholera and Nation*, 59.

96. Vaynig, "Mageyfe-khasenes," 26.

97. Lipiets, *Sefer ha-mat'amim*, 73.

98. Lipiets, *Sefer ha-mat'amim he-hadash*, 61.

99. Albeit ubiquitous in North America in the late nineteenth and early twentieth centuries, freak shows were much less common in eastern Europe. Edward Portnoy, "Freaks, Geeks, and Strongmen: Warsaw Jews and Popular Performance, 1912–1930," *The Drama Review: TDR* 50, no. 2 (2006): 130.

100. Abraham Rechtman, *Yidishe etnografye un folklor: zikhroynes vegn der etnografisher ekspeditsye, ongefirt fun sh. an-ski* (Buenos Aires: Yidisher visnshaftlekher institut, 1958), 132. "Black wedding" came to be another term for referring to the cholera wedding; apparently the huppah itself was sometimes made of black cloth. See Kaspi, "3 hatunot-mitsvah."

101. This is not the only Jewish tale about a righteous person sacrificing himself to save his community from destruction by disease; in sixteenth-century Eretz Israel, the preacher R. Moses de Curiel was said to have died for the sins of the community, which was then saved from a plague that had been decreed against it. Jeffrey Howard Chajes, *Between Worlds: Dybbuks, Exorcists, and Early Modern Judaism* (Philadelphia: University of Pennsylvania Press, 2003), 103. For examples in ancient Greek culture, see Jan N. Bremmer, *Greek Religion and Culture, the Bible, and the Ancient Near East* (Boston: Brill, 2008), 178. For other tales (primarily Irish legends), see Thompson, *Motif-Index of Folk-Literature*, § S260 (esp. S263.5.1, S263.5.2., S276).

102. Rechtman, "Khasen-kale-kvorim," in *Yidishe etnografye un folklor*, 169–71; S. An-ski, "Alte shuhlen un zeyer legende," in id., *Gezamelte shriften*, vol. 15: *Folklor un etnografye* (Vilna: Ferlag "An-ski," 1925), 244. In the latter work, An-ski explained that these were actually the graves of Jews murdered as they took sanctuary in the synagogue. For a translation of the chapter in Rechtman, see *The Dybbuk and the Yiddish Imagination: A Haunted Reader*, ed. Joachim Neugroschel (Syracuse, NY: Syracuse

University Press, 2000), 99–101. The grave of the martyred couple plays an important role in An-ski's *The Dybbuk*. S. An-ski, *The Dybbuk and Other Writings*, ed. David G. Roskies, trans. Golda Werman (New York: Schocken Books, 1992), 21, 25, 28.

103. The biblical reference is explained in *Otsar ha-sifrut* 4 (1892): 445.

104. Shiper, *Geshikhte fun yidisher teater-kunst un drame*, 66.

105. Vaynig, "Mageyfe-khasenes," 30.

106. For a study of the scapegoat ritual in ancient Near Eastern, Israelite, Greek, and early Christian cultures, see Bremmer, *Greek Religion*, 169–214.

107. Ibid., 194.

108. Ibid., 177.

109. Ibid., 180.

110. Ibid., 171–72.

111. Thomassen, "Uses and Meanings of Liminality," 18.

Chapter 5

1. It was not only Jews in the Russian Empire who held such views: Central Asian jadids, the Muslim equivalent of maskilim, likewise lamented the backwardness of Muslim society and encouraged their coreligionists to emulate European and Russian ways. Only thus, they thought , could Muslims in Central Asia achieve "modern knowledge, order, discipline, cleanliness, power—in a word, modernity," Khalid Adeeb writes in "Representations of Russia in Central Asian Jadid Discourse," in *Russia's Orient: Imperial Borderlands and Peoples, 1700–1917*, ed. Edward J. Lazzerini and Daniel R. Brower (Bloomington: Indiana University Press, 1997), 194.

2. Polonsky, *The Jews in Poland and Russia*, 1:399–400; Salo Baron, *The Russian Jew between Tsars and Soviets* (New York: Macmillan, 1964), 113–18.

3. For an exploration of the significant roles that women played in Jewish philanthropy in the Russian Empire, see Natan Meir, "From Communal Charity to National Welfare: Jewish Orphanages in Eastern Europe before and after World War I," *East European Jewish Affairs* 39, no. 1 (April 1, 2009): 23, and id., *Kiev: Jewish Metropolis*, 237–45.

4. Smith, "Charity and Poor Relief," 3: 454. On philanthropy in nineteenth-century Europe, see Peter Mandler, ed., *The Uses of Charity: The Poor on Relief in the Nineteenth-Century Metropolis* (Philadelphia: University of Pennsylvania Press, 1990); Robert Hamlett Bremner, *Giving: Charity and Philanthropy in History* (New Brunswick, NJ: Transaction Publishers, 1994); Thomas Adam, *Philanthropy, Patronage, and Civil Society: Experiences from Germany, Great Britain, and North America* (Bloomington: Indiana University Press, 2004); Larry Frohman, *Poor Relief and Welfare in Germany from the Reformation to World War I* (New York: Cambridge University Press, 2008).

5. Meir, *Kiev, Jewish Metropolis*, 211.

6. Penslar, *Shylock's Children*, 96.

7. Heinz-Dietrich Löwe, "From Charity to Social Policy: The Emergence of Jewish 'Self-Help' Organizations in Imperial Russia, 1800–1914," *East European Jewish Affairs* 27, no. 2 (1997): 59.

8. On self-help, see ibid., 57. On productivization among maskilic and elite circles in western and central Europe, see Penslar, *Shylock's Children*, 110–23.

9. Steven J. Zipperstein, "Odessa," in the *YIVO Encyclopedia of Jews in Eastern Europe*, 2: 1277–8.

10. Steven Zipperstein, *The Jews of Odessa: A Cultural History* (Stanford: Stanford University Press, 1991), 75, 86.

11. Ibid., 75.

12. Ibid., 88; Tobias Grill, "Odessa's German Rabbi—The Paradigmatic Meaning of Simon Leon Schwabacher (1861–1888)," *Jahrbuch des Simon-Dubnow-Instituts* 2 (2003): 202. On the institution of Crown rabbi, see Freeze, *Jewish Marriage and Divorce*, 95–130; Azriel Shochat, *Mosad "ha-rabanut mi-ta'am" be-rusyah* (Haifa: Haifa University Press, 1975).

13. Smith, "Charity and Poor Relief," 3: 456.

14. D-r Shvabakher, "Zametka (o vazhnosti uchrezhdeniia sirotskikh domov)," *Sion*, no. 2 (July 14, 1861): 22–23.

15. Ibid., 24.

16. Ibid., 23.

17. Schwabacher's analysis of the threat posed by the Jewish lumpenproletariat is a variation of the analogous situation in contemporary Germany, where, in Derek Penslar's evaluation, Christian and Jewish philanthropists were motivated by distinct anxieties: the former by unease about a growing and organized proletariat, the latter by fear of a Jewish "rabble" (mostly immigrants from eastern Europe) that threatened the existing social order and bourgeois Jews' precarious position in it. Penslar, *Shylock's Children*, 193. For an instructive parallel in the United States, see Reena Sigman Friedman, *These Are Our Children: Jewish Orphanages in the United States, 1880–1925* (Hanover, NH: Brandeis University Press and University Press of New England, 1994), 21, 108–9.

18. Friedman, *These Are Our Children*, 94–97.

19. Lindenmeyr, *Poverty Is Not a Vice*, 136.

20. Ibid., 137.

21. Penslar, *Shylock's Children*, 99.

22. For a discussion of the theme of Jewish exploitation in the Russian press of the late nineteenth century, see John Klier, *Imperial Russia's Jewish Question, 1855–1881* (New York: Cambridge University Press, 1995), 300–331. For the attitude of the tsarist bureaucracy, see Hans Rogger, "Government, Jews, Peasants and Land after the Liberation of the Serfs," in *Jewish Policies and Right-Wing Politics in Imperial Russia* (Berkeley: University of California Press; London: Macmillan, 1986), 113–75, esp. pp. 146–56. For similar charges by Polish right-wing ideologues, see Brian Porter, *When Nationalism*

Began to Hate: Imagining Modern Politics in Nineteenth Century Poland (Oxford: Oxford University Press, 2000), 227–32.

23. Penslar, *Shylock's Children*, 193

24. For a similar argument that posits blacks, women, and gays as the Other onto whom Jews project what they see as contemptible in themselves once they starts seeing themselves through the eyes of their oppressors, see Daniel Boyarin, "Homophobia and the Postcoloniality of the 'Jewish Science,'" in *Queer Theory and the Jewish Question*, ed. Daniel Boyarin, Daniel Itzkovitz, and Ann Pellegrini (New York: Columbia University Press, 2003), 183.

25. Rupert Brown, *Prejudice: Its Social Psychology* (Cambridge, Mass: Blackwell, 1995), 170–85.

26. Alexander Orbach, *New Voices of Russian Jewry: A Study of the Russian-Jewish Press of Odessa in the Era of the Great Reforms, 1860–1871* (Leiden: Brill, 1980), 166.

27. Stanislawski, *Tsar Nicholas I and the Jews*, 47. On Kisilev and the Jewish Committee, see Nathans, *Beyond the Pale*, 31–38.

28. Stanislawski, *Tsar Nicholas I and the Jews*, 156. Nathans, *Beyond the Pale*, 34, translates this label as "useless."

29. Dubnow, *History of the Jews in Russia and Poland*, 2: 142. See also Iulii Gessen, "Razbor," *Evreiskaia entsiklopediia*, 13: cols. 273–74.

30. Stanislawski, *Tsar Nicholas I and the Jews*, 159; Polonsky, *Jews in Poland and Russia*, 1: 384 (emphasis added).

31. Daniel R. Brower, "Islam and Ethnicity: Russian Colonial Policy in Turkestan," in *Russia's Orient*, ed. Lazzerini and Brower, 129–30. Imperial policy also labeled the "mountaineers" of the northern Caucasus—who were not nomadic—as unproductive. See Irma Kreiten, "A Colonial Experiment in Cleansing: The Russian Conquest of Western Caucasus, 1856–65," *Journal of Genocide Research* 11, no. 2–3 (2009): 213–41.

32. Ginsburg and Marek, *Evreiskie narodnye pesni v Rossii*, 53; Stanislawski, *Tsar Nicholas I and the Jews*, 155.

33. I. Zelenskii, *Materialy dlia geografii i statistiki Rossii: Minskaia guberniia* (St. Petersburg, 1864), 1: 661. Zelenskii made clear elsewhere, however, that he found Jewish morality questionable at best, blaming Jews for much of the criminality in the province, due in large measure to their not being "settled" (ibid., 2: 480).

34. Klier, *Imperial Russia's Jewish Question*, 329.

35. Lev Levanda, "Neskol'ko slov o evreiakh Zapadnogo kraia Rossii," *Razsvet*, no. 1 (May 27, 1860): 8. See also Klier, *Imperial Russia's Jewish Question*, 85, 329. On Levanda, see John D. Klier, "The Jew as Russifier: Lev Levanda's *Hot Times*," *Jewish Culture and History* 4.1 (Summer 2001): 31–52; Shimon Markish, "Lev Levanda between Assimilation and Palestinophilia," *Shevut* 4 (1996): 1–52; 6 (1997): 1–27.

36. Similarly, "during the first half of the nineteenth century the German Jewish press was filled with hostile depictions of the Jewish poor as cheeky beggars and con

artists, a 'cancer,' as one correspondent put it, that require[d] radical treatment" (Penslar, *Shylock's Children*, 100).

37. Levanda, "Neskol'ko slov," 8.

38. See Biale, *Eros and the Jews: From Biblical Israel to Contemporary America* (Berkeley: University of California Press, 1997), 159–62; Paula Hyman, *Gender and Assimilation in Modern Jewish History: The Roles and Representation of Women* (Seattle: University of Washington Press, 1995), 134–35.

39. Berlin, *Ocherk etnografii evreiskago narodonaseleniia v Rossii*, 39.

40. David G. Roskies, "Ayzik-Meyer Dik and the Rise of Yiddish Popular Literature" (Ph.D. diss., Brandeis University, 1975), 208–9.

41. I. Rülf, *Drei Tage in Jüdisch-Russland: Ein Cultur- und Sittenbild* (Frankfurt a/M.: J. Kauffmann, 1882), 21.

42. Ibid., 22.

43. Chubinskii, *Trudy Etnografichesko-statisticheskoi ekspeditsii*, 7: 75. A. S. Dembovetskii's *Opyt opisaniia Mogilevskoi gubernii*, a study of Mogilev province (now part of Belarus), also accused Jews of parasitism, claiming that they chose unproductive work to enrich themselves and impoverish the Christian population (1: 726).

44. The proposal's submission seems to have been sparked by the large-scale survey of Jewish charitable institutions that the tsarist government undertook in the early 1860s. LVIA Vilnius f. 378 B/S 1854, d. 1743 ("Ob ustroistve i soderzhanii evreiskikh bol'nits i bogadelen v Vilenskoi, Kovenskoi, Grodnenskoi i Minskoi guberniiakh," 1854–65), microfilm at CAHJP HM3/224.14.

45. Schwabacher had many models to draw on: centralized Jewish poor care commissions espousing rational methods of providing relief for the needy had been established over the previous half-century in Paris (1809), Amsterdam (1825), Berlin (1837), Vienna (1839), and London (1859). Penslar, *Shylock's Children*, 98–101.

46. RGIA f. 1287, op. 13, d. 1145 ("Ob ustroistve evreiskikh bol'nits i bogadelen v gorodakh i mestechkakh razlichnykh gubernii," 1863–64), ll. 342ob, microfilm at CAHJP HM2/8276.

47. Ibid., l. 343.

48. Ibid., l. 343ob.

49. Ibid., ll. 343ob–345ob; David Ingleby, "Mental Health and Social Order," in *Social Control and the State*, ed. Stanley Cohen and Andrew Scull (New York: St. Martin's Press, 1983), 159.

50. Julie V. Brown, "Social Influences on Psychiatric Theory and Practice in Late Imperial Russia," in *Health and Society in Revolutionary Russia*, ed. Susan Gross Solomon and John F. Hutchinson (Bloomington: Indiana University Press, 1990), 28.

51. Foucault, *Madness and Civilization*, 8–77.

52. Gary Gutting, "Foucault and the History of Madness," in *The Cambridge Companion to Foucault*, ed. Gary Gutting, 2nd ed. (Cambridge: Cambridge University Press, 2006), 54–55.

53. Abramovitsh, "Fishke the Lame," 241.

54. ChaeRan Y. Freeze, "Lilith's Midwives: Jewish Newborn Child Murder in Nineteenth-Century Vilna," *Jewish Social Studies* 16, no. 2 (2010): 6.

55. "Most of the youngsters admitted to these institutions [orphanages], at least in the U.S. in the late 19th and early 20th centuries, were half-orphans, especially the children of widowed or deserted mothers" (*Encyclopedia Judaica*, 1st ed., s.v. "Orphan, Orphanage").

56. Boris Brutskus, *Statistiki evreiskago naseleniia: raspredelenie po territorii, demograficheskie i kul'turnye priznaki evreiskago naseleniia po perepisi 1897 g.* (St. Petersburg: Sever, 1909), 26–27.

57. Ibid., 11.

58. "Talmud-Tora," *Evreiskaia entsiklopediia* 14: cols. 723–25. On elementary Jewish education in the Russian Empire, see Shaul Stampfer, "Heder Study, Knowledge of Torah, and the Maintenance of Social Stratification," in *Families, Rabbis and Education*, 136–66; Iris Parush, "Another Look at 'The Life of "Dead" Hebrew': Intentional Ignorance of Hebrew in Nineteenth-Century Eastern European Jewish Society," *Book History* 7, no. 1 (2004): 171–214.

59. Government documents show that the Talmud-Torah in Mglin (Chernigov province) was also attached to one of the houses of study, as was probably the case in other towns. TsDIAU f. 707, op. 87 (t. 1), spr. 1066 ("Vedemosti o talmud-torakh i khadarimakh, nakhodiashchikhsia v vedenii evreiskikh uchilishchnykh komissii Chernigovskoi Gubernii," 1845), ark. 58zv.

60. From M. Lev., "Pruzhener lebn," in N. Ts., "Lern-anshtaltn in pruzhene in der tsveyter helft fun XIX y"h," in *Pinkes fun der shtot pruzhene* (Pruzhene: Pinkos, 1930), 161–62.

61. See Nathaniel Deutsch, *The Jewish Dark Continent: Life and Death in the Russian Pale of Settlement* (Cambridge, MA: Harvard University Press, 2011), 164. This was an important source of income for many Talmud-Torah societies (Chubinskii, *Trudy Etnografichesko-statisticheskoi ekspeditsii*, 7: 107). In some cases, the custom was for the boys and their teachers to march in the funeral procession upon the death of a member of the religious confraternity that supported the Talmud-Torah; see NBUV IR f. 321, op. 1, od. zb. 27 ("Pinkas relihiinoï shkoly—'Talmud Torah', Volozhyn," 1826–1915), ark. 2zv. A custom with some resemblance was introduced for English charity-school children in the eighteenth century, who processed, prayed, and sang at church services commemorating the anniversary of the schools' establishment, with donors to the schools in attendance (Bremner, *Giving*, 78).

62. Litvak, *Conscription and the Search for Modern Russian Jewry*, 122.

63. S. A. Abramovitsh, "The Little Man; or, Portrait of a Life," in *Classic Yiddish Stories of S. Y. Abramovitsh, Sholem Aleichem, and I. L. Peretz*, ed. and trans. Ken Frieden (Syracuse, NY: Syracuse University Press, 2007), 29. On orphan apprentices, see Chubinskii, *Trudy Etnografichesko-statisticheskoi ekspeditsii*, 7: 107.

64. "Znachenie nashikh Talmud-Tor i neobkhodimost' ikh preobrazovaniia," *Russkii evrei*, July 23, 1880: cols. 1164–5.

65. "Odna iz zhguchikh potrebnostei nashego obshchinnago ustroistva" [editorial], *Russkii evrei* 16 (1883): cols. 2–5.

66. V. Veinshtein, "Pis'mo iz Kremenchuga," *Russkii evrei*, no. 7 (February 13, 1880): cols. 250–51.

67. NBUV IR f. 321, op. 1, od. zb. 71 ("Pinkas relihiinoï shkoly, Ostropil'," 1889, kopiia).

68. Zipperstein, *Jews of Odessa*, 74; Meir, *Kiev, Jewish Metropolis*, 211–60; Löwe, "From Charity to Social Policy."

69. "Korrespondentsiia (Vil'na, Dec. 30, 1897)," *Nedel⊠naia khronika Voskhoda*, no. 3 (January 18, 1898): cols. 101–2.

70. CAHJP JCA/Lon 69/4, "Correspondence regarding the opening of a vocational school 'Talmud Tora' in Bialystok," 1900–1901, annex 1, ad. no. 475.309, p. 6.

71. Obshchestvo popecheniia o bednykh i bezpriiutnykh detiakh g. Belostoka, *Ustav Obshchestva . . . g. Belostoka* (Bialystok, 1905), 11. Similar guardianship systems were set up in Jewish communities throughout the Pale of Settlement and Congress Poland. See, e.g., TsDIAU f. 442, op. 625, spr. 405 ("Ob uchrezhdenii v g. Lutske popechitel'stva nad sirotami i bednymi det'mi evreev," 1896).

72. Scott Ury, *Barricades and Banners: The Revolution of 1905 and the Transformation of Warsaw Jewry* (Stanford: Stanford University Press, 2012), 69.

73. TsDIAU f. 707, op. 317, spr. 26 ("Po khodataistve upolnomochennykh Chernobyl'skago evreiskago obshchestva o razreshenii otkryt' v m. Chernobyle talmud-toru," 1898–1917), ark. 41.

74. TsDIAU f. 707, op. 317, spr. 26, ark. 44.

75. Rokhlin, *Mestechko Krasnopol'e*, 75.

76. Jewish Colonization Association, *Recueil de matériaux*, 2: 319.

77. For an overview of the topic, see Shaul Stampfer, "Gender Differentiation and Education of the Jewish Woman in Nineteenth Century Eastern Europe," in id., *Families, Rabbis and Education*, 166–89.

78. LVIA Vilnius 378 B/S, 1858, d. 907 ("O pozhertvovanii Rubinom Rommom deneg na soderzhanie evreiskago devich'ego priiuta v Vil'no," 1858–61), microfilm at CAHJP HM3/233.4.

79. Eliyana R. Adler, *In Her Hands: The Education of Jewish Girls in Tsarist Russia* (Detroit: Wayne State University Press, 2011), 124–27.

80. "Korrespondentsiia," Vil'na, *Nedel'naia khronika Voskhoda*, cols. 101–2.

81. A. L. Biska, [untitled], *Ha-magid*, no. 10 (March 7, 1901): 3.

82. On the rise of Jewish social science in central Europe, principally as a tool in the hands of Zionists, see Mitchell B. Hart, *Social Science and the Politics of Modern Jewish Identity* (Stanford: Stanford University Press, 2000).

83. Yehiel Yeshaia Trunk, *Poyln: My Life within Jewish Life in Poland, Sketches and Images*, ed. Piotr Wróbel and Robert M. Shapiro, trans. Anna Clarke (Toronto: University of Toronto Press, 2007), 63–64.

84. Maurice Fishberg, *The Jews: A Study of Race and Environment* (New York: Walter Scott, 1911), 360.

85. Subbotin, *V cherte evreiskoi osedlosti*, 1: 134.

86. Ibid., 1: 133–34.

87. S. Ia. Ianovskii, "Evreiskaia blagotvoritel'nost'," *Trudovaia pomoshch'* 12 (1902): 582.

88. Ibid., 582–83.

89. I. Brodovskii, *Evreiskaia nishcheta v Odesse* (Odessa, 1902), 5–6. Brodovskii was clearly pushing back at the depraved image of poor and working-class Odessans painted in many of the city's newspapers. Roshanna P. Sylvester, *Tales of Old Odessa: Crime and Civility in a City of Thieves* (DeKalb: Northern Illinois University Press, 2005), 42.

90. Brodovskii, *Evreiskaia nishcheta v Odesse*, 15.

91. Ibid., 23–24.

92. Jewish Colonization Association, *Recueil de matériaux*, 2: 247.

93. Levitats, *Jewish Community in Russia, 1772–1844*, 260.

94. Epstein, "Caring for the Soul's House," 179–87; Stampfer, "Scientific Welfare and Lonely Old People," 93–95. See also Meir, *Kiev, Jewish Metropolis*, 211–27.

95. Epstein, "Caring for the Soul's House," 186. For an early example of a Bikur Holim society taking upon itself the overhaul of a hekdesh, see Yohanan Petrovsky Shtern, "The Marketplace in Balta," *East European Jewish Affairs* 37, no. 3 (December 1, 2007): 288.

96. Herschberg, *Pinkes byalistok*, 2: 164.

97. *Zaria* no. 37 (September 15, 1885): col. 1006.

98. Guesnet, *Polnische Juden*, 57.

99. Sylvester, *Tales of Old Odessa*, 64–66; Scott Ury, *Barricades and Banners*, 69.

100. *Jewish Encyclopedia*, s.v. "Kovna"; Subbotin, *V cherte evreiskoi osedlosti*, 1: 133 n. 28.

101. In some locales, there was a kind of slippage between the hekdesh and the institution of the old-age home. It was facilitated by the Russian cultural and linguistic context, since the term *bogadel'nia* meant a charitable asylum housing the destitute, which included beggars and the physically disabled and also, by extension, elderly people without a home or support of any kind. Had the latter not been given shelter in the asylum, they would almost certainly have been on the street begging. Jewish Colonization Association, *Recueil de matériaux*, 2: 245. See also Stampfer, "Scientific Welfare and Lonely Old People," 95.

102. Vilenskaia obshchestvennaia evreiskaia bogadel'nia, *Otchet . . . za 1908 god.* ([Vilna], 1909), 4; see also "Evreiskaia obshchestvennaia meditsina g. Vil'ny," *Evreiskii meditsinskii golos*, no. 3–4 (1910): 120–23; Isaac Levitats, *The Jewish Community in Russia, 1844–1917* (Jerusalem: Posner & Sons, 1981), 167.

103. Jewish Colonization Association, *Recueil de matériaux*, 2: 246.

104. Trunk, *Poyln*, 64–65, trans. modified; Yekhiel Yeshaye Trunk, *Poyln: zikhroynes un bilder*, vol. 1 (New York: Farlag medem-klub, 1944), 100–101. It is unclear to what extent, if any, such Jewish groups interacted with Roma (gypsies) in the western provinces of the Russian Empire. See David Crowe, *A History of the Gypsies of Eastern Europe and Russia* (New York: Palgrave Macmillan, 2007), 151–94.

105. For another example of Abramovitsh's fiction being treated as real-life reportage, see Levitats, *Jewish Community in Russia, 1772–1844*, 260.

106. Ken Frieden, *Classic Yiddish Fiction: Abramovitsh, Sholem Aleichem, and Peretz* (Albany: State University of New York Press, 1995), 23.

107. See the discussion of *Poyln* in Roskies, *Bridge of Longing*, 312–18.

108. Leo Rosenberg, "Armenwesen und Soziale Fürsorge im Ostjudentum," *Der Jude* 2, no. 5–6 (1917–18): 333–34.

109. Steven E. Aschheim, *Brothers and Strangers: The East European Jew in German and German Jewish Consciousness, 1800–1923* (Madison: University of Wisconsin Press, 1982), 21.

110. Penslar, *Shylock's Children*, 204–5.

111. Jack Wertheimer, *Unwelcome Strangers: East European Jews in Imperial Germany* (New York: Oxford University Press, 1987), 146, 89.

112. Aschheim, *Brothers and Strangers*, 22.

113. Wertheimer, *Unwelcome Strangers*, 25–27.

114. Penslar, *Shylock's Children*, 199–201, quoted, 201.

115. Ibid., 203. For a detailed evaluation of the operations of the ZJW, see Aharon Bornstein, *Mi-kabtsanim le-dorshei avodah: yehudim navadim be-germanyah, 1869–1914* (Tel Aviv: n.p., 1987), 247–94.

116. M. F. Zeydman, "A farzamlung fun der 'kabtsonim-organizatsye,'" *Der moment*, May 18, 1914, 2.

117. Ibid., 3.

118. Those organizations were the OPE (Society for the Promotion of Culture among the Jews of Russia) and OZE (Society for the Protection of the Health of the Jewish Population). There were, however, local efforts—e.g., an "Anti-Beggary Society" was established in Kalisz in 1899 (Guesnet, *Polnische Juden im 19. Jahrhundert*, 420 n. 264).

119. Leyzer Ran, ed., *Yerusholayim de-lita: ilustrirt un dokumentirt* (New York: Vilner albom komitet, 1974), 1: 148.

120. Smith, "Charity and Poor Relief," 459.

121. Desanka Schwara, "Luftmenschen—ein Leben in Armut," in *Luftmenschen und rebellische Töchter: zum Wandel ostjüdischer Lebenswelten im 19. Jahrhundert*, ed. Heiko Haumann (Cologne: Böhlau, 2003), 216.

Chapter 6

1. Brintlinger, "Introduction," in *Madness and the Mad in Russian Culture*, ed. Brintlinger and Vinitsky, 10.

2. Julie V. Brown, "Peasant Survival Strategies in Late Imperial Russia: The Social Uses of the Mental Hospital," *Social Problems* 34, no. 4 (1987): 314.

3. On Guttmacher and the kvitlekh, see Dynner, *Yankel's Tavern*, 131–35, and for a geographical breakdown, Marcin Wodziński, *Historical Atlas of Hasidism*, Waldemar Spallek, cartographer (Princeton, NJ: Princeton University Press, 2018), 84–85. On the *kvitl* in its original context and as historical source, see Marcin Wodziński, *Hasidism: Key Questions* (New York: Oxford University Press, 2018), 102–5.

4. Sandra Berliant, "Guide to the Papers of Eliyahu Guttmacher (1796–1874), 1840s–1874," in Guide to the YIVO Archives (2007), www.yivoarchives.org/index.php?p=collections/findingaid&id=23957&q= (accessed December 7, 2019).

5. For an analysis of the contents of the Guttmacher petitions, see Wodziński, *Hasidism: Key Questions*, 111–23. Wodziński's sample of about 350 kvitlekh does not include any mention of "demonic possession, dybbuks, demons, *shedim*, *mazikim*, and other typical folk medicine diagnoses," but other petitions include terms that are arguably comparable, such as *ruah ra'ah*.

6. Brown, "Social Influences on Psychiatric Theory and Practice in Late Imperial Russia," 27.

7. Dynner, *Yankel's Tavern*, 131–33.

8. YIVO Archive RG 27 (Papers of Eliyahu Guttmacher), box 2, folder 136.

9. Ibid., box 4, folder 182.

10. As Roy Porter has noted, when writing the history of madness, it often seems that one must choose either to understand mental illness in the sources as a genuine diagnosis (in the tradition of the history of psychiatry) or to analyze descriptions of mental illness entirely in the context of the "discursive formations" from which they emerge, with little or no relationship to the actual cognitive state of the individuals in question. The best place for the historian to come down is somewhere between the two, Porter suggests in the introduction to *The Confinement of the Insane: International Perspectives, 1800–1965*, ed. Porter and David Wright (New York: Cambridge University Press, 2003), 2. See also the essays in *Discovering the History of Psychiatry*, ed. Mark S. Micale and Roy Porter (New York: Oxford University Press, 1994). For an excellent example of this approach, see Midelfort, *History of Madness*, 356–65, on descriptions of mental illness in sixteenth-century petitions for admission to hospitals for the rural poor in Hesse.

11. YIVO Archive RG 27, box 2, folder 118.

12. Morris M. Faierstein, "Possession and Exorcism," in the *YIVO Encyclopedia of Jews in Eastern Europe*, 2: 1442; Gedalyah Nigal, *Magic, Mysticism, and Hasidism: The Supernatural in Jewish Thought* (Northvale, NJ: Jason Aronson, 1994), 67–101.

13. YIVO Archive RG 27, box 1, folder 45.

14. Ibid., box 6, folder 306.

15. Friedrich Paulizky and Bezalel Judah Eliasberg, *Marpe la-am* (Zhitomir, 1868), 1:181. The original title was *Anleitung zu einer vernünftigen Gesundheitspflege*.

16. Foucault, *Madness and Civilization*, 69.

17. NLI DM, Guttmacher Collection, ARC 4° 1069 folder 8 aleph (1868).

18. YIVO Archive RG 27, box 4, folder 178.

19. Ibid., box 6, folder 299.

20. Ibid., box 4, folder 171.

21. On Tatar healers, see Deutsch, *Jewish Dark Continent*, 160.

22. Berlin, *Ocherk etnografii*, 34. For a reference to various folk healers in the shtetl, including "Petrucha, a gentile woman," see Mendele Mocher Sforim, "Of Bygone Days," in *A Shtetl and Other Yiddish Novellas*, ed. Ruth R. Wisse (Detroit: Wayne State University Press, 1986), 292.

23. Jews also went to tsaddikim and "miracle rabbis." For a story of a tsaddik healing a madwoman, see Uri Henis, *Temimei derekh: sipurim me-olam ha-hasidut* (Jerusalem: Ahi'ever, 1959), 18–24. On ba'alei shem, see Immanuel Etkes, "Mekomam shel ha-magiyah u-va'ale shem ba-hevrah ha-ashkenazit be-mifneh ha-me'ot ha-17-ha-18," *Tsiyon* 60, no. 1 (1995): 69–104; Nigal, *Magic, Mysticism, and Hasidism*, 1–31; Yohanan Petrovsky-Shtern, "Ba'ale Shem," in the *YIVO Encyclopedia of Jews in Eastern Europe*, 1: 99–100.

24. Berlin, *Ocherk etnografii*, 34; Chubinskii, *Trudy Etnograficheskо-statisticheskoi ekspeditsii*, 7: 57–58.

25. YIVO Archive RG 27, box 7, folder 328.

26. Hirsz Abramowicz, *Farshvundene geshtaltn* [Disappeared Figures], trans. Eva Zeitlin Dobkin as *Profiles of a Lost World: Memoirs of East European Jewish Life before World War II*, ed. Dina Abramowicz and Jeffrey Shandler (Detroit: Wayne State University Press, 1999), 109.

27. Women also engaged in self-harm. Khaye Sore bas Zelde of Łódź was reported to have been insane for about six months and was now "striking herself and [hitting] her head against the wall." YIVO Archive RG 27, box 9, folder 432.

28. Ibid., box 2, folder 57. For another case of a young Jewish woman whose madness was sparked by fear of dogs, see "Petition to Hospitalize Rivka Gefter of Vil'na for Mental Illness (1902)" in Freeze and Harris, *Everyday Jewish Life*, 300.

29. YIVO Archive RG 27, box 7, folder 328.

30. Ibid., box 4, folder 171.

31. Elior, *Dybbuks and Jewish Women*, 57.

32. Bilu, "Taming of the Deviants and Beyond," in *Spirit Possession in Judaism*, ed. Goldish, 27–40.

33. YIVO Archive RG 27, box 2, folder 118.

34. Ibid., box 6, folder 299.

35. Shaul Stampfer, "Love and Family," in id, *Families, Rabbis and Education*, 41–42.

36. On the other hand, since in Jewish law only a man could initiate divorce proceedings, only female insanity was a valid reason for divorce. Jewish Encyclopedia, s.v. "Insanity"; Freeze, *Jewish Marriage and Divorce*, 185–86; see also Abrams, *Judaism and Disability*, 127. There is anecdotal evidence (Freeze, *Jewish Marriage and Divorce*, 187; Freeze and Harris, *Everyday Jewish Life*, 215–16) that parents of daughters with mental illness or intellectual disabilities sometimes concealed this so as to marry them off, only to have the husband sue for divorce when the truth was later revealed.

37. YIVO Archive RG 27, box 3, folder 138.

38. Ibid., box 1, folder 11.

39. See Yaffa Eliach's comment on such circumstances for a later period: "Most of the mentally ill in the shtetl of Eishyshok were native born, and most lived with their own families, who did the best they could to control their sometimes troublesome relatives." *There Once Was a World: A Nine-Hundred-Year Chronicle of the Shtetl of Eishyshok* (Boston: Little Brown, 1998), 388.

40. NLI DM, Guttmacher Collection, ARC 4° 1069 folder 8 aleph (n.d.).

41. YIVO Archive RG 27, box 4, folder 192.

42. Ibid., box 6, folder 302.

43. Bernstein, *Yudishe shprikhverter un redensarten*, 174–77. The book lists no fewer than seventy-six such sayings s.v. "fool."

44. J. David Bleich, "Mental Incompetence and Its Implications in Jewish Law," *Journal of Halacha and Contemporary Society* 1, no. 2 (1981): 143.

45. I"sh, "Isha keshat ruah," *Ha-yom*, June 1, 1887, 2.

46. TsDIAU f. 385, op. 1, spr. 56 ("O postuplenii i vybytii umalyshennykh i nervnobol'nykh iz Odesskoi gorodskoi bol'nitsy," 1871).

47. Freeze and Harris, *Everyday Jewish Life*, 297–298.

48. Ibid., 293.

49. Ibid., 294.

50. Ibid., 295.

51. Ibid.

52. Ibid., 296–97.

53. BT Baba Batra 12b, cited in Abrams, *Judaism and Disability*, 143.

54. Ibid., 143.

55. Dov Baer ben Samuel, *In Praise of the Baal Shem Tov: The Earliest Collection of Legends about the Founder of Hasidism*, ed. Dan Ben-Amos and Jerome R. Mintz (Northvale, NJ: Jason Aronson, 1993), 34.

56. S. An-ski, "Evreiskoe narodnoe tvorchestvo," *Perezhitoe* 1 (1909): 309.

57. Eliach, *There Once Was a World*, 384.

58. Kalman Marmor, *Mayn lebns-geshikhte* (New York: Ikuf, 1959), 1: 229–30.

59. Israel Klausner, *Vilnah, yerushalayim de-lita: dorot aharonim, 1881–1939* ([Lohame ha-geta'ot:] Beit lohamei ha-geta'ot, 1983), 659.

60. B. Tsegrovski, "An'invazye fun mishegoyim in lemberg," *Haynt*, August 24, 1926, 6.

61. Klausner, *Vilnah, yerushalayim de-lita: dorot aharonim*, 660–61.

62. Selik Rosovsky, "Remembering Bobruisk," trans. Alex Ross, *Belarus SIG Newsletter*, no. 5 (February 3, 2000), www.jewishgen.org/Belarus/newsletters/mogilev/RememberBobruisk/index.html (accessed December 7, 2019).

63. Barukh Domnits, "Mukei goral," in *Pinkas slutsk u-venoteha*, ed. Nahum Hinits and Shimshon Nahmani (Tel Aviv: Yizkor Book Committee, 1962), 132.

64. Abraham Weissbrod, *Death of a Shtetl*, trans. of *Es Shtarbt a Shtetl; Megiles Skalat*, trans. Lusia Milch and Joseph Kofler (Munich: Central Historical Commission of the Central Committee of Liberated Jews in the American Zone of Germany, 1948), www.jewishgen.org/yizkor/Skalat1/ska040.html (accessed December 2, 2019).

65. Yankev Elboym, "Dray doyres vaser-treger," in *Sefer-yizkor li-kehilat radomsk veha-sevivah*, ed. L. Losh (Tel-Aviv: Irgun yots'e radomsk be-yisra'el, 1967), 156; Yakov Elboim, "Three Generations of Water Carriers," in *Memorial Book of the Community of Radomsk and Vicinity*, trans. Gloria Berkenstat Freund (updated 2002) www.jewishgen.org/Yizkor/Radomsko/rad144.html#Generations (accessed December 2, 2019).

66. Matityahu Shpergel, "Moteleh: tipshah shel lizhansk," in *Lizhansk: sefer zikaron li-kedoshe lizhansk she-nispu be-sho'at ha-natsim*, ed. H. Rabin and Matityahu Shpergel ([Tel Aviv]: Irgun olei lizhansk be-yisra'el, 1969), 237; Matityahu Spergel, "Motteleh— The Fool of Lizhensk," in *Memorial Book of the Martyrs of Lezajsk Who Perished in the Holocaust (Leżajsk, Poland)*, trans. Zygmunt Frankel et al. (updated 2002), www.jewishgen.org/Yizkor/Lezajsk/lez234.html (accessed December 2, 2019).

67. "Di meshugene sore," in *Pinkas Bendin*, ed. A. Sh. Shtein (Tel Aviv: Hotsa'at irgun yots'ei bendin be-yisra'el, 1959), 150. *From a Ruined Garden: The Memorial Books of Polish Jewry*, ed. Jack Kugelmass and Jonathan Boyarin (New York: Schocken Books, 1983), 108–9.

68. I. L. Peretz, "The Mad Talmudist," in *A Treasury of Yiddish Stories*, ed. Irving Howe, Eliezer Greenberg, and Ben Shahn, trans. Irving Howe and Eliezer Greenberg, rev. and updated ed. (New York: Viking Press, 1989), 234.

69. Yitskhok Leyb Peretz, "Der meshugener batlen," in id., *Ale verk* (New York: CYCO, 1947), 2: 20 (my trans.).

70. Peretz, "Mad Talmudist," 235.

71. Ibid., 235.

72. Ibid.

73. Ibid., 238.

74. Ibid., 241 (trans. slightly modified).

75. Kh. Shoshkes, "In a mishegoyim-hoyz (rayze-ayndrukn)," *Nayer haynt*, August 21, 1925, 7.

76. Ury, *Barricades and Banners*, 76.

77. A. Novovilaysker, "Vegn novo-vileyker 'hakhnoses orkhim' far mishegoyim (a brif in redaktsiye)," *Der shtern*, no. 36 (April 1, 1913): 2.

78. Tsegrovski, "An'invazye fun mishegoyim."

79. David Wright, "Developmental and Physical Disabilities," in *Encyclopedia of European Social History from 1350 to 2000*, ed. Stearns, 3: 510.

80. Almost one quarter of the beds in the Warsaw and Minsk Jewish hospitals were psychiatric beds, while the same proportion in in the Vilna Hospital was just under 10 percent. L. L. Rokhlin, "O evreiskikh lechebnykh zavedeniiakh v Rossii (Statisticheskie zametki)," *Evreiskii meditsinskii golos*, no. 1 (1908): 5–16.

81. I. K. [Yisroel-Avraham Kahan], "Lodzer kehalishe fragn," *Nayes lodzer morgen-blat*, no. 249 (October 31, 1913): 3.

82. T., "Di mishugoyim-frage in varshe," *Haynt*, no. 182 (August 20, 1913): 5. See also Ury, *Barricades and Banners*, 75, 85.

83. Towarzystwo Opieki nad Ubogimi Nerwowo i Umysłowo Chorymi Żydami, "Sprawozdanie z Czynności Towarzystwa Opieki nad Ubogimi Nerwowo i Umysłowo Chorymi Żydami" (Warsaw, 1906), 2.

84. "Hilf far gaystig-kranke," *Der veg*, June 27, 1906, 3.

85. Novovilaysker, "Vegn novo-vileyker 'hakhnoses orkhim' far mishegoyim (a brif in redaktsiye)"; V. S. Iastrebov, "Organizatsiia psikhiatricheskoi pomoshchi," in *Obsh-chaia psikhiatriia*, ed. A. S. Tiganov (1999), Nauchnyi tsentr psikhicheskogo zdorov'ia: biblioteka, http://psychiatry.ru/lib/53/book/28/chapter/101 (in Russian; accessed December 3, 2019).

86. John M. Efron, *Defenders of the Race: Jewish Doctors and Race Science in Fin-de-Siècle Europe* (New Haven, CT, 1994), 160–70; Gilman, "Jews and Mental Illness."

87. Brutskus, *Statistiki evreiskago naseleniia*, 30–31; Bureau für Statistik der Juden, *Die sozialen Verhältnisse der Juden in Russland* (Berlin-Charlottenburg: Jüdischer Verlag, 1906), 66. Gilman argues persuasively that the statistics used to demonstrate a Jewish predisposition to mental illness "probably reflect the higher incidence of hospitalization of Jews for mental illness resulting from their concentration in urban areas" and the fact that "urban Jews had developed a better network for the identification and treatment of illness" (Gilman, "Mental Illness," 152). Some experts also pointed to statistics that suggested higher rates of "idiocy and imbecility" among Jews than among non-Jews (*Jewish Encyclopedia*, s.v. "Idiocy").

88. Freeze, *Jewish Marriage and Divorce*, 28.

89. Maurice Fishberg, *The Jews: A Study of Race and Environment* (New York: Walter Scott, 1911), 324.

90. John M. Efron, *Medicine and the German Jews: A History* (New Haven, CT: Yale University Press, 2001), 148–49; Gilman, "Jews and Mental Illness," 150–51.

91. Sander L. Gilman, *The Jew's Body* (New York: Routledge, 1991), 76; Gilman, "Jews and Mental Illness," 155. Jewish social scientists often argued that Jewish hysteria might be due in part to endogamy, but they did not use the term "incest."

92. Wright, "Developmental and Physical Disabilities," in *Encyclopedia of European Social History from 1350 to 2000*, ed. Stearns, 3: 511.

93. Ibid., 511.

94. Efron, *Medicine and the German Jews*, 183.

95. Brown, "Social Influences on Psychiatric Theory," 37.

96. Ts. Shabad, "Meshugene Koloniyes," *YIVO Bleter* 7 (1934): 265–67; Abramowicz, *Profiles of a Lost World*, 109–10.

97. Brown, "Sociohistorical Perspective," 181.

98. Martin Engländer, *Die auffallend häufigen Krankheitserscheinungen der jüdischen Rasse* (Vienna: J. L. Pollak, 1902), 12, cited in Gilman, "Jews and Mental Illness," 154.

99. Brown, "Sociohistorical Perspective" 181.

Chapter 7

1. Ury, *Barricades and Banners*, 60–61.

2. Gilman, *Jew's Body*, 63.

3. Marina Mogilner, "Toward a History of Russian Jewish 'Medical Materialism': Russian Jewish Physicians and the Politics of Jewish Biological Normalization," *Jewish Social Studies* 19, no. 1 (2012): 91.

4. Mogilner (ibid., 92) argues that "Jewish 'medical materialism' produced the most integral version of modern Jewish nationalism in the Russian Empire." See also Todd Samuel Presner, *Muscular Judaism: The Jewish Body and the Politics of Regeneration* (New York: Routledge, 2007).

5. Steven J. Zipperstein, "The Politics of Relief: The Transformation of Russian Jewish Communal Life during the First World War," in *The Jews and the European Crisis, 1914–21*, ed. Jonathan Frankel (New York: Oxford University Press, 1988), 22–40.

6. Meir, "From Communal Charity to National Welfare, 27.

7. Keith Ian Weiser, *Jewish People, Yiddish Nation: Noah Prylucki and the Folkists in Poland* (Toronto: University of Toronto Press, 2011), 97–101. See also Barbara Kirshenblatt-Gimblett, "Folklore, Ethnography, and Anthropology," in the *YIVO Encyclopedia of Jews in Eastern Europe*, 1: 521–526; Deutsch, *Jewish Dark Continent*, 32–37.

8. Ginsburg and Marek, *Evreiskie narodnye pesni*, nos. 307, 309, 330.

9. Regina Lilientalowa, "Pieśni ludowe żydowskie," *Wisła: miesięcznik geograficzno-etnograficzny* 17, no. 5 (1903): 581–89.

10. Deutsch, *Jewish Dark Continent*, 261–63 (original in S. An-ski, *Dos yidishe etnografishe program* [Petrograd, 1915]).

11. A. Litvin, "Tsebrokhene neshomes," in *Yudishe neshomes* (New York: Farlag folksbildung, 1916), 2: 1 (vols. 1 and 2 bound together, with separate pagination).

12. Ibid., 2: 5.

13. Herschberg, *Pinkes byalistok*, 2: 163.

14. Litvin, "Tsebrokhene neshomes," in *Yudishe neshomes*, 2: 4.

15. A. Rabinovits, "Me-arei ha-medinah: halinkah (p' grodno)," *Ha-tsefirah*, September 15, 1900, 847; A. Bekenshtain, "Me-arei ha-medinah: slonim," *Ha-tsefirah*, November 27, 1901, 1063.

16. A. Litvin, "Der beykier bokhur-'bal-shem'," in *Yudishe neshomes*, 6: 1.

17. Ibid., 1–2.

18. Ibid., 2–3.

19. Kalman Lichtenstein, "Ha-bahur mi-beyki," in *Pinkas slonim* (Tel Aviv: Irgun olei slonim be-yisra'el, 1961), 1: 124–25. This episode is reminiscent of the Maiden of Ludmir, the "female tsaddik" who lived during the same period as the Bokhur; "accounts of the Maiden's life . . . emphasize that many people were drawn to her because she was such a 'wonder.' The Maiden of Ludmir's strangeness helped to create an aura around her," Nathaniel Deutsch writes. "Neither female nor male, she was an androgyne rebbe who apparently attracted many chronically ill and disabled people in search of healing" (Deutsch, *Jewish Dark Continent*, 141, 143).

20. On the latter, see Edward A. [Eddy] Portnoy, *Bad Rabbi and Other Strange but True Stories from the Yiddish Press* (Stanford: Stanford University Press, 2018).

21. On the popular press offering voyeuristic glimpses into Odessa's working-class neighborhoods, see Sylvester, *Tales of Old Odessa*, 28–80. For a similar phenomenon in London around the same time, see Judith Walkowitz, *City of Dreadful Delight: Narratives of Sexual Danger in Late-Victorian London* (Chicago: University of Chicago Press, 1992), 26–39.

22. Shloymo Berkman, "'Ezras-yesoymim' (tsu ihr hayntigen yontef)," *Haynt*, June 14, 1911. For other examples of Warsaw's Jewish organizations attempting to save the most vulnerable from the street (and especially from prostitution), see Ury, *Barricades and Banners*, 61–67.

23. Ruth R. Wisse, *I. L. Peretz and the Making of Modern Jewish Culture* (Seattle: University of Washington Press, 1991), 56.

24. Mark W. Kiel, "Vox Populi, Vox Dei: The Centrality of Peretz in Jewish Folkloristics," *Polin* 7 (1992): 103.

25. Ibid., 119 n. 122.

26. See Garland-Thomson, "Introduction," in *Freakery*, ed. id., 11–12.

27. Noah Isenberg, "To Pray like a Dervish: Orientalist Discourse in Arnold Zweig's *The Face of East European Jewry*," in *Orientalism and the Jews*, ed. Ivan Davidson Kalmar and Derek Jonathan Penslar (Waltham, MA: Brandeis University Press and University Press of New England, 2005), 95.

28. Wertheimer, *Unwelcome Strangers*, 108; Aschheim, *Brothers and Strangers*, 51–52.

29. Cited in Aharon Bornstein, *Mi-kabtsanim le-dorshei avodah: yehudim navadim be-germanyah, 1869–1914* (Tel Aviv: n.p., 1987). I am grateful to Shaul Stampfer for this reference.

30. I. S. Hertz, "Der bund un di andere rikhtungen" in *Di geshikhte fun bund* (New York: Farlag unzer tsayt, 1960), 1: 351, cited in Ben Halpern and Jehuda Reinharz, *Zionism and the Creation of a New Society* (New York: Oxford University Press, 1998), 135; trans. modified.

31. Theodor Herzl, *Old New Land*, trans. Lotta Levensohn (Princeton, NJ: M. Wiener, 1997), 26, 60, 69–60.

32. Michael Stanislawski, *Zionism and the Fin-de-Siècle: Cosmopolitanism and Nationalism from Nordau to Jabotinsky* (Berkeley: University of California Press, 2001), 195.

33. Derek Jonathan Penslar, *Zionism and Technocracy: The Engineering of Jewish Settlement in Palestine, 1870–1918* (Bloomington: Indiana University Press, 1991), 72. For an example of criticism of the initiative, see Shmul Rozenfeld, "Nokh a mol di 'kehalishe yesoymim,'" *Der fraynd*, no. 80 (April 9, 1904): 2.

34. Shloymo Berkman, "'Ezras-yesoymim' (tsu ihr hayntigen yontef)," *Haynt*, June 14, 1911, § 125.

35. Tara Zahra, "'Each Nation Only Cares for Its Own': Empire, Nation, and Child Welfare Activism in the Bohemian Lands, 1900–1918," *American Historical Review* 111, no. 5 (2006): 1378.

36. *35 yor tetigkeyt fun keshenever yesoymim-hoyz far inglekh (1900–1935)* ([Kishinev (now Chişinău, Moldova)]: [Tekhnik], [1936]), 3.

37. Ibid., 4.

38. Dovid Bergelson, "Der toyber," in id., *Geklibene verk* (Vilna: B. Kletskin, 1929), 1: 95–122; trans. as "The Deaf Man," in *No Star Too Beautiful: Yiddish Stories from 1382 to the Present*, ed. Joachim Neugroschel (New York: Norton, 2002), 424–43.

39. See Dafna Katsnelson-Bank, *Ha-shiga'on ba-sifrut ha-ivrit be-reshit ha-me'ah he-esrim* (Tel-Aviv: Hotsa'at ha-kibuts ha-me'uhad, 2005).

40. I. L. Peretz, "Be-agaf ha-meshuga'im," *Ha-tsefirah* 23, no. 195 (September 2, 1896): 948.

41. Frieden, *Classic Yiddish Fiction*, 272.

42. Peretz, "Be-agaf ha-meshuga'im"; I. L. Peretz, "Fun dul-hoyz," in id., *Ale verk fun y. l. perets* (Vilna: Vilner farlag fun b. kletskin, 1925), 6: 221.

43. Peretz, "Be-agaf ha-meshuga'im" and "Fun dul-hoyz," 6: 219.

44. Peretz, "Fun dul-hoyz," 6: 220.

45. Peretz, "Be-agaf ha-meshuga'im."

46. Roskies, *Bridge of Longing*, 115.

47. Peretz, "Fun dul-hoyz," 6: 227.

48. Peretz, "Be-agaf ha-meshuga'im" and "Fun dul-hoyz," 6: 239. This is a reference to Mishnah Oktsin 3:12: "In the future the Holy One, Blessed be He, will bequeath to each and every righteous person three hundred ten worlds."

49. Peretz, "Be-agaf ha-meshuga'im," *Ha-tsefirah* 23, no. 198 (September 6, 1896): 962; Peretz, "Fun dul-hoyz," 6: 231.

50. Peretz, "Be-agaf ha-meshuga'im," 962; Peretz, "Fun dul-hoyz," 6: 231.

51. Peretz, "Be-agaf ha-meshuga'im," 962; Peretz, "Fun dul-hoyz," 6: 234. This is a reference to the rabbinic midrash that lists the magical objects created on the eve of the first Sabbath, including the rainbow, the manna, the inscription on the Tablets of the Ten Commandments, the Tablets themselves, and, some say, destructive spirits (m. Avot 5:9).

52. Jeffrey A. Shandler, "Christmas," in the *YIVO Encyclopedia of Jews in Eastern Europe*, 1: 330.

53. Peretz, "Be-agaf ha-meshuga'im," 962; Peretz, "Fun dul-hoyz," 6: 235.

54. Perhaps similarly, in the 1870s, S. Y. Abramovitsh played with the idea of a new narrator protagonist named Yisrolik der meshugener (Yisrolik the Madman), who "was at least as close to the Abramovitsh persona as he was to the Mendele one," Dan Miron writes in *From Continuity to Contiguity: Toward a New Jewish Literary Thinking* (Stanford: Stanford University Press, 2010), 439–40.

55. Peretz, "Be-agaf ha-meshuga'im," 963; Peretz, "Fun dul-hoyz," 6: 223.

56. Perets Tsunzer, "Mishegas-motivn in y. l. peretses shafn: kritisher analiz," *Kultur*, January 22, 1926, 3.

57. *Madness and the Mad in Russian Culture*, ed. Brintlinger and Vinitsky, 24.

58. David Ingleby, "Mental Health and Social Order," in *Social Control and the State*, ed. Stanley Cohen and Andrew Scull (New York: St. Martin's Press, 1983), 162.

59. Roskies, *Bridge of Longing*, 115–18 (quote on 118). See also Wisse, *I. L. Peretz*, 55–59.

60. Peretz was surely also influenced by Dostoevsky, who has much to say about madness, as Harriet Murav has shown, noting that in his major novels Dostoevsky used the figure of the holy fool to express resistance to "the age of positivism and science" and as an icon of the degraded condition of humanity and its "need for redemption" (Murav, *Holy Foolishness*, 8).

61. Michael C. Steinlauf, "The Dybbuk," in the *YIVO Encyclopedia of Jews in Eastern Europe*, 1: 434.

62. Avrom Goldfaden, "The Two Kuni-Lemels," in *Landmark Yiddish Plays: A Critical Anthology*, ed. Jeremy Dauber and Joel Berkowitz (Albany: State University of New York Press, 2006), 201–45; David Pinski, "Cripples," in *Ten Plays*, trans. Isaac Goldberg (New York: B. W. Huebsch, 1920), 77–86.

63. Nahma Sandrow, *Vagabond Stars: A World History of Yiddish Theater* (New York: Harper & Row, 1977), 131–32, 141; Michael C. Steinlauf, "Yiddish Theater," in the

YIVO Encyclopedia of Jews in Eastern Europe, 2: 1864. See also Barbara J. Henry, *Rewriting Russia: Jacob Gordin's Yiddish Drama* (Seattle: University of Washington Press, 2011), who suggests that Khasye represents the Jewish people: "motherless, in exile, the child of a loving but distant father who . . . is never around to protect his eldest, best-loved child" (140).

64. Jacob Gordin, *Khashe [Khasye] di yesoyme: a drame in 4 akten* (Warsaw: Ferlag di "yudishe bihne," 1907). The play stirred controversy among critics in North America but not in Europe. See Henry, *Rewriting Russia*, 127–29; Beth Kaplan, *Finding the Jewish Shakespeare: The Life and Legacy of Jacob Gordin* (Syracuse, NY: Syracuse University Press, 2007), 123–26.

65. Gabriella Safran, *Wandering Soul: The Dybbuk's Creator, S. An-Sky* (Cambridge, MA: Belknap Press of Harvard University Press, 2010), 188.

66. The term "ethnographic museum," repurposed by Safran (ibid., 214), was used disparagingly by Hebrew poet Avraham Shlonsky in 1925.

67. S. An-ski, "Tsvishen tsvey velten (der dibek)," in idem, *Gezamelte shriften* (Vilna: S. An-Ski, 1928), 2: 5–6; An-skii, *Mezh dvukh mirov (Dibuk)*, in *Polveka evreiiskogo teatra: 1876–1926*, ed. Boris Entin (Moscow: Dom evreiskoi knigi, 2003), 323-24. For an English translation of the Russian version, see id., "*Between Two Worlds (The Dybbuk)*: Censored Variant," trans. Anne Eakin Moss, in *The Worlds of S. An-Sky: A Russian Jewish Intellectual at the Turn of the Century*, ed. Gabriella Safran and Steven J. Zipperstein (Stanford: Stanford University Press, 2006), 361–435.

68. An-ski, *The Dybbuk and Other Writings*, ed. Roskies, 20–21.

69. Ibid.

70. Ibid., 22 (trans. slightly modified).

71. Ibid. For a description of a traditional Jewish wedding in eastern Europe that included a bride dance (*kale-tants*) with wives of itinerant beggars who were encamped near the author's hometown, see Trunk, *Poyln: My Life*, 66, and *Poyln: zikhroynes un bilder*, 1: 103.

72. An-ski, *The Dybbuk and Other Writings*, ed. Roskies, 23.

73. Ibid., 23.

74. Ibid., 24; An-ski, "Tsvishen tsvey velten," 67; An-skii, *Mezh dvukh mirov (Dibuk)*, 353.

75. For a queer reading of *The Dybbuk*, see Naomi Seidman, "The Ghost of Queer Loves Past: Ansky's 'Dybbuk' and the Sexual Transformation of Ashkenaz," in Boyarin, Itzkovitz, and Pellegrini, *Queer Theory and the Jewish Question*, 228–45.

76. Giora Manor explains that although Vakhtangov invited the choreographer Lev A. Lashchilin to stage the dances, Vakhtangov himself was actually the guiding presence in the choreography of the Dance of the Beggars. Giora Manor, "Extending the Traditional Wedding Dance: Inbal Dance Theater's 'Yemenite Wedding' and the 'Dance of the Beggars' in Habimah National Theater's 'Dybbuk,'" in *Seeing Israeli and Jewish Dance*, ed. Judith Brin Ingber (Detroit: Wayne State University Press, 2011), 218–19.

77. Evgenii Vakhtangov, *The Vakhtangov Sourcebook*, ed. Andrei Malaev-Babel (New York: Routledge, 2011), 59.

78. Ibid., 59. The reference is to the analysis of Soviet actor, director, and pedagogue Aleksandr Karev, published in a 1959 collection of essays about Vakhtangov.

79. N. D. Volkov, *Vakhtangov* (Moscow: Korabl', 1922), 20, cited in Vakhtangov, *Vakhtangov Sourcebook*, 61.

80. D. Tal'nikov, "Pesn' torzhestvuiushchei liubvi," *Teatr i muzyka*, July 10, 1923: 961, cited in Vladislav Ivanov, "An-Sky, Evgeny Vakhtangov, and The Dybbuk," in *Worlds of S. An-Sky*, ed. Safran and Zipperstein, 260.

81. André Levinson, review of *The Dybbuk*, Paris, June 30, 1926 (unidentified clipping from archive of Habimah Theater, Tel Aviv), cited in Manor, "Extending the Traditional Wedding Dance," 219.

82. Manor, "Extending the Traditional Wedding Dance," 219.

83. Grosz, "Intolerable Ambiguity" in *Freakery*, ed. Garland-Thomson, 57 (emphasis in original).

84. J. Brooks Atkinson, "THE PLAY: 'The Dybbuk' in Hebrew," *New York Times*, December 14, 1926.

85. Ivanov, "An-Sky, Evgeny Vakhtangov, and The Dybbuk," 259.

86. Ibid., 263.

87. Michał Waszyński, dir., *Der dibek (Dybuk)*, 1937, 1:18:40.

88. Chaim Grade, *My Mother's Sabbath Days: A Memoir*, trans. Channa Kleinerman Goldstein and Inna Hecker (New York: Knopf, 1986), 100.

89. Seth Wolitz, "Inscribing An-Sky's Dybbuk in Russian and Jewish Letters," in *Worlds of S. An-Sky*, ed. Safran and Zipperstein, 176.

90. On the Civil War-era massacres, see O. V. Budnitskii, *Russian Jews between the Reds and the Whites, 1917–1920* (Philadelphia: University of Pennsylvania Press, 2012); Henry Abramson, *A Prayer for the Government: Ukrainians and Jews in Revolutionary Times, 1917–1920* (Cambridge, MA: Distributed by Harvard University Press for the Harvard Ukrainian Research Institute and Center for Jewish Studies, Harvard University, 1999); *Kniga pogromov: pogromy na Ukraine, v Belorussii i evropeiskoi chasti Rossii v period Grazhdanskoi voiny, 1918–1922 gg.: sbornik dokumentov*, ed. L. B. Miliakova (Moscow: ROSSPEN, 2007); Laura Engelstein, *Russia in Flames: War, Revolution, Civil War, 1914–1921* (New York: Oxford University Press, 2018), 511–40; Peter Kenez, "Pogroms and White Ideology in the Russian Civil War," in *Pogroms: Anti-Jewish Violence in Modern Russian History*, ed. John D. Klier and Shlomo Lambroza (Cambridge: Cambridge University Press, 1991), 293–313.

91. "A Barefoot Beggar Woman," *Forverts*, December 16, 1923, 19.

92. L. Yakhnovitsh, "Odeser rabonim shtelen shvartse khupes oyfn beys oylem als mitel gegen der kholera," *Forverts*, September 30, 1922, 8.

93. Zipperstein, "Politics of Relief," 29–34.

94. Avrom Levinson, "A natsionaler khov," in *Dos elendste kind*, ed. M. Shneyorson (Warsaw: CENTOS, 1927), 8.

95. Smith, "Charity and Poor Relief," in *Encyclopedia of European Social History*, ed. Stearns, 3: 461.

96. Zahra, "'Each Nation Only Cares for Its Own,'" 1382.

97. Mikhail Beizer, *Relief in Time of Need: Russian Jewry and the Joint, 1914–24* (Bloomington, IN: Slavica Publishers, 2015), 97–104; Leon Shapiro, *The History of ORT: A Jewish Movement for Social Change* (New York: Schocken Books, 1980), 132.

98. Beizer, *Relief in Time of Need*, 104–6, 136–37.

99. Hayim Wolnerman, "Benevolent Societies," in *Oswiecim; Auschwitz Memorial Book (Oświęcim, Poland)*, ed. Aviezer Burstim, and Meir Simon Geshuri, (translation of *Sefer Oshpitsin*, 1977), JewishGen Yizkor Book Project, jewishgen.org/yizkor/os-wiecim1/Oswiecim.html (accessed December 2, 2019).

100. Luba (Atkin) Bat, "Through Tears and Laughter (Personal Memoir)," Children of Pruzany and the Surrounding Area (n.d.), http://cpsa.info/pruzany/luba_bat.htm (accessed December 2, 2019).

101. I am grateful to Jeremy Dauber for this insight.

102. Agnon, "Ovadiah ba'al mum," in id., *Kol sipurav shel shemu'el yosef agnon*, 2: 409.

103. Ibid.

104. Ibid.

105. Ibid.

106. Ibid., 410.

107. Shaked, "Three Kalikes," 185.

108. Agnon, "Ovadiah ba'al mum," in id., *Kol sipurav shel shemu'el yosef agnon*, 2: 425.

109. Ibid., 414.

110. Ibid., 416.

111. Ibid., 417.

112. Ibid., 424.

113. Ibid., 418.

114. Ibid., 428.

115. While Gershon Shaked argues that Ovadiah must overcome "the benevolence of the welfare society's hospital that tempted him to escape the hard facts of life," in fact it is precisely that benevolence that, together with Ovadiah's own kind and perhaps naïve nature, induces him to stay with Sheyne Serl and the baby. Shaked, "Three Kalikes," 186.

116. Stanislawski, *Zionism and the Fin-de-Siècle*, 74–97; Hart, *Social Science and the Politics of Modern Jewish Identity*, 108–9; Gilman, "Jews and Mental Illness," 154–57.

117. Hart, *Social Science*, 105–6.

118. Presner, *Muscular Judaism*, 4.

119. See Samuel D. Kassow, *Who Will Write Our History? Emanuel Ringelblum, the*

Warsaw Ghetto, and the Oyneg Shabes Archive (Bloomington: Indiana University Press, 2007), esp. chap. 3; Cecile Esther Kuznitz, *YIVO and the Making of Modern Jewish Culture: Scholarship for the Yiddish Nation* (New York: Cambridge University Press, 2014), chaps. 3 and 5; Natan M. Meir, "Charting the Outer Provinces of Jewry: The Study of East European Jewry's Margins," *Polin* 29 (2017): 89–104.

120. Majer Bałaban, *Dzieje Żydów w Krakowie i na Kazimierzu (1304–1868)* (Kraków: Nakł. Izraelickiej Gminy Wyznaniowej, 1912), 1: 285–87; Majer Bałaban, "Obyczajowość i życie prywatne Żydów w dawnej Rzeczypospolitej," in *Żydzi w Polsce odrodzonej: działalność społeczna, gospodarcza, oświatowa i kulturalna*, ed. Ignacy Schiper (Warsaw, 1932), 1: 348; Shiper, *Geshikhte fun yidisher teater-kunst un drame*, 63–68; Isaiah Trunk, "Le-toldot ha-historiografyah ha-yehudit-polanit," *Gal-Ed* 3 (1976): 263. For Bałaban's influence, see Natalia Aleksiun, "Training a New Generation of Jewish Historians: Majer Bałaban's Seminar on the History of Polish Jews," in *Zwischen Graetz und Dubnow: Jüdische Historiographie in Ostmitteleuropa im 19. und 20. Jahrhundert*, ed. François Guesnet (Leipzig: Akademische Verlagsanstalt, 2009).

121. Emanuel Ringelblum, "Der yidisher opshoym in 18-tn y"h: loyt gerikhtlekhe dokumentn," in *Kapitlen geshikhte fun amolikn yidishn lebn in poyln*, ed. Jacob Shatzky (Buenos Aires: Tsentral-farband fun poylishe yidn in argentine, 1953), 153–67. The article focused on Jewish criminals, mostly petty thieves, in Warsaw. See Samuel D. Kassow, "Historiography: An Overview," in the *YIVO Encyclopedia of Jews in Eastern Europe*, 1: 726; Kassow, *Who Will Write Our History?* 73–74; Trunk, "Le-toldot ha-historiografyah ha-yehudit-polanit," 264.

122. Emanuel Ringelblum, "Shnorers in poyln in di amolike tsaytn," in Shatzky, *Kapitlen geshikhte*, 168–72. Most studies of Jewish deviance focused on contemporary society and, if focused on criminality, often had an apologetic tone. See Rudolf Vaserman, "Di bazunderkeytn fun der kriminalitet bay yidn," *Shriftn far ekonomik un statistik* 1 (1928): 122–28; L. Hersh, "Di farbrekherishkayt bay der yidisher un nit-yidisher bafelkerung fun der poylisher republik," *Ekonomishe shriftn* 2 (1932): 174–200.

123. Itzik Nakhmen Gottesman, *Defining the Yiddish Nation: The Jewish Folklorists of Poland* (Detroit: Wayne State University Press, 2003), 33–34; *Bay unz yuden: zamelbukh far folklor un filologye*, ed. M. Vanvild (Warsaw: Farlag Pinkhes Graubard, 1923).

124. YIVO Etnografishe komisye, *Vos iz azoyns yidishe etnografye?: hantbikhl far zamler* (Vilna: [YIVO], 1929), 10–11.

125. Bill Gladstone, "Toronto Shul Exhibits Photos of Polish Shtetl," *Canadian Jewish News*, September 28, 2012, www.cjnews.com/culture/entertainment/toronto-shul-exhibits-photos-polish-shtetl (accessed December 8, 2019).

126. Deborah Yalen, "Documenting the 'New Red Kasrilevke,'" *East European Jewish Affairs* 37, no. 3 (December 1, 2007): 359.

127. Ibid., 367.

128. Alexander Harkavy, *Navaredok: ihr historye un ihr hayntiger leben* (New York: Navaredoker hilf-komitet in nyu ork, 1921), 42.

129. Ibid., 41–42.

130. See, e.g., "Kalushin" (amateur film, 1935–36), YIVO Archive RG 105, F005 (possible town fool at 1: 17) and amateur footage by Gustave Eisner (1930s), YIVO Archive RG 105, F18, http://yivoencyclopedia.org/article.aspx/Beggars_and_Begging (accessed December 8, 2019). My thanks to Roberta Newman for assistance with the archival citation for the second film.

131. See, e.g., *Want: 100 Postcards from the Collection of John Kasmin* (London: Royal Academy of Arts, 2013), as well as www.delcampe.net/en_GB/collectables/postcards/lithuania/lituanie-n-1739-bettlertypen-in-wilna-beggars-typique-de-vilnius-mendiants-382059005.html (accessed December 1, 2019).

132. Roberta Newman, "Pictures of a Trip to the Old Country," ed. Jack Kugelmass, *YIVO Annual* 21 (1993): 226.

133. Roberta Newman, "Home Movies and the Alte Heym (Old Home): American Jewish Travel Films in Eastern Europe in the 1920s and 1930s," *Jewish Folklore and Ethnology Review* 15, no. 1 (1993): 25.

134. *Forvets*, April 27, 1924, 19; September 6, 1925, 19; February 3, 1924, 20. Other towns whose town fools were featured were Akerman, Łódź, Mława, Pińsk, Płock, and Zwolen.

135. Abraham Icchok Lerner Index to Yiddish periodicals, http://yiddish-periodicals.huji.ac.il; Historic Jewish Press, http://web.nli.org.il/sites/JPress (both accessed December 8, 2019).

136. On the genre of the yizkor book, see Jack Kugelmass and Jonathan Boyarin, "Introduction," in *From a Ruined Garden*, ed. Kugelmass and Boyarin, 1–48; Abraham Wein, "'Memorial Books' as a Source for Research into the History of Jewish Communities in Europe," *Yad Vashem Studies* 9 (1973): 255–72.

137. Rivka Parciak, "The Others in Yizker Books," in *Memorial Books of Eastern European Jewry: Essays on the History and Meanings of Yizker Volumes*, ed. Rosemary Horowitz (Jefferson, NC: McFarland, 2011), 237.

138. See Kugelmass and Boyarin, "Yizker Bikher and the Problem of Historical Veracity," 519–35.

139. Kugelmass and Boyarin, "Introduction," 23–25.

140. M. Vorobeichic, *Rehov ha-yehudim be-vilnah: 65 temunot = Ein Ghetto im Osten—Wilna: 65 Bilder* (Zurich: Orell Füssli, 1931), pl. 63.

141. On Vorobeichic, see Samuel Spinner, "Avant-garde Authenticity: M. Vorobeichic's Photographic Modernism and the East European Jew," in *Writing Jewish Culture: Paradoxes in Ethnography*, ed. Andreas Kilcher and Gabriella Safran (Bloomington, IN: Indiana University Press, 2016), 208–32.

142. On the transformation of Jewish welfare and philanthropy in the interwar

period, see Samuel Kassow, "Jewish Communal Politics in Transition: The Vilna Kehile, 1919–1920," *YIVO Annual* 20 (1991): 61–92; Rebecca Kobrin, *Jewish Bialystok and Its Diaspora* (Bloomington: Indiana University Press, 2010), 131–75. For specific instances of interwar hekdeshim, see Natan M. Meir, "Home for the Homeless? The Hekdesh in Eastern Europe," in *Place in Modern Jewish Culture and Society*, ed. Richard I. Cohen (New York: Oxford University Press, 2018), 11.

143. Hilary Mantel, "Adaption," BBC Reith Lectures 2017, pt. 5, broadcast July 11, 2017, https://medium.com/@bbcradiofour/adaptation-3d6bce51c69 (accessed December 1, 2019).

144. *Encyclopaedia Judaica*, 2nd ed., s.v. "Opatoshu, Joseph."

145. Anita Norich, *The Homeless Imagination in the Fiction of Israel Joshua Singer* (Bloomington: Indiana University Press, 1991), 34.

146. Joseph Opatoshu, "A khasene oyfn beys-oylem," in id., *Gezamelte verk* (Vilne: B. Kletskin, 1931), 12: 102.

147. Ibid., 104.

148. Ibid., 103.

149. Ibid., 104.

150. Ibid.

151. Ibid., 105.

152. Israel Joshua Singer, *Yoshe Kalb* (Warsaw: Grafia, 1932), 244.

153. The Yiddish original has her moaning "like a cow" (ibid., 205).

154. Israel Joshua Singer, *Yoshe Kalb*, trans. Maurice Samuel (New York: Schocken Books, 1988), 152–53.

155. Ibid., 166–67.

156. Singer, *Yoshe Kalb*, 237.

157. Norich, *Homeless Imagination*, 28.

158. J. Hoberman, *Bridge of Light: Yiddish Film between Two Worlds* (Hanover, NH: Dartmouth College and University Press of New England in association with the National Center for Jewish Film, 2010), 302.

159. Ibid., 304.

160. Ibid., 303.

161. Ulmer's wife Shirley recalled that Ulmer "always had sympathy for any outcast or anybody who had a disability or was a fugitive." Noah William Isenberg, *Edgar G. Ulmer: A Filmmaker at the Margins* (Berkeley: University of California Press, 2014), 108.

162. In a quirk of literary and cinematic fate, David Opatoshu, the American actor who played Fishke in the film, was the son of Joseph Opatoshu, author of "A Wedding in the Cemetery."

163. JDC Archives, Records of the New York Office of the American Jewish Joint Distribution Committee, Poland 1933–44, Folder 841b, "Letter from Committee for Medem Sanitarium in Poland [New York] to JDC," 1938.

164. Julian Tuwim, "Little Jew-Boy," trans. Jacob Sonntag, *Jewish Quarterly* 30, no. 4 (1983): 36.

165. For a similar conclusion vis-à-vis the "schlemiel" character in Abramovitsh's works ("in an insane world, the fool may be the only morally sane man"), see Ruth R. Wisse, *The Schlemiel as Modern Hero* (Chicago: University of Chicago Press, 1971), 38–39.

Epilogue

1. "Orphaned alleyways" is Chaim Grade's locution. Grade, *My Mother's Sabbath Days*, 335.

2. Erica T. Lehrer, *Na szczęście to Żyd: Polskie figurki Żydów / Lucky Jews: Poland's Jewish figurines*, trans. Joanna Warchoł, (Kraków: Korporacja Ha!art, 2014), 94–96.

3. Fritz Hippler, dir., *Der ewige Jude = The Eternal Jew* (Deutsche Film Gesellschaft, 1940), 10:59.

4. Wertheimer, *Unwelcome Strangers*, 27–31. Linked to the image of the Jewish beggar was the set of stereotypes associated with the idea of Jewish criminality, central to Nazi antisemitism. See Michael Berkowitz, *The Crime of My Very Existence: Nazism and the Myth of Jewish Criminality* (Berkeley: University of California Press, 2007).

5. Ian Kershaw, *Hitler, 1936–45: Nemesis* (New York: Norton, 2000), 152.

6. Jürgen Matthäus and Emil Kerenji, eds., *Jewish Responses to Persecution, 1933–1946: A Source Reader* (Lanham, MD: Rowman & Littlefield, 2017), 84.

7. Ibid., 85.

8. Parciak, "Others," 236–37.

9. ChaeRan Y. Freeze, "Family," in the *YIVO Encyclopedia of Jews in Eastern Europe*, 1: 499.

10. Emanuel Ringelblum, *Notes from the Warsaw Ghetto; the Journal of Emmanuel Ringelblum* (New York: Schocken Books, 1974), 233–34.

11. Rivke Schiller, "Ceremonia 'czarnego wesela' i jej opisy w księgach pamięci," trans. Piotr Pazinski, *Midrasz*, no. 6 (November–December 2011): 39.

12. Adam Czerniaków, *The Warsaw Diary of Adam Czerniakow: Prelude to Doom*, ed. Raul Hilberg, Stanislaw Staron, and Joseph Kermish (New York: Stein & Day, 1979), 293. Since Yom Kippur fell on October 1 in 1941, the proposal obviously reached Czerniaków much later than the members of the rabbinical council had planned.

13. Paul Weindling, *Epidemics and Genocide in Eastern Europe, 1890–1945* (Oxford: Oxford University Press, 2000), 278.

14. Mochalova, "Istselenie, spasenie, izbavlenie," 104–5.

15. Grade, *My Mother's Sabbath Days*, 99–111.

16. Ibid., 114.

17. Ibid., 338.

18. Abraham Karpinowitz, "Shibele's Lottery Ticket," in *Vilna My Vilna: Stories*, trans. Helen Mintz (Syracuse, NY: Syracuse University Press, 2016), 45.

19. Ibid., 52.

20. Joseph C. Landis, "'Gimpl Tam' and the Perils of Translation," *Yiddish* 14, nos. 2–3 (2006): 112, 114.

21. Edward Alexander, *Isaac Bashevis Singer: A Study of the Short Fiction* (Boston: Twayne, 1990), 52, emphasis in original.

22. David G. Roskies, "Gimpel the Simple and on Reading from Right to Left," in *Arguing the Modern Jewish Canon: Essays on Literature and Culture in Honor of Ruth R. Wisse*, ed. Justin Daniel Cammy et al. (Cambridge, MA: Harvard University Press, 2008), 322.

23. Ibid., 322.

24. Dan Miron, "Passivity and Narration: The Spell of Isaac Bashevis Singer," in id., *Image of the Shtet*, 338.

25. Ibid., 340.

26. Roskies, "Gimpel the Simple and on Reading from Right to Left," in *Arguing the Modern Jewish Canon*, ed. Cammy et al., 336.

27. Gimpel represents all of "poor, bewildered, suffering humanity," Paul N. Siegel argues in "Gimpel and the Archetype of the Wise Fool," in *The Achievement of Isaac Bashevis Singer*, ed. Marcia Allentuck (Carbondale: Southern Illinois University Press, 1969), 173.

Conclusion

1. Rachel Adams, *Sideshow U.S.A.: Freaks and the American Cultural Imagination* (Chicago: University of Chicago Press, 2001), 7.

2. Naomi Seidman, "Reading 'Queer' Ashkenaz: This Time from East to West," *The Drama Review: TDR* 55, no. 3 (October 1, 2011): 50.

3. Levanda, "Neskol'ko slov," 8.

4. Another link between poverty and deviant sexuality, this time in the modern bourgeois moral culture that middle-class Jews shared, was the notion of the destitute Jewish female at risk of becoming a "fallen woman," a locution denoting the transformation from poor but virtuous woman, wife and mother *in potentia*, into a moral cripple.

5. Adams, *Sideshow U.S.A.*, 8.

6. Seidman, "Reading 'Queer' Ashkenaz," 52.

7. Zehavit Stern, "From Jester to Gesture: Eastern European Jewish Culture and the Re-Imagination of Folk Performance" (Ph.D. diss., University of California, Berkeley, 2011), 140. It is telling that Henekh Kohn, the film's composer, described the beggar extras as "undisciplined human material" (*nisht ditsipliniert mentshn-materiel*) (ibid., 140), and see Henekh Kohn, "In film atelye," *Literarishe Bleter* 30 (July 23, 1937): 485.

8. Simi Linton, "The Disability Studies Project: Broadening the Parameters of Diversity," in *End Results and Starting Points: Expanding the Field of Disability Studies,*

ed. Elaine Makas and Lynn Schlesinger (Boston: Society for Disability Studies, 1996), 323–25; cited in Paul K. Longmore and Lauri Umansky, "Introduction: Disability History: From the Margins to the Mainstream," in *The New Disability History: American Perspectives*, ed. Paul K. Longmore and Lauri Umansky (New York: New York University Press, 2001), 7.

SELECTED BIBLIOGRAPHY

Archival Sources

AMERICAN JEWISH JOINT DISTRIBUTION COMMITTEE ARCHIVES

NY Office 1921–32: Poland
Photographic Collection

CENTRAL ARCHIVES FOR THE HISTORY OF THE JEWISH PEOPLE, JERUSALEM (CAHJP)

JCA/Lon (Jewish Colonization Association).
Lithuanian State Historical Archives, Vilnius (LVIA) f. 378, Kantseliariia Vilensk-ogo, Kovenskogo i Grodnenskogo general-gubernatora g. Vil'na (B/S = *bendrasis skyrius* [General Section]); microfilm at CAHJP – HM3/224.14
LVIA f. 620, Vilenskii evreiskii kagal g. Vil'na; microfilm at CAHJP – HM2/9821.2 and 9825.3.
P/166 (An-ski Ethnographic Expedition).
Russian State Historical Archive, St. Petersburg (RGIA), f. 1286, Departament politisii ispol'nitel'noi MVD; microfilm at CAHJP – RU1111
RGIA f. 1287, Khoziastvennyi department MVD; microfilm at CAHJP – HM2/8276

CENTRAL STATE HISTORICAL ARCHIVE OF UKRAINE, KIEV (TSDIAU)

f. 442, Kantseliaria Kievskogo, Podol'skogo i Volynskogo general-gubernatora
f. 533, Kievskii voennyi Gubernator

f. 707, Upravlenie Kievskogo uchebnogo okruga

NATIONAL LIBRARY OF ISRAEL, DEPARTMENT OF MANUSCRIPTS (NLI-DM)

ARC. 4° 1069, Papers of Elihayu Guttmacher

STATE ARCHIVE OF KIEV OBLAST', KIEV (DAKO)

f. 2, Kantseliariia Kievskogo gubernatora

VERNADSKY NATIONAL LIBRARY OF UKRAINE, MANUSCRIPT DIVISION, JUDAICA SECTION (NBUV IR)

f. 321, Kollektsiia evreiskikh rukopisei/Pinkasim Collection

YIVO INSTITUTE FOR JEWISH RESEARCH, NEW YORK

RG 12, Minsk Jewish Community Council Records
RG 27, Papers of Eliyahu Guttmacher (1796–1874)
RG 30, Russia and the Soviet Union Collection (Vilna Archives)
YIVO Photo Archive

Periodical Literature

Der fraynd
Der moment
Der shtern
Der veg
Di varhayt (Die Wahrheit)
Folkstsaytung
Forverts
Ha-karmel
Ha-magid
Ha-melits
Ha-tsefira
Haynt
Ha-yom
Kol mevaser
Nayer haynt
Nayes lodzer morgenblat
Nedel'naia khronika Voskhoda
New York Times

Razsvet

Russkii evrei

Sion

Zaria

Primary Sources

Abramovitsh, S. Y. [pseud. Mendele Moykher-Sforim; Mendele Mokher-Sefarim].
"Fishke der krumer." In *Geklibene verk*, 3: 5–161. New York: IKUF Farlag, 1947.

———. "Fishke the Lame: A Book of Jewish Poorfolk." In *Tales of Mendele the Book
Peddler: Fishke the Lame and Benjamin the Third*, edited by Dan Miron and Ken
Frieden, translated by Ted Gorelick, 1–297. New York: Schocken Books, 1996.

———. "Fishke the Lame." In *Selected Works of Mendele Moykher-Sforim*, edited by
Marvin S. Zuckerman, Gerald Stillman, and Marion Herbst, translated by Gerald Stillman, 169–312. Malibu, CA: Joseph Simon / Pangloss Press, 1991.

———. "The Little Man; or, Portrait of a Life." In *Classic Yiddish Stories of S. Y.
Abramovitsh, Sholem Aleichem, and I. L. Peretz*, edited and translated by Ken
Frieden, 3–31. Syracuse, NY: Syracuse University Press, 2007.

———. "Of Bygone Days." In *A Shtetl and Other Yiddish Novellas*, edited by Ruth R.
Wisse. Detroit: Wayne State University Press, 1986.

———. "Sefer ha-kabtsanim." In *Kol kitvei mendele mokher sefarim*, 89–142. Tel-
Aviv: Dvir, 1947.

Abramowicz, Hirsz. *Farshvundene geshtaltn* [Disappeared Figures]. Translated by
Eva Zeitlin Dobkin as *Profiles of a Lost World: Memoirs of East European Jewish
Life before World War II*. Edited by Dina Abramowicz and Jeffrey Shandler. De-
troit: Wayne State University Press, 1999.

Agnon, Shmuel Yosef. "Ovadiah ba'al mum." In *Kol sipurav shel shemu'el yosef agnon*,
2: 408–28. Jerusalem: Schocken, 1967.

Aleksandrov, H. "Fun minsker arkhivn." *Tsaytshrift far yidisher geshikhte, demografye
un ekonomik, literatur-forshung, shprakhvisnshaft un etnografye (Institut far vaysruslendisher kultur, yidisher sektor)* 2–3 (1928): 763–78.

Ans-ski, S. [Shloyme Zanvl Rappoport, pseud.]. "Alte shuhlen un zeyer legende."
In id., *Gezamelte shriften*, vol. 15: *Folklor un etnografiye*. Vilna: Ferlag "An-ski,"
1925.

———. "*Between Two Worlds (The Dybbuk)*: Censored Variant." Translated by Anne
Eakin Moss. In *The Worlds of S. An-Sky: A Russian Jewish Intellectual at the Turn
of the Century*, edited by Gabriella Safran and Steven J. Zipperstein, 361–435.
Stanford: Stanford University Press, 2006.

———. *The Dybbuk and Other Writings*. Edited by David G. Roskies. Translated by
Golda Werman. New York: Schocken Books, 1992.

———. "Evreiskoe narodnoe tvorchestvo." *Perezhitoe* 1 (1909): 276–314.

———. *Mezh dvukh mirov (Dibuk)*. In *Polveka evreiiskogo teatra: 1876–1926*, edited by Boris Entin, 319–81. Moscow: Dom evreiskoi knigi, 2003.

———. "Tsvishen tsvey velten (der dibek)." In An-ski, *Gezamelte shriften*, 2: 5–105. Vilna: Ferlag "An-ski," 1928.

Appelfeld, Aharon. "Bertha." In *Truth and Lamentation: Stories and Poems on the Holocaust*, edited by Milton Teichman and Sharon Leder, 149–59. Urbana: University of Illinois Press, 1994.

Arkhangel'skii, Grigorii Ivanovich. *Kholernyia epidemii v Evropeiskoi Rossii*. St. Petersburg, 1874.

Avron, Dov. *Pinkas ha-kesherim shel kehilat Pozna (Acta electorum communitatis Judaeorum Posnaniensium, 1621–1835)*. Jerusalem: Memorial Foundation for Jewish Culture, 1966.

Bergelson, Dovid. "Der toyber." In id., *Geklibene verk*, 1: 95–122. Vilna: B. Kletskin, 1929. Translated by Joachim Neugroschel as "The Deaf Man" in *No Star Too Beautiful: Yiddish Stories from 1382 to the Present*, ed. Neugroschel, 424–43 (New York: Norton, 2002).

Berlin, M. *Ocherk etnografii evreiskago narodonaseleniia v Rossii*. St. Petersburg, 1861.

Brafman, Iakov. *Kniga kagala*. 2 vols. St. Petersburg, 1875.

Brodovskii, I. *Evreiskaia nishcheta v Odesse*. Odessa, 1902.

Brutskus, Boris. *Statistiki evreiskago naseleniia: raspredelenie po territorii, demograficheskie i kul'turnye priznaki evreiskago naseleniia po perepisi 1897 g.* St. Petersburg, 1909.

Bureau für Statistik der Juden. *Die sozialen Verhältnisse der Juden in Russland*. Berlin-Charlottenburg: Jüdischer Verlag, 1906.

Craigie, David. "On the Progress of Cholera through the West of Russia to Poland." *Supplement to the Edinburgh Medical and Surgical Journal* 37 (February 1832): cxxxii–cli.

Czerniaków, Adam. *The Warsaw Diary of Adam Czerniakow: Prelude to Doom*. Edited by Raul Hilberg, Stanislaw Staron, and Joseph Kermish. New York: Stein & Day, 1979.

Darewski, Israel Nahum. *Le-korot ha-yehudim be-kiyov*. Berdichev: H. Y. Sheftil, 1902.

Dembovetskii, A. S. *Opyt opisaniia Mogilevskoi gubernii v istoricheskom, fiziko-geograficheskom, etnograficheskom, promyshlennom . . . otnosheniiakh*. 3 vols. Mogilev: Tip. Gub. pravleniia, 1882.

Dik, Ayzik M. *Di nakht fun tes-vav kislev*. Vilna, 1867.

Dillon, Emile Joseph. *The Jews in Russia*. [London], 1890.

Dov Baer ben Samuel. *In Praise of the Baal Shem Tov = (Shivhei Ha-Besht): The Earliest Collection of Legends about the Founder of Hasidism*. Edited by Dan Ben-Amos and Jerome R. Mintz. Northvale, NJ: Jason Aronson, 1993.

———. *Sefer shivhei ha-besht*. Edited by Samuel A. Horodezky. Berlin: Ayanot, 1922.

Dubnow, Simon, ed. *Pinkas ha-medinah o pinkas va'ad ha-kehilot ha-rashiyot bi-medinat lita*. Berlin: Ayanot, 1925.

"Evreiskaia obshchestvennaia meditsina g. Vil'ny." *Evreiskii meditsinskii golos*, nos. 3–4 (1910): 100–135.

35 yor tetigkeyt fun keshenever yesoymim-hoyz far inglekh (1900–1935). [Kishinev]: [Tekhnik], [1936].

Fishberg, Maurice. *The Jews: A Study of Race and Environment*. New York: Walter Scott, 1911.

Friedberg, A. S. *Sefer ha-zikhronot*. 2 vols. Warsaw: Shuldberg ve-shutafo, 1899.

Gaster, Moses, ed. *Ma'aseh Book*. 2 vols. Philadelphia: Jewish Publication Society of America, 1934.

Ginsburg, Saul M., and P. S. Marek, eds. *Evreiskie narodnye pesni v Rossii*. St. Petersburg: Redaktsiia "Voskhoda," 1901.

Goldfaden, Avrom. "The Two Kuni-Lemels." In *Landmark Yiddish Plays: A Critical Anthology*, edited by Jeremy Dauber and Joel Berkowitz, 201–45. Albany: State University of New York Press, 2006.

Gordin, Jacob. *Khashe [Khasye] di yesoyme: a drame in 4 akten*. Warsaw: Ferlag di "yudishe bihne," 1907.

Grade, Chaim. *My Mother's Sabbath Days: A Memoir*. Translated by Channa Kleinerman Goldstein and Inna Hecker. New York: Knopf, 1986.

Greenfield, Patrick, and Sarah Marsh. "Revealed: Homeless People Given One-Way Tickets to Other Areas." *Guardian*, December 28, 2018.

Halfan, Avraham Matityahu. *Tal orot*. Odessa, 1890.

Harkavy, Alexander. *Navaredok: ihr historye un ihr hayntiger leben*. New York: Navaredoker hilf-komitet in Nyu York, 1921.

Hartland, E. Sidney. "The Sin-Eater." *Folklore* 3, no. 2 (1892): 145–57.

Heine, Heinrich. *The Works of Heinrich Heine*. Translated by Charles Godfrey Leland. 20 vols. New York: Croscup & Sterling, 1892.

Henis, Uri. *Temimei derekh: sipurim me-olam ha-hasidut*. Jerusalem: Ahi'ever, 1959.

Herschberg, A. S. *Pinkes byalistok: grunt-materyaln tsu der geshikhte fun di yidn in byalistok biz nokh der ershter velt-milkhome*. Edited by Yudel Mark. 2 vols. New York, 1949.

Hersh, L. "Di farbrekherishkayt bay der yidisher un nit-yidisher bafelkerung fun der poylisher republik." *Ekonomishe shriftn* 2 (1932): 174–200.

Hippler, Fritz, dir. *Der ewige Jude: ein Dokumentarfilm über das Weltjudentum = The Eternal Jew*. Deutsche Film Gesellschaft, 1940.

Hirshovitz, Abraham Eliezer. *Otsar kol minhagei yeshurun*. St. Louis, MO, 1919.

Ianovskii, S. Ia. "Evreiskaia blagotvoritel'nost'." *Trudovaia pomoshch'* 12 (1902): 570–615.

Imperatorskoe russkoe geograficheskoe obshchestvo. *Trudy Etnografichesko-statis- ticheskoi ekspeditsii v Zapadno-Russkii krai snariazhennoi Imperatorskim Russkim geograficheskim obshchestvom (IUgo-Zapadnyi otdel); materialy i izsledovaniia.* Ed- ited by Pavel Chubinskii. 7 vols. St. Petersburg, 1872.

Jewish Colonization Association. *Recueil de matériaux sur la situation économique des Israélites de Russie, d'après l'enquête de la Jewish Colonization Association.* 2 vols. Paris: F. Alcan, 1906.

Karpinowitz, Abraham. "Shibele's Lottery Ticket." In *Vilna My Vilna: Stories,* trans- lated by Helen Mintz, 41–52. Syracuse, NY: Syracuse University Press, 2016.

Kolp, Tsvi Hirsh Lifshits. *Sefer mi-dor le-dor.* Warsaw: N. Sokolov, 1901.

Kopff, Wiktor. *Wspomnienia z ostatnich lat Rzeczypospolitej Krakowskiej.* Kraków: Druk. "Czasu," 1906.

Kotik, Yekhezkel. *Journey to a Nineteenth-Century Shtetl: The Memoirs of Yekhezkel Kotik.* Translated by David Assaf. Detroit: Wayne State University Press in co- operation with the Diaspora Research Institute, Tel Aviv University, 2002.

———. *Mayne zikhroynes.* Vol. 1. Warsaw: Klal-farlag, 1913. Vol. 2. Berlin: Klal- farlag, 1922.

Kovenskii evreiskii sirotskii dom imeni uchenago ravvina Itskhok-Elkhonona Spe- ktora. *Otchet . . . za vse vremia ego sushchestvovaniia do 1-go Ianvaria 1907 goda.* Kovna [Kaunas], 1907.

Levanda, Lev. "Neskol'ko slov o evreiakh Zapadnago kraia Rossii." *Razsvet,* no. 1 (May 27, 1860).

Levinson, Avrom. "A natsionaler khov." In *Dos elendste kind,* edited by M. Shneyor- son, 14–22. Warsaw: CENTOS, 1927.

Lipiets, Meir Yehiel. *Sefer ha-mat'amim.* Warsaw, 1890.

———. *Sefer ha-mat'amim he-hadash.* Warsaw, 1895.

Litvin, A. "Der beykier bokhur-'bal-shem'." In *Yudishe neshomes,* 6: 1–5. New York: Farlag folksbildung, 1916.

———. "Tsebrokhene neshomes." In *Yudishe neshomes,* vol. 2 (bound together with vol. 1). New York: Farlag folksbildung, 1916.

Margolis, O. *Geshikhte fun yidn in rusland: etyudn un dokumentn.* Moscow: Tsentraler felker-farlag fun F.S.S.R., 1930.

Marmor, Kalman. *Mayn lebns-geshikhte.* 2 vols. New York: Ikuf, 1959.

Melamed, Samuel Max. "The Hekdesh and Its People." *American Jewish Chronicle,* April 6, 1917, 2.

Nahman of Bratslav. *The Tales.* Translated by Arnold J. Band. New York: Paulist Press, 1978.

Neugroschel, Joachim, ed. *The Dybbuk and the Yiddish Imagination: A Haunted Reader*. Syracuse, NY: Syracuse Press, 2000.

Obshchestvo popecheniia o bednykh i bezpriiutnykh detiakh g. Belostoka, *Ustav Obshchestva . . . g. Belostoka*. Bialystok, Poland, 1905.

Opatoshu, Joseph. "A khasene oyfn beys-oylem." In id., *Gezamelte verk*, 12: 100–105. Vilna: B. Kletskin, 1931.

Paulizky, Friedrich, and Bezalel Judah Eliasberg. *Marpe la-am*. Zhitomir: A. S. Shodov, 1868.

Pavlovskaia, L. *Kholernye gody v Rossii: istoricheskii ocherk*. St. Petersburg: Izd. K. L. Rikkera, 1893.

Peretz, I. L. "Be-agaf ha-meshuga'im." *Ha-tsefirah* 23, no. 195 (September 2, 1896): 948; no. 196 (September 3, 1896): 952; no. 198 (Sepember 6, 1896): 962–63.

——. "Fun dul-hoyz." In Peretz, *Ale verk fun y. l. perets*, 6: 206–38. Vilna: Vilner farlag fun b. kletskin, 1920.

——. "The Mad Talmudist." In *A Treasury of Yiddish Stories*, edited by Irving Howe, Eliezer Greenberg, and Ben Shahn, translated by Irving Howe and Eliezer Greenberg, rev. and updated ed., 234–42. New York: Viking Press, 1989.

——. "Der meshugener batlen." In Peretz, *Ale verk*, 2: 18–29. New York: CYCO, 1947.

——. *Ver es vil nisht, shtarbt nisht oyf kholi-ra*. Warsaw: Varshoyer yudishen hilfs komitet gegen kholi-ra, 1893.

Pinkerton, Robert. *Russia, or, Miscellaneous Observations on the Past and Present State of That Country and Its Inhabitants*. London: Seeley & Sons, 1833.

Pinski, David. "Cripples." In *Ten Plays*, translated by Isaac Goldberg, 77–86. New York: B. W. Huebsch, 1920.

Rechtman, Abraham. "Khasen-kale-kvorim." In *Yidishe etnografye un folklor: zikhroynes vegn der etnografisher ekspeditsye, ongefirt fun sh. an-ski*, 169–71. Buenos Aires: Yidisher visnshaftlekher institut, 1958.

——. *Yidishe etnografye un folklor: zikhroynes vegn der etnografisher ekspeditsye, ongefirt fun sh. an-ski*. Buenos Aires: Yidisher visnshaftlekher institut, 1958.

Rokhlin, L. L. *Mestechko Krasnopol'e Mogilevskoi gub.: opyt statistiko-ekonomicheskago opisaniia tipichnago mestechka cherty evreiskoi osedlosti*. St. Petersburg, 1909.

——. "O evreiskikh lechebnykh zavedeniiakh v Rossii (Statisticheskie zametki)." *Evreiskii meditsinskii golos*, no. 1 (1908): 5–16.

Rombro, Ia. "Kholernaia svad'ba." *Voskhod* 4, no. 6 (June) (1884): 10–45.

Rosenberg, Leo. "Armenwesen und Soziale Fürsorge im Ostjudentum." *Der Jude* 1, no. 11 (February 1917): 737–50; 2, no. 5–6 (1917–18): 321–39.

Rülf, I. *Drei Tage in Jüdisch-Russland: Ein Cultur- und Sittenbild*. Frankfurt a/M.: J. Kauffmann, 1882.

Rymanower, Zevi Hirsh. *Sefer be'erot ha-mayim*. Przemyśl, 1894.

Samuels, David. "A Last Conversation with Aharon Appelfeld." *Tablet*, January 5, 2018. www.tabletmag.com/jewish-arts-and-culture/books/228475/last-conversation-aharon-appelfeld. Accessed December 2, 2019.

Schammes, Jousep. *Minhagim de-k.k. vermaisa.* 2 vols. Jerusalem, 1648.

Seyfarth, Carly. *Aberglaube und Zauberei in der Volksmedizin Sachsens: ein Beitrag zur Volkskunde des Königreichs Sachsen.* Leipzig: Heims, 1913.

Shabad, Ts. "Meshugene koloniyes." *YIVO Bleter* 7 (1934): 265–67.

Singer, Israel Joshua. *Yoshe Kalb.* Warsaw: Grafia, 1932.

———. *Yoshe Kalb.* Translated by Maurice Samuel. New York: Schocken Books, 1988.

Subbotin, A. P. *V cherte evreiskoi osedlosti: otryvki iz ekonomicheskikh izsledovanii v Zapadnoi i IUgo-zapadnoi Rossii za leto 1887 g.* Vol. 1. 2 vols. St. Petersburg: Ekonomicheskii Zhurnal, 1888.

Towarzystwo Opieki nad ubogimi nerwowo i umysłowo chorymi Żydami. "Sprawozdanie z czynności Towarzystwa Opieki nad ubogimi nerwowo i umysłowo chorymi Żydami." Warsaw, 1906.

"Tramps, Mediæval and Modern." *Westminster Review* 129, no. 5 (May 1888): 587–99.

Trunk, Yehiel Yeshaia. *Poyln: My Life within Jewish Life in Poland, Sketches and Images.* Edited by Piotr Wróbel and Robert M. Shapiro. Translated by Anna Clarke. Toronto: University of Toronto Press, 2007.

———. *Poyln: zikhroynes un bilder.* Vol. 1. New York: Farlag medem-klub, 1944.

Tsherikover, E. "Der arkhiv fun shimen dubnov." *Historishe shriftn,* 1 (1929): 565–604.

Tsukerman, N. "Pinkes fun der pruzhener kehile." In *Pinkes fun der shtot Pruzhene.* Pruzhene: Pinkos, 1930.

Tuwim, Julian. "Little Jew-Boy." Translated by Jacob Sonntag. *Jewish Quarterly* 30, no. 4 (1983): 36.

Urinski, G. "A dokument vegn der kholere in pruzhene." In *Pinkes fun der shtot Prushene.* Pruzhene: Pinkos, 1930.

Ustav Obshchestva popecheniia o bednykh i bezpriiutnykh detiakh g. Belostoka. 1905.

Vanvild, M., ed. *Bay unz yuden: zamelbukh far folklor un filologye.* Warsaw: Farlag Pinkhes Graubard, 1923.

Vaserman, Rudolf. "Di bazunderkeytn fun der kriminalitet bay yidn." *Shriftn far ekonomik un statistik* I (1928): 122–28.

Vilenskaia obshchestvennaia evreiskaia bogadel'nia. *Otchet . . . za 1908 god.* [Vilna], 1909.

Viner, Meyer, ed. *Folklor-lider: naye materyaln-zamlung.* 2 vols. Moscow: Emes, 1936.

Vorobeichic, M. [Moshé Raviv-Vorobeichic]. *Rehov ha-yehudim be-vilnah: 65 temunot = Ein Ghetto im Osten (Wilna): 65 Bilder.* Zurich: Orell Füssli, 1931.

Want: 100 Postcards from the Collection of John Kasmin. London: Royal Academy of Arts, 2013.

Waszyński, Michał, dir. *Der dibek (Dybuk).* 1937. *The Dybbuk = Der Dibuk.* Waltham, MA: National Center for Jewish Film, 2007.

Weinreich, Beatrice, ed. *Yiddish Folktales.* New York: Pantheon Books, 2007.

YIVO Etnografishe komisye. *Vos iz azoyns yidishe etnografye? hantbikhl far zamler.* Vilna: [Yivo], 1929.

Yudishe shprikhverter un redensarten: folshtendige groyse oysgabe. Edited by Ignatz Bernstein. Warsaw: Universal, 1912.

Zelenskii, I. *Materialy dlia geografii i statistiki Rossii: Minskaia guberniia.* 2 vols. St. Petersburg, 1864.

Zweig, Arnold. *Das ostjüdische Antlitz.* 1920. Reprint. Wiesbaden: Fourier, 1988. Edited and translated by Noah Isenberg as *The Face of East European Jewry* (Berkeley: University of California Press, 2004).

Yizkor Book Literature

Bat, Luba (Atkin). "Through Tears and Laughter (Personal Memoir)." Children of Pruzany and the Surrounding Area. http://cpsa.info/pruzany/luba_bat.htm. Accessed December 2, 2019.

Blatman, Leon S. "The Wedding at the Cemetery." In *Kamenetz-Podolsk: A Memorial to a Jewish Community Annihilated by the Nazis in 1941*, edited by Leon S. Blatman, 85–86. New York: n.p., 1966.

Domnits, Barukh. "Mukei goral." In *Pinkas slutsk u-venoteha*, edited by Nahum Hinits and Shimshon Nahmani, 132. Tel Aviv: Yizkor Book Committee, 1962.

Elboym, Yankev [Yakov Elboim]. "Dray doyres vaser-treger." In *Sefer-yizkor li-kehilat radomsk veha-sevivah*, edited by L. Losh, 156. Tel-Aviv: Irgun yots'e radomsk be-yisra'el, 1967. Translated as "Three Generations of Water Carriers," in *Memorial Book of the Community of Radomsk and Vicinity*, translated by Gloria Berkenstat Freund. Accessed May 16, 2017. http://www.jewishgen.org/Yizkor/Radomsko/rad144.html#Generations. Accessed December 2, 2019.

Garmi (Grimtlikht), Yisrael. "Ha-hupah ha-shehorah." In *Sefer yizkor le-kehilat luboml*, edited by Berl Kagan, 89–90. Tel Aviv, 1974.

Kalman Lichtenstein. "Ha-bahur mi-beyki." In *Pinkas slonim*, 124–25. Tel Aviv: Irgun olei slonim be-yisra'el, 1961.

Khazen, M. "A khupe ofn beys-oylem." In *Shumsk: sefer zikaron le-kedoshe shumsk she-nispu be-sho'at ha-natsim bi-shenat 1942*, edited by Chaim Rabin, 382–86. Tel Aviv: n.p., 1968.

Krumerkop, Nokhem. "Der yidisher yishev in tarnogrod." In *Yizker-bukh: nokh der khorev-gevorener yidisher kehile tarnogrod*, edited by Shimon Kanc, 51–118. Tel Aviv: Tarnogroder landslayt in yisroel, 1966.

Kugelmass, Jack, and Jonathan Boyarin, eds. *From a Ruined Garden: The Memorial Books of Polish Jewry*. New York: Schocken Books, 1983.

Oswiecim; Auschwitz Memorial Book (Oświęcim, Poland). Translation of *Sefer Oshpitsin: Oshviyents'im-Oshvits*, edited by Hayim Wolnerman, Aviezer Burstim, and Meir Simon Geshuri. Jerusalem: Oshpitsin Society, 1977. www.jewishgen.org/yizkor/oswiecim1/Oswiecim.html. Accessed December 2, 2019.

Rabin, H., and Matityahu Shpergel, eds. "Motele: tipshah shel lizhansk." In *Lizhansk: sefer zikaron li-kedoshe lizhansk she-nispu be-sho'at ha-natsim*, 236–38. [Tel Aviv]: Irgun olei lizhansk be-yisra'el, 1969.

Rosin, Yosef, and Esther Etinger. "Shkud." In *Pinkas ha-kehilot. Lita*, edited by Dov Levin and Yosef Rosin, 690–93. Jerusalem: Yad Vashem, 1996.

Rosovsky, Selik. "Remembering Bobruisk." Translated by Alex Ross. *Belarus SIG Newsletter*, no. 5 (February 3, 2000). www.jewishgen.org/Belarus/newsletters/mogilev/RememberBobruisk/index.html. Accessed December 2, 2019.

Shevah, Chaim. "Ha-dibuk." In *Piesk ve-most: sefer yizkor*, 150–52. Tel Aviv, 1975.

Shtein, A. Sh., ed. "Di meshugene sore." In *Pinkas Bendin*, 150–51. Tel Aviv: Hotsa'at irgun yots'e bendin be-yisra'el, 1959.

Spergel, Matityahu. "Motteleh—The Fool of Lizhensk." In *Memorial Book of the Martyrs of Lezajsk Who Perished in the Holocaust (Leżajsk, Poland)*, translated by Zygmunt Frankel, Jerrold Landau, Bat-Zion Susskind, and Tuvia Litzman. www.jewishgen.org/Yizkor/Lezajsk/lez234.html. Accessed December 2, 2019.

Taytl, Pinye. "A 'shvartse' khasene in apt." In *Apt (Opatow); sefer zikaron le-ir va-em be-yisrael*, edited by Z. Yasheev, 106–7. Tel Aviv: Apt Organizations in Israel, U.S.A., Canada, and Brazil, 1966.

Weissbrod, Abraham. *Death of a Shtetl*. Translation by Lusia Milch and Joseph Kofler of *Es Shtarbt a Shtetl; Megiles Skalat*. Munich: Central Historical Commission of the Central Committee of Liberated Jews in the American Zone of Germany, 1948. www.jewishgen.org/yizkor/Skalat1/ska040.html. Accessed December 2, 2019.

Wolnerman, Hayim, Aviezer Burstim, Meir Simon Geshuri, and Natan Goldfinger, eds. "Ayarati." In *Sefer Oshpitsin: Oshviyents'im-Oshvits*, 371–76. Jerusalem: Irgun yots'ei oshpitsin be-yisra'el, 1977.

Secondary Literature

Abrams, Judith. *Judaism and Disability: Portrayals in Ancient Texts from the Tanach through the Bavli*. Washington, DC: Gallaudet University Press, 1998.

Abramson, Henry. *A Prayer for the Government: Ukrainians and Jews in Revolutionary*

Times, 1917–1920. Cambridge, MA: Distributed by Harvard University Press for the Harvard Ukrainian Research Institute and Center for Jewish Studies, Harvard University, 1999.

Adam, Thomas. *Philanthropy, Patronage, and Civil Society: Experiences from Germany, Great Britain, and North America*. Bloomington: Indiana University Press, 2004.

Adams, Rachel. *Sideshow U.S.A.: Freaks and the American Cultural Imagination*. Chicago: University of Chicago Press, 2001.

Adeeb, Khalid. "Representations of Russia in Central Asian Jadid Discourse." In *Russia's Orient: Imperial Borderlands and Peoples, 1700–1917*, edited by Edward J. Lazzerini and Daniel R. Brower, 188–202. Bloomington: Indiana University Press, 1997.

Adelman, Rachel. "'Passing Strange'—Reading Transgender across Genre: Rabbinic Midrash and Feminist Hermeneutics on Esther." *Journal of Feminist Studies in Religion* 30, no. 2 (September 25, 2014): 81–97.

Adler, Eliyana R. *In Her Hands: The Education of Jewish Girls in Tsarist Russia*. Detroit: Wayne State University Press, 2011.

Afanasyeva, Anna. "Quarantines and Copper Amulets: The Struggle against Cholera in the Kazakh Steppe in the Nineteenth Century." *Jahrbücher für Geschichte Osteuropas* 61, no. 4 (2013): 489–512.

Aleksiun, Natalia. "Training a New Generation of Jewish Historians: Majer Bałaban's Seminar on the History of Polish Jews." In *Zwischen Graetz und Dubnow: Jüdische Historiographie in Ostmitteleuropa im 19. und 20. Jahrhundert*, edited by François Guesnet. Leipzig: Akademische Verlagsanstalt, 2009.

Alexander, Edward. *Isaac Bashevis Singer: A Study of the Short Fiction*. Boston: Twayne, 1990.

Aschheim, Steven E. *Brothers and Strangers: The East European Jew in German and German Jewish Consciousness, 1800–1923*. Madison: University of Wisconsin Press, 1982.

Ashley, Susan A. *"Misfits" in Fin-de-Siècle France and Italy: Anatomies of Difference*. London: Bloomsbury Academic, 2017.

Assaf, David. *Untold Tales of the Hasidim: Crisis and Discontent in the History of Hasidism*. Translated by Dena Ordan. Waltham, MA: Brandeis University Press and University Press of New England, 2010.

Backhaus, Fritz. "'Im Heckhuß die Lahmen, Blinden, Hungerleider . . .': Die sozialen Institutionen in der Frankfurter Judengasse." In *Juden und Armut in Mittel- und Osteuropa*, edited by Stefi Jersch-Wenzel, Gertrud Pickhan, Andreas Reinke, Desanka Schwara, and François Guesnet, 31–54. Cologne: Böhlau, 2000.

Bakhtin, Mikhail. *Rabelais and His World*. Translated by Hélène Iswolsky. Cambridge, MA: MIT Press, 1968.

Bałaban, Majer. *Dzieje Żydów w Krakowie i na Kazimierzu (1304–1868)*. 2 vols. Kraków, 1912.

———. "Obyczajowość i życie prywatne Żydów w dawnej Rzeczypospolitej." In *Żydzi w Polsce odrodzonej: działalność społeczna, gospodarcza, oświatowa i kulturalna*, edited by Ignacy Schiper, 1: 345–74. Warsaw, 1932.

Baldwin, Peter. *Contagion and the State in Europe, 1830–1930*. New York: Cambridge University Press, 1999.

Baranowski, Bohdan. *Ludzie gościńca w XVII–XVIII w.* Łódź: Wydawn. Łódzkie, 1986.

Barber, E. J. W. *The Dancing Goddesses: Folklore, Archaeology, and the Origins of European Dance*. New York: Norton, 2013.

Bar-Levav, Avriel. "We Are Where We Are Not: The Cemetery in Jewish Culture." *Jewish Studies*, no. 41 (2002): 15–46.

Baron, Salo. *The Jewish Community: Its History and Structure to the American Revolution*. 3 vols. Philadelphia: Jewish Publication Society of America, 1942.

———. *The Russian Jew between Tsars and Soviets*. New York: Macmillan, 1964.

Beizer, M. (Mikhail). *Relief in Time of Need: Russian Jewry and the Joint, 1914–24*. Bloomington, IN: Slavica Publishers, 2015.

Belova, Ol'ga. "Narodnaia magiia v regionakh etnokul'turnykh kontaktov slavian i evreev." In *Narodnaia meditsina i magiia v slavianskoi i evreiskoi kul'turnoi traditsii: sbornik statei*, edited by O. V. Belova. Moscow: Tsentr nauchnykh rabotnikov i prepodavatelei iudaiki v vuzakh "Sefer" and Institut slavianovedeniia Rossiiskoi Akademii Nauk, 2004.

Bergmann, Yehuda. *Ha-tsedakah be-yisra'el: toldoteha u-mosdoteha*. Jerusalem, 1944.

Berkowitz, Michael. *The Crime of My Very Existence: Nazism and the Myth of Jewish Criminality*. Berkeley: University of California Press, 2007.

Berliant, Sandra. "Guide to the Papers of Eliyahu Guttmacher (1796–1874), 1840s–1874," Guide to the YIVO Archives (2007). www.yivoarchives.org/index.php?p=collections/findingaid&id=23957&q=. Accessed December 2, 2019.

Biale, David. *Eros and the Jews: From Biblical Israel to Contemporary America*. Berkeley: University of California Press, 1997.

Bilu, Yoram. "Dybbuk and Maggid: Two Cultural Patterns of Altered Consciousness in Judaism." *AJS Review* 21, no. 2 (1996): 341–66.

———. "Ha-dibuk ba-yahadut: hafra'ah nafshit ke-mash'av tarbuti." *Jerusalem Studies in Jewish Thought / Mehkerei yerushalayim be-mahshevet yisra'el* 2, no. 4 (1983): 529–63.

———. "The Taming of the Deviants and Beyond: An Analysis of Dybbuk Possession and Exorcism in Judaism." In *Spirit Possession in Judaism: Cases and Contexts from the Middle Ages to the Present*, edited by Matt Goldish, 27–40. Detroit: Wayne State University Press, 2003.

Bleich, J. David. "Mental Incompetence and Its Implications in Jewish Law." *Journal of Halacha and Contemporary Society* 1, no. 2 (1981): 123–43.

Bornstein, Aharon. *Mi-kabtsanim le-dorshei avodah: yehudim navadim be-germanyah, 1869–1914.* Tel Aviv: n.p., 1987.

Boyarin, Daniel. "Homophobia and the Postcoloniality of the 'Jewish Science.'" In *Queer Theory and the Jewish Question*, edited by Daniel Boyarin, Daniel Itzkovitz, and Ann Pellegrini, 166–98. Columbia University Press, 2003.

Bradley, Joseph. *Muzhik and Muscovite: Urbanization in Late Imperial Russia.* Berkeley: University of California Press, 1985.

Bremmer, Jan N. *Greek Religion and Culture, the Bible, and the Ancient Near East.* Boston: Brill, 2008.

Bremner, Robert Hamlett. *Giving: Charity and Philanthropy in History.* New Brunswick, NJ: Transaction Publishers, 1994.

Breuer, Mordechai, and Michael Graetz. *Tradition and Enlightenment, 1600–1780.* Translated by William Temple. Vol. 1 of *German-Jewish History in Modern Times*, edited by Michael A. Meyer and Michael Brenner. New York: Columbia University Press, 1996.

Briggs, Asa. "Cholera and Society in the Nineteenth Century." *Past & Present*, no. 19 (April 1, 1961): 76–96.

Brintlinger, Angela. "Introduction: Approaching Russian Madness." In *Madness and the Mad in Russian Culture*, edited by Angela Brintlinger and Ilya Vinitsky, 3–19. Toronto: University of Toronto Press, 2007

Bronisław Geremek. *The Margins of Society in Late Medieval Paris.* New York: Cambridge University Press, 1987.

Bronner, Leila Leah. "Esther Revisited: An Aggadic Approach." In *A Feminist Companion to Esther, Judith and Susanna*, edited by Athalya Brenner. Sheffield, England: Sheffield Academic Press, 1995.

Brower, Daniel R. "Islam and Ethnicity: Russian Colonial Policy in Turkestan." In *Russia's Orient: Imperial Borderlands and Peoples, 1700–1917*, edited by Edward J. Lazzerini and Daniel R. Brower, 115–35. Bloomington: Indiana University Press, 1997.

Brown, Julie V. "Peasant Survival Strategies in Late Imperial Russia: The Social Uses of the Mental Hospital." *Social Problems* 34, no. 4 (1987): 311–29.

———. "Social Influences on Psychiatric Theory and Practice in Late Imperial Russia." In *Health and Society in Revolutionary Russia*, edited by Susan Gross Solomon and John F. Hutchinson, 27–44. Bloomington: Indiana University Press, 1990.

———. "Societal Responses to Mental Disorders in Prerevolutionary Russia." In *The Disabled in the Soviet Union: Past and Present, Theory and Practice*, edited by

William O. McCagg and Lewis H. Siegelbaum, 13–37. Pittsburgh: University of Pittsburgh Press, 1989.

———. "A Sociohistorical Perspective on Deinstitutionalization: The Case of Late Imperial Russia." *Research in Law, Deviance & Social Control* 7 (1985): 167–88.

Brown, Rupert. *Prejudice: Its Social Psychology.* Cambridge, MA: Blackwell, 1995.

Budnitskii, Oleg V. *Russian Jews between the Reds and the Whites, 1917–1920.* Philadelphia: University of Pennsylvania Press, 2012.

Chajes, Jeffrey Howard. *Between Worlds: Dybbuks, Exorcists, and Early Modern Judaism.* Philadelphia: University of Pennsylvania Press, 2003.

Chevalier, Louis, ed. *Le choléra, la première épidémie du XIXe siècle.* La Roche-sur-Yon: Impr. centrale de l'Ouest, 1958.

Clark, Katerina. *Mikhail Bakhtin.* Cambridge, MA: Belknap Press of Harvard University Press, 1984.

Cohen, Israel. *Vilna.* Philadelphia: Jewish Publication Society of America, 1943.

Cohen, Mark R. *Poverty and Charity in the Jewish Community of Medieval Egypt.* Princeton, NJ: Princeton University Press, 2005.

———. *The Voice of the Poor in the Middle Ages: An Anthology of Documents from the Cairo Geniza.* Princeton, NJ: Princeton University Press, 2013.

Collins, Felicity. "Brazen Brides, Grotesque Daughters, Treacherous Mothers: Women's Funny Business in Australian Cinema from *Sweetie* to *Holy Smoke*." Senses of Cinema, December 2002. http://sensesofcinema.com/2002/feature-articles/women_funny_oz. Accessed December 3, 2019.

Constantinou, Stavroula. "Grotesque Bodies in Hagiographical Tales: The Monstrous and the Uncanny in Byzantine Collections of Miracle Stories." *Dumbarton Oaks Papers* 64 (2010): 43–54.

Covey, Herbert C. *Social Perceptions of People with Disabilities in History.* Springfield, IL: Charles C. Thomas, 1998.

Crowe, David. *A History of the Gypsies of Eastern Europe and Russia.* New York: Palgrave Macmillan, 2007.

Cuffel, Alexandra. *Gendering Disgust in Medieval Religious Polemic.* Notre Dame, IN: University of Notre Dame Press, 2007.

Dan, Joseph. *Ha-sipur ha-hasidi.* Jerusalem: Keter yerushalayim, 1975.

Dancoine, Pierre. *Mendiants, vagabonds et prostituées dans le nord au XVIIIème siècle.* Steenvoorde: Foyer culturel de l'Houtland, 1996.

Dauber, Jeremy. *In the Demon's Bedroom: Yiddish Literature and the Early Modern.* New Haven, CT: Yale University Press, 2010.

Davis, John P. "The Struggle with Cholera in Tsarist Russia and the Soviet Union, 1892–1927." Ph.D diss., University of Kentucky, 2012.

Delaporte, François. *Disease and Civilization: The Cholera in Paris, 1832.* Cambridge, MA: MIT Press, 1986.

Deutsch, Nathaniel. *The Jewish Dark Continent: Life and Death in the Russian Pale of Settlement.* Cambridge, MA: Harvard University Press, 2011.

Douglas, Mary. *Purity and Danger: An Analysis of the Concepts of Pollution and Taboo.* London: Ark, 1984.

Dubnow, Simon. *History of the Jews in Russia and Poland.* 3 vols. Philadelphia: Jewish Publication Society of America, 1916.

Durey, Michael. *The Return of the Plague: British Society and the Cholera, 1831–2.* Dublin: Gill & Macmillan; New York: Humanities Press, 1979.

Dynner, Glenn. *Yankel's Tavern: Jews, Liquor, and Life in the Kingdom of Poland.* New York: Oxford University Press, 2014.

Efron, John M. *Defenders of the Race: Jewish Doctors and Race Science in Fin-de-Siècle Europe.* New Haven, CT: Yale University Press, 1994.

———. *Medicine and the German Jews: A History.* New Haven, CT: Yale University Press, 2001.

Eliach, Yaffa. *There Once Was a World: A Nine-Hundred-Year Chronicle of the Shtetl of Eishyshok.* Boston: Little Brown, 1998.

Elior, Rachel. *Dybbuks and Jewish Women in Social History, Mysticism and Folklore.* Jerusalem: Urim Publications, 2008.

Elizabeth Grosz. "Intolerable Ambiguity: Freaks as/at the Limit." In *Freakery: Cultural Spectacles of the Extraordinary Body,* edited by Rosemarie Garland-Thomson, 55–66. New York: New York University Press, 1996.

Engelstein, Laura. *Russia in Flames: War, Revolution, Civil War, 1914–1921.* New York: Oxford University Press, 2018.

Ephraim Shoham-Steiner. *On the Margins of a Minority: Leprosy, Madness, and Disability among the Jews of Medieval Europe.* Translated by Haim Watzman. Detroit: Wayne State University Press, 2014.

Epstein, Lisa. "Caring for the Soul's House: The Jews of Russia and Health Care, 1860–1914." Ph.D diss., Yale University, 1995.

Erica T. Lehrer. *Na szczęście to Żyd: Polskie figurki Żydów / Lucky Jews: Poland's Jewish figurines.* Translated by Joanna Warchoł. Kraków: Korporacja Ha!art, 2014.

Etkes, Immanuel. "Mekomam shel ha-magiyah u-va'ale shem ba-hevrah ha-ashkenazit be-mifneh ha-me'ot ha-17-ha-18." *Tsiyon* 60, no. 1 (1995): 69–104.

———. *Rabbi Israel Salanter and the Mussar Movement: Seeking the Torah of Truth.* Philadelphia: Jewish Publication Society, 1993.

Evans, Richard J. *Death in Hamburg: Society and Politics in the Cholera Years, 1830–1910.* Oxford: Clarendon Press, 1987.

———. "Introduction: The 'Dangerous Classes' in Germany from the Middle Ages to the Twentieth Century." In *The German Underworld: Deviants and Outcasts in German History,* edited by Richard J. Evans, 1–28. New York: Routledge, 1988.

———. "Review Article: Blue Funk and Yellow Peril: Cholera and Society in

Nineteenth-Century France." *European History Quarterly* 20, no. 1 (January 1, 1990): 111–26.

Evreiskaia entsiklopediia: svod znanii o evreistve i ego kulture v proshlom i nastoiash-chem. 16 vols. St. Petersburg: Obschestvo dlia nauchnykh evreiskikh izdanii i iz-vo Brokgauz-Efron, 1906–13.

Feldman, David M. "Deafness and Jewish Law and Tradition." In *The Deaf Jew in the Modern World*, edited by Jerome D. Schein and Lester J. Waldman, 12–23. New York: Ktav Publishing House for the New York Society for the Deaf, 1986.

Foucault, Michel. *Madness and Civilization: A History of Insanity in the Age of Reason.* Translated by Richard Howard. London: Routledge, 2001.

Frančić, Mirosław. *Ludzie luźni w osiemnastowiecznym Krakowie.* Wrocław: Zakład Narodowy im. Ossolińskich, 1967.

Freeze, ChaeRan Y. *Jewish Marriage and Divorce in Imperial Russia.* Hanover, NH: Brandeis University Press and University Press of New England, 2002.

———. "Lilith's Midwives: Jewish Newborn Child Murder in Nineteenth-Century Vilna." *Jewish Social Studies* 16, no. 2 (2010): 1–27.

Freeze, ChaeRan Y., and Jay Michael Harris, eds. *Everyday Jewish Life in Imperial Russia: Select Documents, 1772—1914.* Waltham, MA: Brandeis University Press, 2013.

Freud, Sigmund. *The Uncanny.* Translated by David McLintock. New York: Penguin Books, 2003.

Frieden, Ken. *Classic Yiddish Fiction: Abramovitsh, Sholem Aleichem, and Peretz.* Albany: State University of New York Press, 1995.

Frieden, Nancy M. "The Russian Cholera Epidemic, 1892–93, and Medical Professionalization." *Journal of Social History* 10, no. 4 (1977): 538–59.

Friedman, Reena Sigman. *These Are Our Children: Jewish Orphanages in the United States, 1880–1925.* Hanover, NH: University Press of New England and Brandeis University Press, 1994.

Frisch, Ephraim. *An Historical Survey of Jewish Philanthropy.* New York: Cooper Square Publishers, 1969.

Frohman, Larry. *Poor Relief and Welfare in Germany from the Reformation to World War I.* New York: Cambridge University Press, 2008.

Gajerski, Stanislaw. "Szpitale żydowskie na Rusi Czerwonej w XVI–XVIII w." *Biuletyn Żydowskiego Instytutu Historycznego*, no. 4 (1979): 25–33.

Galai, Iu. G. *Nishchenstvo i brodiazhnichestvo v dorevoliutsionnoi Rossii: zakonodatel'nye i prakticheskie problemy.* Nizhnii Novgorod: Nizhegorodskaia pravovaia akademiia, 2012.

Geremek, Bronisrod: *Poverty: A History.* Oxford: Blackwell, 1994.

Gessen, Iulii. *Istoriia evreiskogo naroda v Rossii.* 2 vols. in one. Leningrad, 1925. Reprint, Moscow: Evreiiskii universitet, 1993.

Gilbert, Pamela K. *Cholera and Nation: Doctoring the Social Body in Victorian England*. Albany: State University of New York Press, 2008.

Gilman, Sander L. "Jews and Mental Illness: Medical Metaphors, Anti-semitism, and the Jewish Response." *Journal of the History of the Behavioral Sciences* 20, no. 2 (1984): 150–59.

———. *The Jew's Body*. New York: Routledge, 1991.

Ginsburg, Shoyl. "Vi unzere elter-zeydes hoben gekemft gegen der kholere-mageyfe." In id., *Historishe verk*, edited by Isaac Rivkind, 1: 229–37. New York: Shoyl ginzburg 70-yohriger yubiley komitet, 1937.

Glanz, Rudolf. *Geschichte des niederen jüdischen Volkes in Deutschland; eine Studie über historisches Gaunertum, Bettelwesen und Vagantentum*. New York: n.p., 1968.

Glick, Shmuel. *Or nagah alehem: ha-zikah she-ben minhagei nisu'in le-minhagei avelut be-masoret yisra'el*. Efrat, Israel: Keren Ori, 1997.

Goeing, Anja-Silvia. "Chandling the Scholar." H-Ideas, May 28, 2018. https://networks.h-net.org/node/6873/blog/premodern-universities/1871241/chandling-scholar. Accessed December 3, 2019.

Goldberg, Jakub. "Armut unter den Juden im alten Polen." In *Juden und Armut in Mittel- und Osteuropa*, edited by Stefi Jersch-Wenzel, Gertrud Pickhan, Andreas Reinke, Desanka Schwara, and François Guesnet, 71–89. Cologne: Böhlau, 2000.

Goldberg, Sylvie Anne. *Crossing the Jabbok: Illness and Death in Ashkenazi Judaism in Sixteenth- through Nineteenth-Century Prague*. Berkeley: University of California Press, 1996.

Goldstein, Bluma. *Enforced Marginality: Jewish Narratives on Abandoned Wives*. Berkeley: University of California Press, 2007.

Gottesman, Itzik Nakhmen. *Defining the Yiddish Nation: The Jewish Folklorists of Poland*. Detroit: Wayne State University Press, 2003.

Grill, Tobias. "Odessa's German Rabbi—The Paradigmatic Meaning of Simon Leon Schwabacher (1861–1888)." *Jahrbuch des Simon-Dubnow-Instituts* 2 (2003): 199–222.

Grochowski, Piotr. *Dziady: rzecz o wędrownych żebrakach i ich pieśniach*. Toruń, Poland: Wydawn. Naukowe Uniwersytetu Mikołaja Kopernika, 2009.

Guesnet, François. "Jüdische Armut und ihre Bekämpfung im Königreich Polen: Grundzüge und Entwicklungen im 19. Jahrhundert." In *Juden und Armut in Mittel- und Osteuropa*, edited by Stefi Jersch-Wenzel, Gertrud Pickhan, Andreas Reinke, Desanka Schwara, and François Guesnet. Cologne: Böhlau, 2000.

———. *Polnische Juden im 19. Jahrhundert: Lebensbedingungen, Rechtsnormen und Organisation im Wandel*. Cologne: Böhlau, 1998.

Guggenheim, Yacov. "Meeting on the Road: Encounters between German Jews and Christians on the Margins of Society." In *In and Out of the Ghetto:*

Jewish-Gentile Relations in Late Medieval and Early Modern Germany, edited by R. Po-chia Hsia and Hartmut Lehmann, 125–36. Washington, DC: German Historical Institute; Cambridge: Cambridge University Press, 1995.

———. "Von den Schalantjuden zu den Betteljuden: jüdische Armut in Mittel-europa in der Frühen Neuzeit." In *Juden und Armut in Mittel- und Osteuropa*, edited by Stefi Jersch-Wenzel, Gertrud Pickhan, Andreas Reinke, Desanka Schwara, and François Guesnet, 55–69. Cologne: Böhlau, 2000.

Gutting, Gary. "Foucault and the History of Madness." In *The Cambridge Companion to Foucault*, 2nd ed., edited by Gary Gutting, 47–70. New York: Cambridge University Press, 2006.

Halliday, Stephen. "Death and Miasma in Victorian London: An Obstinate Belief." *BMJ: British Medical Journal* 323, no. 7327 (December 22, 2001): 1469–71.

Halpern, Ben, and Jehuda Reinharz. *Zionism and the Creation of a New Society*. New York: Oxford University Press, 1998.

Halpern, Israel. "Havarot shel sho'avei mayim." In *Yehudim ve-yahadut be-mizrah eiropa: mehkarim be-toldotehem*, 186–94. Jerusalem: Magnes Press, 1968.

———. "Tosafot u-milu'im le-pinkas medinat lita (hotsa'at dubnov)." *Horev* 2, no. 1 (1935): 69–86.

Hamlin, Christopher. *Cholera: The Biography*. Oxford: Oxford University Press, 2009.

Hart, Mitchell B. *Social Science and the Politics of Modern Jewish Identity*. Stanford: Stanford University Press, 2000.

Hays, J. N. *Epidemics and Pandemics: Their Impacts on Human History*. Santa Barbara, CA: ABC-CLIO, 2005.

Henry, Barbara J. *Rewriting Russia: Jacob Gordin's Yiddish Drama*. Seattle: University of Washington Press, 2011.

Henze, Charlotte. *Disease, Health Care and Government in Late Imperial Russia: Life and Death on the Volga, 1823–1914*. Hoboken, NJ: Taylor & Francis, 2010.

Hippel, Wolfgang von. *Armut, Unterschichten, Randgruppen in der frühen Neuzeit*. Munich: Oldenbourg, 1995.

Hirshhoyt, Yekhiel. "Mendele Moykher-Sforim (Sholem-Yankev Abramovitsh)." In *Leksikon fun der nayer yidisher literatur*, vol. 4. New York: Congress for Jewish Culture, 1956.

Hitchcock, David. *Vagrancy in English Culture and Society, 1650–1750*. London: Bloomsbury Academic, 2016.

Hoberman, J. *Bridge of Light: Yiddish Film between Two Worlds*. Hanover, NH: Dartmouth College and University Press of New England in association with the National Center for Jewish Film, 2010.

Horn, Klaus-Peter, and Bianca Frohne. "On the Fluidity of 'Disability' in Medieval and Early Modern Societies: Opportunities and Strategies in a New Field of Research." In *The Imperfect Historian: Disability Histories in Europe*, edited by

Sebastian Barsch, Anne Klein, and Pieter Verstraete. Frankfurt a/M.: Peter Lang, 2013.

Horowitz, Elimelekh [Elliot]. "Va-yihyu aniyim (hagunim) benei veitekha: tsedakah, aniyim u-fiku'ah hevrati be-kehilot yehudei eiropa ben yemei ha-veinayim le-reishit ha-et ha-hadashah." In *Dat ve-khalkala: yahase gomlin*, edited by Menahem Ben-Sasson, 209–31. Jerusalem: Merkaz zalman shazar le-toldot yisra'el, 1995.

Horowitz, Elliott S. "Speaking to the Dead: Cemetery Prayer in Medieval and Early Modern Jewry." *Journal of Jewish Thought & Philosophy* 8, no. 2 (1999): 303–17.

Hundert, Gershon. *The Jews in a Polish Private Town*. Baltimore: Johns Hopkins University Press, 1992.

———. *Jews in Poland-Lithuania in the Eighteenth Century: A Genealogy of Modernity*. Berkeley: University of California Press, 2004.

———, ed. *The YIVO Encyclopedia of Jews in Eastern Europe*. 2 vols. New Haven, CT: Yale University Press, 2008.

Hutchinson, John F. *Politics and Public Health in Revolutionary Russia, 1890–1918*. Baltimore: Johns Hopkins University Press, 1990.

Hyman, Paula. *Gender and Assimilation in Modern Jewish History: The Roles and Representation of Women*. Seattle: University of Washington Press, 1995.

Iangoulova, Lia. "The *Osvidetel'stvovanie* and *Ispytanie* of Insanity: Psychiatry in Tsarist Russia." In *Madness and the Mad in Russian Culture*, edited by Angela Brintlinger and Ilya Vinitsky, 46–58. Toronto: University of Toronto Press, 2007.

Iastrebov, V. S. "Obshchaia psikhiatriia." In *Obshchaia psikhiatriia*, ed. A. S. Tiganov (1999). Nauchnyi tsentr psikhicheskogo zdorov'ia: biblioteka. http://psychiatry.ru/lib/53/book/28/chapter/101. Accessed December 3, 2019.

Ingleby, David. "Mental Health and Social Order." In *Social Control and the State*, edited by Stanley Cohen and Andrew Scull, 141–88. New York: St. Martin's Press, 1983.

Isenberg, Noah William. *Edgar G. Ulmer: A Filmmaker at the Margins*. Berkeley: University of California Press, 2014.

———. "To Pray Like a Dervish: Orientalist Discourse in Arnold Zweig's *The Face of East European Jewry*." In *Orientalism and the Jews*, edited by Ivan Davidson Kalmar and Derek Jonathan Penslar, 94–108. Waltham, MA: Brandeis University Press and University Press of New England, 2005.

Ivanov, Sergey A. *Holy Fools in Byzantium and Beyond*. New York: Oxford University Press, 2006.

Ivanov, Vladislav. "An-Sky, Evgeny Vakhtangov, and The Dybbuk." In *The Worlds of S. An-Sky: A Russian Jewish Intellectual at the Turn of the Century*, edited by

Gabriella Safran and Steven J. Zipperstein, 252–65. Stanford: Stanford University Press, 2006.

Kaplan, Beth. *Finding the Jewish Shakespeare: The Life and Legacy of Jacob Gordin.* Syracuse, NY: Syracuse University Press, 2007.

Kaspi, Y. "3 hatunot-mitsvah be-shedlits." *Reshumot,* n.s., 2 (1946): 101–2.

Kassow, Samuel D. "Jewish Communal Politics in Transition: The Vilna Kehile, 1919–1920." *YIVO Annual* 20 (1991): 61–92.

———. *Who Will Write Our History? Emanuel Ringelblum, the Warsaw Ghetto, and the Oyneg Shabes Archive.* Bloomington: Indiana University Press, 2007.

Katsnelson-Bank, Dafna. *Ha-shiga'on ba-sifrut ha-ivrit be-reshit ha-me'ah he-esrim.* Tel Aviv: Hotsa'at ha-kibuts ha-me'uhad, 2005.

Katz, Jacob. *Tradition and Crisis: Jewish Society at the End of the Middle Ages.* New York: New York University Press, 1993.

Kenez, Peter. "Pogroms and White Ideology in the Russian Civil War." In *Pogroms: Anti-Jewish Violence in Modern Russian History,* edited by John D. Klier and Shlomo Lambroza, 293–313. Cambridge: Cambridge University Press, 1991.

Kershaw, Ian. *Hitler, 1936–45: Nemesis.* New York: Norton, 2000.

Kiel, Mark W. "Vox Populi, Vox Dei: The Centrality of Peretz in Jewish Folkloristics." *Polin* 7 (1992): 89–120.

Kittredge, George Lyman. *Witchcraft in Old and New England.* New York: Russell & Russell, 1956.

Klausner, Israel. *Toldot ha-kehilah ha-ivrit be-vilnah.* Jerusalem: n.p., 1938.

———. *Vilnah, yerushalayim de-lita: dorot aharonim, 1881–1939.* Lohamei ha-geta'ot: Beit lohamei ha-geta'ot, 1983.

———. *Vilnah, yerushalayim de-lita: dorot rishonim, 1495–1881.* Lohamei ha-geta'ot: Beit lohamei ha-geta'ot, 1988.

Klier, John. *Imperial Russia's Jewish Question, 1855–1881.* New York: Cambridge University Press, 1995.

———. *Russia Gathers Her Jews: The Origins of the "Jewish Question" in Russia, 1772–1825.* DeKalb: Northern Illinois University Press, 1986.

Kobrin, Rebecca. *Jewish Bialystok and Its Diaspora.* Bloomington: Indiana University Press, 2010.

Kreiten, Irma. "A Colonial Experiment in Cleansing: The Russian Conquest of Western Caucasus, 1856–65." *Journal of Genocide Research* 11, no. 2–3 (2009): 213–41.

Kudlick, Catherine J. "Disability History: Why We Need Another 'Other.'" *American Historical Review* 108, no. 3 (June 2003): 763–93.

Kugelmass, Jack, and Jonathan Boyarin. "Introduction." In *From a Ruined Garden: The Memorial Books of Polish Jewry,* edited by Jack Kugelmass and Jonathan Boyarin, 1–48. New York: Schocken Books, 1983.

———. "Yizker Bikher and the Problem of Historical Veracity: An Anthropological Approach." In *The Jews of Poland Between Two World Wars*, edited by Israel Gutman, Ezra Mendelsohn, Jehuda Reinharz, and Chone Shmeruk, 519–35. Hanover, NH: Published for Brandeis University Press by University Press of New England, 1989.

Kuznitz, Cecile Esther. *YIVO and the Making of Modern Jewish Culture: Scholarship for the Yiddish Nation*. New York: Cambridge University Press, 2014.

Landis, Joseph C. "'Gimpl Tam' and the Perils of Translation." *Yiddish* 14, no. 2–3 (2006): 110–15.

Lederhendler, Eli. *The Road to Modern Jewish Politics: Political Tradition and Political Reconstruction in the Jewish Community of Tsarist Russia*. New York: Oxford University Press, 1989.

Levie Bernfeld, Tirtsah. *Poverty and Welfare among the Portuguese Jews in Early Modern Amsterdam*. Portland, OR: Littman Library of Jewish Civilization, 2012.

Levinski, Yomtov. "'Hatunot mageifah' be-minhagei ashkenaz." *Mahanayim*, no. 83 (1963): 60–63.

Levitats, Isaac. *The Jewish Community in Russia, 1772–1844*. New York: Octagon Books, 1970.

———. *The Jewish Community in Russia, 1844–1917*. Jerusalem: Posner & Sons, 1981.

Lewis, Justin Jaron. *Imagining Holiness: Classic Hasidic Tales in Modern Times*. Montreal: McGill–Queen's University Press, 2009.

"Lik na kholeru." *Etnohrafichnyi zbirnyk* 33 (1912): 228.

Lilientalowa, Regina. "Pieśni ludowe żydowskie." *Wisła: miesięcznik geograficzno-etnograficzny* 17, no. 5 (1903): 581–89.

———. "Wierzenia, przesady i praktyki ludu żydowskiego." *Wisła* 19, no. 2 (March–April) (1905): 148–76.

Lindenmeyr, Adele. *Poverty Is Not a Vice: Charity, Society, and the State in Imperial Russia*. Princeton, NJ: Princeton University Press, 1996.

Linton, Simi. "The Disability Studies Project: Broadening the Parameters of Diversity." In *End Results and Starting Points: Expanding the Field of Disability Studies*, edited by Elaine Makas and Lynn Schlesinger. Boston: Society for Disability Studies, 1996.

Lipsker, Avidav. "Ha-kalah ve-shiv'at ha-kabtsanim—le-she'elat mekorotav shel sipur-hamisgeret shel 'mayse meha-7 betlirs.'" *Jerusalem Studies in Jewish Folklore* 13–14 (1992): 229–48.

Litvak, Olga. *Conscription and the Search for Modern Russian Jewry*. Bloomington: Indiana University Press, 2006.

Longmore, Paul K., and Lauri Umansky. "Introduction: Disability History: From the Margins to the Mainstream." In *The New Disability History: American*

Perspectives, edited by Paul K. Longmore and Lauri Umansky, 1–29. New York: New York University Press, 2001.

Löwe, Heinz-Dietrich. "From Charity to Social Policy: The Emergence of Jewish 'Self-Help' Organizations in Imperial Russia, 1800–1914." *East European Jewish Affairs* 27, no. 2 (1997): 53–75.

Mahler, Raphael. *Hasidism and the Jewish Enlightenment: Their Confrontation in Galicia and Poland in the First Half of the Nineteenth Century*. Philadelphia: Jewish Publication Society of America, 1985.

Mandler, Peter, ed. *The Uses of Charity: The Poor on Relief in the Nineteenth-Century Metropolis*. Philadelphia: University of Pennsylvania Press, 1990.

Manor, Giora. "Extending the Traditional Wedding Dance: Inbal Dance Theater's 'Yemenite Wedding' and the 'Dance of the Beggars' in Habimah National Theater's 'Dybbuk.'" In *Seeing Israeli and Jewish Dance*, edited by Judith Brin Ingber, 213–21. Detroit: Wayne State University Press, 2011.

Marcus, Jacob R. *Communal Sick-Care in the German Ghetto*. Cincinnati: Hebrew Union College Press, 1947.

Mark, Zvi. "Dybbuk and Devekut in the *Shivhe Ha-Besht*: Towards a Phenomenology of Madness in Early Hasidism." In *Spirit Possession in Judaism: Cases and Contexts from the Middle Ages to the Present*, edited by Matt Goldish, 257–301. Detroit: Wayne State University Press, 2003.

Marx, Tzvi. *Disability in Jewish Law*. New York: Routledge, 2002.

Matthäus, Jürgen, and Emil Kerenji, eds. *Jewish Responses to Persecution, 1933–1946: A Source Reader*. Lanham, MD: Rowman & Littlefield, 2017.

McGrew, Roderick. *Russia and the Cholera, 1823–1832*. Madison: University of Wisconsin Press, 1965.

Meir, Natan M. "Charting the Outer Provinces of Jewry: The Study of East European Jewry's Margins." *POLIN: Studies in Polish Jewry* 29 (2017): 89–104.

———. "From Communal Charity to National Welfare: Jewish Orphanages in Eastern Europe before and after World War I." *East European Jewish Affairs* 39, no. 1 (April 1, 2009): 19–34.

———. "Home for the Homeless? The Hekdesh in Eastern Europe." In *Place in Modern Jewish Culture and Society*, edited by Richard I. Cohen, 3–16. Studies in Contemporary Jewry 30. New York: Oxford University Press, 2018.

———. *Kiev, Jewish Metropolis: A History, 1859–1914*. Bloomington: Indiana University Press, 2010.

Micale, Mark S., and Roy Porter, eds. *Discovering the History of Psychiatry*. New York: Oxford University Press, 1994.

Michałowska, Anna. *The Jewish Community: Authority and Social Control in Poznań and Swarzędz, 1650–1793*. Translated by Alicja Adamowicz. Warsaw: Wydawn. Uniwersytetu Wrocławskiego, 2008.

Midelfort, H. C. Erik. *A History of Madness in Sixteenth-Century Germany*. Stanford: Stanford University Press, 1999.

Miron, Dan. *From Continuity to Contiguity: Toward a New Jewish Literary Thinking*. Stanford: Stanford University Press, 2010.

———. "Introduction." In *Tales of Mendele the Book Peddler: Fishke the Lame and Benjamin the Third*, edited by Dan Miron and Ken Frieden, vii–lxx. New York: Schocken Books, 1996.

———. "The Literary Image of the Shtetl." In Miron, *The Image of the Shtetl and Other Studies of Modern Jewish Literary Imagination*, 1–48. Syracuse, NY: Syracuse University Press, 2000.

———. "Passivity and Narration: The Spell of Isaac Bashevis Singer." In Miron, *The Image of the Shtetl and Other Studies of Modern Jewish Literary Imagination*, 339–51. Syracuse, NY: Syracuse University Press, 2000.

———. "Sh. Y. Abramovitsh and His 'Mendele.'" In Miron, *The Image of the Shtetl and Other Studies of Modern Jewish Literary Imagination*, 81–127. Syracuse, NY: Syracuse University Press, 2000.

Mishani, Dror. "'Kol yisrael kabtsan hu'—huts meha-soharim, ba'alei ha-bayit vekha-yotse ba-eileh: he'arot le-shihzur ha-dibur ha-ma'amadi be-'sefer kabt-sanim'." In *Sifrut u-ma'amad: likrat historiografiyah politit shel ha-sifrut ha-ivrit ha-hadashah*, edited by Amir Benbaji and Hannan Hever, 102–16. Jerusalem and Bnai Brak: Van Leer Institute and Hakibbutz Hameuchad, 2014.

Mochalova, Viktoriia. "Istselenie, spasenie, izbavlenie v evreiskoi traditsii i magicheskaia praktika (evreiskii obriad kladbishchenskoi svad'by i ego slavianskie paralleli)." In *Narodnaia meditsina i magiia v slavianskoi i evreiskoi kul'turnoi traditsii: sbornik statei*, edited by O. V. Belova. Moscow: Tsentr nauchnykh rabotnikov i prepodavatelei iudaiki v vuzakh "Sefer" and Institut slavianovedeniia Rossiiskoi Akademii Nauk, 2007.

Mogilner, Marina. "Toward a History of Russian Jewish 'Medical Materialism': Russian Jewish Physicians and the Politics of Jewish Biological Normalization." *Jewish Social Studies* 19, no. 1 (2012): 70–106.

Mollat, Michel. *The Poor in the Middle Ages: An Essay in Social History*. Translated by Arthur Goldhammer. New Haven, CT: Yale University Press, 1986.

Morris, R. J. *Cholera, 1832: The Social Response to an Epidemic*. New York: Holmes & Meier, 1976.

Mühlauer, Elisabeth. *Welch' ein unheimlicher Gast: Die Cholera-Epidemie 1854 in München*. Münster: Waxmann, 1996.

Murav, Harriet. *Holy Foolishness: Dostoevsky's Novels & the Poetics of Cultural Critique*. Stanford: Stanford University Press, 1992.

N. Ts. "Lern-anshtaltn in pruzhene in der tsveyter helft fun XIX y"h." In *Pinkes fun der shtot pruzhene*, 157–68. Pruzhene: Pinkos, 1930.

Nadav, Mordekhai. *The Jews of Pinsk, 1506 to 1880*. Edited by Mark Mirsky and Murray Jay Rosman. Stanford: Stanford University Press, 2008.

Nathans, Benjamin. *Beyond the Pale: The Jewish Encounter with Late Imperial Russia*. Berkeley: University of California Press, 2002.

Newman, Roberta. "Home Movies and the Alte Heym (Old Home): American Jewish Travel Films in Eastern Europe in the 1920s and 1930s." *Jewish Folklore and Ethnology Review* 15, no. 1 (1993): 22–28.

———. "Pictures of a Trip to the Old Country." Edited by Jack Kugelmass. *YIVO Annual* 21 (1993): 223–39.

Nigal, Gedalyah. *Ha-"aher" ba-sipur ha-hasidi*. Jerusalem: Ha-makhon le-heker ha-sifrut ha-hasidit, 2007.

———. *The Hasidic Tale*. Oxford: Littman Library of Jewish Civilization, 2008.

———. *Leksikon ha-sipur ha-hasidi*. Yerushalayim: Ha-makhon le-heker ha-sifrut ha-hasidit, 2005.

———. *Magic, Mysticism, and Hasidism: The Supernatural in Jewish Thought*. Northvale, NJ: Jason Aronson, 1994.

Norich, Anita. *The Homeless Imagination in the Fiction of Israel Joshua Singer*. Bloomington: Indiana University Press, 1991.

Orbach, Alexander. *New Voices of Russian Jewry: A Study of the Russian-Jewish Press of Odessa in the Era of the Great Reforms, 1860–1871*. Leiden: Brill, 1980.

Parciak, Rivka. "The Others in Yizker Books." In *Memorial Books of Eastern European Jewry: Essays on the History and Meanings of Yizker Volumes*, edited by Rosemary Horowitz, 222–43. Jefferson, NC: McFarland, 2011.

Parush, Iris. "Another Look at 'The Life of "Dead" Hebrew': Intentional Ignorance of Hebrew in Nineteenth-Century Eastern European Jewish Society." *Book History* 7, no. 1 (2004): 171–214.

Penslar, Derek J. *Shylock's Children: Economics and Jewish Identity in Modern Europe*. Berkeley: University of California Press, 2001.

———. *Zionism and Technocracy: The Engineering of Jewish Settlement in Palestine, 1870–1918*. Bloomington: Indiana University Press, 1991.

Petrovskii-Shtern, Iokhanan. *Evrei v russkoi armii: 1827–1914*. Historia Rossica. Moscow: Novoe literaturnoe obozrenie, 2003.

Petrovsky-Shtern, Yohanan. *The Golden Age Shtetl: A New History of Jewish Life in East Europe*. Princeton, NJ: Princeton University Press, 2014.

———. *Jews in the Russian Army, 1827–1917: Drafted into Modernity*. New York: Cambridge University Press, 2009.

———. "The Marketplace in Balta." *East European Jewish Affairs* 37, no. 3 (December 1, 2007): 277–98.

Pinsker, Shachar. "The Language That Was Lost on the Roads: Discovering Hebrew through Yiddish in Aharon Appelfeld's Fiction." *Journal of Jewish Identities* 7, no. 1 (2014): 129–41.

Polishchuk, Mikhail. *Evrei Odessy i Novorossii: sotsial'no-politicheskaia istoriia evreev Odessy i drugikh gorodov v Novorossii: 1881–1904*. Moscow: Mosty kul'tury, 2002.

Polonsky, Antony. *The Jews in Poland and Russia*. 3 vols. Oxford: Littman Library of Jewish Civilization, 2010.

Porter, Brian. *When Nationalism Began to Hate: Imagining Modern Politics in Nineteenth Century Poland*. New York: Oxford University Press, 2000.

Porter, Roy. "Foucault's Great Confinement." *History of the Human Sciences* 3, no. 1 (1990): 47–54.

———. "Introduction." In *The Confinement of the Insane: International Perspectives, 1800–1965*, edited by Roy Porter and David Wright, 1–19. New York: Cambridge University Press, 2003.

———. *A Social History of Madness: The World through the Eyes of the Insane*. New York: Weidenfeld & Nicolson, 1988.

Portnoy, Edward A. [Eddy]. *Bad Rabbi and Other Strange but True Stories from the Yiddish Press*. Stanford: Stanford University Press, 2018.

———. "Freaks, Geeks, and Strongmen: Warsaw Jews and Popular Performance, 1912–1930." *TDR: The Drama Review* 50, no. 2 (2006): 117–35.

Presner, Todd Samuel. *Muscular Judaism: The Jewish Body and the Politics of Regeneration*. New York: Routledge, 2007.

Ramer, Samuel C. "Traditional Healers and Peasant Culture in Russia, 1861–1917." In *Peasant Economy, Culture, and Politics of European Russia, 1800–1921*, edited by Esther Kingston-Mann, Timothy Mixter, and Jeffrey Burds. Princeton, NJ: Princeton University Press, 1991.

Ran, Leyzer, ed. *Yerusholayim de-lita: ilustrirt un dokumentirt*. 2 vols. New York: Vilner albom komitet, 1974.

Ringelblum, Emanuel. "Der yidisher opshoym in 18-tn y"h: loyt gerikhtlekhe dokumentn." In *Kapitlen geshikhte fun amolikn yidishn lebn in poyln*, edited by Jacob Shatzky, 153–67. Buenos Aires: Tsentral-farband fun poylishe yidn in argentine, 1953.

———. *Notes from the Warsaw Ghetto: The Journal of Emmanuel Ringelblum*. New York: Schocken Books, 1974.

———. "Shnorers in poyln in di amolike tsaytn." In *Kapitlen geshikhte fun amolikn yidishn lebn in poyln*, edited by Jacob Shatzky, 168–72. Buenos Aires: Tsentral-farband fun poylishe yidn in argentine, 1953.

Roczniak, Wladyslaw. "Preserving the Poor: Pre-Modern Polish Hospitals, Twelfth to Eighteenth Century." Ph.D. diss., City University of New York, 2004.

Rogger, Hans. "Government, Jews, Peasants and Land after the Liberation of the

Serfs." In *Jewish Policies and Right-Wing Politics in Imperial Russia*, 113–75. Berkeley: University of California Press; London: Macmillan, 1986.

Rosemarie Garland-Thomson. "Introduction: From Wonder to Error—A Genealogy of Freak Discourse in Modernity." In *Freakery: Cultural Spectacles of the Extraordinary Body*, edited by Rosemarie Garland-Thomson, 1–19. New York: New York University Press, 1996.

Rosenberg, Charles E. *The Cholera Years: The United States in 1832, 1849, and 1866*. Chicago: University of Chicago Press, 1962.

Roskies, David G. "Ayzik-Meyer Dik and the Rise of Yiddish Popular Literature." Ph.D. diss., Brandeis University, 1975.

———. *A Bridge of Longing: The Lost Art of Yiddish Storytelling*. Cambridge, MA: Harvard University Press, 1995.

———. "Gimpel the Simple and on Reading from Right to Left." In *Arguing the Modern Jewish Canon: Essays on Literature and Culture in Honor of Ruth R. Wisse*, edited by Justin Daniel Cammy, Dara Horn, Alyssa Quint, and Rachel Rubinstein, 319–40. Cambridge, MA: Harvard University Press, 2008.

Rubin, Ruth. *Voices of a People: The Story of Yiddish Folk Song*. Philadelphia: Jewish Publication Society, 1979.

Ryan, William F. *The Bathhouse at Midnight: An Historical Survey of Magic and Divination in Russia*. University Park: Pennsylvania State University Press, 1999.

Safran, Gabriella. *Wandering Soul: The Dybbuk's Creator, S. An-Sky*. Cambridge, MA: Belknap Press of Harvard University Press, 2010.

Sagiv, Gadi. "Hasidism and Cemetery Inauguration Ceremonies: Authority, Magic, and Performance of Charismatic Leadership." *Jewish Quarterly Review* 103, no. 3 (2013): 328–51.

Sandrow, Nahma. *Vagabond Stars: A World History of Yiddish Theater*. New York: Harper & Row, 1977.

Schainker, Ellie R. *Confessions of the Shtetl: Converts from Judaism in Imperial Russia, 1817–1906*. Stanford: Stanford University Press, 2017.

Schiller, Rivke. "Ceremonia 'czarnego wesela' i jej opisy w księgach pamięci." Translated by Piotr Pazinski. *Midrasz*, no. 6 (November–December 2011): 36–39.

Schiper, Ignacy. *Studya nad stosunkami gospodarczymi Żydów w Polsce podczas średniowiecza*. Lwów: Nakł. Funduszu konkursowego im. Wawelberga; gl. skład: W Księgarni polskiej B. Polonieckiego, 1911.

Schleicher, Marianne. *Intertextuality in the Tales of Rabbi Nahman of Bratslav: A Close Reading of Sippurey Ma'asiyot*. Boston: Brill, 2007.

Scholem, Gershom. *On the Kabbalah and Its Symbolism*. London: Routledge and K. Paul, 1965.

———. "The Tradition of the Thirty-Six Hidden Just Men." In *The Messianic Idea in Judaism and Other Essays on Jewish Spirituality*, 251–56. New York: Schocken Books, 1995.

Schwara, Desanka. "Luftmenschen—ein Leben in Armut." In *Luftmenschen und rebellische Töchter: zum Wandel ostjüdischer Lebenswelten im 19. Jahrhundert*, edited by Heiko Haumann. Cologne: Böhlau, 2003.

Scott Ury. *Barricades and Banners: The Revolution of 1905 and the Transformation of Warsaw Jewry*. Stanford: Stanford University Press, 2012.

Seidman, Naomi. "The Ghost of Queer Loves Past: Ansky's 'Dybbuk' and the Sexual Transformation of Ashkenaz." In *Queer Theory and the Jewish Question*, edited by Daniel Boyarin, Daniel Itzkovitz, and Ann Pellegrini, 228–45. Columbia University Press, 2003.

———. "Reading 'Queer' Ashkenaz: This Time from East to West." *The Drama Review: TDR* 55, no. 3 (October 1, 2011): 50–56.

Shaked, Gershon. *Bein sehok le-dema: iyunim be-yetsirato shel mendele mokher-sefarim*. Tel-Aviv: Agudat ha-sofrim be-yisra'el le-yad hotsa'at masadah, 1965.

———. "Dickens' *Oliver Twist* and Mendele's *The Book of Beggars*." In id., *The New Tradition: Essays on Modern Hebrew Literature*, 173–82. Cincinnati: Hebrew Union College Press, 2006.

———. "A Groan from a Broken Heart: Mendele's *Fishke the Lame*." In *The New Tradition: Essays on Modern Hebrew Literature*, 194–215. Cincinnati: Hebrew Union College Press, 2006.

———. "Three Kalikes: A Comparative Study of Mendele, Agnon, and Bashevis." In *The New Tradition: Essays on Modern Hebrew Literature*, 183–93. Cincinnati: Hebrew Union College Press, 2006.

Shapiro, Leon. *The History of ORT: A Jewish Movement for Social Change*. New York: Schocken Books, 1980.

Shiper, Yitskhok. *Geshikhte fun yidisher teater-kunst un drame: fun di eltste tsaytn biz 1750*. Warsaw: Kultur-lige, 1927.

Shochat, Azriel. "Ha-hanhagah be-kehilot rusyah im bitul ha-kahal." *Tsiyon* 42 (1977): 143–233.

———. *Mosad "ha-rabanut mi-ta'am" be-rusyah*. Haifa: Haifa University Press, 1975.

Shulvass, Moses A. *From East to West: The Westward Migration of Jews from Eastern Europe during the Seventeenth and Eighteenth Centuries*. Detroit: Wayne State University Press, 1971.

Siegel, Paul N. "Gimpel and the Archetype of the Wise Fool." In *The Achievement of Isaac Bashevis Singer*, edited by Marcia Allentuck, 159–73. Carbondale: Southern Illinois University Press, 1969.

Skinner, Frederick W. "Odessa and the Problem of Urban Modernization." In *The City in Late Imperial Russia*, edited by Michael F. Hamm, 209–48. Bloomington: Indiana University Press, 1986.

Smith, Timothy B. "Charity and Poor Relief: The Modern Period." In *Encyclopedia of European Social History from 1350 to 2000*, edited by Peter N. Stearns, 3: 453–65. New York: Scribner, 2001.

———. "Marginal People." In *Encyclopedia of European Social History from 1350 to 2000*, edited by Peter N. Stearns, 3: 175–86. New York: Scribner, 2001.

Snowden, Frank M. *Naples in the Time of Cholera, 1884–1911.* New York: Cambridge University Press, 1995.

Sperber, Daniel. *Minhagei yisra'el: mekorot ve-toldot.* 8 vols. Jerusalem: Mossad Harav Kook, 1994.

Sperber, Haim. "Agunot, 1851–1914. An Introduction." *Annales de démographie historique* 136, no. 2 (2018): 107–35.

Stampfer, Shaul. "Gender Differentiation and Education of the Jewish Woman in Nineteenth Century Eastern Europe." In id., *Families, Rabbis and Education: Traditional Jewish Society in Nineteenth-Century Eastern Europe*, 166–89. Oxford: Littman Library of Jewish Civilization, 2010.

———. "Heder Study, Knowledge of Torah, and the Maintenance of Social Stratification." In id,, *Families, Rabbis and Education: Traditional Jewish Society in Nineteenth-Century Eastern Europe*, 136–66. Oxford: Littman Library of Jewish Civilization, 2010.

———. "Love and Family." In id., *Families, Rabbis and Education: Traditional Jewish Society in Nineteenth-Century Eastern Europe*, 26–55. Oxford: Littman Library of Jewish Civilization, 2010.

———. "Scientific Welfare and Lonely Old People: The Development of Old Age Homes among Jews in Eastern Europe." In id., *Families, Rabbis and Education: Traditional Jewish Society in Nineteenth-Century Eastern Europe*, 86–101. Oxford: Littman Library of Jewish Civilization, 2010.

Stanislawski, Michael. *Tsar Nicholas I and the Jews: The Transformation of Jewish Society in Russia, 1825–1855.* Philadelphia: Jewish Publication Society of America, 1983.

———. *Zionism and the Fin-de-Siècle: Cosmopolitanism and Nationalism from Nordau to Jabotinsky.* Berkeley: University of California Press, 2001.

Stearns, Peter N. *European Society in Upheaval: Social History since 1750.* Toronto: Maxwell Macmillan Canada, 1992.

Stern, Zehavit. "From Jester to Gesture: Eastern European Jewish Culture and the Re-Imagination of Folk Performance." Ph.D. diss., University of California, Berkeley, 2011.

Stevens, Donald F. "Eating, Drinking, and Being Married: Epidemic Cholera and the Celebration of Marriage in Montreal and Mexico City, 1832–1833." *Catholic Historical Review* 92, no. 1 (January 1, 2006): 74–94.

Stiker, Henri-Jacques. *A History of Disability*. Translated by William Sayers. Ann Arbor: University of Michigan Press, 1999.

Stutchkoff, Nahum. *Der oytser fun der yidisher shprakh*. Edited by Max Weinreich. New York: Yidisher Visnshaftlekher Institut–YIVO, 1950.

Sylvester, Roshanna P. *Tales of Old Odessa: Crime and Civility in a City of Thieves*. DeKalb: Northern Illinois University Press, 2005.

Tartakower, Aryeh. "Al ofi ha-oni ha-yehudi veha-tsedakah ha-yehudit." In *Kelal yisra'el: perakim ba-sotsyologyah shel ha-am ha-yehudi*, edited by Ben Zion Dinur, Aryeh Tartakower, and Jacob Lestschinsky. Jerusalem: Mosad Bialik, 1954.

Ta-Shma, Israel M. *Minhag ashkenaz ha-kadmon: heker ve-iyun*. Jerusalem: Magnes Press, 1999.

———. "'Tsadikim einam metam'in"—al halakah ve-agadah.'" *JSIJ —Jewish Studies, an Internet Journal* 1 (2002): 45–53.

Thomas, Keith. *Religion and the Decline of Magic: Studies in Popular Beliefs in Sixteenth and Seventeenth Century England*. London: Weidenfeld & Nicolson, 1971.

Thomassen, Bjørn. "The Uses and Meanings of Liminality." *International Political Anthropology* 2, no. 1 (2009): 5–28.

Thompson, Stith. *Motif-Index of Folk-Literature: A Classification of Narrative Elements in Folktales, Ballads, Myths, Fables, Mediaeval Romances, Exempla, Fabliaux, Jest-Books, and Local Legends*. 4 vols. Bloomington: Indiana University Press, 1955.

Trachtenberg, Joshua. *The Devil and the Jews: The Medieval Conception of the Jew and Its Relation to Modern Antisemitism*. Philadelphia: Jewish Publication Society, 1993.

———. *Jewish Magic and Superstition: A Study in Folk Religion*. Philadelphia: University of Pennsylvania Press, 2004.

Trunk, Isaiah. "Le-toldot ha-historiografyah ha-yehudit-polanit." *Gal-Ed* 3 (1976): 245–68.

Trunk, Sh. "A yidishe kehile in poyln baym sof XVIII yorhundert, kutne." *Bleter far geshikhte* 1 (1934): 87–140.

Tsukerovich, Meir. "Kalat ha-ir be-zambrov." *Yeda am* 1, no. 1 (1948): 13–14.

Tsunzer, Perets. "Mishegas-motivn in y. l. peretses shafn: kritisher analiz." *Kultur*, January 22, 1926, 3.

Turner, Victor W. "Betwixt and Between: The Liminal Period in *Rites de Passage*." In *The Forest of Symbols: Aspects of Ndembu Ritual*, 93–111. Ithaca, NY: Cornell University Press, 1967.

———. "Liminality and Communitas." In *The Ritual Process: Structure and Anti-Structure*, 94–130. Chicago: Aldine, 1969.

Vakhtangov, Evgenii. *The Vakhtangov Sourcebook*. Edited by Andrei Malaev-Babel. New York: Routledge, 2011.

Vanhemelryck, Fernand. *Marginalen in de geschiedenis: over beulen, joden, hoeren, zigeuners en andere zondebokken.* Leuven: Davidsfonds, 2004.

Vaynig, N. "Mageyfe-khasenes." *Sotsyale meditsin* 10, no. 9–10 (1937): 24–32.

Walkowitz, Judith. *City of Dreadful Delight: Narratives of Sexual Danger in Late-Victorian London.* Chicago: University of Chicago Press, 1992.

Węgrzynek, Hanna. "Shvartze Khasene: Black Weddings among Polish Jews." In *Holy Dissent: Jewish and Christian Mystics in Eastern Europe,* edited by Glenn Dynner, 55–68. Detroit: Wayne State University Press, 2011.

Weindling, Paul. *Epidemics and Genocide in Eastern Europe, 1890–1945.* Oxford: Oxford University Press, 2000.

Weiser, Keith Ian. *Jewish People, Yiddish Nation: Noah Prylucki and the Folkists in Poland.* Toronto: University of Toronto Press, 2011.

Wertheimer, Jack. *Unwelcome Strangers: East European Jews in Imperial Germany.* New York: Oxford University Press, 1987.

Wigzell, Faith. "Folklore and Russian Literature." In *The Routledge Companion to Russian Literature,* edited by Neil Cornwell. London; New York: Routledge, 2001.

Wiskind-Elper, Ora. *Tradition and Fantasy in the Tales of Reb Nahman of Bratslav.* Albany: State University of New York Press, 1998.

Wisse, Ruth R. *I. L. Peretz and the Making of Modern Jewish Culture.* Seattle: University of Washington Press, 1991.

———. *The Schlemiel as Modern Hero.* Chicago: University of Chicago Press, 1971.

Wodziński, Marcin. *Hasidism: Key Questions.* New York: Oxford University Press, 2018.

———. *Historical Atlas of Hasidism.* Waldemar Spallek, cartographer. Princeton, NJ: Princeton University Press, 2018.

Wolff, Eberhard. "Juden als Verkörperung von Armut und Unsauberkeit in ärztlichen Berichten über die Choleraepidemie in Osteuropa 1830/31." In *Juden und Armut in Mittel- und Osteuropa,* edited by Stefi Jersch-Wenzel, Gertrud Pickhan, Andreas Reinke, Desanka Schwara, and François Guesnet, 123–48. Cologne: Böhlau, 2000.

Wolitz, Seth. "Inscribing An-Sky's Dybbuk in Russian and Jewish Letters." In *The Worlds of S. An-Sky: A Russian Jewish Intellectual at the Turn of the Century,* edited by Gabriella Safran and Steven J. Zipperstein, 164–202. Stanford: Stanford University Press, 2006.

Wright, David. "Developmental and Physical Disabilities: The 'Blind,' 'Deaf and Dumb,' and 'Idiot.'" In *Encyclopedia of European Social History from 1350 to 2000,* edited by Peter N. Stearns, 3: 507–15. New York: Scribner, 2001.

Yalen, Deborah. "Documenting the 'New Red Kasrilevke.'" *East European Jewish Affairs* 37, no. 3 (December 1, 2007): 353–75.

Zahra, Tara. "'Each Nation Only Cares for Its Own': Empire, Nation, and Child Welfare Activism in the Bohemian Lands, 1900–1918." *American Historical Review* 111, no. 5 (2006): 1378–1402.

Zalkin, Mordechai. "'Ha-ketsavim de-po parku ol': me'afyenim u-megamot be-fe'ilut ma'arekhet ha-revahah be-kehilat vilnah be-reshit ha-me'a ha-tesha esreh." In *Mi-vilna le-yerushalayim: mehkarim be-toldotehem uve-tarbutam shel yehudei mizrah eiropah mugashim le-profesor shemu'el verses*, edited by David Assaf, Israel Bartal, Avner Holtzman, Chava Turniansky, Shmuel Feiner, and Yehuda Friedlander, 25–42. Jerusalem: Magnes Press, 2002.

Zimmels, Hirsch Jacob. *Magicians, Theologians and Doctors: Studies in Folk-Medicine and Folk-Lore as Reflected in the Rabbinical Responsa (12th–19th Centuries)*. London: Edward Goldston & Son, 1952.

Zipperstein, Steven J. *The Jews of Odessa: A Cultural History*. Stanford: Stanford University Press, 1991.

———. "The Politics of Relief: The Transformation of Russian Jewish Communal Life during the First World War." In *The Jews and the European Crisis, 1914–21*, edited by Jonathan Frankel, 22–40. Studies in Contemporary Jewry 4. New York: Oxford University Press, 1988.

INDEX

Abramovitsh, Sholem Yankev (Mendele Moykher Sforim): Agnon comparison, 85, 200; cholera wedding, 105–6, 106–7, 108, 114, 215, 220–21, 238; *Fishke der krumer*, 74–75, 77–83, 105–6, 114, 128–29, 142–43, 184, 200, 220–21; Friedberg comparison, 106–7; on hekdesh, 77–82; literary works, 5, 63, 74–77; "The Little Man" (*Dos kleyne mentshele*), 130–31; madman protagonist, 289n54; on marginal individual in Jewish narrative, 82–85, 87; portrayal of Jewish vagrants, 142–43, 144; schlemiel (fool) character, 296n165; on scientific philanthropy, 128–29; *Sefer ha-kabtsanim* (The Book of Beggars), 75, 81, 84; Singer comparison, 215, 221; Trunk comparison, 143; Tuwim comparison, 226; Vaynig comparison, 114
Abramowicz, Hirsz, 156
Abrams, Judith, 30–31, 163
Adams, Rachel, 36, 237, 239
Adler, Eliyana, 135

Agnon, Shmuel Yosef, 63, 85–87, 200–205, 239
Alexander II, Russian Emperor, 118, 137
almsgiving: in Christian world, 248n24; condemnation of, 121; increase in seekers of, 45; insufficiency of, 137–38; itinerant religious singers and, 40; under Peter the Great, 41; *Pletten* system, 21, 49, 248n24, 257n50; in premodern Europe, 38; private alms, 4; reliance on, 7
An-ski, S. (S. Z. Rappoport, pseud.), 112, 134 fig.5.1, 135 fig.5.2, 140 fig.5.3, 144 fig.5.4, 163, 176, 178, 190–95, 272n102
antisemitism, 13, 121, 227–28; displacement of onto marginal people, 13, 81–83, 87–88, 129, 226
Appelfeld, Aharon, 1–2, 178
Ashkenazi Jews, 20, 31, 35, 61, 108–9, 119, 239, 252n100
Ashley, Susan A., 245n13

Bakhtin, Mikhail, 80–81, 106, 107
Baldwin, Peter, 95
Bar-Levav, Avriel, 70

Stanford Studies in Jewish History and Culture
David Biale and Sarah Abrevaya Stein, Editors

This series features novel approaches to examining the Jewish past in the form of innovative work that brings the field into productive dialogue with the newest scholarly concepts and methods. Open to a range of disciplinary and interdisciplinary approaches, from history to cultural studies, this series publishes exceptional scholarship balanced by an accessible tone, illustrating histories of difference and addressing issues of current urgency. Books in this list push the boundaries of Jewish Studies and speak compellingly to a wide audience of scholars and students.

For a complete listing of titles in this series, visit the Stanford University Press website, www.sup.org.

Made in the USA
Middletown, DE
11 April 2021